MASTERING EXCEL
ON THE MACINTOSH

MASTERING EXCEL
ON THE MACINTOSH™

CARL TOWNSEND

Second Edition

San Francisco • Paris • Düsseldorf • London

Cover art by Thomas Ingalls & Associates
Cover photography by Casey Cartwright
Series design by Julie Bilski

To Sandy
for helping to keep the ship on course as the book was written.

ACKNOWLEDGMENTS

I would like to express my appreciation to the many people who helped make this book possible.

At Microsoft, thanks to the Excel group, Marty Taucher, and others for providing the software and documentation and providing help in many other ways.

To Apple Corporation, thanks for the hardware and software support. All of the examples in the book were done on a Macintosh SE.

At SYBEX special thanks to Bonnie Gruen for editing the book. Thanks also to Mark Taber, technical reviewer; John Kadyk, word processor; Gladys Varon, typesetter; and Lynne Bourgault, proofreader.

TABLE OF CONTENTS

P A R T   2   FUNDAMENTALS OF EXCEL ────

P A R T   3   *DATABASE MANAGEMENT*

PART 4 *USING SPECIAL TECHNIQUES*

P A R T 6   *USING EXCEL PRODUCTIVELY*

INTRODUCTION

"There are corporate executives, wholesalers, retailers, and small-business owners who talk about their business lives in two time periods: before and after the electronic spreadsheet."

Steven Levy

BACKGROUND

Before the invention of the personal-computer spreadsheet program, it was not unusual for a financial vice-president of a company to spend the night manually preparing the company's financial projections for an annual meeting, using nothing more than a hand calculator. If even a small error was made, it would ripple endlessly through all subsequent calculations on the entire spreadsheet. Spreadsheet programs did exist for large mainframe computers, but they were often cumbersome to use, and the computers were not very accessible to most employees.

VisiCalc, invented by Robert Frankston and Dan Bricklin in 1978 for the Apple II computer, suddenly changed all this. For the first time, a business manager could inexpensively set up an entire financial model and analyze any number of scenarios quickly and accurately.

The popularity and capabilities of personal-computer spreadsheet programs grew at a rapid rate. Sorcim's SuperCalc (1980), Microsoft's Multiplan (1982), and Lotus' 1-2-3 (1983) each added new features, capabilities, and integrated tools. These products represented important milestones in the evolution of the spreadsheet, but spreadsheet users still wanted more capabilities.

Users today need more cells in their spreadsheets to build larger models, and they want to be able to link spreadsheets to form hierarchical relationships. They also want to able to control the appearance of their output. The popularity of bit-mapped displays has encouraged users to explore the possibility of altering fonts and character attributes to make presentation-quality graphs, charts, and displays. Users have found macros to be the most powerful feature in spreadsheet programs, yet they have been cumbersome to use in the products that included them, and they have not been included at all in some spreadsheet programs marketed as late as 1985. In 1985 Microsoft released Excel for the Macintosh, the first spreadsheet program designed specifically to address the needs of users who manage many types of data—those frustrated by the limitations of the numerical analysis products currently available.

THE PHILOSOPHY OF EXCEL

Before you begin using Excel, it is important to understand some of the philosophy in the design of the product. It is not, as many spreadsheet products, intended as integrated software that combines many applications, such as Jazz or AppleWorks. Rather, Excel is limited to three applications—spreadsheet (or worksheet), database, and graphics—and it does each of these in a depth that is not available in competitive products.

Excel is an example of a contextually integrated product. That is, it combines the applications that are frequently used in the same context by users whose primary task is analyzing and processing numerical data. This contextual integration permits a user to quickly move from one application to another to see the results of an analysis.

Because Excel is specifically designed for users working with data in a large variety of numerical analysis contexts, it supports the data-processing application more thoroughly than any other personal-computer software product. However, Excel users are not restricted by the program's narrow range of applications. The Switcher, which comes with the Excel package, offers the user the capability to integrate Excel with many other software products, such as word processors and communication programs.

BOOK ORGANIZATION

The book is divided into seven parts. The first part (Chapters 1 through 3) provides an introduction to the worksheet concept and leads you through a simple example. In the second part (Chapters 4 through 9) you will learn the basic principles of working with Excel worksheets. The third part (Chapters 10 through 12) covers database management, and the fourth part (Chapters 13 through 17) explains the special features of Excel. The fifth part covers charting and graphics and teaches you how to create effective graphs.

Part 6 includes four chapters on application design (Chapters 20 through 23). Using invoicing, financial management, and trend analysis applications, you will gain some understanding of how to use Excel to solve specific problems.

Finally, Part 7 describes macros and how to use them. It includes examples to help you design your own macros and a chapter that lists all the macro functions with a brief description of each.

The appendix section is extensive, and it is intended to be used as a reference manual. The appendices include a glossary, a summary of all the commands, and a summary of Excel functions.

Throughout this book, you will be given many tutorial examples showing how Excel can be used to meet a variety of needs. I encourage you to try these examples. Each of them will give you valuable insights about the special features of Excel.

P A R T 1

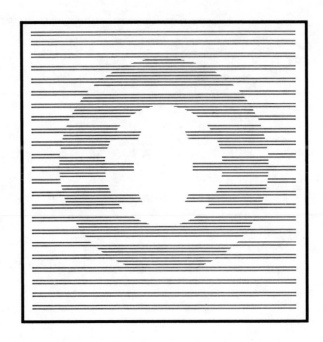

EXCEL: A FIRST VIEW

PART 1 OF THIS BOOK IS FOR THOSE OF YOU WHO want to start using Excel quickly without learning a lot of commands and instructions. First you will learn how to get Excel up and running. Then you will jump right in and use it. Chapter 3 guides you through the creation of a simple worksheet and chart.

INTRODUCTION TO EXCEL

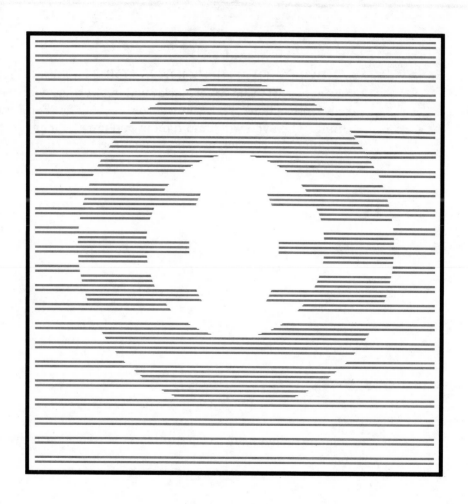

CHAPTER 1

EXCEL IS AN ADVANCED WORKSHEET (OR SPREAD-sheet) product for the Macintosh that also provides database and graphics functions.

A worksheet program is essentially a replacement for the columnar pad, pencil, and calculator. The computer displays a two-dimensional worksheet, configuring the workspace into rows and columns. Each intersection of a row and a column is called a cell. An on-screen worksheet may look very similar to a paper one. However, the size of an electronic worksheet can be much, much larger than its paper counterpart. Excel has over 4 million cells available in 256 columns of 16,384 rows.

Excel can also be used with Switcher, which makes it easy for users to integrate Excel with other programs, such as Microsoft Word. Using Switcher, you can easily switch back and forth between Excel and a word processing system on the screen.

THE FEATURES OF EXCEL

The features of Excel can be grouped into two classifications: analysis features and presentation features. Analysis features are used to obtain the output information of the worksheet. Presentation features provide a variety of ways to present information to the user.

ANALYSIS FEATURES

Excel offers several analysis features that competing worksheets do not offer:

- Excel can link worksheets and develop hierarchical relationships among them. For example, marketing and production worksheets could be developed independently by department managers as components of a larger corporate worksheet, and these component worksheets could be linked hierarchically. Changes in a linked document are reflected in all linked worksheets dependent on the change.

- When calculating, Excel only includes the cells that have changed since the last calculation. This provides quick worksheet updating.

- Excel can be used for array processing and to solve multiple-value problems. Using arrays, functions can operate on a series of values or return a series of values.

- Excel offers users the capability to simulate many, many possibilities, with input data values changed in each simulation. This is done through the use of a single table that controls input.

- Repetitive worksheet tasks can be automated with Excel's easy-to-use macros and user-definable functions. Macros can be created automatically by recording keystrokes using the Recorder feature.

- Excel users can make use of data already used with other worksheet software, even from other computers. Excel offers two-way file capability with Multiplan, Chart, Lotus 1-2-3, and any program using the Microsoft SYLK format.

- Excel includes integrated full-featured charting and on-screen databases with querying, extracting, and sorting functions.

PRESENTATION FEATURES

Excel can produce presentation-quality worksheet documentation, and it offers users a wide selection of fonts and formats. Its presentation features include the following:

- Variable fonts and font sizes
- Boldface and italics available at the cell level
- Five border styles
- 19 predefined number formats
- User-definable formatting
- 42 built-in chart formats

- Flexibility in adding legends, text, arrows, patterns, scaling, and symbols
- Capability to view multiple charts on the screen simultaneously
- Complete support of AppleTalk network, LaserWriter, Imagewriter, and other printers

SWITCHER

Using Switcher, you can run two or more programs on the Macintosh at the same time and switch back and forth between them. You can work with Excel and a word processor or external database-management system by moving data quickly to and from the different programs.

When using Switcher, all programs currently in use are in the Macintosh memory; that is, the memory is partitioned so that each application program has a slice of memory. The number of programs that you can run simultaneously is limited by the amount of memory in the Macintosh. More information on Switcher is included in Chapter 20 and in Appendix F.

WHAT CAN I DO WITH EXCEL?

Any type of application that involves numerical data processing can take advantage of Excel's extensive worksheet capabilities. For administration and record-keeping purposes, you can use Excel for check registers, expense reports, annual reports, and five-year forecasts. Excel's financial applications include amortization schedules, cash-flow projections, general ledgers, accounts receivable, accounts payable, comparative investment analysis, personal net worth statements, balance sheets, and tax planning. Some examples of sales and marketing applications are sales comparisons, marketing analyses, product line summaries, and sales-forecast and linear-regression analyses. For operations, you can use Excel for inventory-management systems, material-requirement planning, inventory-rate-of-turnover analyses, and last-in-first-out (LIFO) analyses.

Here are some ways users might apply their Excel systems:

- Donald, a building contractor involved in competitive bidding, puts all his cost factors into an Excel worksheet. Then he alters each factor to see how it affects his final proposed bid. He can then study and analyze each factor that controls his cost to produce a final bid that is as low as possible.

- Susan is trying to conserve energy in her home. She creates a "model" of her house on an Excel worksheet. This model includes factors that control heating and cooling costs, such as attic insulation, window caulking, and a high-efficiency furnace. She can also calculate the cost of installing each of these energy-saving features. Using this, she can analyze the results to see how long it would take her to recover the costs of each energy-saving idea.

- Carol invests in the stock market, commodities, and bonds. She uses Excel worksheets to create investment models and to perform "what-if" analyses to try to find the best investment opportunities.

- George is in charge of labor negotiations for his company. Every few years, the union contracts are renegotiated. George has to be able to study proposals quickly from the unions and determine how they would affect the company earnings on both a short-term and a long-term basis. Using a worksheet, he can create a financial model of the company and quickly see how the union proposals will affect company earnings.

- John likes to do a little real-estate business from his home. He has several rental properties, and he needs to manage the rental costs as a factor of upkeep, taxes, and depreciation. He also has to know when to buy and sell the properties that he manages. The Excel worksheet gives him instant information on his profits as these factors change.

- Widget Manufacturing has a large sales staff, and the Sales Department needs to keep tabs on sales productivity as it relates to specific target goals. It also needs to send monthly reports to the Administrative Department, which uses the numbers to create corporate reports that control planning factors for other departments, such as the status of the inventory and costs of advertising. The company uses an entire collection of Excel worksheets, all interlinked. There is also a company summary worksheet, which enables the company president to make quick decisions as the market changes.

All of these applications can be grouped into one of two broad classifications: reporting on what has happened or forecasting what could happen (called what-if analysis). In the first case, the user is taking data that describe something that has often happened in the past (such as the last three-months' sales of a product in three areas of the country) and putting these data into a form that can be analyzed (such as a pie chart). From this, the user can make a decision (such as the marketing strategy for next month). In the second case, the user is changing one or more variables and seeing how these changes will affect a specific goal (such as changing various cost factors to see how this affects the bid on a project).

Now that you have some idea of what Excel is and what it can do, it's time to get started using it.

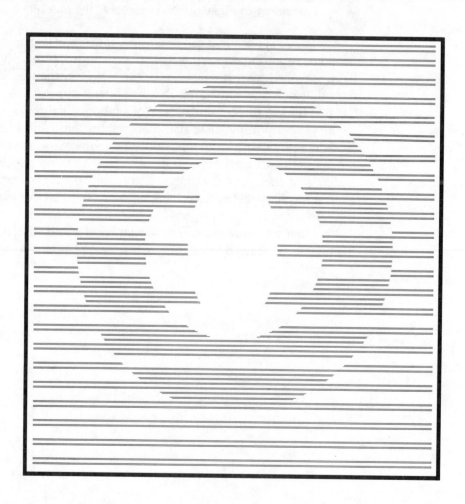

CHAPTER 2

BEGINNING TO USE EXCEL IS, WITHOUT DOUBT, AN
exciting adventure. Before starting, however, you should be sure that
you have everything that you will need. You should also take certain
initial precautions, as you would when beginning to use any new computer program.

This chapter provides step-by-step instructions on how to make copies of the disks that come with your Excel package and how to start up
Excel. It also includes a brief review of Macintosh window techniques,
such as scrolling and moving windows around on the screen.

Other important points covered in this chapter are how to set up a
printer and how to get on-screen help if you need it.

WHAT DO I NEED?

Before starting Excel, be sure that you have the following hardware:

- A Macintosh computer with at least 512K of memory
- A hard disk drive
- A printer

Although the printer and hard disk drive are listed by Microsoft as
optional, they are almost essential for using Excel effectively.

You also need the Excel program and data disks, extra disks, and
the documentation that came with Excel. When you purchase Excel,
you will receive one 800K disk. If you are using an older Macintosh
with a 400K disk drive, the package contains instructions for obtaining a copy on two 400K disks.

INSTALLING EXCEL

The Excel disk is not copy-protected, so you can install it on your hard disk using conventional means:

1. Start your Macintosh from the hard disk.

2. Create, if you wish, a folder on the Macintosh for the Excel program and data. Name it Excel. If a folder was created, open the folder.

3. Insert the Excel disk.

4. Drag the Excel disk icon to the hard disk or folder directory window.

CREATING BACKUP COPIES

Before starting to use Excel, you should create a backup copy of the Excel disk.

1. Start the Macintosh from the internal disk drive.

2. Put a blank disk in the disk drive (800K disk).

3. Initialize the disk.

4. Copy the programs in the Excel folder to the blank disk.

STARTING EXCEL

Microsoft Excel

Turn your Macintosh on. If necessary, open the Excel folder. Your screen should look like Figure 2.1. Be sure that the window for the Excel program is active, then double-click the Excel icon. The Excel program should start and display a worksheet, as shown in Figure 2.2. Now quit the program by pulling down the File menu and choosing Quit.

Restart the program by double-clicking the Excel icon. Wait for Excel to load. A blank worksheet will be displayed again. Once you

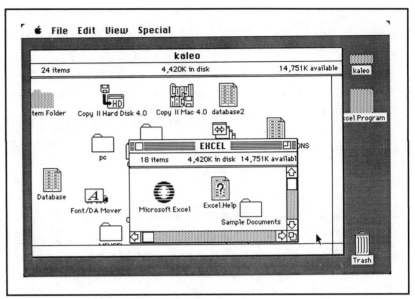

Figure 2.1: Starting Excel

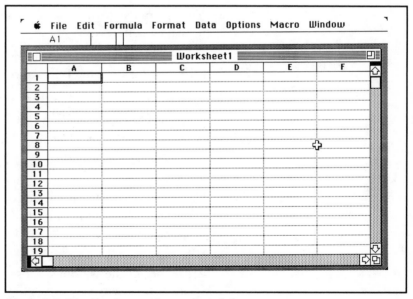

Figure 2.2: The Excel menu bar and worksheet

Worksheet1

Resume Excel

have used Excel to create worksheets, charts, and other files, you can start Excel in any one of three ways:

- Double-click the Excel icon, as you just did

- Double-click the icon for any worksheet, chart, or macro file

- Double-click the Resume Excel icon, which will start the program with the last document that was in use when you quit Excel

THE WORKSHEET WINDOW

Excel's worksheet window is much like any other window that is displayed on the Macintosh screen. Try a few things now with the displayed window (refer to Figure 2.2):

1. You can change the size of the window by dragging the size box in the lower right and moving the mouse up or down, left, or right.

2. You can move the window around on the screen by dragging it by its title bar.

3. You can scroll left or right in the worksheet using the scroll arrows at the bottom of the window in the scroll bar.

4. You can move the window up or down in the worksheet using the scroll arrows at the right of the window in the scroll bar.

5. You can use the scroll boxes at the right or the bottom to quickly move the window to any place in the worksheet.

6. If more than one window is displayed, you can click any displayed window to make it active. Pull down the Window menu from the menu bar and choose Show Clipboard. You will now see the Clipboard window.

7. You can close any window using the close box in the upper-left corner of the window. Close the Clipboard window by clicking its close box.

Experiment with these Macintosh window features until you are comfortable with how they work in Excel.

SETTING UP THE PRINTER

Before using your printer to print any worksheets, you must set up the program interface to the printer. Pull down the Apple menu and choose Chooser. The contents of the dialog box that appears depend on which type of printer you are using. Figure 2.3 shows a dialog box for an Imagewriter. Click on the icon that represents your printer and then click on the icon that represents your printer port.

GETTING HELP

If you need help at any time while you're using Excel, pull down the Apple menu and choose About Microsoft Excel. You will then

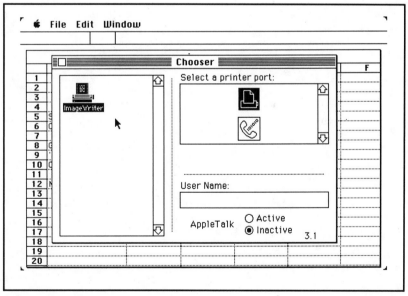

Figure 2.3: Configuring the printer

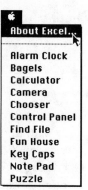

see the Help dialog box. Select the topic about which you need help, then click Help. You will see a window that shows the information you need. Click Next to see the next topic, Previous to see the last topic, Topics to return to the list of choices, or Cancel to return to your worksheet.

If you are working on a document, you can also get help by pressing the Command key and the question mark key at the same time. The cursor will change to a question mark. Move this question mark to the window area, dialog box query, or command about which you need help. Then click or choose the command to get help. To return to your work, click Cancel.

A QUICK TOUR OF EXCEL

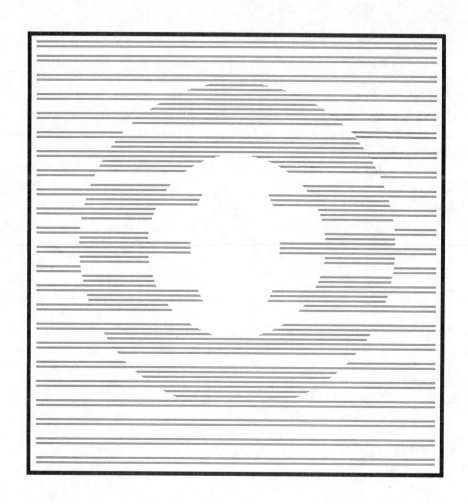

CHAPTER 3

ALTHOUGH EXCEL CAN SOLVE VERY COMPLICATED problems, it is actually quite easy to use. You'll discover this for yourself right now if you follow along with the quick exercise in this chapter. In this chapter you will use Excel to do the following:

- Create a worksheet, complete with formulas
- Format the worksheet
- Save the worksheet
- Print the worksheet
- Create a chart using the worksheet

This exercise will give you a feel for Excel and let you learn what it can do. Don't worry too much about how or why you did things— you'll learn the details in later chapters.

CREATING AN EXCEL WORKSHEET

Bring up the Excel program by selecting the Excel icon from the display. Double-click the icon to start the program. Excel creates an empty window, as shown in Figure 3.1.

WORKSHEET WINDOW FEATURES

Notice several things about this window before you do anything:

- Columns are defined by letters and rows by numbers. Each cell is shown as a box. Cells are designated by the column letter and row number. For example, cell B4 refers to the intersection of the fourth row with the second column.

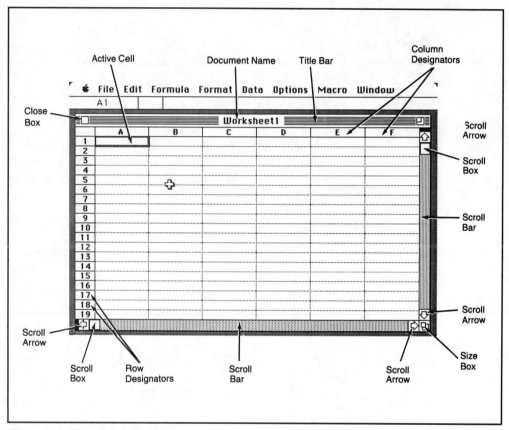

Figure 3.1: The worksheet window

- A cursor (in the shape of a cross) is on one cell.

- The first cell, A1, is highlighted with bold lines. This is the *active cell.*

- The window has a title: Worksheet1.

- Now refer to Figure 3.2. There is a display line under the menu bar that contains the name of the active cell (C1). There is also a second entry area, called the *formula bar,* which displays any text entered from the keyboard into the active cell.

Move the mouse about, and you will see the cursor move around the worksheet. The highlighted cell does not change, and neither does the active-cell designator on the display line under the menu bar.

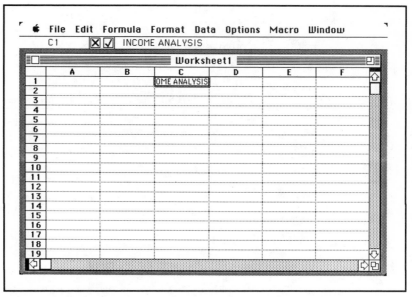

Figure 3.2: Entering the worksheet title

SCROLLING

Place the cursor on the scroll box in the scrolling bar at the right of the window. The cursor is now in the shape of an arrow. Click and drag the box downward. Notice that the active cell designator in the upper left changes, always showing the current row number as you drag the scroll box. When you release the mouse button, the last row number displayed will be at the top of the worksheet.

Drag the scroll box to the top of the scroll bar so that row 1 is at the top of the worksheet. Now, click the scroll box in the scroll bar at the bottom of the window and drag it to the right. Watch the designator under the menu bar change to indicate the current column letter. Release the mouse button and see where the last displayed column is now located. Finally, drag the scroll box all the way to the left so that column A is the first column.

ENTERING TITLES

Move the cursor back to the worksheet, and it becomes cross-shaped again. Use the mouse to move the cursor to cell C1, then click. Cell C1 is now highlighted, and the active-cell designator on the display line changes to C1. Use the keyboard to enter the title for your worksheet as **INCOME ANALYSIS**.

Notice that, as you enter your data, two new boxes appear near the formula bar: the enter box with a check ($\checkmark$) and a cancel box with an X, as shown in Figure 3.2. The entire title appears in the formula bar, and the portion that will fit appears in cell C1. After you enter the title, press the Return key or click the enter box to complete the entry. You will now see the entire title on the worksheet.

Enter the titles for the rows next:

1. Click cell A5 and drag to cell A12 (see Figure 3.3)

2. Type **Sales** and press Return

3. Type **Cost of Goods Sold** and press Return twice (to skip one row)

4. Type **Gross Margin** and press Return twice

5. Type **Operating Expenses** and press Return twice

6. Type **Net Income** and press Return

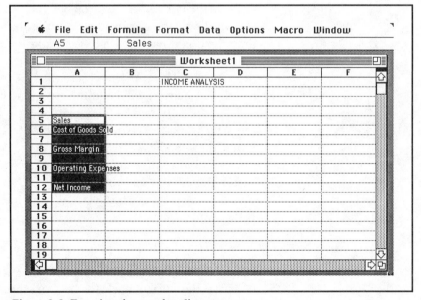

Figure 3.3: Entering the row headings

If you make a mistake in typing any title before you press Return, you can use the Backspace key to backspace and correct the entry. If you notice a mistake after you've pressed Return, go ahead and finish entering the row titles, then click the cell to be corrected and reenter the title.

After you have entered the row headings, you will notice that column A is not wide enough for two of the row titles. To widen the column:

1. Click once on cell A1

2. Pull down the Format menu and select Column Width

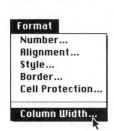

3. When you see the Column Width dialog box shown in Figure 3.4, click Standard Width, enter 15 as the new width, then click OK

You will see column A widen to accommodate your titles, as shown in Figure 3.5.

Now enter the column titles shown in Figure 3.6:

1. Click cell B4 and drag to cell D4

2. Type **1986** and press Return

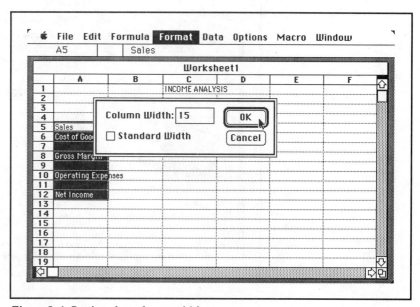

Figure 3.4: Setting the column width

3. Type **1987** and press Return

4. Type **1988** and press Return

ENTERING DATA

Now click cell B5 and enter the numbers shown in Figure 3.7 into rows 5, 6, and 10. (Do not enter data into rows 8 or 12.) You can include commas in the numbers if you wish, but they will disappear each time you press Return.

ENTERING FORMULAS

Enter the first formula by clicking cell B8 and typing **= B5 – B6**. Remember to type the equal sign first. This tells Excel to subtract the amount in B6 from the amount in B5. After you enter the formula, press Return. The gross margin, 240000, will appear in cell B8. If you make a mistake, click cell B8 and try entering the formula again.

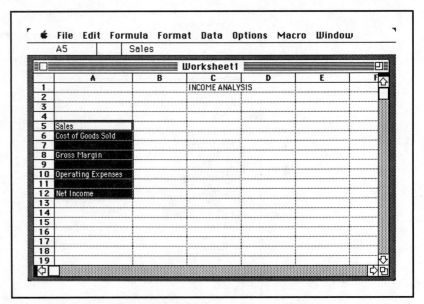

Figure 3.5: Column widths adjusted

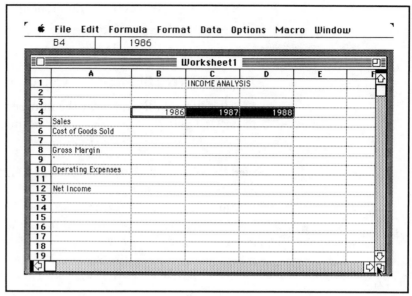

Figure 3.6: Entering the column headings

	A	B	C	D	E	F
1			INCOME ANALYSIS			
2						
3						
4		1986	1987	1988		
5	Sales	800000	850000	830000		
6	Cost of Goods Sold	560000	590000	580000		
7						
8	Gross Margin					
9	'					
10	Operating Expenses	170000	190000	184000		
11						
12	Net Income					

Figure 3.7: Entering the data

Now you can try a slightly different approach for entering the formula into cell B12:

1. Click cell B12 and enter an equal sign (=)
2. Click cell B8 and enter a minus sign (–)
3. Click cell B10 and press Return

The net income, 70000, will appear in cell B12.

To enter the formulas in rows 8 and 12, you can use a faster method. Click cell B8 and drag to cell D8. Pull down the Edit menu and choose Fill Right. The correct totals are now in row 9. Click cell B12 and drag to cell D12. Pull down the Edit menu and choose Fill Right. The correct totals are now in row 12. In both cases, as the formula is copied, the cells referenced are automatically changed to reflect the new columns. Select cell C8 and examine the formula in the formula bar. Compare this with the formula shown when you select cell B8.

After you've entered all the formulas, your worksheet should look like Figure 3.8.

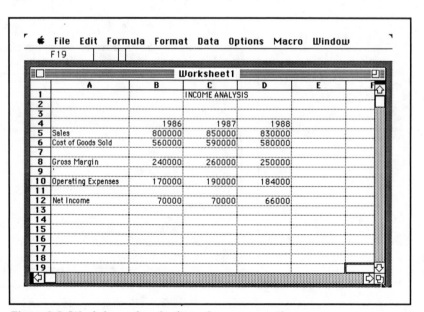

Figure 3.8: Worksheet after the formulas are entered

FORMATTING THE WORKSHEET

Now you can format the worksheet. Excel stores two things for each cell in the worksheet: the value (constant or formula) and information about how the value is to be displayed. Data are now displayed with text left-justified and numbers right-justified. Place the cursor on cell B5 and drag to cell D12. All the numeric cells should be highlighted. Pull down the Format menu and select Number. The Format Number dialog box shown in Figure 3.9 appears. Select the first currency format (the one highlighted in the figure), then click OK. The display will now show all numeric values in the selected range with a dollar sign in front and a comma every third digit.

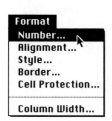

You can do a few more things to make the worksheet more readable. First, put the title in bold print:

1. Click cell C1

2. Pull down the Format menu and choose Style

3. When the Style dialog box shown in Figure 3.10 appears, click Bold, then OK

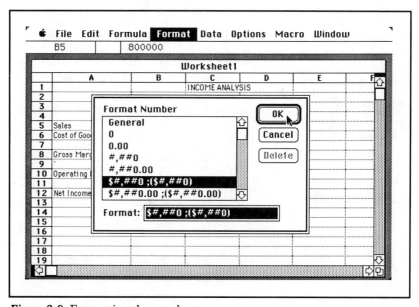

Figure 3.9: Formatting the numbers

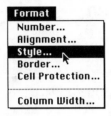

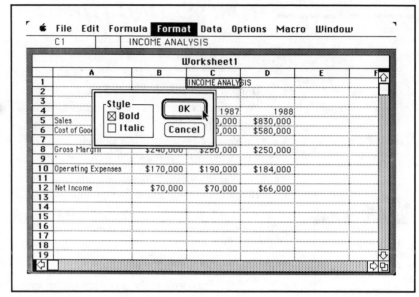

Figure 3.10: Putting the title in boldface print

Next, center the column titles:

1. Click cell B4 and drag to cell D4

2. Pull down the Format menu and choose Alignment

3. When the Alignment dialog box shown in Figure 3.11 appears, click Center, then OK

Finally, you can add some hyphens to separate the totals from the other numbers:

1. Click cell B7 and enter ten hyphens to fill the cell

2. Click cell B7 and drag to cell D7

3. Pull down the Edit menu and choose Fill Right

4. Repeat steps 1 through 3 for row 11 (cells B11 through D11)

Your final worksheet should look like the one shown in Figure 3.12.

You can now experiment by changing the values in rows 5, 6, and 10. You'll see that the numbers in rows 8 and 12 automatically change to reflect the new values.

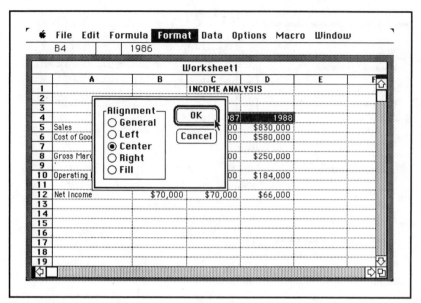

Figure 3.11: Aligning the column titles

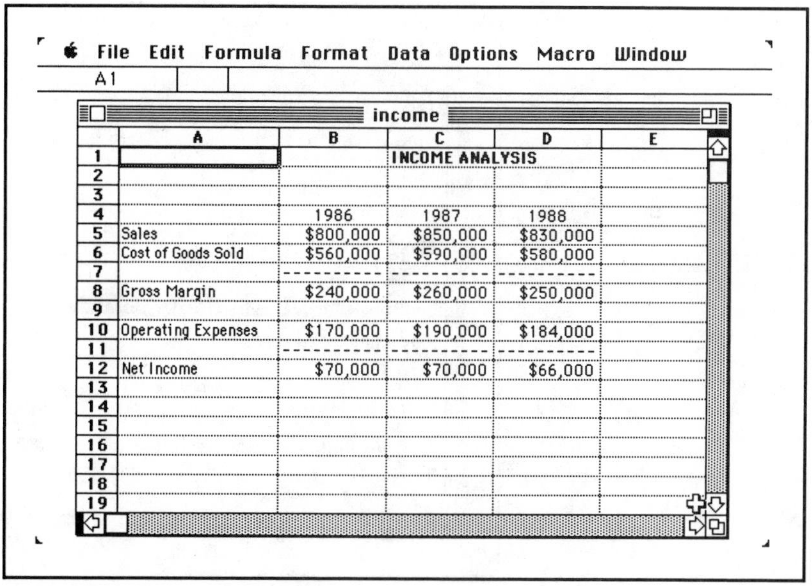

Figure 3.12: The final worksheet

PRINTING THE WORKSHEET

To print the worksheet, you should first turn off the row and column designators on the printout. Pull down the File menu and choose Page Setup. The dialog box shown in Figure 3.13 appears. Click both Print Row & Column Headings and Print Gridlines to turn these options off, then Click OK.

Now print the worksheet. Pull down the File menu and choose Print. Be sure that the printer is on and selected. When the Print dialog box shown in Figure 3.14 is displayed, click OK. The final output is shown in Figure 3.15.

SAVING THE WORKSHEET

Before quitting Excel, you should save the worksheet. Be sure that the data in rows 5, 6, and 10 are correct. Pull down the File menu and choose Save As. When the Save dialog box shown in Figure 3.16 is displayed, be sure that the data disk is active. If not, click Drive. Now enter the title **Income** and click Save.

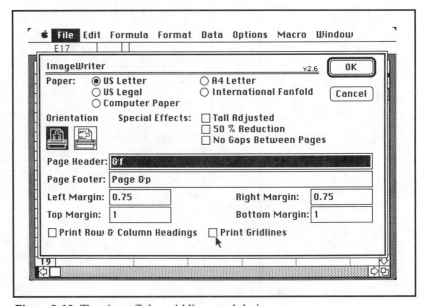

Figure 3.13: Turning off the grid lines and designators

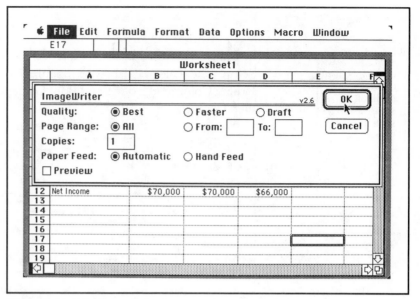

Figure 3.14: The Print dialog box

	1986	1987	1988
	INCOME ANALYSIS		
Sales	$800,000	$850,000	$830,000
Cost of Goods Sold	$560,000	$590,000	$580,000
Gross Margin	$240,000	$260,000	$250,000
Operating Expenses	$170,000	$190,000	$184,000
Net Income	$70,000	$70,000	$66,000

Figure 3.15: The printout

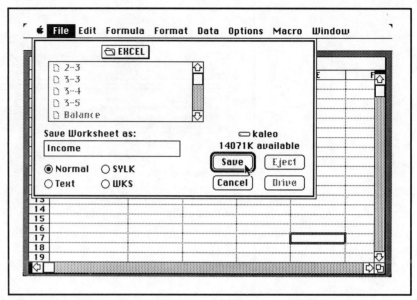

Figure 3.16: Saving the document

If you wish to make changes and save the document again, clicking Save will save it under the same name, and you will not see the dialog box. Clicking Save As permits you to enter a new name for the document or to change the disk drive.

CREATING A GRAPH

Now you can create a graph (or chart) from the sales figures on your Income worksheet. You will find that it takes only a few clicks of the mouse.

Follow these steps:

1. Click the heading for row 4 and drag to row 5 to designate the data to use for the graph, as shown in Figure 3.17.

2. Pull down the File menu and choose New.

3. When the dialog box shown in Figure 3.18 is displayed, click Chart, then click OK.

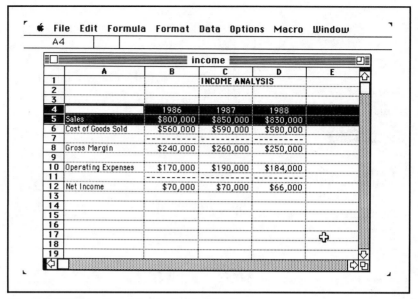

Figure 3.17: Selecting the data for the chart

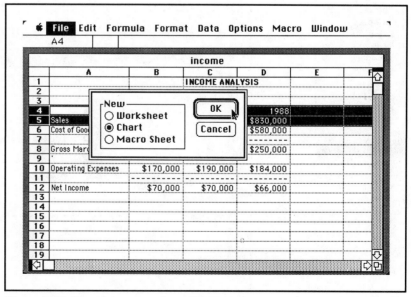

Figure 3.18: Opening a new chart document

Excel will draw the chart shown in Figure 3.19 in a new window on the screen. Notice that a different menu bar for charts is now displayed. You can improve the chart by selecting another graph type:

1. Pull down the Gallery menu and choose Column.

2. When the chart selection is displayed, as shown in Figure 3.20, double-click the third chart.

Excel will redraw the chart, as shown in Figure 3.21. You can print this chart by following the steps that you used to print the worksheet. When you are finished with the chart, click the close box in the chart window. When the dialog box shown in Figure 3.22 appears, click No to indicate that you do not want to save the chart.

QUITTING EXCEL

When you wish to leave Excel, there are only two simple steps: save your work and then exit. After using Save or Save As to save the document, pull down the File menu and choose Quit.

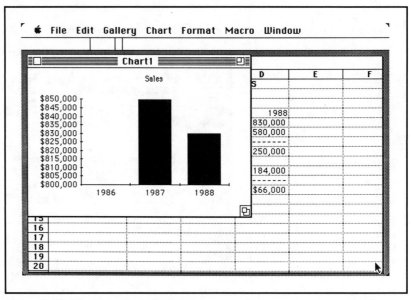

Figure 3.19: The first chart draft

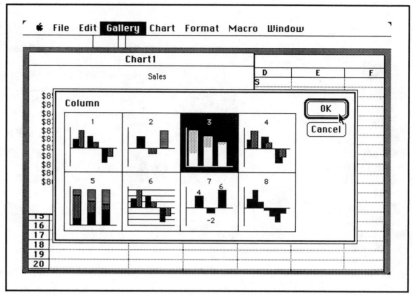

Figure 3.20: The column chart selection

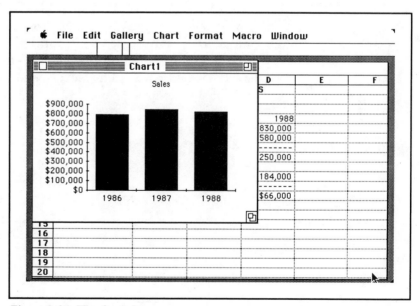

Figure 3.21: The final chart

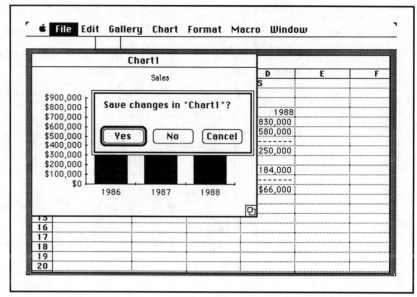

If you forget to save your document before quitting, Excel will catch this and prompt you with a dialog box, giving you another chance. Your best insurance, however, is to always save your document before quitting Excel.

Figure 3.22: Closing the chart document

SUMMARY

You have now created a simple worksheet that includes formulas and a chart using some of the data on that worksheet. You also learned how to do some formatting, how to print the worksheet, and how to save it to disk. In the next chapter, you will learn how to use additional worksheet features.

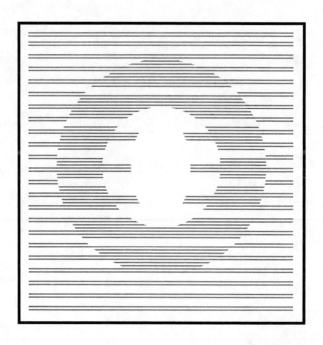

FUNDAMENTALS OF
EXCEL

THE PROCESS OF MAKING A WORKSHEET IS DIVIDED into four steps: creating, editing, formatting, and printing. For each of these steps there are several rules and procedures of which you must be aware in order to work with any type of worksheet. This section will introduce you to the basic rules by teaching you how to create, edit, format, and print a simple balance sheet. Even if you have created worksheets before, take the time to work through these exercises. You will be surprised at how much easier it is to do them with Excel than with any other spreadsheet program that you have used.

After you've created and printed the basic worksheet, this part will introduce you to a few other basic features: window control, formulas and functions, and naming cells.

CREATING THE WORKSHEET

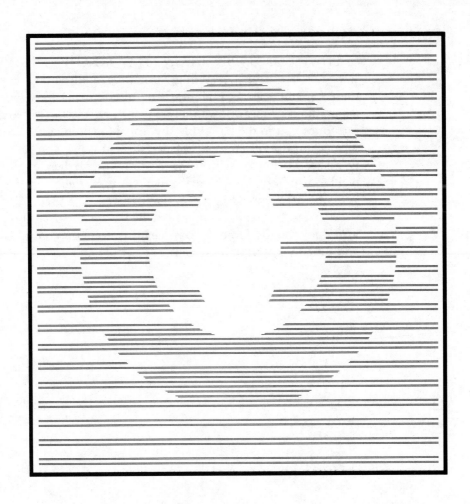

CHAPTER *4*

IN THIS CHAPTER YOU WILL LEARN HOW TO CREATE a worksheet. Do not be too concerned about any errors that you make when entering data. In the next chapter, you will learn how to correct those errors. First, let's review the basic parts of a worksheet and the techniques used in creating one.

THE WORKSHEET

The basic parts of the worksheet are shown in Figure 4.1. Excel provides 16,384 rows with 256 columns in each row. Thus, Excel makes 256 times 16,384, or 4,194,304, cells available to the user. The columns are designated by the letters of the alphabet (A through Z, then AA through IV), and rows are designated by numbers.

You can select a single cell or a range of cells for any operation. If a single cell is selected, it is the active cell, and its cell designator is displayed in the upper left under the menu bar.

The formula bar also appears under the menu bar. Anything you type on the keyboard is entered into the active cell and displayed in the formula bar. Once anything is typed, the enter box and cancel box appear on the formula bar. Clicking the enter box or pressing the Return key completes the entry.

The worksheet display is a window, and you can move this window to view or work with any area of the worksheet. To view various parts of the worksheet, you can scroll the window to that area. When you scroll around in the worksheet, the hidden parts of the worksheet are not erased; they are kept in the computer memory. When you're printing or saving a worksheet, all the worksheet (not just the visible part) is available.

You can enter text, numbers, or formulas into any cell of the worksheet. A *formula* is used to define the cell contents as a function of other cells on the worksheet. The contents of a cell with a formula will

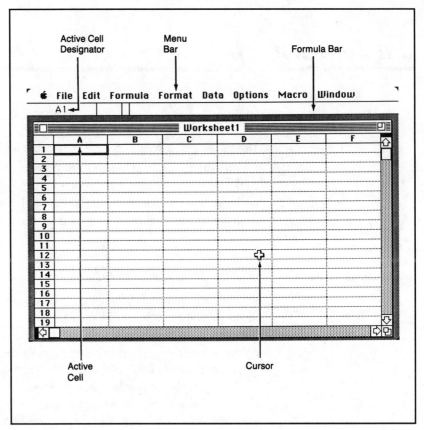

Figure 4.1: The Excel worksheet

change automatically to reflect any changes in the cells on which the formula cell is dependent. For example, you could define cell B6 as the sum of cells B2 and B3. If you alter the contents of cell B2 or B3, the value in cell B6 will automatically change to the new total.

BASIC WORKSHEET TECHNIQUES

To enter data to a cell, you must do three things:

- Make the cell active
- Enter the data with the keyboard
- Lock the data to the cell

In its simplest form, the procedure involves making the cell active by clicking on the desired cell, entering the data from the keyboard, and locking the data to the cell by pressing the Return key.

With Excel, however, you have plenty of flexibility in data entry. The basic techniques for entering data into a worksheet are described in the next three sections. You will then use these techniques to begin to create a more complex worksheet than the simple one that you set up in Chapter 3.

MAKING THE CELL ACTIVE

The active cell is the cell in which data will be entered when you start typing on the keyboard. You may select one or more cells (such as a cell range), but only one cell can be the active cell at a time. The active cell is indicated by a heavy border. The name of the active cell always appears in the active cell designator box.

When you want to enter data or perform an operation on a cell or cell range, you must first select the cell or range. Each time that you select a new cell or range, the previous selection is canceled. You can tell which cell, or cells, is selected at any given time because it is highlighted. You can select a single cell, a range of cells (rectangular area), a row of cells, or a column.

Selecting a cell or range of cells does not change the contents of the cell or cells. The cell contents will only be changed if you enter data from the keyboard after the cell is selected.

SELECTING CELLS AND RANGES   There are eight ways to select cells using Excel:

- You can select a single cell by placing the cursor on the cell and clicking once. A heavy border will appear around the cell and the cell's reference letter and number will appear in the active cell designator box to the left of the formular bar.

- You can select a cell range by placing the cursor on the first cell in the range, clicking the mouse button, and dragging the cursor to the last cell in the range. To select cells in more than one column or row, start the selection in the upper left and drag to the lower right. If the final cell of the desired range will be beyond the window border, the window will automatically scroll as you drag the cursor beyond the border. When you select a range of cells, the first cell from which you define the range becomes the active cell. The range is indicated in black, and the active cell remains in white. While defining the range, the active cell designator will display the size of the range. When the mouse button is released, however, the designator displays only the active cell. If you select a row or column, the first cell of that row or column in the displayed window will be the active cell.

- You can select an entire row by placing the cursor on the row designator at the left of the window and clicking once.

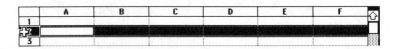

- You can select an entire column by placing the cursor on the column designator and clicking once.

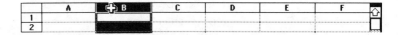

- You can select the entire worksheet by placing the cursor on the small box to the left of the column headings and above the row headings and clicking once.

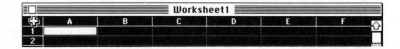

- You can select a range of rows by clicking a row designator and dragging to another row. In the same way, you can select a range of columns by selecting a column designator and dragging to another column.

- You can select a rectangular cell range by clicking on the cell in one diagonal, then holding down the Shift key and clicking the cell at the opposite diagonal.

- You can make multiple range selections by clicking your first selection and then holding down the Command key while you click to select additional cells or cell ranges. Multiple ranges selected in this way are called discontinuous ranges.

Before continuing, you should practice making each type of selection listed above.

If you want to move the active cell one cell in any direction, use the direction keys or the following:

To the right	Tab
To the left	Shift-Tab
Down	Return
Up	Shift-Return

If a range is selected, these keys still work but the active cell will only move within the range.

MOVING A RANGE Once you have selected a cell or cell range on the worksheet, you can move the range across the worksheet using the following key combinations:

To the right	Command-Tab
To the left	Shift-Command-Tab
Down	Command-Return
Up	Shift-Command-Return

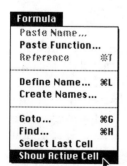

FINDING THE ACTIVE CELL If you are working with a large worksheet, the active cell may not be visible on the screen. To find it, pull down the Formula menu and choose Show Active Cell. To find the last cell in the worksheet, pull down the Formula menu and choose Select Last Cell.

ENTERING DATA

Once an active cell is selected, the next step is entering data into the cell. You can either enter a constant value or a formula. There are four basic types of constant values that can be entered: text, numbers, dates and times, and logical values.

When you select a blank cell, a flashing vertical bar appears in the formula bar. As you enter characters, the bar will move in front of the characters. This bar is called the insertion point. Later you will learn how to move this insertion point for editing purposes.

As soon as you begin typing the cell entry, the enter box (✔) and cancel box (x) icons appear at the formula bar. The enter box can be used like the Return key to lock the data into the cell after entry. The cancel box can be clicked if you wish to clear the data entry without locking the data to the cell.

You can also enter data into a selected cell or cell range by using the mouse to point to other cells or names that you have defined. You will learn more about this technique later in this chapter and in Chapter 9.

ENTERING NUMBERS   You can enter numbers in one of three formats:

FORMAT	*EXAMPLES*
Integer	1, 45, −45
Decimal fraction	43.5, −56.75
Scientific notation	25E23, 4E −3

You can use a minus sign or parentheses to enter negative numbers. Dollar signs, percent signs, the letter E, and commas can also be used as a part of numeric entry. Unless you select otherwise, numbers are right-justified in a cell. If a number has too many characters to fit in a specific cell, Excel will display ###### in that cell to indicate the overflow or will try to display the entry in scientific notation.

Regardless of how numbers are displayed, they are always stored with 14 digits of accuracy unless you use the Precision As Displayed command on the Options menu to change the display.

ENTERING DATES AND TIMES   Excel stores both dates and times as serial numbers. The serial number that is stored for the date represents the number of days since January 1, 1904. This makes it possible for Excel to calculate the number of days between two dates by subtracting the earlier date from the later one. However, when you type in a date or select any cell in which a date is already stored, it is displayed on the formula bar as a date, not a serial number.

You can enter dates in mm/dd/yy format using slashes or hyphens or you can spell them out, for example, September 1, 1987 or Sept 1,

1987. You can also enter dates in any of three other formats: dd/mm/yy (e.g., 25/May/85), dd/mm (e.g., 25/May), or mm/yy (e.g., May/86). If you enter a date in any other format, Excel will not display an error message; it will simply store it as text rather than as a serial number.

You can enter time values in either standard (e.g., 3:30:30 PM) or military (e.g., 13:15:45) format. The seconds entry is optional, and you can use A or P instead of AM or PM. You can enter both a date and time into a single cell.

Dates and times can only be used as constants. They cannot be entered into formulas. If you need to use a date or time in a formula, enter it as text (inside quotation marks). Excel will convert any date in a valid date format into a serial number when it evaluates the formula.

ENTERING LOGICAL VALUES   You can enter the logical values true or false in upper- or lowercase, but they will be stored and displayed in uppercase by Excel. The use of logical values is discussed in Chapter 8.

ENTERING TEXT   Any characters that Excel cannot interpret as a number, date, time, logical value, or formula are considered text. Unless you select otherwise, text data are always left-justified in a cell. You can enter up to 255 characters in a cell.

If any part of a numeric string is nonnumeric, Excel will assume the entire string is text. For example, **234 Fox Drive** would be assumed to be a text string, even though it begins with a number. You can enter numbers as text by enclosing them in quotation marks. You can enter text in formulas by enclosing the text in quotation marks.

ENTERING FORMULAS   The real power of Excel lies in its ability to calculate the value of a cell from the values in other cells. This is accomplished by entering formulas in cells. You use formulas to tell Excel exactly how to calculate a cell value from the values in other cells. You can even use a formula to calculate a cell value based on formulas in other cells. A worksheet, then, can become a very complex system of interwoven formulas and values. Changing one value on the worksheet can initiate a complex chain of calculations that will change cells throughout the entire worksheet.

Creating Formulas   To create a formula, first select the cell or cell range that you want to contain the value calculated by the formula. You can enter the formula into the cell in one of three ways:

- Type in the formula from the keyboard. First, type an equal sign, then type the formula. Complete the entry by clicking the enter box on the formula bar or by pressing the Return key.

- Click the cells that are referenced in the formula. For example, to enter cell B5 minus cell B7, you would type an equal sign, place the cursor on cell B5 and click, type a minus sign, and then place the cursor on cell B7 and click. To complete the formula, click the enter box or press the Return key. You can only use this method with relative cell referencing (see Chapter 8).

- Type or paste the name that you assigned to a cell or range of cells. Once you've defined names for cells (see Chapter 9), you can use the Paste Name command on the Formula menu to enter the formula (Excel will automatically begin the formula with an equal sign). Alternately, you can type an equal sign and then type in the formula using the names. Again, click the enter box or press the Return key to complete the formula.

Remember to begin each formula with an equal sign and to complete the entry by clicking the enter box on the formula bar or by pressing the Return key. If you make a mistake while you're entering a formula, click the cancel box on the formula bar or backspace to the error. Methods for building and using formulas are discussed in detail in Chapters 8 and 9.

Formula Operators   When you create formulas, you must use operators to indicate how Excel is to produce new values from other cell values. The mathematical operators are:

OPERATOR	*FUNCTION*
+	Addition

–	Subtraction
*	Multiplication
/	Division
^	Exponentiation

You can also use an ampersand (&) as an operator with text fields to join two text values to create a new text value. For example *"Mr." &* *"Smith"* becomes *Mr. Smith*.

You can also use a formula to compare cell values. The result of using comparison operators is always a logical value—TRUE or FALSE. The following comparison operators are available:

OPERATOR	*FUNCTION*
=	Equal to
<	Less than
< =	Less than or equal to
>	Greater than
> =	Greater than or equal to
< >	Not equal to

Reference operators are used to refer to two or more cells in formulas and in function arguments. There are three reference operators available:

OPERATOR	*FUNCTION*
:	Range: references all cells in the given range
,	Union: includes two references
space	Intersection: includes cells common to two references

For example, to indicate the range from cell A1 to cell A10, you could use A1:A10. With reference operators, you can combine relative and absolute referencing (see Chapter 8). You can also use the names that you assigned to a cell or range of cells (see Chapter 9).

If you don't type in an operator, Excel will automatically insert a plus sign.

LOCKING THE ENTRY

Once data are entered in a cell, you must lock them to that cell. There are three ways to lock the data:

- Press the Return key. The active cell designator does not change.

- Press any key that moves the active cell: Tab, Shift-Tab, Return, or Shift-Return. Each of these will lock the data to the cell, then activate the adjacent cell. You can also use any of the direction keys to lock the entry and move the cursor in the direction of the arrow.

- Click on the enter box.

If you are entering data into a series of cells, use the second locking method. That way, you activate the adjacent cell after the data entry and are ready to enter subsequent data.

THE CELL DATA DISPLAY

An Excel cell can hold up to 255 characters. However, often the actual cell width displayed is much shorter (the standard is 10). Therefore, there are rules as to what Excel will display.

The true cell value and the displayed value are two different things. Excel always remembers whatever you type exactly as you type it. This is the true cell value. If you type a 50 character text string to be entered in a cell with a width of 10, Excel remembers the entire text string but displays only 10 characters if the cell to the right contains data. To see the entire text string, click on the cell and you will see the entire text string in the formula bar.

If you enter a large number into a small cell, the number is always stored with 14 digits of accuracy. Excel will try to display it all using scientific notation. You can also use the format command to alter what is displayed, as you will learn later. For example, if you enter the number 14.3245, you could format it to display as 14.32. The entire number, though, is still stored as the cell value and will be used in calculations. You could also change the format to display more decimal places of the number.

A displayed calculation on a cell range may not appear to be the right answer, as the displayed values are not necessarily the true cell values. This will be discussed further in Chapter 6.

SPECIAL WORKSHEET TECHNIQUES

When creating a worksheet, there are several special techniques that are important to learn. These include clearing, filling, copying, and changing column widths.

CLEARING THE WORKSHEET

If you have some practice entries on your worksheet and you want to start over with a clean worksheet, you can clear it by following these steps:

1. Select the entire worksheet, as described in the Basic Worksheet Techniques section of this chapter

2. Pull down the Edit menu and choose Clear, click All and OK

FILLING

You can enter the same value into all the cells in a horizontal or vertical range by using the Fill commands. To use a Fill command:

1. Select the range, including the cell that already contains the value

2. Pull down the Edit menu and choose Fill Right or Fill Down, as appropriate

Excel moves the value into each cell selected and automatically adjusts formulas that contain relative addressing.

There is a short-hand way of filling right and down (using the Option key), as described in the tip in the next section.

MOVING AND COPYING

When you copy, you take a value or a formula in one cell and copy it into a cell or range of cells. Moving is similar, except that the original cells are cleared. When you use the Fill Right or Fill Down command, you are copying. Excel does provide, however, an even more versatile approach.

To move data, select the source cell range, pull down the Edit menu, and choose Cut. This moves a copy of the current range data to the Clipboard. Click the first cell of the destination range (or the entire range). The source range will remain marked with a dotted line. Pull down the Edit menu and choose Paste. The source cells will clear, and the destination cells will now contain the data. Source and destination ranges can overlap if necessary.

To copy data, select the source range, pull down the Edit menu, and choose Copy. This creates a copy of the source range data in the Clipboard. Click the first cell of the destination range (or the entire range). Again, the source range remains marked. Pull down the Edit menu and choose Paste. The destination range will now contain the same data as the source range. The data is still in the Clipboard. You can do more pastes with the same source range without using the Copy command.

When formulas are copied into other cells, the formula references change to reflect their new position. This default method is called relative addressing. It is possible to prevent this adjustment to formulas by using absolute addressing. See Chapter 8 for more about relative and absolute addressing. As with moving, you can designate the destination range by selecting the upper-left corner of the range as a single cell. You can also specify a destination range that is an integer multiple of the source cells and create multiple copies. For example, if the source range is two cells, the destination range must contain two, four, six, or another even number of cells. The destination range must be a single cell or an integer multiple of the source range. Do not use overlapping copy ranges.

CHANGING COLUMN WIDTHS

In creating worksheets, you will often need to change the width of a column to display the entire cell contents or to improve the appearance of the worksheet. You can change column widths either by using the Column Width command on the Format menu or by dragging the column.

CHANGING THE COLUMN WIDTH USING A COMMAND   To change the width by using the Column Width command, pull down the Format menu and choose Column Width. When the Column Width

---

When moving, save time by designating the destination range by a single cell—the upper-left corner of the destination range. The entire range will still be moved.

In creating a worksheet, there is a quick way to copy or fill formulas or data. Before entering the original formula (or data) select the entire range to which the formula will be applied (such as cells B13 to D13). Enter the formula into the formula bar, hold down the Option key, then press the Return key to complete the entry. Excel will move the formula (or data) into each cell of the range.

To see the size of a selected range, use the Clipboard. Copy the range to the Clipboard. Pull down the Window menu and choose Show Clipboard. The Clipboard will indicate the range size. You can use this trick when copying to be sure the source and destination ranges are the same size.

dialog box appears, type in the new width from the keyboard, and then click OK. The column width will change to reflect the value entered. The contents of the cells in that column will not be changed.

CHANGING THE COLUMN WIDTH BY DRAGGING To change the width by dragging, move the cursor to the line between the column heading designators. The shape of the cursor will change to a vertical line. Click and drag the cursor to the right. The width of the column on the left will follow the cursor. Release the mouse button at the desired width.

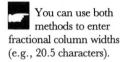
You can use both methods to enter fractional column widths (e.g., 20.5 characters).

SAVING THE WORKSHEET

After you have created the worksheet, you will need to save it on your disk. Although the worksheet is displayed on the screen, it is only stored in the computer memory. If you turn the computer off or load another worksheet, the current worksheet will be lost. To save the worksheet on disk, pull down the File menu and choose Save As. Enter the name of the worksheet in the dialog box, be sure that the disk designator is correct (click Drive if necessary), and then click Save.

As a general rule, while you're creating a worksheet, you should save it approximately every 20 minutes. This will protect your work against power failures, hardware failures, or inadvertent user mistakes. Use Save As on the File menu only the first time that you save your file. On subsequent saves, pull down the File menu and choose Save. With Save, Excel won't display the dialog box. It saves the worksheet under the same name that you used previously.

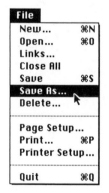

THE BALANCE WORKSHEET

During this and the next two chapters, you will create the worksheet shown in Figure 4.2. In this chapter, you will use the techniques described so far to enter the worksheet data and formulas. When you're done, your worksheet should look like the one in Figure 4.3. In comparing the two figures, notice the difference in the quality of presentation that is achieved by formatting, which you will learn in Chapter 6.

ACME MANUFACTURING COMPANY

Balance Sheet for 1987
(Figures in Thousands of Dollars)

	Qtr 1	Qtr 2	Qtr 3	Qtr 4
Current Assets				
Cash	$28,653	$42,894	$64,882	$91,053
Accounts Receivable	$35,700	$44,150	$48,450	$55,230
Inventory	$11,400	$12,930	$14,500	$16,490
Total Current Assets	*$75,753*	*$99,974*	*$127,832*	*$162,773*
Fixed Assets				
P,P, and E				
Furniture, Fixtures	$12,100	$12,100	$12,100	$12,100
Equipment	$6,500	$16,600	$21,100	$42,300
Office Equipment	$4,100	$4,100	$4,100	$4,100
Gross P, P, and E	$22,700	$32,800	$37,300	$58,500
Accumulated Depreciation	$6,600	$8,700	$11,400	$13,400
Total Fixed Assets	*$16,100*	*$24,100*	*$25,900*	*$45,100*
Total Assets	**$91,853**	**$124,074**	**$153,732**	**$207,873**
Current Liabilities				
Accounts Payable	$17,340	$41,000	$42,300	$75,200
Income Taxes Payable	$4,043	$6,132	$7,301	$9,245
Total Current Liabilities	$21,383	$47,132	$49,601	$84,445
Non-current Liabilities				
Long-term debt	$22,000	$20,000	$18,000	$16,000
Total Liabilities	*$43,383*	*$67,132*	*$67,601*	*$100,445*
Common Stock, $1 per var	$40,000	$40,000	$40,000	$40,000
Retained Earnings	$8,470	$16,942	$46,131	$67,428
Total Liabilities & Equity	**$91,853**	**$124,074**	**$153,732**	**$207,873**

Figure 4.2: The final Balance worksheet

	Qtr 1	Qtr 2	Qtr 3	Qtr 4
ACME MANUFACTURING COMPANY				
Balance Sheet for 1987 (Figures in Thousands of Dollars)				
Current Assets				
Cash	28653	42894	64882	91053
Accounts Receivable	35700	44150	48450	55230
Inventory	11400	12930	14500	16490
Total Current Assets	75753	99974	127832	162773
Fixed Assets				
P,P, and E				
Furniture, Fixtures	12100	12100	12100	12100
Equipment	6500	16600	21100	42300
Office Equipment	4100	4100	4100	4100
Gross P, P, and E	22700	32800	37300	58500
Accumulated Depreciation	6600	8700	11400	13400
Total Fixed Assets	16100	24100	25900	45100
Total Assets	91853	124074	153732	207873
Current Liabilities				
Accounts Payable	17340	41000	42300	75200
Income Taxes Payable	4043	6132	7301	9245
Total Current Liabilities	21383	47132	49601	84445
Non-current Liabilities				
Long-term debt	22000	20000	18000	16000
Total Liabilities	43383	67132	67601	100445
Common Stock, $1 per var	40000	40000	40000	40000
Retained Earnings	8470	16942	46131	67428
Total Liabilities & Equity	91853	124074	153732	207873

Figure 4.3: The Balance worksheet before formatting

Microsoft Excel

In this and the following data entries, do not be too concerned about mistakes. If you make a mistake, continue to create your worksheet working around it. In the next chapter, I will show you how to edit the worksheet and correct your mistakes.

CREATING THE WORKSHEET

To get started, put the Excel disks in your Macintosh and double-click the Excel icon. You will see Excel load a blank worksheet called Worksheet1.

Now start creating the worksheet by selecting cells A8 through A43. Enter the row titles shown in Figure 4.4. Press the Return key after you've typed each title. Press the Return key twice to skip a line.

Expand the width of column A by pulling down the Format menu and choosing Column Width. When the dialog box shown in Figure 4.5 appears, click OK.

Next, drag the cursor from cell B6 to cell E6 and enter the column headings shown in Figure 4.4. Press Return after each entry. Add a title to the worksheet by selecting cell C1 and entering **ACME MANUFACTURING COMPANY** from the keyboard. Select cell C3 and enter **Balance Sheet for 1987**. Select cell C4 and enter **(Figures in Thousands of Dollars)**.

To enter the horizontal separators, first place one hyphen in the left-most column (as B12). Then click Format, Alignment, and Fill. Then copy the separator to the other three by selecting B12 to E12, pulling down the Edit menu, and selecting Fill Right.

Now enter the numbers shown in Figure 4.4 into the worksheet. Do not enter the values for rows 13, 21, 24, 26, 32, 37, and 43. You'll use formulas to fill these in, as described below.

Enter the following formulas for column B:

SELECT	TYPE
B13	= B9 + B10 + B11
B21	= B17 + B18 + B19
B24	= B21 − B22
B26	= B13 + B24
B32	= B29 + B30
B37	= B32 + B35
B43	= B37 + B39 + B41

In Figure 4.6, you can see how the worksheet lists these formula values; see, for example, cell B13.

	A	B	C	D	E
1			ACME MANUFACTURING COMPANY		
2					
3			Balance Sheet for 1987		
4			(Figures in Thousands of Dollars)		
5					
6		Qtr 1	Qtr 2	Qtr 3	Qtr 4
7					
8	Current Assets				
9	Cash	28653	42894	64882	91053
10	Accounts Receivable	35700	44150	48450	55230
11	Inventory	11400	12930	14500	16490
12		----------	----------	----------	----------
13	Total Current Assets				
14					
15	Fixed Assets				
16	P,P, and E				
17	Furniture, Fixtures	12100	12100	12100	12100
18	Equipment	6500	16600	21100	42300
19	Office Equipment	4100	4100	4100	4100
20		----------	----------	----------	----------
21	Gross P, P, and E				
22	Accumulated Depreciation	6600	8700	11400	13400
23		----------	----------	----------	----------
24	Total Fixed Assets				
25					
26	Total Assets				
27					
28	Current Liabilities				
29	Accounts Payable	17340	41000	42300	75200
30	Income Taxes Payable	4043	6132	7301	9245
31		----------	----------	----------	----------
32	Total Current Liabilities				
33					
34	Non-current Liabilities				
35	Long-term debt	22000	20000	18000	16000
36		----------	----------	----------	----------
37	Total Liabilities				
38					
39	Common Stock, $1 per var	40000	40000	40000	40000
40					
41	Retained Earnings	8470	16942	46131	67428
42		----------	----------	----------	----------
43	Total Liabilities & Equity				

Figure 4.4: Entering text and numbers

Edit	
Can't Undo	⌘Z
Cut	⌘H
Copy	⌘C
Paste	⌘U
Clear...	⌘B
Paste Special...	
Delete...	⌘K
Insert...	⌘I
Fill Right	⌘R
Fill Down	⌘D

Now you need to fill in the formulas. Click cell B13 and drag to cell E13. Pull down the Edit menu and choose Fill Right. Repeat this procedure for all the rows with formulas.

Before you continue, save the worksheet. Pull down the File menu and choose Save As. Enter the name **Balance** into the dialog box that

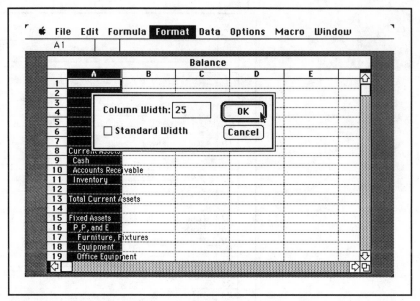

Figure 4.5: Changing the column width

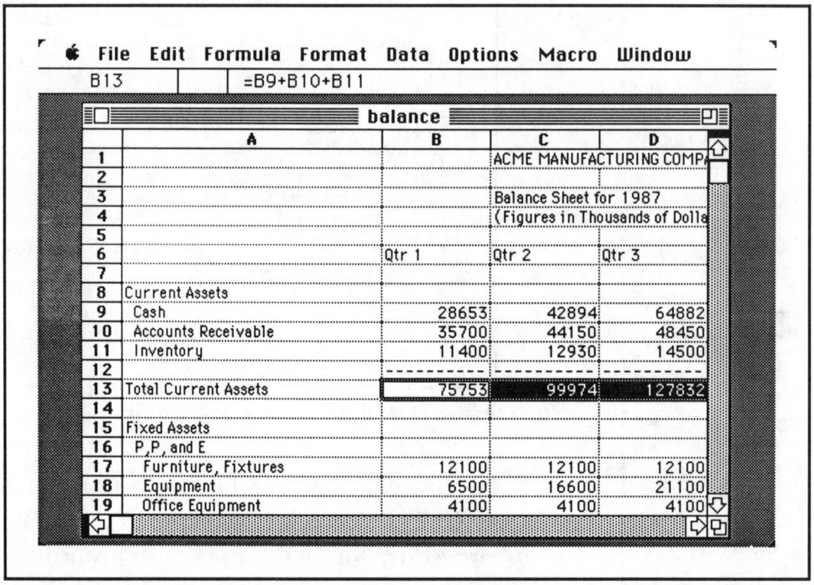

Figure 4.6: The worksheet after entering a formula

appears (see Figure 4.7). Be sure that the disk designator shows the data disk (otherwise, click Drive), then click Save.

EXPERIMENTING WITH THE WORKSHEET

Now you can try some different techniques. First, try copying a formula. Instead of entering the formulas for cells C13, D13, and E13 using the Fill Right command as you did, copy the formula from cell B13 into the rest of the row. First, click cell B13. Pull down the Edit menu and choose Copy. Notice that the highlighting on cell B13 changes. Now, click cell C13 and drag to cell E13. Although cells C13, D13, and E13 are now selected, cell B13 is still marked to indicate the "from" cell range for the copy. Now pull down the Edit menu again and choose Paste. The correct totals will immediately show in the rest of the row.

Notice that the totals in cells C13, D13, and E13 are correct. The formula in cell C13 was automatically adjusted for the new columns when it was moved. To check this, click cell C13 and look at the formula in the formula bar at the top of the page (see Figure 4.8).

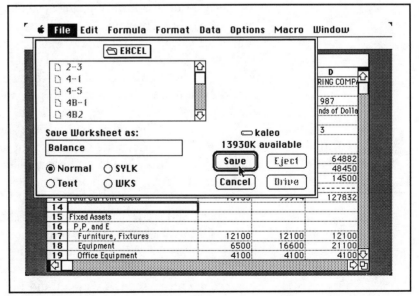

Figure 4.7: Saving the document

Figure 4.8: Examining a formula created by a copy command

Now, just for practice, move row 43 to row 44. First, select row 43 by placing the cursor on the row designator and clicking once. Pull down the Edit menu and choose Cut. Notice that the entire range is marked. Place the cursor on the designator for row 44 and click once. Pull down the Edit menu again and choose Paste. Row 43 will move to row 44 (row 43 will be cleared). Notice that the formulas are automatically adjusted. Recover the former worksheet by pulling down the Edit menu and choosing Undo Paste.

You use the Clipboard for both cutting and copying. You can watch the Clipboard change during a cut and paste operation. First, make the worksheet window a little smaller by dragging the size box in the lower-right corner up and to the left slightly. Then, pull down the Window menu and choose Show Clipboard. The Clipboard window opens and is the active window, as shown in Figure 4.9.

The Clipboard can be moved, scrolled, and closed, like any other active window. Again, repeat the cut exercise described above. Watch the active window switch back to the worksheet and the Clipboard contents change as you cut and paste. The cutting operation

❖ File Edit Window

	A	B	C	D
		Balance		
1				ACME MANUFACTURING COMPANY
2				
3				Balance Sheet for 1987
4				(Figures in Thousands of Dollars)
5				
6			Qtr 1	Qtr 2	Qtr 3	Qt
7				
8	Current Assets			
9	Cash		28653	42894	64882
10	Accounts Receivable		35700	44150	48450
11	Inventory		11400	12930	14500
12					
13	Total Current Assets		75753	99974	127832
14					

☐☐ Clipboard ☐☐

es	12100	12100	12100
	6500	16600	21100
	4100	4100	4100

Figure 4.9: The Clipboard window

clears the Clipboard. The pasting operation does not clear the contents of the Clipboard—you can do two pastes from one Copy command. Once you have completed pasting, make the Clipboard window active, click its close box, and then adjust the worksheet window again to fill the entire display. Be sure that the total appears on row 43.

As a last experiment, change the width of column A by dragging. Move the cursor to the line between column A and column B. Click and drag the cursor, which now appears as a vertical line, as shown in Figure 4.10. Release the mouse button when the column is wider. Before going on, be sure that the column width of column A is 25 characters.

During this chapter and the next two chapters, you will be changing this document in a series of exercises. When you leave Excel (by pulling down the File menu and choosing Quit), you will see a dialog box. The box indicates that the document has been changed and asks if you wish to save the new document. If you do not wish to save the altered document, click No.

File	
New...	⌘N
Open...	⌘O
Links...	
Close All	
Save	⌘S
Save As...	
Delete...	
Page Setup...	
Print...	⌘P
Printer Setup...	
Quit	⌘Q

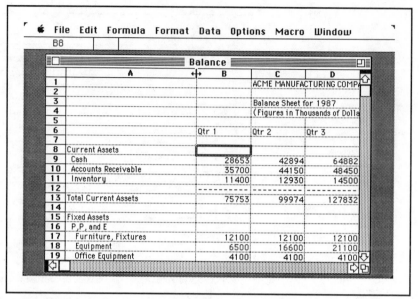

Figure 4.10: Changing the column width by dragging

WORKSHEET DESIGN STRATEGIES

The following are some general guidelines for creating useful worksheets:

1. Work out the general worksheet idea on paper first before using Excel.

2. Always use a heading. It should contain, as a minimum, a descriptive title and version number. Generally, you will also want to include the date of the last modification (see Chapters 8 and 26 for more information about how to add a date).

3. Use more formulas to link cells and avoid using absolute values unless necessary. For example, the worksheet may have a price that affects several cells and changes periodically. Put the price in a separate block on the page and use a formula to move it to other cells in the worksheet.

4. Avoid large worksheets. Instead, try to use a series of small worksheets and, if necessary, link them together (see Chapter 16).

5. Use blank rows, columns, and cells liberally to improve worksheet readability.

6. Add special documentation and notes at the end of the page as text if you need to explain any special features of the worksheet.

7. Use the Fill and Copy commands to enter new columns and rows when possible. Use the Option key to enter the same value or formula into many cells.

8. Check the worksheet over carefully before printing it. People have used electronic worksheets to make major decisions based on incorrect data. If the input data are wrong or if a formula is wrong, the results will be wrong. The computer can only do what you tell it to do.

EDITING THE WORKSHEET

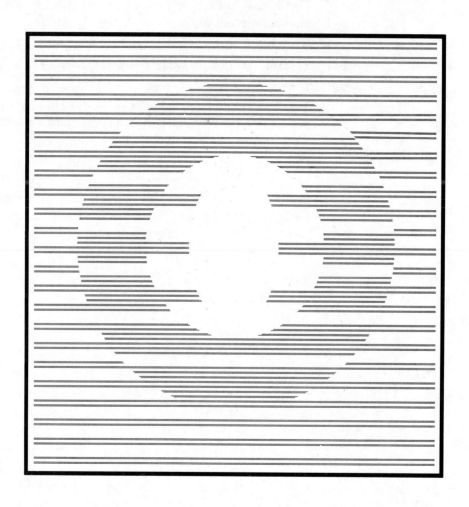

CHAPTER 5

EXCEL HAS MANY EDITING FEATURES THAT CAN make your work easier. You can clear a cell or cell range, recover from an accidental cut, delete or clear, and insert or delete rows and columns. You can also use standard Macintosh editing techniques to edit any data in the formula bar.

In this chapter, you will learn the basic editing skills to use with Excel worksheets. These will enable you to correct any mistakes that you might have made in the last chapter. Even if your worksheet does not have any mistakes, take the time to try some of the editing described here.

This chapter also includes information about adding comments to worksheets, using other commands for editing, and saving your edited worksheet. More advanced editing techniques are discussed in Chapter 14.

EDITING TECHNIQUES

A variety of worksheet editing techniques are available to the Excel user. They make it easy for you to keep your worksheets up-to-date and accurate, as well as to use one basic worksheet structure for many purposes.

The process of using a basic worksheet structure for many purposes is called *templating*. A master worksheet is created that contains all the data and formatting for several problems. This master worksheet is then saved and used as the template for successive worksheets that are created.

Now let's examine how you can edit a worksheet. The techniques discussed in this section include:

- Clearing cells

- Undoing various operations

- Editing cells

- Editing formulas

- Inserting and deleting rows and columns

LOADING THE WORKSHEET

Balance

To begin editing, start up Excel by double-clicking the Balance icon on the data disk. In a few minutes, you will see the Balance worksheet that you created in the last chapter.

CLEARING A CELL OR CELL RANGE

Sometimes, when you've entered data into the wrong range of cells, the easiest way to correct the error is to clear the entire range. To clear a cell, the simplest method is to select the cell, then press the Backspace key. Then press Return or click the enter box. (If you press the Backspace key accidentally, click the cancel box to restore the cell's contents.)

If you wish to replace a cell value instead of clearing it, see Editing a Cell Value in this chapter.

To clear a range of cells, first select the cell range that you want to clear. Pull down the Edit menu and choose Clear. The Clear dialog box shown in Figure 5.1 appears. Click All, then OK. The cell range will be cleared. This will also work to clear a single cell.

You can try this now with your Balance worksheet. Select cells C13, D13, and E13. Pull down the Edit menu, choose Clear, click

Figure 5.1: Clearing a cell or cell range

All, then OK. The cells will clear. You will also notice that two totals in row 26 change, as you have just changed the data that are used to compute these totals. Before going on to anything else, pull down the Edit menu and choose Undo Clear (undoing is discussed below).

The Clear dialog box also has options for clearing formulas only and format only. Clearing a format puts the range in the default General number template. Clearing formulas clears the data in the cell, but not the format. Clearing All clears both format and data.

UNDOING

If you make a mistake while you're changing a worksheet, you can recover the previous version by using the Undo command. The Undo command applies to almost any type of operation: inserting, deleting, moving, copying, and pasting. However, only the last operation can be undone—once you have gone on to something else, the undo capability is lost. For example, if you did a cut and paste operation with the Clipboard window open (as you did in the last chapter), closing the Clipboard would cause you to lose the capability to undo the cut and paste. Each time that you select the Edit menu, if the Undo command is available, it will be shown in boldface, and the function that you can undo will be the second word, such as **Undo Cut** or **Undo Paste**.

You can see how this works by moving row 13 to row 14 and then undoing the operation:

1. Select row 13

2. Pull down the Edit menu and choose Cut

3. Select row 14

4. Pull down the Edit menu and choose Paste; row 13 has now moved to row 14

5. Pull down the Edit menu and choose Undo Paste; row 14 is now moved back to row 13

Notice that the window is still marked for another paste operation. As shown in Figure 5.2, row 13 is marked as a *from* range and row 14 is marked as a *to* range. You can select another paste range and paste again (without cutting). Alternately, you can select another cell or cell range and start a new operation (enter cell contents, cut, copy, etc.).

To clear an entire worksheet, it is faster to pull down the File menu, choose New, and create a new worksheet. Another way to clear the whole worksheet is to: (1) select the entire worksheet by clicking the empty square above the row 1 designator, (2) pull down the Edit menu, and (3) choose All, then Clear.

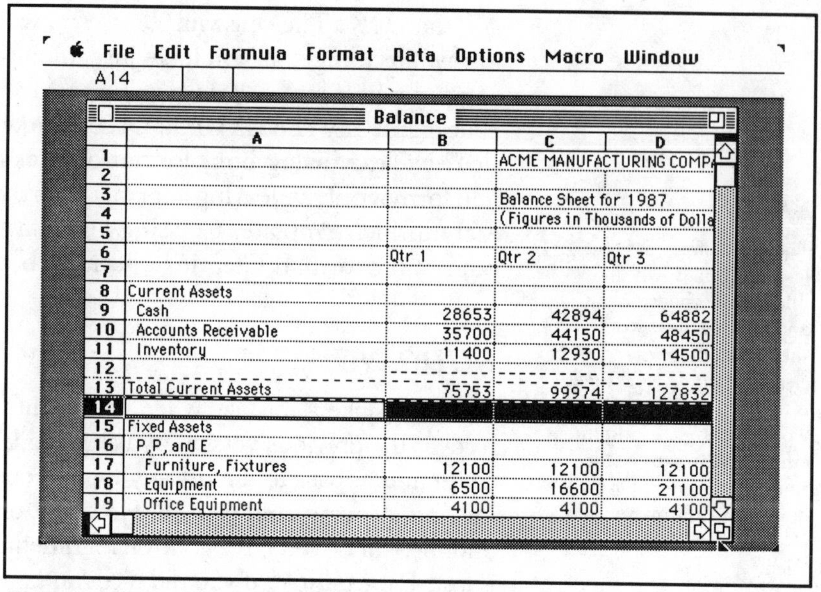

Figure 5.2: The worksheet after undoing a paste

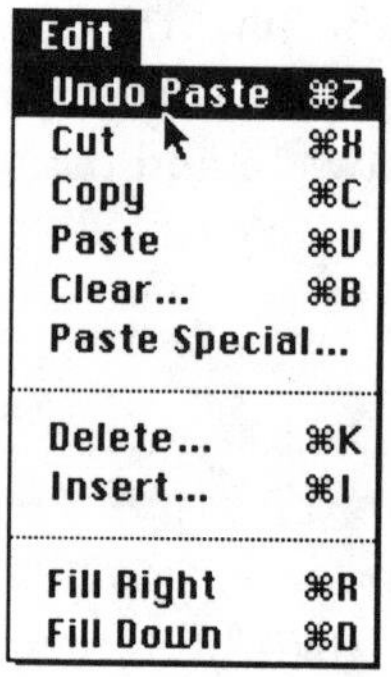

Before leaving this section, be sure that the Total Current Assets row is row 13 on the Balance worksheet.

EDITING A CELL VALUE

You can edit cell values that appear in the formula bar in three ways: you can reenter the entire value, edit the current formula, or copy something into the cell from another cell.

To reenter the entire value, simply click the cell that you wish to edit and enter the new value into the formula bar. The new data will replace the old. Notice that the cell must be active before it can be edited.

Try this now with cell B10 of your Balance worksheet. Click the cell. The current value (35700) is displayed in the formula bar. Now, reenter the same value. When you enter the first number, the formula bar clears, and you will see a *3*.

While editing, you can move the cursor into the formula bar and click at any point on the value. Notice that the cursor changes to an

I-beam form when it is in the formula bar. You can then enter characters from the keyboard, and they will be inserted at the cursor position. The remaining characters will be moved over. You can also use the Backspace key to remove characters in the formula bar. Another way to delete characters in the formula bar (and thus in the active cell) is to click anywhere in the formula bar and drag the cursor over the characters that you wish to delete. Then, pull down the Edit menu and choose Cut. The Cut, Copy, and Paste commands work with characters in the formula bar in the same way that they work with entire cell contents.

The third method of editing a cell is to copy something from another cell to that cell. If a formula is wrong in a cell, for example, it is often easier to copy the correct formula to the cell from another cell where it is already correct than to edit the formula bar or reenter the formula.

If the entry is long, your best approach is generally to edit the current value. For shorter entries, you may save time by replacing the entire value.

EDITING FORMULAS

You can edit formulas that appear in the formula bar in the same way that you edit cell values; that is, you can reenter the entire formula, edit the current formula, or copy and paste a formula from another cell.

To reenter a formula, first select the cell that contains the formula that you want to edit. Now reenter the entire formula, then press Return or click the enter box.

To edit the current formula, use the formula bar and insert or delete characters. Whenever the formula bar is active, you can click the cell that you want to reference in the formula instead of typing it in from the keyboard. To use this technique, first click the cursor in the formula bar where you want the reference to be inserted, then click that cell in the worksheet. If you insert the new cell reference immediately after an existing reference, without including an operator, Excel will automatically insert a plus sign between the two. (If you insert a cell reference immediately after an existing operator, a plus sign will not be added.)

Any time that you click the formula bar, the cancel and enter boxes are displayed, along with the contents of the active cell. Click the enter box to enter the edited formula or click the cancel box to revert to the original formula. You can undo any editing if you make a mistake.

On your Balance worksheet, try editing the equation in cell B21:

1. Select the cell

2. Enter the equal sign into the formula bar

3. Click cells B17 and B18, then click cell B19; you will see each cell name appear in the formula bar preceded with a plus sign

4. Click the enter box

As before, the equation in cell B21 contains the correct total.

As with editing cell values, you can use the Undo command to recover the previous entry after locking the cell (pressing Return) if this is necessary.

Alternately, you can use the Copy and Paste commands to replace the entire current contents. When a formula is copied and pasted in this way, the cell references are automatically adjusted for the new cell (see Chapter 14).

INSERTING AND DELETING ROWS AND COLUMNS

When you're creating a worksheet, you may find that you need to add or delete rows and columns. With Excel, this is as easy as two clicks. For example, you can add a new blank row just after the Total Current Assets row (row 13). New rows are always inserted *before* the selected row. Therefore, you need to select row 14. Click the row 14 designator, pull down the Edit menu, and choose Insert. Excel will create a new row just before the previous row 14, as shown in Figure 5.3.

Notice that the row numbers below the added row have been increased by one. Excel also automatically adjusts the formulas to compensate for the new row.

To delete a row, use the Delete command on the Edit menu. Now you can delete the row that you just added. Select row 14, pull down the Edit menu, and choose Delete. The rows will move up, and the worksheet will be as it was before.

Try this again with a row that contains data and see what happens. Select row 13, which contains the Total Current Assets. Pull down the Edit menu and choose Delete. Row 13 vanishes, and the rows below

Figure 5.3: Adding a row

move up and assume new numbers. Recover the deleted row before doing anything else by pulling down the Edit menu and choosing Undo Delete.

You can insert or delete columns by using the same method: click the column designator, then choose Insert or Delete on the Edit menu.

You can also insert or delete portions of columns or rows. To do this, select a cell or cell range rather than a row or column designator. Then choose Insert or Delete on the Edit menu. Figure 5.4 shows the Insert dialog box. Excel asks if other cells or rows should be moved to adjust for the insertion or deletion. Click the appropriate response, then click OK.

Try this with your Balance worksheet:

1. Select cells B17 through B19

2. Pull down the Edit menu and choose Delete

3. When the dialog box appears, click Shift Cells Up, then click OK

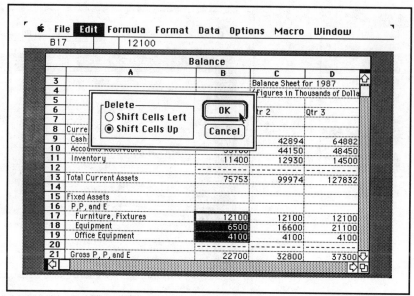

Figure 5.4: The Insert/Delete dialog box

4. The cells will be shifted, and several error messages will appear on your worksheet

5. To recover the deleted cells, pull down the Edit menu and choose Undo Delete

If you delete a cell or range of cells on which the values of other cells depend (because they are based on a formula that uses the deleted cell), the dependent cells will display *REF!* indicating that the formula references a deleted cell. You will then need to correct the formula that used the deleted cell. You can see how this works by deleting row 21 from the Balance worksheet. Because the values in what will be rows 23 and 25 after the deletion depend on the values that were in row 21, you will see REF! in rows 23 and 25, as shown in Figure 5.5. Now restore row 21 by pulling down the Edit menu and selecting Undo Delete.

COMMENTING CELLS

Sometimes you may wish to add a comment about a cell that will be useful to someone entering data into the worksheet. However, you

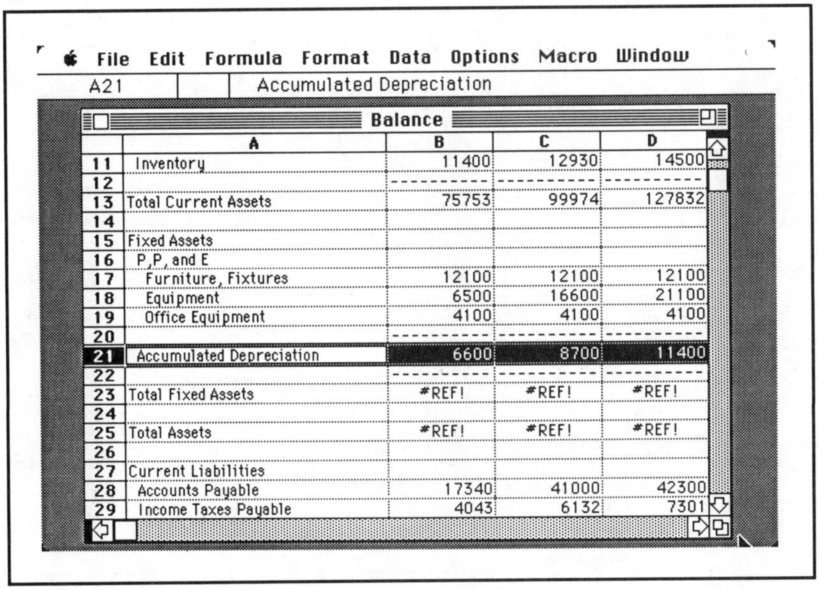

Figure 5.5: Deleting cells on which other cells depend

do not want the comment to appear on the worksheet. Here is one way to add such a comment with Excel:

1. Add a new column immediately after the column that contains the cell or cells about which you wish to comment. You will comment on cell B11, so select column C, pull down the Edit menu, and choose Insert.

2. Change the width of this column to a single character. Pull down the Format menu, choose Column Width, enter 1 in the dialog box, and click OK.

3. Select the single-character cell immediately to the right of the cell about which you're commenting (cell C11).

4. Press the spacebar three times and then enter your comment. (You can use the comment shown in Figure 5.6 or make up your own.) Click the enter box. The comment will not show on the worksheet.

You will be able to see the entire comment in the formula bar whenever you select the single-character cell, as shown in Figure 5.6. If

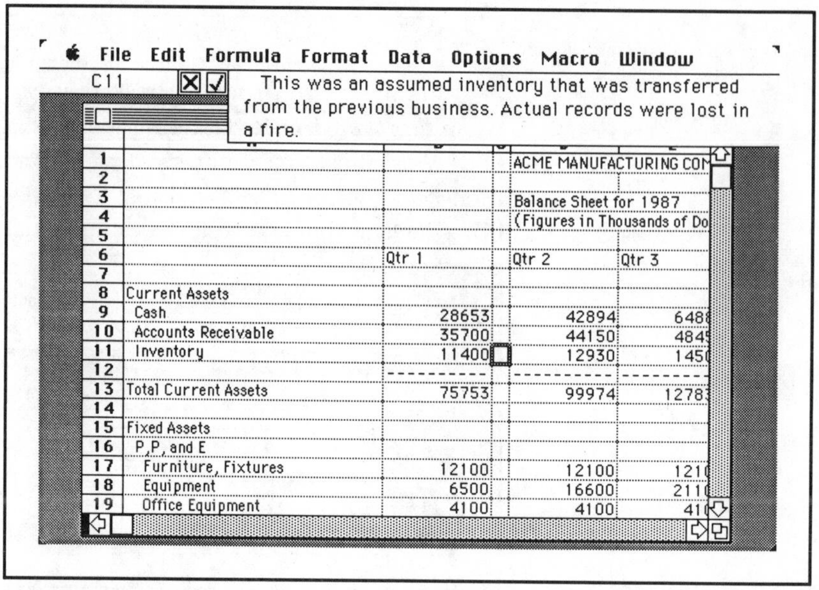

Figure 5.6: Adding comments

you wish, you can enter a column width of 0.5 and enter only two spaces before the comment.

If you try this little experiment, you will see that you can actually enter rather large comments into the tiny cell. The size of the formula bar will adjust automatically to accommodate large comments. The maximum comment size is 255 characters.

OTHER OPERATIONS

Many of the commands on the Edit menu that you used in creating the worksheet are also available for editing it. You can move data from one cell to another using the Cut and Paste commands. You can copy data from one cell to another using the Copy and Paste commands or the Fill Right or Fill Down commands. Refer to Chapter 4 if you need to learn how to use these commands. You will learn about the more advanced editing commands in Chapter 14.

SAVING YOUR EDITS

Whenever you are editing, remember to save your worksheet when you have finished making changes. The first time that you save your worksheet after it is created, you need to pull down the File menu and select Save As. Enter the document name in the dialog box, be sure that the disk designator is the data disk (click Drive if necessary), and then click Save. On subsequent saves, you can simply use the Save command on the File menu. You won't see a dialog box, and Excel will save the document under the name that you gave it previously.

When you're editing a worksheet, save your work approximately every 20 minutes.

RESUMING EXCEL

When using Excel with several windows open, clicking Resume Excel is a quick way to restart and open everything again.

Each time you quit Excel, a document named Resume Excel is created. You can double-click this icon to restart Excel with the same documents and windows open you were using before.

FORMATTING AND PRINTING THE WORKSHEET

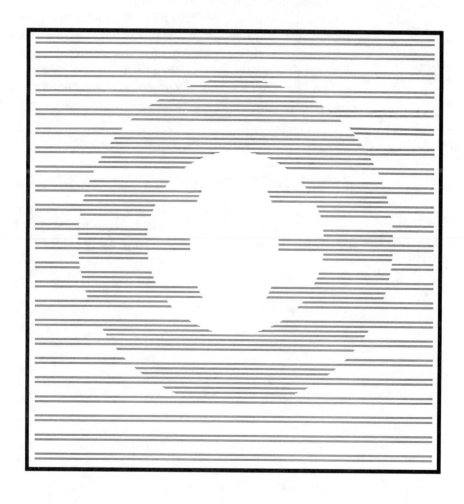

CHAPTER 6 _____

IN THIS CHAPTER, YOU WILL LEARN HOW TO control the appearance of your worksheets. There are two things that Excel stores for each cell in a worksheet: the cell's value (constant or formula) and the cell's formatting information. The formatting information, which controls the appearance of the cell's display, includes the following:

- How numbers are to be displayed (the cell's template)
- The alignment of the cell's display (left, center, or right)
- The style of the cell's display (regular, boldface, or italics)
- The font used in the cell's display (Chicago, New York, Geneva, or Monaco)

In addition, you can control the display of the worksheet's grid lines and you can add borders around the whole worksheet or just certain areas. When a worksheet is well-formatted, it is easier to read and understand; the conclusions you wish to portray are emphasized so they stand out from the rest of the worksheet; and it becomes a presentation-quality document. Excel offers you extensive formatting control, so you can exercise your creativity in setting up your worksheets.

FORMATTING YOUR WORKSHEET ____

To clear a format without clearing the values, select Edit Clear. Then click Format. To clear the values without clearing the format, select Edit Clear. Then click Formulas.

When you format your worksheet, you define the appearance of a cell or range. As you would expect, you will find most of the formatting commands on the Format menu. You can define the format before or after a cell entry. If you define a format before a cell entry is made, there will be no visible indication, of course, until a cell value or formula is entered. Once a cell is formatted, the format remains the same

To clear both contents and format, click All on the same Clear dialog box.

Formats are copied with the values when you copy, fill, or use the Series command. Take advantage of this fact by formatting before you copy.

Plan your worksheet ahead and choose your templates before data entry whenever you can. Format by range to save formatting time. Because numeric templates do not affect text cells, you can often apply a single numeric template for a whole worksheet.

You can change the default format by creating a blank worksheet with the default template, alignment, and styles you wish. Then save it as a *template worksheet* to use for solving different problems in the future. You can also define default column widths and fonts in a template.

even if you change the value or formula in the cell. The format will only change if you select a new one.

SETTING UP TEMPLATES

Templates are the displays Excel provides for numbers, dates, or time in your worksheet. Excel includes 19 predefined templates for cell display: 10 for numeric displays and 9 for dates and times. In addition, you can define new templates, which are useful for worksheets that involve special values, such as foreign currency.

PREDEFINED TEMPLATES   Excel's predefined templates give you the following choices:

- How many digits appear to the right of the decimal
- Whether commas are used in numbers
- Whether a dollar sign appears with currency
- Whether a percent sign is used with percentages
- Whether dates and times appear with hyphens, dashes, or colons

In the default mode (when Excel is first started up), Excel displays all cells using the General template. The General template shows all numbers as precisely as possible. In other words, if you enter 123, the cell will display 123; if you enter 123.23, the cell will display 123.23. If a General template number is too large for the current column width, Excel will attempt to display the number in scientific notation. For example, if you entered the value 10 billion (a one followed by 10 zeros) into a blank cell of standard width (10 characters), Excel would display **1E + 10** in that cell. It would use scientific notation because the 11-digit number would not fit in a 10-character cell.

To choose another predefined template for a cell or range of cells, follow these steps:

1. Select the cell or range of cells that you want to reformat.
2. Pull down the Format menu and choose Number.

3. The Format Number dialog box shown in Figure 6.1 appears. Click the format that you wish to use. If you need to, you can click the scroll arrows or drag the scroll box to see other templates listed in the box.

4. Click OK, and the cell or cell range will be formatted according to the template that you selected.

Here are some examples of how the predefined templates can be used to format a particular display:

ENTRY	*TEMPLATE*	*DISPLAY*
123	0.00	123.00
123.67	0	124
123	$#,##0.00	$123.00

Numeric templates will not affect the display of a text cell.

Most of the templates are self-explanatory. The only confusing ones are perhaps the percentage templates, which multiply the entered value by 100; that is, if you enter .1534 it will be displayed as 15.34%.

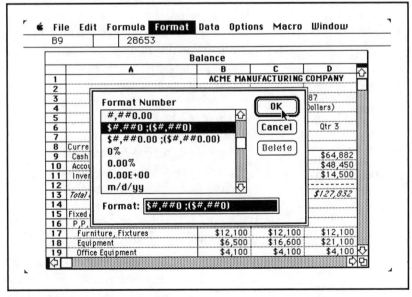

Figure 6.1: Selecting a template

DEFINING NEW TEMPLATES Instead of using a predefined template, you can create your own. For example, if you need to enter social security numbers, you can define a template that automatically puts in the dashes. Other uses for new templates include telephone numbers and foreign currencies. You can even create a template that uses text (such as "lbs").

As an example, you can set up a template that puts *No.* in front of any number entered into a cell. First, start up Excel with your Balance worksheet by double-clicking the Balance icon. Then, follow the steps below:

1. Select a blank cell or cell range on the screen

2. Pull down the Format menu and choose Number

3. In the entry bar at the bottom of the Format Number dialog box, enter **"No."** #### and click OK

Now, enter a few numbers and see what happens. Remember that only the cells or cell range that you selected will use the new template.

Now that you have defined this new template for the Balance worksheet, it will appear as one of your choices in the Format Number dialog box that is displayed when this worksheet is active. You can easily format other cells using the new template by simply selecting it from the dialog box. However, the new template that you define for a particular worksheet will not be available to other worksheets unless you enter it into the Format Number dialog box when you're formatting that worksheet.

Table 6.1 lists the symbols that you can use for creating your own templates. You can delete templates from the Format Number dialog box by selecting the format that you want to remove and then clicking Delete (see Figure 6.1).

Now you can set up a template for the numeric cells in your Balance worksheet:

1. Select cell B9.

2. Pull down the Formula menu and choose Goto. When the Reference box is displayed, enter E43. Hold down the Shift key and click OK. You have selected cells B9 through E43.

3. Pull down the Format menu and choose Number.

Balance

You can use an asterisk in a format to define a repeating character. Follow the asterisk with a character that you want to be repeated as many times as necessary to fill the blank space in the cell. For example, the format ##,##0.00*@ would display $123.23 as 123.23@@@, with the @ symbol filling the cell. This is useful for printing a check in which the entire check amount field must be filled.

SYMBOL	MEANING
0	Template for a single numeric digit. If the number has less digits on either side of the decimal point than there are zeros in the template on either side of the decimal point, Excel displays the extra zeros. If the number has more zeros to the right of the decimal than zeros in the template to the right of the decimal, Excel rounds the number of zeros to the right of the decimal. If the number has more digits to the left of the decimal than zeros in the template to the left, the extra digits are displayed. Example: Template: 0.0; Entry: .8; Displayed: 0.8.
#	Template for a single numeric digit. Follows the rules for 0 above, except extra zeros are not displayed to the right and left of the decimal. Example: Template: #.#; Entry: 8; Displayed: .8.
.	Decimal point. Will display as in the template.
%	Multiply by 100 and add a percent sign.
,	Thousands separator. Thousands are separated by commas if this is included in the template surrounded by zeros.
E− , E+ , e− , e+	Scientific format notation.
:, $, − , + , ( )	Display the character.
space	Display the character.

Table 6.1: Symbols Used for Creating New Templates

SYMBOL	MEANING
*	Repeat next character to fill cell width.
"XXXX"	Display characters within quotation marks as text.
m, mm, mmm, mmmm	Display month in number format.
d, dd, ddd, dddd	Display the day.
yy, yyyy	Display the year.
h, hh	Display the hour without leading zeros.
m, mm	Display the minutes without leading zeros (must be after hours).
s, ss	Display seconds without leading zeros (must be after minutes).
AM, PM, A, P	Display hours using 12-hour clock with am or pm.

Notes:

1. Two templates can be entered for a cell separated by a colon(s). With one colon, the first applies to positive numbers and the second to negative. If you use two colons, the third template will be applied to numbers equal to zero.

2. If you do not want negative numbers displayed, enter the format for positive numbers followed by a semicolon. If you do not want any numbers displayed, use two semicolons.

Table 6.1: Symbols Used for Creating New Templates (continued)

    4. Click the first currency format (highlighted in Figure 6.1) in the Format Number dialog box, then click OK.

All the numbers are now displayed as currency, with dollar signs but without decimals and cents.

You can also create new templates from existing ones. When the dialog box is displayed, the template that will be selected by clicking OK will be at the bottom of the box. You can put an insertion point in this box and edit it. When you click OK, the cell or range will be formatted to the new template. The new template will be added to the end of the template list, permitting you to use it for other cells in the worksheet.

To delete a custom template, use the Format Number command to display the Format Number dialog box. Select the template to delete and click delete.

CHANGING THE TEMPLATE FOR A CELL   If you need to change a current template, select the cell or cell range, then use the Format Number command to display the dialog box. Then click the new template desired.

ALIGNMENT

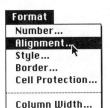

Excel offers you a choice of five alignments within a cell:

- General, which left-justifies text and right-justifies numbers
- Left, which left-justifies all entries (numbers, dates, and text)
- Right, which right-justifies all entries
- Center, which centers each entry
- Fill, which repeats the entry until the cell is filled

When you first start up Excel, all cells are set to General alignment. To change the alignment of text or numbers, first select the cell or cell range that you want to realign. Then, pull down the Format menu and choose Alignment. The dialog box shown in Figure 6.2 appears. Click the alignment that you want, then click OK.

To center the information at the top of your Balance worksheet follow these steps:

1. Select cells A1 through E6 by dragging

2. Pull down the Format menu and choose Alignment

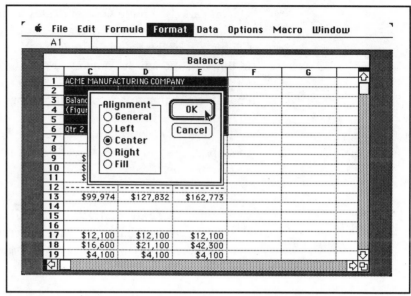

Figure 6.2: Selecting the alignment

> 3. Click Center (shown with a dot in the circle next to it in Figure 6.2) in the Alignment dialog box, then click OK

All the text in the selected cell range is now centered.

STYLE

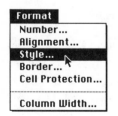

You can display your worksheet entries in boldface, italics, or both, as well as in regular style, which is the default (no bold or italics). Different styles can be selected for the individual cells or for a range of cells. To change the style, select the cell or cell range that you want to display in the different style. Pull down the Format menu and choose Style. The Style dialog box shown in Figure 6.3 appears. Click Bold, Italic, or both. These options are *toggles,* so you can turn each of these styles on and off by successive clicking. When you've made your selection, click OK.

The X next to Bold or Italic in the Style dialog box marks the current style of the selected cell or cell range. If the cells in the selected range are in more than one style, the box next to the style of the active

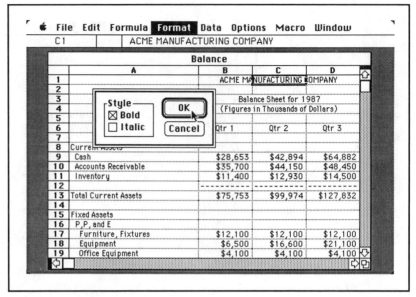

Figure 6.3: Changing the style

cell will be shaded in gray (as shown in Figure 6.4) to indicate the mixed styles of the range.

Now you can change the styles on parts of your Balance worksheet. The title should be in boldface; the Total Current Assets, Total Fixed Assets, and Total Liabilities rows should be in italics; and the Total Assets and Total Liabilities & Equity rows should be in both boldface and italics. Follow these steps:

1. Click cell C3 to select the title.

2. Pull down the Format menu and choose Style.

3. Click Bold, then click OK.

4. Click the designator for row 13. Hold down the Command key and click the designators for rows 24 and 37. All three rows are now selected.

5. Pull down the Format menu and choose Style.

6. Click Italic, then click OK.

7. Click the designator for row 26. Hold down the Command key and click the designator for row 43. Both rows are selected.

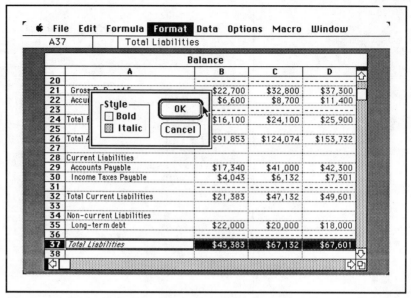

Figure 6.4: Showing mixed styles in a cell range

    8. Pull down the Format menu and choose Style.

    9. Click both Bold and Italic, then click OK.

The totals on your Balance worksheet now stand out from the rest of the entries.

USING THE OPTIONS MENU

The commands on the Options menu, unlike the Format menu, affect the entire worksheet, instead of specific, selected cells.

CHANGING THE FONT

You can change the font and font size of the worksheet entries, but you cannot control the font of individual cells or cell ranges. Whatever font and font size you select will be applied to the entire worksheet. Remember the general rule: the Format menu changes cells or cell ranges. The Options menu changes the entire worksheet.

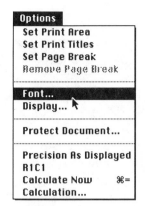

Options
Set Print Area
Set Print Titles
Set Page Break
Remove Page Break

Font...
Display...

Protect Document...

Precision As Displayed
R1C1
Calculate Now   ⌘=
Calculation...

Each of the fonts is displayed best at a certain size. If you use another size for a particular font, you will lose some of the image quality. If the display looks ragged or otherwise of poor quality, experiment with another font size.

Excel offers a choice of the Chicago, New York, Geneva, or Monaco fonts. The default font is 10-point Geneva. You can add other fonts using the Font/DA Mover program in the Macintosh System Folder.

To change the worksheet font:

1. Pull down the Options menu and choose Font.

2. When the Font dialog box shown in Figure 6.5 appears, click the font that you want. Excel then displays the available sizes for that particular font. You can use the scroll arrows to scroll through the list of font sizes.

3. Select the font size that you want and then click OK.

The entire worksheet will be displayed on the screen (and eventually printed out) in the new font. Whatever styles that you selected from the Style dialog box will remain in effect. The cell size is automatically adjusted to accommodate the new font size.

CHICAGO   NEW YORK   GENEVA   MONACO VENICE   LONDON   ATHENS

Figure 6.5: Changing the font and font size

CONTROLLING GRID LINES

On the worksheet screen display, cells are separated by vertical and horizontal grid lines. You may want to turn the grid lines off to see how a worksheet looks without them.

To turn off the grid lines, pull down the Options menu and choose Display. The Display dialog box shown in Figure 6.6 appears. Click Gridlines to remove the X in the box next to it, then click OK. The Gridlines option is a toggle that switches the grid-line display on and off. If an X is displayed, the option is on; if not, it is off. By clicking the option, you can switch between the two conditions. However, no matter what you select in this dialog box, the grid lines will still be printed. You can only control the *screen display* of the grid lines this way.

You use the Page Setup command on the File menu to turn off the grid lines on the printed worksheet. If you want to print your Balance worksheet without grid lines, follow these steps:

1. Pull down the File menu and choose Page Setup.

Figure 6.6: The Display dialog box

2. The Page Setup dialog box shown in Figure 6.7 appears. Click Print Gridlines to remove the X in the box next to that option (this is a toggle like the options in the Display dialog box). Click OK.

The grid lines will still appear on the screen display while you work with the worksheet, but they will not show on the printed version.

CONTROLLING DESIGNATORS

At the top of each column is a column designator—A, B, C, and so on to IV. At the left edge are the row designators, numbered from 1 to 16,384. Like the grid lines, you can turn these off so that they don't appear on the worksheet screen display. To turn off the display of designators, pull down the Options menu and choose Display. When the Display dialog box shown in Figure 6.6 appears, click Row & Column Headings (another toggle). This removes the X in the box next to that

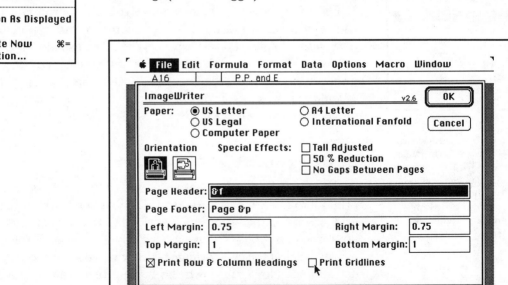

Figure 6.7: The Page Setup dialog box

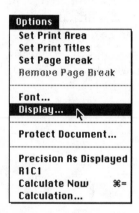

If you need a print-out of the formulas, use the Display command to display the formulas. Print the worksheet as usual (using the Print command on the File menu).

option. Click OK. Remember, the Display dialog box options only control the screen display, not the printed output.

To eliminate the designators on the printed worksheet, you use the Page Setup command on the File menu. To eliminate the row and column designators from your printed Balance worksheet, follow the steps below:

1. Pull down the File menu and choose Page Setup.

2. When the Page Setup dialog box (shown in Figure 6.7) appears, click Print Row & Column Designators. This removes the X in the box next to that option (another toggle). Click OK.

The row and column designators will still be displayed on the screen, but you won't see them on the printed worksheet.

DISPLAYING FORMULAS

There may be times when you need to see the formulas associated with a particular worksheet. To display the formulas, pull down the Options menu and choose Display. When the Display dialog box (see Figure 6.6) appears, click Formulas and then click OK. The screen display will then show the formulas. Each column will now be twice as wide as it was in your normal display to permit room for the formulas. You can switch the display back by repeating this operation.

ADDING BORDERS

You may wish to add a border to parts of the worksheet display or printout to make it easier to read. To add a border, first turn off the grid lines using the procedure described earlier. (If the grid lines are not turned off, you will have a hard time seeing the borders on the display.) Select the cell or range of cells that you want to put the border around. Now pull down the Format menu and select Border. When the Border dialog box shown in Figure 6.8 appears, click one or more options, then click OK.

Excel offers these choices for borders:

- Outline, which outlines the entire range with a border

- Left, which draws a vertical line at the left of each cell

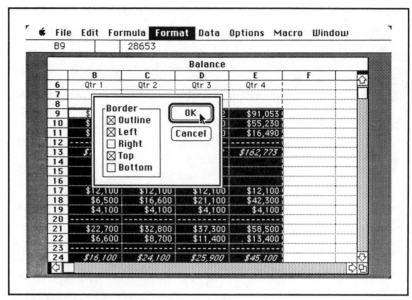

Figure 6.8: Selecting borders

- Right, which draws a vertical line at the right of each cell

- Top, which draws a horizontal line at the top of each cell

- Bottom, which draws a horizontal line at the bottom of each cell

You can choose one or more of these border options for the selected cells. The added borders appear on both the screen display and the printed worksheet. By using a combination of styles and borders, you can emphasize any values on your worksheets. Figure 4.2 in Chapter 4 shows how bordering can be used effectively.

Now you can put the borders shown in Figure 4.2 on your Balance worksheet:

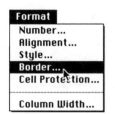

Be sure that the grid lines are turned off, or it will not be easy to see the borders.

1. Select cell B9.

2. Pull down the Formula menu, choose Goto, enter E24 into the Reference box, hold down the Shift key, and click OK. You have selected cells B9 through E24.

3. Pull down the Format menu. Choose Border, then click Outline, and then click OK.

Borders are useful for dividing your worksheet into areas to draw attention to specific cell ranges. You can also use them to create tables, calendars, and forms with Excel.

4. Select the range of cells B29 to E41 by using the method described in step 2.

5. Pull down the Format menu. Choose Border, then click Outline, and then click OK.

6. Clear row 42 by selecting the row designator, pulling down the Edit menu, choosing Clear, and then clicking OK.

Your worksheet should now have borders defining two separate parts of the sheet.

CONTROLLING THE PRECISION

Excel stores all the numbers that you enter into your worksheets with a full 14-digit precision. (*Precision* refers to the number of decimal places to which a value is carried when it is stored or displayed.) It performs all calculations with this full precision, without regard to how the number is displayed. In some cases, you may wish to switch this so that Excel stores the numbers and performs calculations only with the precision displayed. For example, you may want to switch the precision when the results of formulas do not seem to match the numbers used to calculate them. You can change the precision for all templates except the General template, which always stores numbers with full precision.

To switch from full precision to the displayed precision, pull down the Options menu and choose Precision as Displayed. To switch back, pull down the Options menu and choose Full Precision.

HIDING A COLUMN

There may be times when you want to hide a column on a worksheet so that it is not displayed or printed. For example, you may not want to print some constants that you put in one area of a worksheet to use as a part of formulas in other areas of that worksheet.

To hide columns, you change the column width to zero. This can be done in one of two ways:

*   Pull down the Format menu, choose Column Width, and type in a zero for the width.

If you use dragging to restore a hidden column, be sure to drag from the *right* side of the column designator. If you drag from the left side, instead of restoring the hidden column, you will widen the column to the left of it.

- Place the cursor on the right edge of the designator of the column to be hidden (the cursor will change to the shape of a line). Drag it left until it overlaps the left edge of the column.

To recover a column, do just the opposite: enter a new nonzero column width or drag the column designator edge back to the right.

PRINTING THE WORKSHEET

To print an entire document, pull down the File menu and choose Print. When the Print dialog box shown in Figure 6.9 appears, click OK.

Many of the features already discussed affect the printed worksheet. Remember that grid lines and column and row designators are turned off and on using the Page Setup command on the File menu. If you add borders, they will also be printed. Your selection of fonts and styles also applies to both the screen display and the printout of the worksheet. For more information on printing options, see Chapter 17.

File	
New...	⌘N
Open...	⌘O
Links...	
Close All	
Save	⌘S
Save As...	
Delete...	
Page Setup...	
Print...	⌘P
Printer Setup...	
Quit	⌘Q

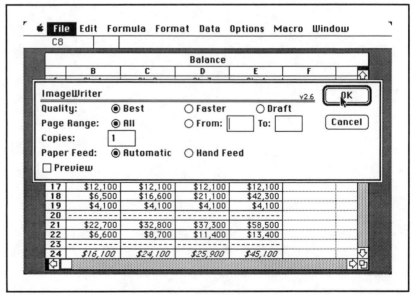

Figure 6.9: The Print dialog box

THE FINAL BALANCE WORKSHEET

If you followed along with the examples in this chapter, you have done the following with your Balance worksheet:

- Put the title in boldface print
- Centered all column headings
- Put rows 13, 24, and 37 in italics
- Put rows 26 and 43 in boldface and italics
- Turned off the grid lines and row and column designators in the printout
- Added borders

Your final printout should look like Figure 4.2.

DOCUMENT AND
WINDOW CONTROL

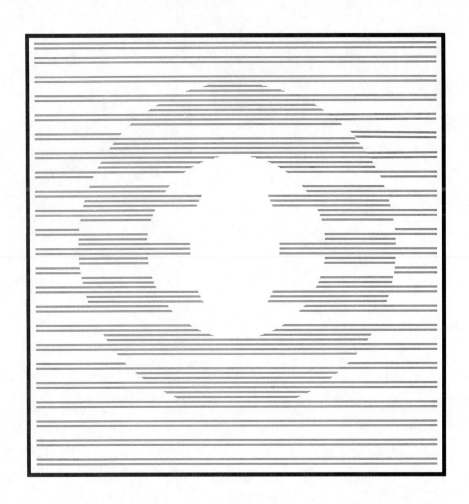

CHAPTER 7

THE WORKSHEET DOCUMENT IS ALWAYS DISPLAYED as a window. With Excel, you can have several windows (worksheets) displayed simultaneously. Although only one window can be active at a time, other windows can be partially active.

Because you create and edit all documents using windows, learning how to control windows is an important part of managing your worksheets. In this chapter, you will learn some of the special Excel window-management techniques, including

- Opening and closing windows
- Switching between windows
- Opening additional windows in the same document
- Creating panes in a window for entering data into large worksheets

WORKING WITH WINDOWS

The worksheet document is always displayed as a window. You also use windows to display almost any type of Excel data: charts, databases, and even macros. The basic Macintosh window-management commands apply to any type of Excel document. You can scroll a window using the scroll bars, move a window by dragging its title bar, and resize a window by dragging the size box in the lower-right corner of the window.

As you are working with Excel, you will use windows to open, close, and delete documents.

OPENING DOCUMENTS

To create a new document, pull down the File menu and choose New. The New dialog box shown in Figure 7.1 appears. As this figure shows, Worksheet is already selected as the type of document. To create a new worksheet, click OK. Excels displays a blank worksheet titled Worksheet1 (if a worksheet with this title already is open, the new document will be Worksheet2).

To open a document that you have already created and stored on the disk, pull down the File menu and choose Open. The dialog box shown in Figure 7.2 appears. It lists the names of the documents currently on the disk. You can use the scroll bar to see additional documents on the same disk. The name of the currently active disk drive is in the upper right of the dialog box. The active drive should always be the one with a data disk. If it is not, click Drive. The dialog box will then list the names of the documents on the data disk. You can complete the command either by double-clicking the document name or by clicking the name and then clicking OK.

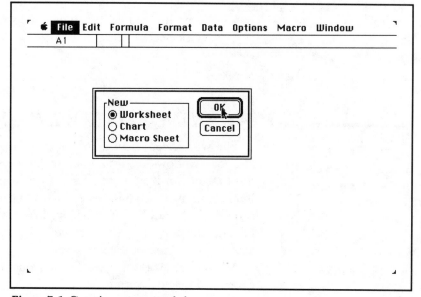

Figure 7.1: Creating a new worksheet

Excel allows you to have more than one window open. If you are working on a worksheet and need to open another document, pull down the File menu and choose New or Open again. You will then see the windows for both documents on the screen.

CLOSING DOCUMENTS

When you are finished working with an Excel document, you should close the document. The document, as displayed, is only in the computer memory. It has not, as yet, been written to the disk where it can be stored when the computer power is off.

There are five ways to store a document to disk:

- Click the close box in the upper left of the window's title bar. This will save the document under the name currently displayed on the worksheet (for example, Worksheet1). If the document has already been saved under this name, Excel will ask whether you want to save any changes. When you close a

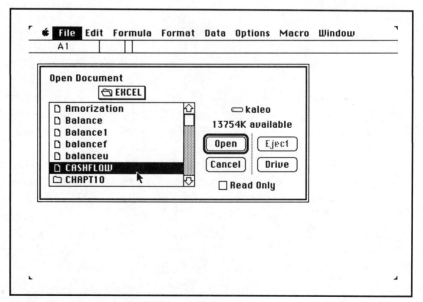

Figure 7.2: Opening an existing worksheet

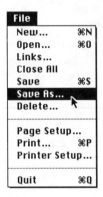

If you inadvertently save a document under a wrong or misspelled name, there is another way to correct it that is quicker than exiting Excel. Use the Save As command on the File menu to save it under the correct name. Then use the Delete command on the File menu to delete the old document with the incorrect name.

document this way, you do not automatically exit Excel. After the window is closed, a short menu bar is displayed. You can use the commands on the File menu to open or create another document. This method is useful if you have finished working with one document and you wish to work on another.

- Pull down the File menu and choose Quit. You will be asked whether you want to save your document. Click the appropriate response. This method is a quick way to exit Excel and save changes.

- Pull down the File menu and choose Save. This will save the current worksheet under the name displayed on the worksheet. The window remains active. This method is useful for saving the worksheet periodically as you work on it.

- Pull down the File menu and select Close All. This works the same as closing a window, except that all windows that were displayed will be closed so you should use it if more than one window is open.

- Pull down the File menu and choose Save As. You will then see a dialog box with the current worksheet name, as shown in Figure 7.3. Enter the name that you wish to assign to the document. Be sure that the disk assignment is correct; click Drive if necessary to select the drive with the data disk. Then click OK. This is the only method that permits you to save a document under a name that you assign.

You cannot change the name of a document that you previously stored using any of the commands on the File menu. To rename a document, you must exit Excel using the Quit command on the File menu. Then, click the icon representing the document that you want to rename and enter the new name from the keyboard. Then press Return.

A quicker way to correct a wrong or misspelled document name is to use the Save As command on the File menu to save it under the correct name. Then use the Delete command on the File menu to delete the old document with the incorrect name.

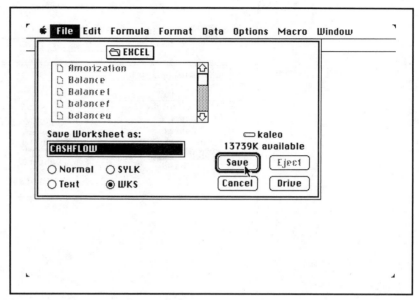

Figure 7.3: Saving the document

DELETING DOCUMENTS

To delete a document from the disk, pull down the File menu and choose Delete. You will then see the Delete Document dialog box shown in Figure 7.4. If necessary, scroll to the document that you wish to delete. Click Drive if you need to switch to another disk. Click the name of the document that you want to delete, then click OK.

USING ADDITIONAL WINDOWS

There may be times when you need to open additional windows. Excel's multiple window feature permits you to view two or more documents at once and to move data from one document to another. The other windows may be into other documents or into the same document, as described later in this section.

The commands on the Edit menu are still available when you have more than one window open, so you can easily move data and

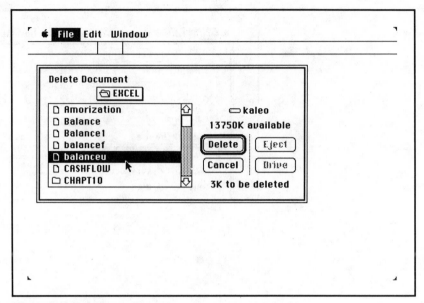

Figure 7.4: Deleting a document

formulas between windows. Use the Copy and Paste or Cut and Paste commands, just as if you were working with a single window.

Linking worksheets in different windows is discussed in Chapter 16.

OPENING WINDOWS INTO OTHER DOCUMENTS

Any time that you are using one window and then want to open a second window into another document, pull down the File menu and choose Open, just as you did to open the first document. Only one window can be active at a time. You can switch active windows by clicking anywhere on the window that you wish to make active.

Another way to switch between windows is to pull down the Window menu and choose the name of the window that you want to make active. The Window menu always lists all the open documents.

OPENING ADDITIONAL WINDOWS INTO THE SAME DOCUMENT

There may be times when you need to open a second window into the same worksheet. Multiple windows are primarily useful with large worksheets in which one part of the worksheet is dependent upon another part of the same worksheet. If you can look at both parts of the worksheet at once, you can edit or change values in one part of the worksheet and immediately see the effect in the other window. This reduces the need to do excessive scrolling. Each window can be controlled independently by using the scroll bars on that window.

You can try this now with your Balance worksheet:

1. Open the worksheet by double-clicking the Balance icon

2. Make the window smaller (see Figure 7.5) by dragging the size box in the lower right

3. Pull down the Window menu and select New Window

4. When the new window opens, make it smaller, too, as shown in Figure 7.5

Notice that the new window is titled Balance:2, and your original window has become Balance:1. You now have two windows into the same worksheet.

The New Window command on the Window menu opens an additional window to the *same* worksheet. No new worksheet is created. Any change made through any open window on a worksheet affects the single underlying worksheet. The New command on the File menu, in contrast, creates a new worksheet.

It is not necessary to make a window active to move it. Just press the Command key and drag the title bar. To resize a window, however, the window must be active.

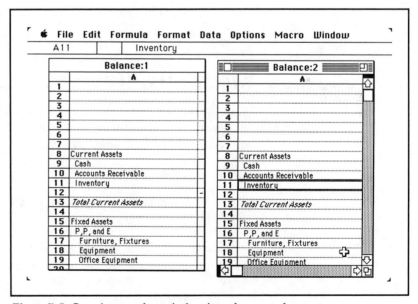

Figure 7.5: Opening another window into the same document

If you have more than one window open from different documents and you click New Window, Excel will create a new window into the worksheet that is currently active.

ZOOMING IN

If you are working with a small window, you can temporarily expand the window to fill the screen by double-clicking the title bar. To return the window to a smaller size, double click the title bar again.

DELETING WINDOWS

To delete a window when more than one window is on the screen, simply make the window active and click the close box of the window. This deletes the active window and renumbers the remaining windows. Deleting a window does not cause the loss of any worksheet data, as the underlying worksheet still remains in memory. If you try to delete the last window, Excel assumes you wish to close the file. It then displays a dialog box that asks whether you want to save the file.

SPLITTING WINDOWS

In the next two sections, you will learn some strategies for working with windows when you have large worksheets. In most applications, you can simplify your work by using *panes*.

CREATING THE CASH-FLOW ANALYSIS WORKSHEET

To understand how to work with panes, you need a large worksheet. You should create the worksheet shown in Figure 7.6. This is a Cash-Flow Analysis worksheet for a twelve-month cycle—a very common type of worksheet application. Figure 7.7 shows the formulas for the

WIDGET MANUFACTURING
CASH FLOW ANALYSIS - 1987

Assump:
Interest Rate	9%
Cost of Goods/Sale of Goods	0.55
Advertising/Sales	0.1

	Jan-87	Feb-87	Mar-87	Apr-87	May-87	Jun-87	Jul-87	Aug-87	Sep-87	Oct-87	Nov-87	Dec-87	Totals
CASH ON HAND	$43,000	$34,236	$63,507	$80,761	$162,282	$176,211	$179,147	$179,754	$224,074	$255,279	$271,356	$286,063	
INCOME													
Sale of Goods	$83,394	$110,237	$114,563	$117,239	$123,291	$108,345	$98,234	$132,874	$143,819	$132,764	$123,127	$131,872	$1,419,759
Sale of Services	$6,432	$10,234	$11,784	$76,123	$10,523	$11,239	$9,272	$11,555	$10,234	$12,812	$13,916	$14,123	$198,247
Total Sales	$89,826	$120,471	$126,347	$193,362	$133,814	$119,584	$107,506	$144,429	$154,053	$145,576	$137,043	$145,595	$1,618,006
Interest Income	$323	$323	$257	$476	$606	$1,217	$1,322	$1,344	$1,348	$1,681	$1,915	$2,035	$12,845
Total Income	$90,149	$120,794	$126,604	$193,838	$134,420	$120,801	$108,828	$145,773	$155,401	$147,257	$138,958	$748,030	$1,630,851
EXPENSES													
Cost of Goods	$45,867	$45,867	$60,630	$63,010	$64,481	$67,810	$59,590	$54,029	$73,081	$79,100	$73,020	$67,720	$754,205
Rent	$11,543	$8,923	$8,923	$8,923	$8,923	$8,923	$8,923	$8,923	$8,923	$8,923	$8,923	$8,923	$109,696
Salaries	$19,894	$15,234	$15,234	$15,234	$15,234	$15,234	$15,234	$15,234	$15,234	$15,234	$15,234	$15,234	$187,468
Taxes	$1,204	$1,094	$1,094	$1,094	$1,094	$1,094	$1,094	$1,094	$1,094	$1,094	$1,094	$1,094	$13,238
Supplies	$2,050	$2,050	$2,050	$2,050	$2,050	$2,050	$2,050	$2,050	$2,050	$2,050	$2,050	$2,050	$24,600
Repairs	$2,873	$2,873	$2,873	$2,873	$2,873	$2,873	$2,873	$2,873	$2,873	$2,873	$2,873	$2,873	$34,476
Advertising	$8,983	$8,983	$12,047	$12,635	$19,336	$13,381	$11,958	$10,751	$14,443	$15,405	$14,558	$13,704	$156,184
Insurance	$734	$734	$734	$734	$734	$734	$734	$734	$734	$734	$734	$734	$8,808
Utilities	$2,345	$2,345	$2,345	$2,345	$2,345	$2,345	$2,345	$2,345	$2,345	$2,345	$2,345	$2,345	$28,140
Emp. Benefits	$1,234	$1,234	$1,234	$1,234	$1,234	$1,234	$1,234	$1,234	$1,234	$1,234	$1,234	$1,234	$14,808
Dues, Subscriptions	$254	$254	$254	$254	$254	$254	$254	$254	$254	$254	$254	$254	$3,048
Travel	$1,432	$1,432	$1,432	$1,432	$1,432	$1,432	$1,432	$1,432	$1,432	$1,432	$1,432	$1,432	$17,184
Miscellaneous	$500	$500	$500	$500	$500	$500	$500	$500	$500	$500	$500	$500	$6,000
Total Expenses	$98,912	$91,522	$109,350	$112,317	$120,491	$117,864	$108,221	$101,452	$124,197	$131,179	$124,251	$118,097	$1,357,854
Net Income	($8,764)	$29,271	$17,253	$81,521	$13,929	$2,937	$606	$44,320	$31,205	$16,078	$14,707	$29,933	$272,996
Net Cash on Hand	$34,236	$63,507	$80,761	$162,282	$176,211	$179,147	$179,754	$224,074	$255,279	$271,356	$286,063	$315,996	

Figure 7.6: Cash-Flow Analysis worksheet

first three columns. You can use a Fill Right command from column B to complete the other columns. When printed, the worksheet should look like Figure 7.8. To get it on a single page, you will need to use a size 12 font, print horizontally, and use a 50% reduction.

	A	B	C
7		30316	30347
8			
9	CASH ON HAND	43000	=B37
10			
11	INCOME		
12	Sale of Goods	83394	110237
13	Sale of Services	6432	10234
14	Total Sales	=B12+B13	=C12+C13
15	Interest Income	=($L$3/12)*B9	=($L$3/12)*B9
16		-	-
17	Total Income	=B14+B15	=C14+C15
18			
19	EXPENSES		
20	Cost of Goods	=$L$4*B12	=$L$4*B12
21	Rent	11543	8923
22	Salaries	19894	15234
23	Taxes	1204	1094
24	Supplies	2050	2050
25	Repairs	2873	2873
26	Advertising	=$L$5*B14	=$L$5*B14
27	Insurance	734	734
28	Utilties	2345	2345
29	Emp. Benefits	1234	1234
30	Dues, Subscriptions	254	254
31	Travel	1432	1432
32	Miscellaneous	500	500
33		-	-
34	Total Expenses	=SUM(B20:B32)	=SUM(C20:C32)
35			
36	Net Income	=B17-B34	=C17-C34
37	Net Cash on Hand	=B9+B36	=C9+C36
38			

Figure 7.7: Formulas and data for the Cash-Flow Analysis worksheet

WIDGET MANUFACTURING
CASH FLOW ANALYSIS - 1987

Assump:	Interest Rate	9%
	Cost of Goods/Sale of Goods	0.55
	Advertising/Sales	0.1

	Jan-87	Feb-87	Mar-87	Apr-87	May-87	Jun-87	Jul-87	Aug-87	Sep-87	Oct-87	Nov-87	Dec-87	Totals
CASH ON HAND	$43,000	$34,236	$63,507	$80,761	$162,282	$176,211	$179,147	$179,754	$224,074	$255,279	$271,356	$286,063	
INCOME													
Sale of Goods	$83,394	$110,237	$114,563	$117,239	$123,291	$108,345	$98,234	$132,874	$143,819	$132,764	$123,127	$131,872	$1,419,759
Sale of Services	$6,432	$10,234	$11,784	$76,123	$10,523	$11,239	$9,272	$11,555	$10,234	$12,812	$13,916	$14,123	$198,247
Total Sales	$89,826	$120,471	$126,347	$193,362	$133,814	$119,584	$107,506	$144,429	$154,053	$145,576	$137,043	$145,995	$1,618,006
Interest Income	$323	$323	$257	$476	$606	$1,217	$1,322	$1,344	$1,348	$1,681	$1,915	$2,035	$12,845
Total Income	$90,149	$120,794	$126,604	$193,838	$134,420	$120,801	$108,828	$145,773	$155,401	$147,257	$138,958	$148,030	$1,630,851
EXPENSES													
Cost of Goods	$45,867	$45,867	$60,630	$63,010	$64,481	$67,810	$59,590	$54,029	$73,081	$79,100	$73,020	$67,720	$754,205
Rent	$11,543	$8,923	$8,923	$8,923	$8,923	$8,923	$8,923	$8,923	$8,923	$8,923	$8,923	$8,923	$109,696
Salaries	$19,894	$15,234	$15,234	$15,234	$15,234	$15,234	$15,234	$15,234	$15,234	$15,234	$15,234	$15,234	$187,468
Taxes	$1,204	$1,094	$1,094	$1,094	$1,094	$1,094	$1,094	$1,094	$1,094	$1,094	$1,094	$1,094	$13,238
Supplies	$2,050	$2,050	$2,050	$2,050	$2,050	$2,050	$2,050	$2,050	$2,050	$2,050	$2,050	$2,050	$24,600
Repairs	$2,873	$2,873	$2,873	$2,873	$2,873	$2,873	$2,873	$2,873	$2,873	$2,873	$2,873	$2,873	$34,476
Advertising	$8,983	$8,983	$12,047	$12,635	$19,336	$13,381	$11,958	$10,751	$14,443	$15,405	$14,558	$13,704	$156,184
Insurance	$734	$734	$734	$734	$734	$734	$734	$734	$734	$734	$734	$734	$8,808
Utilities	$2,345	$2,345	$2,345	$2,345	$2,345	$2,345	$2,345	$2,345	$2,345	$2,345	$2,345	$2,345	$28,140
Emp. Benefits	$1,234	$1,234	$1,234	$1,234	$1,234	$1,234	$1,234	$1,234	$1,234	$1,234	$1,234	$1,234	$14,808
Dues, Subscriptions	$254	$254	$254	$254	$254	$254	$254	$254	$254	$254	$254	$254	$3,048
Travel	$1,432	$1,432	$1,432	$1,432	$1,432	$1,432	$1,432	$1,432	$1,432	$1,432	$1,432	$1,432	$17,184
Miscellaneous	$500	$500	$500	$500	$500	$500	$500	$500	$500	$500	$500	$500	$6,000
Total Expenses	$98,912	$91,522	$109,350	$112,317	$120,491	$117,864	$108,221	$101,452	$124,197	$131,179	$124,251	$118,097	$1,357,854
Net Income	($8,764)	$29,271	$17,253	$81,521	$13,929	$2,937	$606	$44,320	$31,205	$16,078	$14,707	$29,933	$272,996
Net Cash on Hand	$34,236	$63,507	$80,761	$162,282	$176,211	$179,147	$179,754	$224,074	$255,279	$271,356	$286,063	$315,996	

Figure 7.8: Final printout of the Cash-Flow Analysis worksheet

The concept of absolute and relative cell addressing is discussed in Chapter 8. This example will be used again in that chapter. For the moment, it is only necessary to enter the equations as indicated.

Notice that the key parameters for the analysis (interest rate, cost and sale of goods, and advertising and sales) are stored at the top of column L. These are then used as absolute references in the various columns. If these assumptions are changed, the entire worksheet will change to reflect the new assumptions. This allows you to do a what-if analysis to see how changing a factor influences the year's cash flow.

CREATING PANES

When you try to enter the data and formulas for this worksheet, you will quickly discover a difficulty. Entering the data for the first few months is easy, but what happens when you try to enter the data for a later part of the year? As Figure 7.9 shows, you no longer see the row headings. What happens when you enter the last part of the data for any particular month? You will not be able to see the column headings. With Excel, you can solve this problem by splitting the window into panes. Panes let you view two parts of the same worksheet and scroll them together.

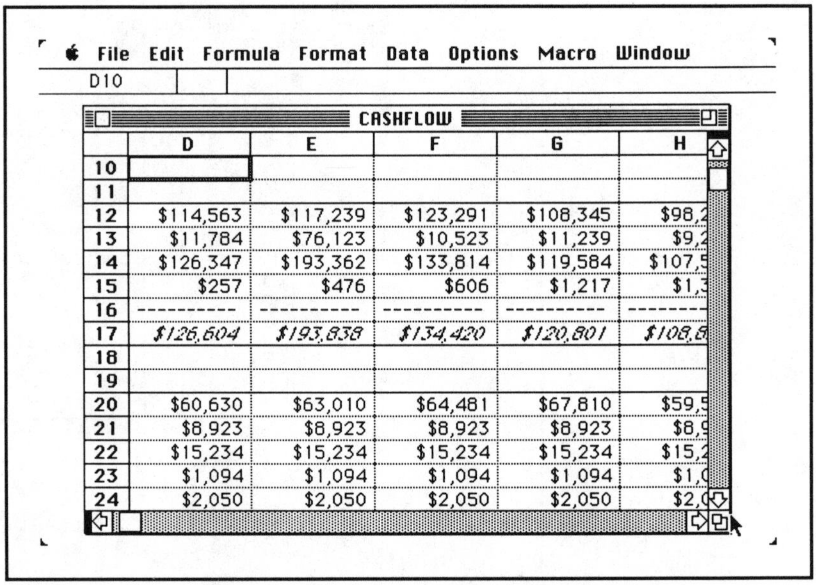

	D	E	F	G	H
10					
11					
12	$114,563	$117,239	$123,291	$108,345	$98,2
13	$11,784	$76,123	$10,523	$11,239	$9,2
14	$126,347	$193,362	$133,814	$119,584	$107,5
15	$257	$476	$606	$1,217	$1,3
16	----------	----------	----------	----------	-------
17	*$126,604*	*$193,838*	*$134,420*	*$120,801*	*$108,8*
18					
19					
20	$60,630	$63,010	$64,481	$67,810	$59,5
21	$8,923	$8,923	$8,923	$8,923	$8,9
22	$15,234	$15,234	$15,234	$15,234	$15,2
23	$1,094	$1,094	$1,094	$1,094	$1,0
24	$2,050	$2,050	$2,050	$2,050	$2,0

Figure 7.9: The Cash-Flow Analysis worksheet without panes

You can experiment with your Balance worksheet. Open that worksheet. Place the cursor on the small black box in the lower left. The cursor will change into the shape of two vertical bars. Drag it to the right until this split bar is between columns A and B. Release the mouse button.

You now have two panes in a single window. Each pane has its own horizontal scroll bar, but there is only one vertical scroll bar. Leave the left pane as it is. Scroll the right pane so that only the four columns for each of the four quarters are visible, as shown in Figure 7.10. Now scroll vertically until the row with the column headings is at the top of the window.

Now you can create four panes. Split the window again by placing the cursor on the small black box at the top of the vertical scroll bar. Drag it down so that the new split bar is just under the top row that displays the column headings. Release the mouse button. Scroll the lower right pane one row so that the columns are shown only once, as shown in Figure 7.11.

Now there are four panes. The only pane that you will have to scroll for data entry is in the lower right. Scroll this vertically and horizontally. You will see that the headings for both the rows and

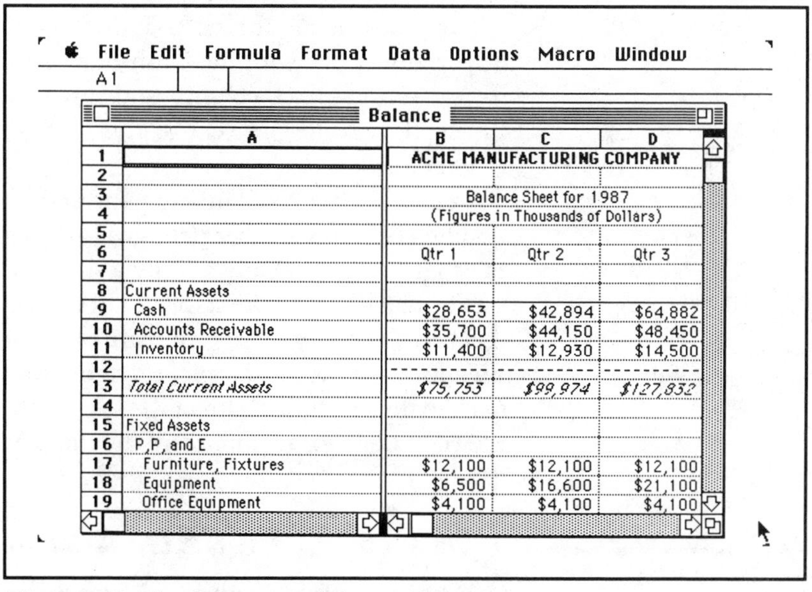

Figure 7.10: The Balance worksheet with two panes

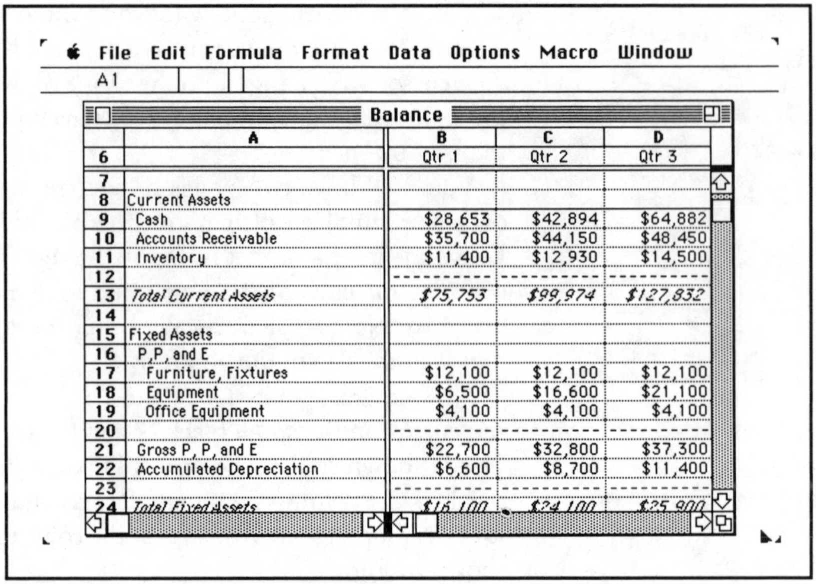

Figure 7.11: The Balance worksheet with four panes

columns are always displayed in the adjacent panes as you enter data into the pane in the lower right.

Now look at Figure 7.12. This shows how the use of panes can help you to work with the Cash-Flow Analysis worksheet. By using panes, you can lock column and row headings, which permits you to scroll around the rest of the worksheet while the headings remain displayed.

You can select a cell in any pane and enter new data. The corresponding cells in the other panes will also show the new data. Remember that you are looking at only a single window.

The black bars in the scroll boxes that separate the panes are called *split bars*. You can close any pane by dragging the split bar. In our Balance worksheet example, dragging the lower split bar all the way back to the left closes both of the left panes. Dragging the split bar on the right back to the top closes the top panes.

> Use panes to lock row and column headings when working with large worksheets.

QUITTING EXCEL

When you wish to exit Excel, pull down the File menu and choose Quit. You will see the dialog box shown in Figure 7.13, asking

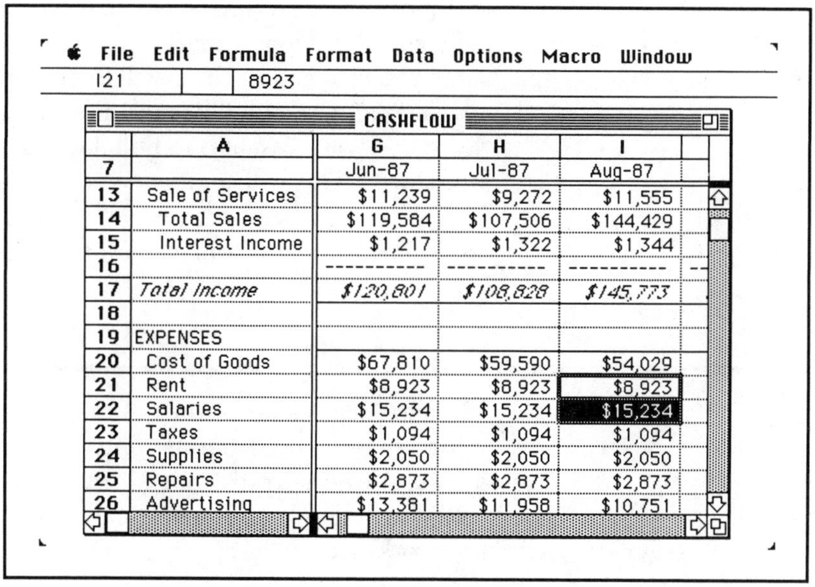

Figure 7.12: The Cash-Flow Analysis worksheet with panes

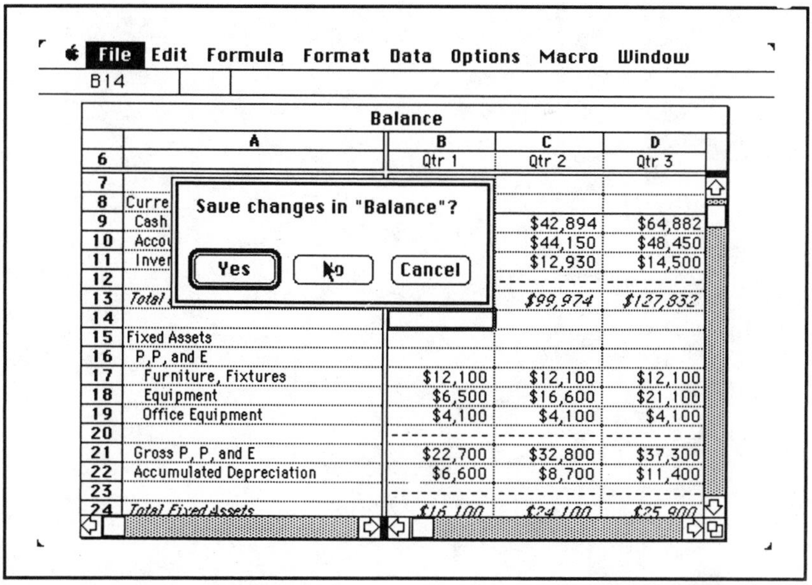

Figure 7.13: Quitting Excel

whether you want to save your changes. Click Yes if you wish to save them; click No if you want the document to revert back to how it was before you changed it. Excel will then quit, saving the changes if that is what you requested. Once the disk window is displayed, the easiest way to end your session is to pull down the Special menu and choose Shut Down. This will complete your exit and eject the disks.

When a worksheet is saved, all of the current windows are saved just as they were last displayed on the screen.

SUMMARY

You have now learned the basics of creating and using worksheets. By now, you should be opening and closing worksheet windows with confidence. You've also learned how to split windows, open multiple windows, and create panes to simplify entering data into large worksheets.

USING WORKSHEET
FORMULAS
AND FUNCTIONS

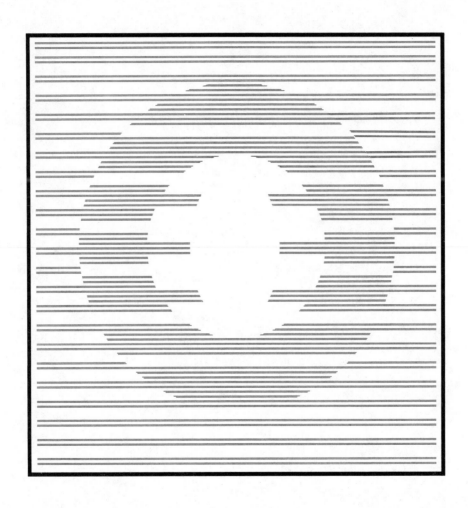

CHAPTER 8 _____

FUNCTIONS ARE ABBREVIATIONS OF FORMULAS THAT enable you to perform a task quickly that would take much longer (or could not be done at all) using other operations. Excel provides a total of 86 functions. In most worksheets, you will want to use one or more of these functions to calculate cell values.

In this chapter, you will use some of Excel's functions to create a very useful amortization schedule. Amortizing something means, literally, to put it to death. That is what you do when you pay off a car loan or house mortgage. In amortizing a loan, you make a series of equal payments for a fixed period of time. During this time, however, the proportion that you pay for the principle increases while the proportion that you pay for the interest decreases. If you are purchasing anything on credit, you may need to evaluate your loan consistently to calculate your taxes or to plan for refinancing. In this chapter, you will learn how Excel can help you to perform this evaluation.

However, before you can use this example and Excel's functions, you need to understand some of the basics of cell addressing and how functions work. The first part of this chapter provides that information. After the example, you will find an overview of all of Excel's functions and a summary of how to use each.

CELL ADDRESSING

With formulas and functions, you can use either relative, absolute or mixed cell addressing. In the example in this chapter, you will use all three kinds of cell addressing.

RELATIVE CELL ADDRESSING

The Income worksheet that you created in Chapter 3 and the Balance worksheet that you created in Chapters 4 through 6 both used *relative cell addressing.* In Chapter 3, you created the following formula for cell B8:

    = (B5 + B6)

What you really stored in cell B8 was a formula that said "Add the value of the cell three cells up to the value of the cell two cells up." This is why you could copy the formula to other cells and it would still work correctly. Relative cell addresses store references to other cells by their position in relation to the active cell.

You can enter relative cell addresses into formulas by typing them in from the keyboard or by clicking the appropriate cells on the worksheet.

ABSOLUTE CELL ADDRESSING

There may be times when you want to store a reference in a cell that will not change with a copy, move, or fill operation. In other words, if you used B5 as a part of a formula and then copied it into another cell, it should still be B5 in the formula in the new cell. The concept of using a specific cell reference that does not change as a part of a formula or function is called *absolute cell addressing.*

To indicate this kind of addressing, you must insert a dollar sign before both the row and column designators of the referenced cell, as in:

    = $B$5 + $B$6

If you copied or moved this formula, cells B5 and B6 would still be referenced in the new cell. Absolute cell references are generally entered from the keyboard. (Chapter 14 describes an alternative method.)

The Cash-Flow Analysis worksheet shown in Figure 7.6 uses absolute cell addressing. Near the title, in column L, is a list of assumed parameters that were used in computing the projected interest, cost of goods, and advertising costs. The formulas in column C used these parameters. When these formulas were copied into the remainder of the row, it was important that the referenced cells in column L were not changed during the fill or copy operation. Thus, these formulas used absolute cell references: advertising costs, for example, in column C were $L$6*B14. This makes it easy to change the parameter values and see how the entire worksheet is affected. (Column B, however, could not contain these formulas, as each formula references a previous month.)

MIXED CELL ADDRESSING

There may be times when you need to use a combination of absolute and relative cell addressing in a single cell. Excel allows you to make either the row or column relative and the other absolute. For example, B$5 refers to a relative column B and an absolute row 5, and $B5 refers to an absolute column B and a relative row 5. This is called *mixed cell addressing*. Mixed cell references are generally entered from the keyboard.

WHAT IS A FUNCTION?

A *function* is an abbreviation of a formula. Functions provide a quick way to calculate the value of a cell that would otherwise use a long formula. In some cases, functions allow you to perform calculations that could not be done at all using formulas. For example, in your Income worksheet of Chapter 3, you used the following formula for cell B8:

    =(B5 + B6)

Now suppose that you wanted to use a total that was the sum of many cells, for example:

    =(B5 + B6 + B7 + B8 + B9)

You can imagine that it would be difficult to get the entire formula into the cell. Instead, you could use the SUM function and specify a range of cells as the input of the function:

    = SUM(B5:B9)

See how much shorter the entry has become?

Try this now with your Income worksheet. Enter = **SUM(B5:B6)** from the keyboard as the formula for cell B8. You will get the same answer as you did before. The new formula, which uses a function, can be copied or filled into cells C8 and D8, just as you did with the earlier formula. Try it.

FUNCTION ARGUMENTS

Arguments are values that are used as the input to a function to calculate the value of the function. With the SUM function, for example, you can have as many as 14 cells or cell ranges as arguments for the function. The number of arguments used by a particular function depends on the function. Some functions do not use any arguments.

Each function expects each of its arguments to be of a certain type. For example, the SUM function expects all of its arguments to be numeric. There are ten argument types that can be used by Excel functions. These are listed in Table 8.1.

The arguments of an Excel function must be in a certain order, which is determined by the function. The appropriate ordering of arguments for each function is listed at the end of this chapter. Be sure to check the appropriate order because Excel's argument order may differ from other worksheet programs, such as Lotus 1-2-3.

USING FUNCTIONS

The following general rules apply for entering functions into your worksheet:

- Always begin a function entry with an equal sign. This informs Excel you are entering a function, not a text string.

- The cells referenced can contain other functions, making it possible to create hierarchies of calculations.

- Separate the arguments with a comma. For example,

  SUM(B1:B5,B9:B10,B14:B15)

ARGUMENT	DEFINITIONS
Number	Anything that produces a number: numeric value, numeric formula, or a reference to a cell with a numeric value
Text	Anything that produces text: text, a text formula, or a reference to a cell containing text
Logical	Anything that produces a logical value
Ref	Anything that produces a reference
Value	Anything that produces a value
Array	Anything that produces an array
Vector	Anything that produces a one-dimensional array

Note: Text arguments must be enclosed in quotation marks.

Table 8.1: Types of Excel Arguments

- You can use up to 14 arguments in a function.

- You can use a maximum of 255 characters in a function (the cell limit).

- You can use any of the reference operators (see Chapter 4) to define the input for a function. For example, another way to define the formula for cell B8 is = SUM(B5,B6). This would store the sum of cells B5 and B6 in cell B8.

- Instead of cell references in a formula, you can use a constant value of the same type as the cell referenced. For example, B8 = SUM(100 + B5) would store the value of the contents of cell B5 plus 100 in cell B8.

- You can also use functions as arguments:

```
= SUM(ROUND(A3,0),ROUND(C1,0))
```

ENTERING FUNCTIONS

There are two ways to enter a function into a cell. One is to type the function in as a part of your formula. The second way is to paste the function name to the formula and then enter the arguments from the keyboard or by clicking.

Formula	
Paste Name...	
Paste Function...	
Reference	⌘R
Define Name...	⌘L
Create Names...	
Goto...	⌘G
Find...	⌘H
Select Last Cell	
Show Active Cell	

1. To manually enter a function, simply type the name. For example, find a blank cell on a worksheet and enter

   = ROUND(2.34,1)

   Notice the cell displays 2.3, the value rounded to one decimal place.

2. To paste a function name into a formula, use the Formula Paste Function command. Try the last example this way. Click on a blank cell, pull down the Formula menu, and select Paste Function. Scroll to the ROUND function name, double click on the function, then enter the arguments from the keyboard. Notice it was not necessary to enter the equal sign.

AN EXAMPLE USING FUNCTIONS

If you know the name of the function you want to paste, you don't have to scroll through all the functions. When the scroll box is displayed, just type the first letter of the function you want. For example, type **R** to get to the first function name beginning with R. Then double-click on ROUND.

Figure 8.1 shows an example worksheet that you can use to experiment with functions. In this example, $8,000.00 is borrowed at 9 percent interest, and Excel is used to calculate the monthly payments, the total amount paid, and the amortization schedule. This example makes extensive use of both the PMT (periodic payment) and PV (present value) functions, which are used frequently for financial analyses. Once you create the worksheet, you can change the amount borrowed, the interest, and the term to see how it affects the schedule. This makes the example much more than a simple tutorial—you can save it and use it to calculate the schedule whenever you purchase something on credit. (You will find more information on the PMT and PV functions in Chapter 22.)

Note that the data-entry area for the user, marked in the upper-left corner of the worksheet, consists of only three cells: B6, B7, and B8. Normally, you would want the rest of the worksheet protected so that

Amortization

AMORTIZATION SCHEDULE BY MONTH
Amortization Payment Schedule by Month

9/10/87
3:21 PM

```
***************  ***************  **
Data Entry Area                   *
Principle        $8,000.00        *
Interest         9.00%            *
Term             48 Months        *
***************  ***************  **

Payment:         $199.08
Total Paid:      $9,555.86
```

Month	Beginning Balance	Ending Balance	Payment	Total Paid	Tot. Princ. Paid	Tot. Interest Paid
1	$8,000.00	$7,860.92	$199.08	$199.08	$139.08	$60.00
2	$7,860.92	$7,720.80	$199.08	$398.16	$279.20	$118.96
3	$7,720.80	$7,579.62	$199.08	$597.24	$420.38	$176.86
4	$7,579.62	$7,437.39	$199.08	$796.32	$562.61	$233.71
5	$7,437.39	$7,294.09	$199.08	$995.40	$705.91	$289.49
6	$7,294.09	$7,149.71	$199.08	$1,194.48	$850.29	$344.20
7	$7,149.71	$7,004.26	$199.08	$1,393.56	$995.74	$397.82
8	$7,004.26	$6,857.71	$199.08	$1,592.64	$1,142.29	$450.35
9	$6,857.71	$6,710.06	$199.08	$1,791.72	$1,289.94	$501.78
10	$6,710.06	$6,561.31	$199.08	$1,990.80	$1,438.69	$552.11
11	$6,561.31	$6,411.44	$199.08	$2,189.88	$1,588.56	$601.32
12	$6,411.44	$6,260.44	$199.08	$2,388.96	$1,739.56	$649.40
13	$6,260.44	$6,108.31	$199.08	$2,588.04	$1,891.69	$696.36
14	$6,108.31	$5,955.05	$199.08	$2,787.12	$2,044.95	$742.17
15	$5,955.05	$5,800.63	$199.08	$2,986.21	$2,199.37	$786.83
16	$5,800.63	$5,645.05	$199.08	$3,185.29	$2,354.95	$830.34
17	$5,645.05	$5,488.31	$199.08	$3,384.37	$2,511.69	$872.68
18	$5,488.31	$5,330.39	$199.08	$3,583.45	$2,669.61	$913.84
19	$5,330.39	$5,171.29	$199.08	$3,782.53	$2,828.71	$953.82
20	$5,171.29	$5,010.99	$199.08	$3,981.61	$2,989.01	$992.60
21	$5,010.99	$4,849.50	$199.08	$4,180.69	$3,150.50	$1,030.18
22	$4,849.50	$4,686.79	$199.08	$4,379.77	$3,313.21	$1,066.55

Figure 8.1: The Amortization worksheet

users can only change these three cells (worksheet protection is described in Chapter 14). The user enters values into these cells, and Excel automatically calculates all the values on the remainder of the worksheet.

Begin creating the Amortization worksheet by entering the titles in cells C1 and C2. Create the data-entry area in cells A5 through B8 and enter the input values shown in Figure 8.2 into this area. Remember to enter a percent sign each time that you insert a value for cell B7. This enables Excel to calculate the schedule with the cell value as a percent.

Enter **Payment:** into cell A10 and **Total Paid** into cell A11. Use the following formulas and functions below the data-entry area:

CELL   *ENTRY*

B10   = PMT($B$7/12,$B$8, –$B$6)

B11   = ($B$8 * $B$10)

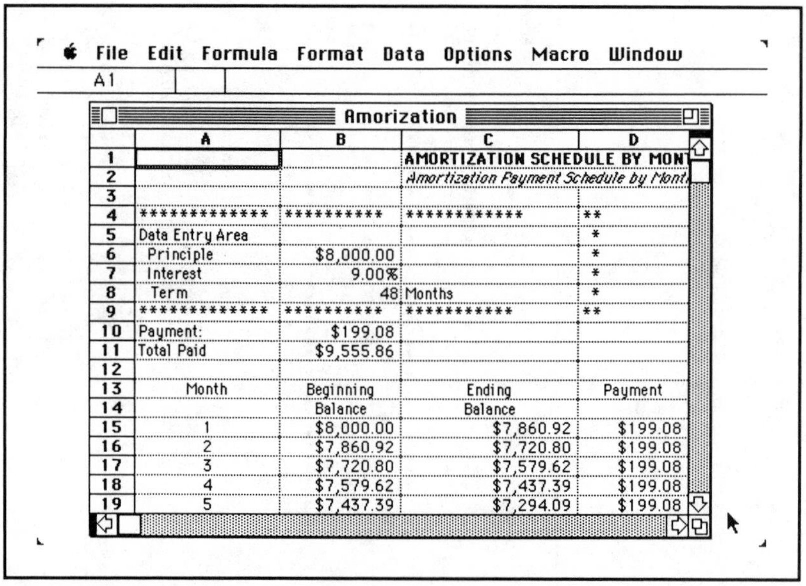

Figure 8.2: Creating the Amortization worksheet

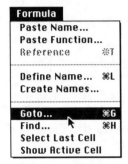 If you have been using Lotus 1-2-3, you will notice that the order of the arguments in Excel is slightly different from the Lotus convention. Excel's financial functions follow the HP-12C Financial Calculator's conventions.

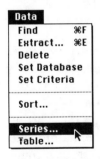

Now, enter the column headings into cells A13 through G14. Then, enter the month numbers into column A.

Chapter 14 describes a quick way to enter the month numbers into column A by using the Series command. Here is a summary if you wish to use this method now:

1. Enter 1 into cell A15

2. Select cell A15, pull down the Formula menu and choose Goto

3. Enter A62 into the Reference box, hold down the Shift key, and click OK

4. Pull down the Data menu, choose Series, and click OK.

Enter these formulas for the values for the first row:

CELL	ENTRY
B15	= \$B\$6
C15	= $-\mathrm{PV}(\$B\$7/12,(\$B\$8-A15),\$B\$10)$
D15	= \$B\$10
E15	= D15
F15	= B15 − C15
G15	= E15 − F15

Copy C15 to C16 and enter:

CELL	ENTRY
B16	= C15
E16	= E15 + D16
F16	= F15 + B16 − C16

Now, you can have Excel calculate the remainder of the amortization schedule by using the Fill Down command on the Edit menu for each column except the first. For columns B, E, and F, you will need to fill from the second row down. On the remaining rows, fill from

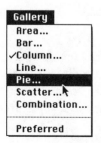

the first row down. The resulting values should be the same as those shown in Figure 8.1.

Format the worksheet, set up the alignments, and set the styles for the titles, as shown in Figure 8.1. Refer to Chapter 6 if you need help. Now, do one more thing: add a date and time stamp. To do this, add the following function entry into *both* cells E5 and E6:

= NOW( )

Use the Number command on the Format menu to change the format of cell E5 to m/d/yy. Change the format of cell E6 to h:mm AM/PM. Now, each time that you update the worksheet, the date and time on the worksheet will be updated automatically. If you don't want the date and time to be updated, see the explanation of how to prevent this in Chapter 17. The NOW function that you used to calculate the date and time is described in the section on date functions later in this chapter. The PMT and PV functions that you used earlier are described in the section on financial functions, later in this chapter and in Chapter 22.

Once you have set up the worksheet, save it using the name **Amortization**. Then, prepare for printing a copy by pulling down the File menu, selecting Page Setup, and setting the Printout Orientation to Sideways. Now print out the worksheet.

You can try changing any of the values in the data-entry area to see what happens to the amortization schedule. Remember to use the percent sign when you enter a different interest rate. Notice that Excel calculates the entire schedule in only a few seconds.

This is a valuable worksheet. Save it for calculating the schedule whenever you purchase something on credit—a house, automobile, computer, or whatever. It calculates the proper interest for income-tax purposes, as well as giving you the status of the principle in case you wish to refinance a loan.

If you are the adventurous type, you can try to create a pie chart from your amortization worksheet showing the relative percentages paid of principle and interest on a 48-month loan. Select only cells F62 and G62, which contain the final totals. Pull down the File menu, choose New, and double-click Chart. Use the Gallery menu to change the bar chart that was automatically created into a pie chart. Change the interest on the worksheet, and watch the chart change. If you get stuck, refer to Chapters 18 and 19.

TYPES OF FUNCTIONS

There are 86 functions available to the Excel user. These can be classified into nine types: mathematical, statistical, database, trigonometric, logical, text, financial, date, and special-purpose. Each function is described by type in the remainder of this chapter.

MATHEMATICAL FUNCTIONS

The following are Excel's mathematical functions:

FUNCTION	DESCRIPTION
ABS(*number*)	Returns the absolute value of *number*.
EXP(*number*)	Returns e raised to the power of *number*. EXP is the reverse of the *LN* (natural logarithm) function. To calculate the power to other bases, use the exponentiation operator.
INT(*number*)	Returns the largest integer less than or equal to *number*. For example: INT(7.6) is 7.
LN(*number*)	Returns the natural logarithm of *number*. *Number* must be positive. LN is the inverse of EXP.
LOG10(*number*)	Returns the base 10 logarithm of *number*.
MOD(*number, divisor number*)	Returns the remainder after *number* is divided by *divisor number*. The result has the same sign as divisor number.
PI( )	Returns the value of pi. There is no argument.
RAND( )	Returns a random number between 0 and 0.999.... The value

	will change each time the worksheet is recalculated. There is no argument.
ROUND(*number, number of digits*)	Returns *number* rounded to *number of digits*.
SIGN(*number*)	Returns 1 if *number* is positive, 0 if *number* is 0, and −1 if *number* is negative.
SQRT(*number*)	Returns the square root of *number*. *Number* must be positive.

STATISTICAL FUNCTIONS

Excel has the following statistical functions:

FUNCTION	*DESCRIPTION*
AVERAGE(*number 1, number 2, …*)	Returns the average of the numeric arguments.
COUNT(*number 1, number 2, …*)	Returns the number of numbers in a list of arguments. Example: COUNT(A1:A5,A8) equals 6.
GROWTH(*Y array, X array, x array*)	Returns an array with the y values as the exponential curve of regression $y = b*m \char`\^ x$ for two variables represented by *X array* and *Y array*.
LINEST(*Y array, X array*)	Returns the horizontal array of two elements, the slope and y intercept of the line of regression for $y = mx + b$ for two variables X and Y represented by *X array* and *Y array*.
LOGEST(*Y array, X array*)	Returns a horizontal array of two elements, the parameters of m and b in the exponential curve of regression $y = b*m \char`\^ x$ for two

	variables represented by *X array* and *Y array*.
MAX(*number 1, number 2, ...*)	Returns the largest number in a list of arguments.
MIN(*number 1, number 2, ...*)	Returns the smallest number in a list of arguments.
STDEV(*number 1, number 2, ...*)	Returns the standard deviation of the numbers in a list of arguments.
SUM(*number 1, number 2, ...*)	Returns the sum of the numbers in a list of arguments.
TREND(*Y array, X array, x array*)	Returns an array, the y values on the line of regression, $y = mx + b$, for the two variables X and Y represented by X array and Y array.
VAR(*number 1, number 2, ...*)	Returns the variance of the numbers in the list of arguments.

For more information on using the statistical functions, see Chapter 22.

DATABASE FUNCTIONS

The following are Excel's database functions:

FUNCTION	DESCRIPTION
DAVERAGE(*database, field name, criteria*)	Returns the average of the numbers in a particular field of the database that meet the specified criteria.
DCOUNT(*database, field name, criteria*)	Returns the count of the numbers in a particular field of a database that meet the specified criteria.
DMAX(*database, field name, criteria*)	Returns the largest of the numbers in a particular field of a database that meet the specified criteria.

DMIN(*database, field name, criteria*)	Returns the smallest of the numbers in a particular field of a database that meet the specified criteria.
DSTDEV(*database, field name, criteria*)	Returns the standard deviation of the numbers in a particular field of a database that meet the specified criteria.
DSUM(*database, field name, criteria*)	Returns the sum of the numbers in a particular field of a database that meet the specified criteria.
DVAR(*database, field name, criteria*)	Returns the variance of the numbers in a particular field of a database that meet the specified criteria.

For more information on using the database functions, see Part 3 of this book.

TRIGONOMETRIC FUNCTIONS

Excel has the following trigonometric functions:

FUNCTION	*DESCRIPTION*
ACOS(*number*)	Returns the arccosine of *number*. The value is returned in radians. To convert to degrees, multiply by 180/PI().
ASIN(*number*)	Returns the arcsine of number (see ACOS).
ATAN(*number*)	Returns the arctangent of number (see ACOS).
ATAN2(*x number, y number*)	Returns the arctangent of *x number* and *y number*.
COS(*number*)	Returns the cosine of *number*.

SIN(*number*)   Returns the sine of *number*.

TAN(*number*)   Returns the tangent of *number*.

Excel measures angles in radians rather than degrees. To convert radians to degrees, use the following equation:

Angle in radians *(180/&p) = Angle in degrees

LOGICAL FUNCTIONS

The following are Excel's logical functions:

FUNCTION	DESCRIPTION
AND(*logical 1, logical 2, ...*)	Returns TRUE if all logical values in the list of arguments are true. If any of the values are false, the function will return a value of FALSE.
CHOOSE(*index, value 1, value 2, ...*)	Returns the value from the list of arguments based on the value of *index*. If *index* is 1, *value 1* is returned.
FALSE( )	Returns the value of FALSE. Useful as an argument in the CHOOSE function.
IF(*logical, value if true, value if false*)	Returns *value if true* if *logical* is TRUE, otherwise returns *value if false*.
ISERROR(*value*)	Returns TRUE if *value* is any Excel error value, otherwise returns FALSE.
ISNA(*value*)	Returns TRUE if *value* is #N/A, (not available— see Appendix D), otherwise returns FALSE.

Use the ISNA and ISERROR functions to trap errors in your worksheet. This is especially useful in macros (see Part 7), as error conditions will terminate a macro execution. Using these functions, you can test and skip on an error condition.

ISREF(*value*)	Returns TRUE if *value* is a reference or reference formula, otherwise returns FALSE.
NOT(*logical*)	Returns FALSE if *logical* is TRUE, TRUE if *logical* is FALSE.
OR(*logical 1, logical 2, ...*)	Returns TRUE if any of the logical values in the list of arguments is TRUE. If all logical values in the list are FALSE, it returns FALSE.
TRUE( )	Returns a logical value of TRUE. Used with CHOOSE function. There is no argument.

TEXT FUNCTIONS

The following are Excel's text functions:

FUNCTION	DESCRIPTION
DOLLAR(*number, number of digits*)	Rounds *number* to *number of digits*, formats it to currency format, and returns a text result.
FIXED(*number, number of digits*)	Rounds *number* to *number of digits*, formats to a decimal format with commas, and returns a text result.
LEN(*text*)	Returns a number equal to the length of *text*.
MID(*text, start position, number of characters*)	Extracts *number of characters* from *text*, starting with *start position*.
REPT(*text, number of times*)	Repeats *text* for *number of times*.
TEXT(*number, format text*)	Formats *number* to *format text* and returns it as text.
VALUE(*text*)	Converts *text* to a number. (Not necessary to use in a formula, as Excel converts it automatically if necessary.)

The TEXT function is useful for displaying numeric text in a special format or alignment. For example,

   = TEXT(C1,"##0.00")

would display "123.3" in C1 as 123.30. Unlike a right-aligned number, however, the value would be left aligned. Text always has a default left alignment. You can use most of the formatting symbols (see Chapter 6), but you cannot use the asterisk in the format to force a repeating symbol to fill a cell. As another example, you could use

   = TEXT(230," " "Please remit: " "$#,##0.00")

to display

   Please remit: $230.00

In this case two quotes (around the text string) are used to represent one internal quote.

Sometimes it is easier to use the DOLLAR and FIXED functions than the TEXT function to display currency values. For example, either of the following displays $123.00, but which is easier to enter?

   DOLLAR(123,2)
   TEXT(123,"$#,##0.00")

Both DOLLAR and FIXED automatically round the displayed value.

FINANCIAL FUNCTIONS

The following are Excel's financial functions:

FUNCTION	DESCRIPTION
FV(*rate, nper, pmt, pv, type*)	Returns the future value of an investment (see PV).
IRR(*values, guess*)	Returns internal rate of return of a series of cash flows, represented by values. *Guess* is an optional argument, specifying the starting point for the iteration. If *guess* is

	omitted, it is assumed to be 0.1 or 10%. *Values* should be an array or reference that contains numbers.
MIRR(*values, safe, risk*)	Returns a modified internal rate of return of a series of cash flows, represented by the numbers in *values,* given *safe* and *risk.* *Safe* is the rate returned by the investment that will finance the negative cash flows. *Risk* is the rate at which the positive cash flows can be reinvested.
NPER(*rate, pmt, pv, fv, type*)	Returns the number of periods of an investment involving constant cash flows (see PV).
NPV(*rate, values 1, values 2, ...*)	Returns net present value of a series of future cash flows, represented by the numbers in the list of values, discounted at a constant interest rate specified by *rate.*
PMT(*rate, nper, pv, fv, type*)	Returns the periodic payment on an investment involving constant cash flows (see PV and the example in this chapter).
PV(*rate, nper, pmt, fv, type*)	Returns the present value. The arguments are as follows: *rate:* interest rate per period *nper:* number of periods *pmt:* periodic payment *fv:* future value *type:* indicates whether payments occur at the beginning or end of the period. If *type* = 0, first payment is at the end of the first period. If *type* = 1, payment is at beginning. If argument is omitted, it is assumed to be 0.

| RATE(*nper, pmt, pv, fv, type, guess*) | Returns the interest rate per period of an investment involving constant cash flows. (See PV.) *Guess* is an optional argument that specifies the starting value for the iteration. If omitted, it is assumed to be 0.1 or 10%. |

The functions PV, FV, NPER, PMT, and RATE are all interrelated; you can calculate one given the value of the others. See the example in this chapter. For more information on the financial functions, see Chapter 22.

DATE FUNCTIONS

The following are Excel's date functions:

FUNCTION	DESCRIPTION
DATE(*year, month, day*)	Returns the serial number of the specified day.
DAY(*serial number*)	Converts *serial number* to the day of the month.
HOUR(*serial number*)	Converts *serial number* to an hour of the day.
MINUTE(*serial number*)	Converts *serial number* to a minute.
MONTH(*serial number*)	Converts *serial number* to a month of the year.
NOW( )	Returns the *serial number* of the current date and time. There is no argument.
SECOND(*serial number*)	Converts *serial number* to second.
TIME(*hour, minute, second*)	Returns the *serial number* for the specified time.
WEEKDAY(*serial number*)	Converts *serial number* to the day of the week.
YEAR(*serial number*)	Converts *serial number* to a year.

You can enter a date in a cell using the date function. For example, =DATE(87,04,15) stores the equivalent serial number for April 15, 1987 in the cell. If you enter an illegal date, Excel will try to calculate a serial date based on the number. For example, if you enter a day of 32 for a month with 31 days, the serial number returned will be for the first day of the next month. You will get no error message. Once a date is entered, use the Format Number command to format the serial number to the desired date form.

You can also enter a date by clicking the cell and typing the date in the desired format. The cell will be formatted automatically. You can use a built-in date or preassigned custom date this way.

You can use formulas to calculate the difference between any two dates. The calculations will be performed on the serial date numbers. The result will be the true date difference in days. To get the difference in weeks, divide by 7.

The TIME function works in a similar way. You can enter a time and then format it. For example,

= TIME(3,15,)

becomes 3:15 A.M. You can also enter a time in any valid time format and it will be automatically formatted. The time is stored as a fractional number, and represents the fraction of the day that has elapsed. For example, 8:00 A.M. is stored as .333.

You can also take the difference of two times. The difference, when multiplied by 24, will give you the true time difference in hours. (Remember that the fraction represents the fractional part of 24 hours that has elapsed.) To convert a fractional hour to minutes, multiply by 60. Use the INT function to extract the fractional part of a date or to get the fractional part of an hour.

The NOW( ) function is useful for time-stamping your worksheets. Use the special format that includes both the date and time: m/d/yy h:mm. This will be wider than a standard cell width, so put it in a wide cell. The date and time will be updated each time you calculate the worksheet.

Sometimes you may wish to freeze the date stamp. Without freezing the value, the date will be calculated each time you load the worksheet. In most cases, you will wish the date of the last update to be

For dates in the twenty-first century, use a three digit year number. =DATE(101,4,1) is April 1, 2001. You can use any year up to 2040 with this method.

If the number of seconds is not important, you can omit the third argument. Be sure to keep the comma. Example: =TIME(7,15,).

displayed instead. If you want to freeze the date stamp so it will not change, use either of these methods:

- Click on the cell, pull down the Edit menu, and choose Copy. Pull down Edit again and choose Click Paste Special. Click the Values option. The cell now contains a pure value—no function. For more information on this method see Chapter 17.

- Click on the cell, drag through all the characters in the formula bar, then pull down the Options menu and choose Calculate Now.

Both methods convert the date to a value and the value (not the equation) is stored in the cell.

Another, simpler way to put the date and time stamps on your worksheets is to use the Command key. To put the date in a cell as a constant, type Command – . To put the time in a cell, use Command = ;. Both can be put in the same cell. Both are constant values and will not change on calculating.

Using the techniques of Chapter 6, you can create your own custom date and time formats.

The WEEKDAY(date) function returns a number that is the day of the week, with Sunday returned as 1. Notice that you have functions that can return the year, month, or day of a date in a cell or the hour, minute, and second of a time in a cell.

SPECIAL-PURPOSE FUNCTIONS

Excel's special-purpose functions are the following:

FUNCTION	DESCRIPTION
AREAS(*ref*)	Returns the number of areas in *ref*. *Ref* can refer to multiple areas. Example: AREAS(A1:A5,B1) equals 2.
COLUMN(*ref*)	Returns the column number of *ref*. If *ref* is omitted, it returns the column number of the current

	cell. *Ref* cannot refer to multiple areas.
COLUMNS(*array*)	Returns the number of columns in *array*.
HLOOKUP(*lookup value, compare array, index number*)	Searches the first row of *compare array* for the largest value that is less than or equal to *lookup value*. The function moves down the column by the amount specified by *index number* and returns the value found there.
INDEX(*ref, row, column, area*)	Returns the cell that is defined in *ref* by row and column. If *ref* refers to multiple areas, *area* defines the areas from which the cell is to be obtained.
INDEX(*array, row, column*)	Returns the value of a single element within *array*, selected by *row* and *column*.
LOOKUP(*lookup value, compare vector, result vector*)	Searches *compare vector* for largest value less than or equal to *lookup value*. The function returns the corresponding value of *result vector*. The values in *compare vector* can be text, numbers, or logical, but they must be in ascending order. Microsoft recommends using this version of LOOKUP rather than the next one.
LOOKUP(*lookup value, compare array*)	Searches first row or column of *compare array* for largest value that is less than or equal to *lookup value*. The function returns the corresponding value in the last row or column of *compare array*. Whether the first row or column is searched

depends on the size of the array. If it is square or has more rows than columns, LOOKUP searches the first column and gives a value from the corresponding last column. If there are more columns than rows, the first row is searched and LOOKUP gives the value of the corresponding cell in the last row. The values in the array can be text, numbers, or logical, but they must be in ascending order.

MATCH(*lookup value, compare vector, type*)

Returns the corresponding number of the comparison value in *compare vector* that matches *lookup value*. Example: If the look-up value matches the second comparison value, MATCH returns a 2.

NA( )

Returns the error value of #N/A (value not available—see Appendix D). There is no argument.

ROW(*ref*)

Returns the row number of *ref* if *ref* references a single cell. If *ref* refers to a range of cells, a vertical array is returned. If the argument is omitted, the row of the current cell is returned. ROW cannot refer to multiple areas.

ROWS(*array*)

Returns the number of rows in *array*.

TRANSPOSE(*array*)

Returns an array that is the transpose of *array*. That is, the rows become columns and the columns become rows.

TYPE(*value*)

Returns a code defining the type of *value:* 1 for number, 2 for text, 4

	for logical, 16 for error, and 64 for an array.
VLOOKUP(*lookup value, compare array, index number*)	Identical to HLOOKUP, except that it searches the first column of *compare array,* moving right in that row by the amount specified by *index number.*

For more information on the lookup functions, refer to Chapter 14.

NAMING CELLS AND RANGES

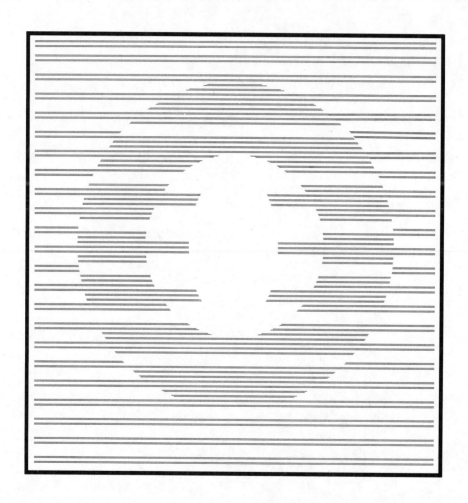

CHAPTER 9 _____

WHEN YOU'RE CREATING WORKSHEETS, YOU MAY often find it an advantage to use names to identify a cell or cell range. Names make worksheets and formulas easier to work with and read. Using names also reduces user errors because the purpose of calculations becomes much clearer.

Once you have defined a name, you can use it in functions and formulas, just as you would use a cell or cell range reference. Some functions, such as the database ones, *require* the use of names. You can also use names with the Goto command to simplify moving to a cell or cell range.

In this chapter, you will learn how to define and paste names by using the simple Income worksheet that you created in Chapter 3. The same techniques can be applied to more complex worksheets of any type.

NAMING CELLS _____

You can use names for absolute, relative, or mixed cell references, although, generally, names are used for absolute references. For example, the Cash-Flow Analysis worksheet that you created in Chapter 7 used a series of constants in column L (near the top of the page). These were part of the worksheet calculations for each month (see Figure 7.6). These could be named Interest, Cost_of_Goods _Ratio, and Advertising_Ratio. The formula for cell C26, the advertising cost for February, would be

= Advertising_Ratio * B12

where B12 is the previous month's sale of goods. You could also give cell B12 a name. You would, however, have to use relative cell addressing in defining that name if you wanted to use a Copy or Fill command to copy the formula into other cells.

There are three different ways that you can define names for cells or for cell ranges:

- Use the Create Names command on the Formula menu to designate row or column titles as names

- Use the Define Name command on the Formula menu to create a name for any cell or cell range

- Use the Define Name window to assign a name to constants used in formulas

NAMING ROWS AND COLUMNS

The easiest way to define a name is to use a row or column title as a name for all the cells in a row or column. First, select the entire row or column. Then, pull down the Formula menu and select Create Names. The Create Names dialog box shown in Figure 9.1 appears.

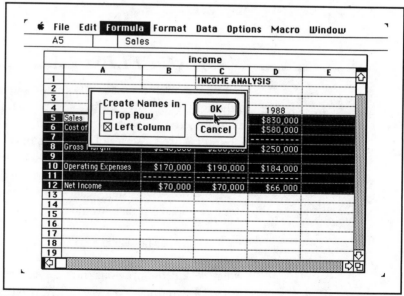

Figure 9.1: The Create Names dialog box

Click Top Row if you wish to use column titles as names; click Left Column if you wish to use row titles as names. You can use both row and column titles by clicking both Top Row and Left Column. After you've made your selection, click OK.

As an example, let's use the simple Income worksheet that you created in Chapter 3. Double-click the Income icon, or use the Open command on the File menu if Excel is already started, and open this worksheet. Figure 9.2 shows the Income worksheet.

Now try the following exercise:

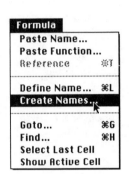

1. Select rows 5 through 12 by clicking the designator for row 5 and dragging to row 12. Be sure that the entire rows are selected.

2. Pull down the Formula menu and choose Create Names.

3. When the Create Names dialog box shown in Figure 9.1 is displayed, click Left Column, then click OK.

4. Click cell B8. The cell's current formula is displayed in the formula bar, as shown in Figure 9.3.

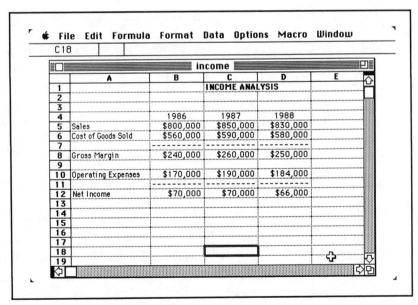

Figure 9.2: The Income worksheet

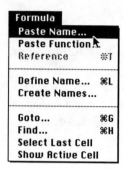

5. Pull down the Formula menu and choose Paste Name. The Paste Name dialog box shown in Figure 9.4 appears. It lists the names that are currently available. These names are the row titles that you selected in step 1. Notice that Excel automatically converted all the spaces that were in the names into underlines. This is because you cannot use spaces in names.

6. Double-click Sales. The formula bar clears, and an equal sign and the name Sales are entered into the formula bar, as shown in Figure 9.5.

7. Enter a minus sign into the formula bar from the keyboard.

8. Pull down the Formula menu again and choose Paste Name again. This time, when the Paste Name dialog box appears, double-click Cost_of_Goods_Sold. This name will appear in the formula bar along with = Sales, as shown in Figure 9.6.

9. Click the enter box in the formula bar, and the correct total will appear in cell B8.

	File	**Edit**	**Formula**	**Format**	**Data**	**Options**	**Macro**	**Window**

B8		=B5-B6

income

	A	B	C	D	E
1			INCOME ANALYSIS		
2					
3					
4		1986	1987	1988	
5	Sales	$800,000	$850,000	$830,000	
6	Cost of Goods Sold	$560,000	$590,000	$580,000	
7					
8	Gross Margin	$240,000	$260,000	$250,000	
9					
10	Operating Expenses	$170,000	$190,000	$184,000	
11					
12	Net Income	$70,000	$70,000	$66,000	
13					
14					
15					
16					
17					
18					
19					

Figure 9.3: The selected cell's current formula displayed in the formula bar

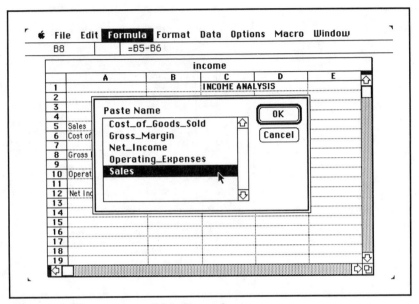

Figure 9.4: The names available for pasting

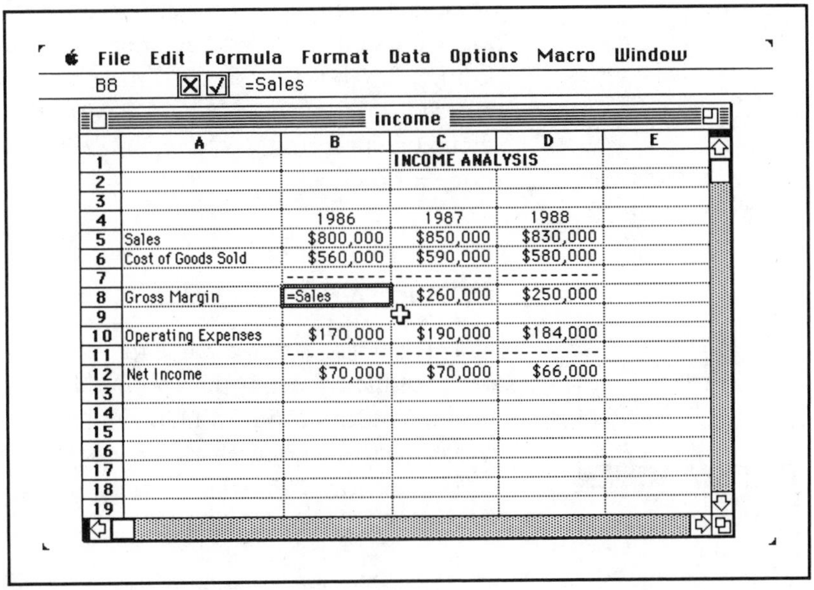

Figure 9.5: Pasting a name in a formula

File Edit Formula Format Data Options Macro Window

| B8 | ☒ ☑ | =Sales-Cost_of_Goods_Sold |

	A	B	C	D	E
1			INCOME ANALYSIS		
2					
3					
4		1986	1987	1988	
5	Sales	$800,000	$850,000	$830,000	
6	Cost of Goods Sold	$560,000	$590,000	$580,000	
7					
8	Gross Margin	of_Goods_Sold	$260,000	$250,000	
9					
10	Operating Expenses	$170,000	$190,000	$184,000	
11					
12	Net Income	$630,000	$70,000	$66,000	
13					
14					
15					
16					
17					
18					
19					

Figure 9.6: The formula bar after the second name is pasted

 You do not assign the name with the Create Names command. The name is taken from the first cell in the row or column. Spaces are converted to underlines. If you wish to assign your own name, see the next section.

You can use the Option key to enter the same name for a range of cells. For example, select cells B8 to D8. Repeat the above steps starting with step 4. However, when you reach step 9, hold down the Option key before you click the enter box. The new name will be entered for the entire range. Select cells C8 and D8 and examine their current formulas. Now, enter the formulas for row 12 using the same procedure.

CREATING A NAME

You can also assign a name to a cell or cell range that is not a row or column title by using the Define Name command on the Formula menu. You can choose a name and assign it to any type of worksheet range, even a discontinuous range.

Try creating a name now by naming row 8 of your Income worksheet:

1. Select the range to name by clicking the row 8 designator

2. Pull down the Formula menu and choose Define Name

Formula

Paste Name...	
Paste Function...	
Reference	⌘T
Define Name...	**⌘L**
Create Names...	
Goto...	⌘G
Find...	⌘H
Select Last Cell	
Show Active Cell	

3. The Define Name window shown in Figure 9.7 is now displayed. It lists the names that are currently active and shows the cell range that you just selected in the Refers to box. Enter **Gross_Sales** at the cursor location in the Name box, then press Return or click OK. Remember to use an underline rather than a space to separate the two words.

The new name has been added to the name list. You can see the name by pulling down the Formula menu and choosing Define Name again. Notice that what appears (Figure 9.7) is actually a window, not just a dialog box. You can move it around on the screen, but you cannot resize it. It does not have a close box so you must click Cancel to return to your worksheet.

When creating your own names, keep the following rules in mind:

- Only one name can be defined each time that the Define Name command is used

- The first character must be a letter

- Spaces are not allowed

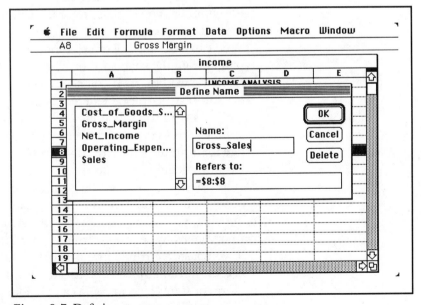

Figure 9.7: Defining a name

- Except for the first character, letters, digits, periods, and underlines can be used

- Names can be up to 255 characters long

- Upper- or lowercase letters can be used

- The name cannot look like an absolute, relative, or mixed cell reference

If you try to use a name that breaks any of these rules, Excel will display an ''illegal name'' message.

USING THE DEFINE NAME WINDOW

Instead of selecting a cell or cell range, you can use the Refers to box on the Define Name window to define the range to which a name refers. You can even enter formulas or other names as a part of the reference.

Any cells that you select before you use the Define Name command will appear in the Refers to box when the window is displayed. You can change that entry, and your new cell or cell range will replace the previous selection. You can clear the Refers to box by placing the cursor at the end of the current entry and backspacing to the beginning. You can also clear the box by selecting the entire contents and backspacing once.

You can enter the cell or cell range into the Refers to box either by typing it from the keyboard, or by clicking the cell you want to reference in the worksheet. If you click a cell to enter its reference into the Refers to box, it will be entered as an absolute cell reference. (The opposite is true when you click a cell to reference it in the formula bar—then it is a relative cell reference.) You can, of course, enter a cell reference from the keyboard as an absolute, relative, or mixed cell address when defining a name.

The commands on the Edit menu are not available for editing the Define Name window. Although you can mark a portion for cutting or moving, you will not be able to execute any operation because you cannot make any selections from the Edit menu.

If you paste a formula from a cell that references a cell in the worksheet, the formula will be updated if the cell is edited. You can use this to store constants for a formula calculation, just as you used constants in Chapter 7.

WORKING WITH NAMES

Once you have named a cell or cell range, you can work with that name in many ways. You can use cut, copy, and fill operations just as you used them with other types of cell referencing. You can also use the Paste Name command on the Formula menu to enter names into formulas, and you can use names with the Goto command.

PASTING NAMES

You can also paste names into formulas by using the following procedure:

1. Click the cursor on the insertion point in the formula bar.

2. Pull down the Formula menu and choose Paste Name. The Paste Name dialog box shown in Figure 9.4 will then be displayed. Scroll through the box until the name that you want to use is visible.

3. Double-click the name, or click the name and then click OK.

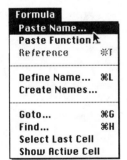

You can also paste names from one worksheet into formulas in other worksheets. The reference to the other worksheet can be entered in either of two ways:

- You can enter the name from the keyboard by preceding it with the worksheet name and an exclamation point, such as:

    BALANCE!CASH

- You can select the cell or cell range that will contain the formula on the alternate worksheet. With the original worksheet active, use the Paste Name command to point at a name in the alternate worksheet's Paste Name dialog box. The name will be entered into the formula bar of the original worksheet, preceded by the worksheet name and an exclamation point, as in the example above.

When you use the Paste Name command to enter a name into a formula, an equal sign is entered into the formula bar automatically

on the first paste. On subsequent pastes, if no operator precedes the cursor location, a plus sign will be added before the name. If an operator precedes the cursor location, a plus sign will not be added.

USING NAMES WITH THE GOTO COMMAND

You can also use names with the Goto command. This command moves you directly to any specific cell or cell range.

You can try using the Goto command with your Income worksheet, with the row titles defined as names. Pull down the Formula menu and select Goto. When the Goto dialog box shown in Figure 9.8 is displayed, double-click Net Income. The cursor will move to this row on the screen.

EDITING AND DELETING NAMES

Excel does not delete the old name when you edit the spelling of a name. Formulas change correctly, but you should take the time to delete the old name and double-check your formulas.

Before deleting a name, use the Formula Find command to locate all references to the name. When the dialog box is displayed, type the name you will delete in the Find What field. Check Formulas and Part and either option in the Look By column. When you click OK, the first occurrence will be displayed. Use Command-H to find successive occurrences.

To edit a name that you have already defined, pull down the Formula menu and choose Define Name. The Define Name window (Figure 9.7) will be displayed. Scroll until the name that you want to edit is visible, then click it. The current name will be displayed in the Name box, and the current reference will be in the Refers to box. The contents of either box can be edited. Click OK when you have completed your editing.

If you want to delete a name that you previously defined, use the following procedure:

1. Edit any cell references using the name

2. Pull down the Formula menu and choose Define Name

3. When the Define Name window is displayed, click the desired name

4. Click Delete

As an exercise, delete the Gross_Sales name that you defined earlier.

If you delete a name defined to a range, all cells referencing that name will display an error message. Edit the cells first, then delete the name.

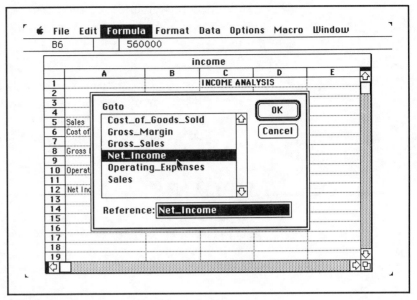

Figure 9.8: The Goto dialog box

NAMING PRECAUTIONS

Keep the following precautions, notes, and tips in mind when naming cells:

- Deleting a cell name that is used in worksheet cells will create worksheet error messages. Edit the cells first.

- Avoid inserting or deleting a row or column in a named range. The results are unpredictable. If necessary to insert or delete, check the name definition after the insertion or deletion.

- If you cut and paste an entire named range, the definition will be changed accordingly.

- When using named formulas, you can use relative, absolute, and mixed references.

- Be very careful when you use relative references in naming ranges and formulas. The result will depend on the active cell when the name is defined. The result will also change if you copy or move the cell in which the name is used.

- If you have a named range of one column or one row, you can refer to individual cells in the range by the range name. For example, you can copy the contents of a named row to another row by first pasting the range name to the first cell in the destination row and then selecting the remaining cells in the destination row and copying the first cell to them.

SUMMARY

You have now defined and pasted names using a simple worksheet. The same techniques can be applied to any type of document. You will probably use names quite often to clarify your worksheet formulas and function arguments.

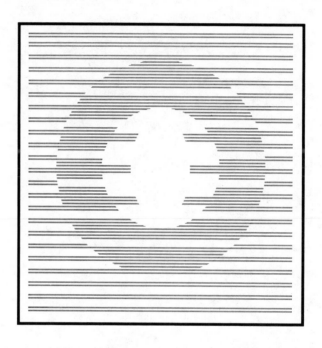

DATABASE MANAGEMENT

ONE OF EXCEL'S MOST USEFUL FEATURES IS ITS capacity for database management. You can use databases for any sort of application that requires the management of groups of items with numerous components, such as the management of mailing lists, prospect lists, or personnel registers. In the case of the mailing list, for example, each database item is a member address that includes the name, street address, city, state, zip, and telephone number.

Excel's on-screen database-management capability allows you to create a database as part of a worksheet and use it to calculate cell values in other parts of the worksheet. For example, you could create an inventory database with the total inventory value used in another part of the worksheet for financial cash flow projections. As the inventory changes, the financial cash-flow projections also change to reflect the current inventory.

Part 3 consists of three chapters. Chapter 10 discusses the fundamentals of database management. You will create a database and learn how to add, edit, and delete records in this database. In later chapters, this same database example will be used to create complex reports and charts. Chapter 11 discusses how to find a record or records in the database that meet a specific criterion. Chapter 12 discusses the techniques of sorting and ordering your database. In all three chapters you will find examples of how you can apply database management to specific problems.

BASIC DATABASE
TECHNIQUES

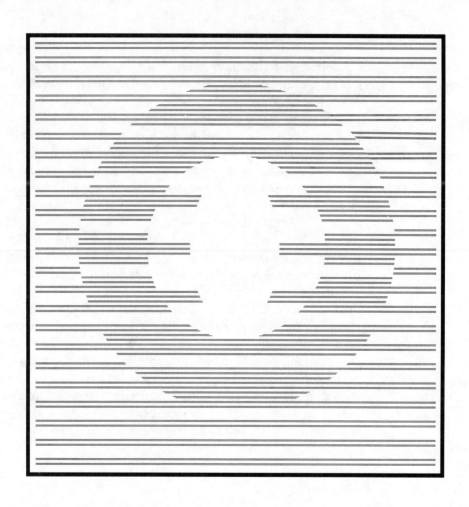

CHAPTER 10

THE EXCEL ON-SCREEN DATABASE-MANAGEMENT system can be viewed much like an electronic filing system. A database is a structured collection of data. The data may be about people, products, events—in short, any type of information that you would like to store. The primary use of a database is to manage the collection of data for reporting and making decisions.

DATABASE APPLICATIONS

You probably use one or more databases every day, although they are perhaps not electronic. Your address book, the telephone book, the recipe box, and the dictionary are all examples of commonly used databases. Each is a collection of data. In each case the database is ordered so that you can find the information you want quickly. Because none of these are electronic, however, they are relatively cumbersome to update.

Excel, however, permits you to create electronic databases that are easy to use and update. Here are some typical applications for an Excel database:

- Financial: General ledgers, accounts-receivable, and accounts-payable systems

- Sales and marketing: Contract management, sales projections, expense accounts, and prospect lists

- Business: Personnel registers, telephone-extension directories, inventory listings, low-inventory reports, and material-requirement planning

- Home: Cataloging of books, records, and tapes; nutrition analyses; mailing lists; and address management

EXCEL VERSUS OTHER DATABASE PRODUCTS

You should be aware that databases created with Excel are different from databases created with single-application database management systems, such as dBASE III PLUS or R:BASE System V. In single-application database management systems, data are stored on the disk and listed or extracted from the disk. The amount of data that can be stored in the database is limited only by the size of the disk storage. As a result, you can create very large databases and do very complex operations on the database. You cannot, however, directly carry data from the database to a worksheet calculation.

When you are working with Excel's database, *all* the database data are stored in the computer memory at the same time. As a result, the size of the database that you can create is limited by the amount of computer memory available. (When Excel is not in use, data are stored in a file on the disk, just as in a single-application system.) Because of this storage system, the entire database is in memory at once and database operations are much faster than in comparable single-application products. You can also directly use the database information in calculations in other areas of the worksheet without having to import it.

If you have a very large database that requires complex reporting and processing, you might want to consider using an external database management system to store the data and using Excel to manage a portion of the database. For example, suppose that you are managing a pension fund for a company. You could keep the annual data for each employee in an Excel database and use an Excel worksheet to calculate the earnings for the year for each employee. After you've calculated the earnings for the year using Excel, you could transfer the results to an external database (using the procedure described in Chapter 20), which would store all the historical information and produce summary reports.

THE DATABASE COMPONENTS

Figure 10.1 shows a sample Excel database. Notice that it is really nothing more than a rectangular range of worksheet cells. In Excel, a *database* is two or more rows of cells that span at least one column.

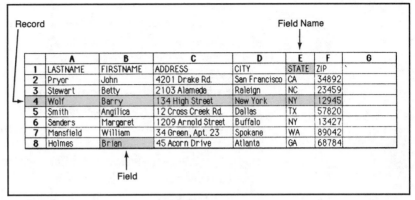

Figure 10.1: The database components

Each row represents a single item, or *record*. In this case there are seven records stored in the database. Each piece of data that you store about an item is called a *field*. In this sample database, the fields are LASTNAME, FIRSTNAME, ADDRESS, CITY, STATE, and ZIP. The first row of the database is used to define the field names. In the worksheet analogy, the records are rows and the fields are columns. Notice that the rows do not have titles.

You can put as many as 16,383 records in an Excel database (the top row must be used for the field names). All of the database must be able to fit in memory along with the Excel program.

WORKING WITH DATABASES

The fact that an on-screen database looks very much like a worksheet makes the Excel database easy to use. There are only two primary differences between the database and the worksheet: in a database, the rows no longer have a title and each of the columns (including the first) has a name that represents a field name.

The features and commands that are available for working with worksheets are the same as those available for databases. The menu bar at the top of the screen also remains the same. You can define any part of a worksheet for a database and use the remainder for worksheet functions, or you can define the entire worksheet as a database. You can add, edit, and delete records and fields in a database in the same way that you work with cells in a worksheet. You can move data from a database to somewhere else on the worksheet (or from somewhere else on the worksheet to the database) using the familiar Copy, Cut, and Paste commands.

A database can be sorted so that the rows are in any desired order. For example, a mailing list might be sorted in zip-code order to prepare some mailing labels, then sorted again alphabetically by last name to print an alphabetical directory. You can also extract information based on a particular criterion; for example, from a mailing list, you could extract all the addresses that are local. In this chapter, you will learn the basics of creating the database. In later chapters you will learn how you can extract information (Chapter 11), how to sort the database to any order (Chapter 12), how to link databases with worksheets or other databases (Chapter 16), and how to create charts from databases (Chapter 19). Finally, you will learn how to use macros to execute repetitive database operations, and to write database management programs (Part 7).

CREATING AN EXCEL DATABASE

Widget Manufacturing had a staff of sales representatives in four areas of the country. Each sales representative had a sales target, and the sum of the targets for the representatives in each area represented the sales target for that particular area. Widget also tracked sales performance by representative during each three-month cycle. These data were recorded in a database and used for a variety of reports. Management used these reports to track the sales performance of representatives and the performance of each sales area.

The sales target for each of the sales representatives is shown in Figure 10.2 as an Excel database. Notice that the records (rows) do not have titles, but each field (column), including the first, has a name.

Now you can create the Sales Projections database. There are four steps involved in creating and using a database:

1. Defining the fields

2. Entering the data

3. Formatting any data that is necessary

4. Defining the database range (that part of the worksheet that will be used as the database)

SALES PROJECTIONS

	A	B	C	D
1				
2				
3				
4				
5				
6				
7				
8				
9				
10				
11	LAST	FIRST	TARGET	REGION
12	Adams	Chuck	$118,000	South
13	Allen	Ellen	$90,000	East
14	Atkins	Lee	$113,000	East
15	Conners	Paul	$142,000	West
16	Ellis	Nancy	$122,000	East
17	Ford	Carl	$191,000	Midwest
18	Glenn	John	$80,000	South
19	Harris	Ken	$176,000	West
20	Jackson	Robert	$112,000	East
21	Keller	Janet	$105,000	West
22	Kennedy	Sandra	$135,000	East
23	Linn	Vera	$80,000	Midwest
24	Parker	Greg	$196,000	South
25	Peterson	Tom	$98,000	Midwest
26	Stevens	Carla	$110,000	East

Figure 10.2: Widget sales targets

DEFINING THE FIELDS

You start creating a database exactly as you would create a worksheet. Open a new worksheet for the database. Pull down the File menu and choose New. You will see the New dialog box, as shown in Figure 10.3. Leave Worksheet selected (because a database is a part of a worksheet) and click OK. Excel displays an empty worksheet.

Enter the field names shown in Figure 10.2. Start in row 11, as you will need some working space at the top later. You may use any text (to a maximum of 255 characters) for field names, but it is a good idea to keep the names short to simplify future searches. You can also use functions that produce text to create field names, however you cannot use numbers or functions that produce numbers as field names.

ENTERING THE DATA

Now enter the worksheet data as shown in Figure 10.2. It is a good idea to enter an entire record before entering the data for any other records. This minimizes errors on data entry. Use the Tab key after each entry to move to the next field.

Plan your database before entering the fields. In most cases, for example, you will want separate fields for first and last names. This permits you to treat each part of the name as a separate component. You could then use the first name field in a form letter; for example, Dear Vera:. Any piece of data you might use for a search criterion should be put in a separate field.

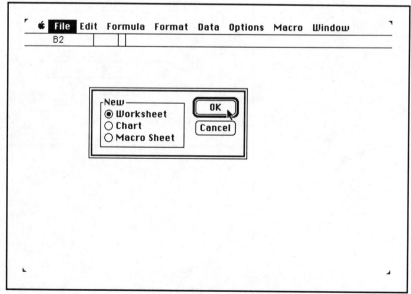

Figure 10.3: Opening a worksheet window for a database

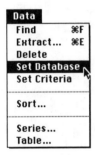

When using formulas in calculated fields, use absolute references or names to refer to cells outside the database range and relative references to refer to cells inside the database range.

Format databases by column to save time, as all formats in the same column are the same. The column width should normally be equal to or greater than the longest field length expected in that field.

Data	
Find	⌘F
Extract...	⌘E
Delete	
Set Database	
Set Criteria	
Sort...	
Series...	
Table...	

FORMATTING THE DATA

You should now format any data in the database that is necessary just as you would format any other cell or cell range in the worksheet (Format menu, Number option). If any field width change is necessary, use the Column Width option on the Format menu. Change any alignments necessary (Format menu, Alignment option). You can also align the field titles if you wish or change the style of the name. Fonts are set from the Options menu, and a single font applies to the entire worksheet. However, you can set the style in which the font is displayed for an individual cell, a column, or a range.

DEFINING THE DATABASE RANGE

Now you must define the area of the worksheet that will serve as your database:

1. Click cell A11 and scroll to row 26.

2. Hold down the Shift key and click cell D26. You have now selected the entire database area, including the field names. (See Figure 10.4.)

```
 File  Edit  Formula  Format  Data  Options  Macro  Window
   A11              LAST
========================= SALES PROJECTIONS =========================
         A            B          C           D           E          F
10 |
11 | LAST       | FIRST    | TARGET    | REGION    |           |
12 | Adams      | Chuck    | $118,000  | South     |           |
13 | Allen      | Ellen    | $90,000   | East      |           |
14 | Atkins     | Lee      | $113,000  | East      |           |
15 | Conners    | Paul     | $142,000  | West      |           |
16 | Ellis      | Nancy    | $122,000  | East      |           |
17 | Ford       | Carl     | $191,000  | Midwest   |           |
18 | Glenn      | John     | $80,000   | South     |           |
19 | Harris     | Ken      | $176,000  | West      |           |
20 | Jackson    | Robert   | $112,000  | East      |           |
21 | Keller     | Janet    | $105,000  | West      |           |
22 | Kennedy    | Sandra   | $135,000  | East      |           |
23 | Linn       | Vera     | $80,000   | Midwest   |           |
24 | Parker     | Greg     | $196,000  | South     |           |
25 | Peterson   | Tom      | $98,000   | Midwest   |           |
26 | Stevens    | Carla    | $110,000  | East      |           |
27 |
28 |
29 |
```

Figure 10.4: Selecting the database range

3. Pull down the Data menu and choose Set Database. This assigns the name Database to the worksheet area that you defined. You can use the name Database in commands and in formulas.

There is really nothing special about what you have just done. You simply defined a range and then named that range Database. You could also have done it with the Define Name command, but the Set Database command is easier. If you pull down the Formula menu and choose Paste Name, you will see Database listed as one of the available names now. This name is used by the commands on the Database menu to determine what area of the worksheet to operate on.

EDITING A DATABASE

Editing a database is the process of adding records and fields, deleting records and fields, and moving records and fields. These processes are described below.

ADDING RECORDS

To eliminate the need to update the database range and format new data, put a dummy record as the last record. This record should contain data that will always keep it at the end after any sort. It should also be formatted correctly. Any records inserted before the dummy end record will automatically extend the range and be formatted. Name the last row so that you can use the Goto command to quickly get to this row.

There are two ways to add records to an Excel database: adding a record to the end of the database or inserting it in the middle.

To add a record to the end of the database, select all fields in the empty row at the end, and click on the first blank cell (the first field) of the row. (See Figure 10.5.) Type in the data for the new record. Repeat this procedure for every record you want to add.

After you have entered all the new records, you must extend the database range because Excel does not automatically expand the range to include the new records. Define the range for the new database by pulling down the Data menu and choosing Set Database. You will also need to format any new data you enter because it will be set automatically in the default General format.

To add a record to the middle of the database, click the row number where you wish to enter the record. Pull down the Edit menu and choose Insert. A blank row will be inserted. Enter the data for the

File Edit Formula Format Data Options Macro Window

A27

SALES PROJECTIONS

	A	B	C	D	E	F
10						
11	LAST	FIRST	TARGET	REGION		
12	Adams	Chuck	$118,000	South		
13	Allen	Ellen	$90,000	East		
14	Atkins	Lee	$113,000	East		
15	Conners	Paul	$142,000	West		
16	Ellis	Nancy	$122,000	East		
17	Ford	Carl	$191,000	Midwest		
18	Glenn	John	$80,000	South		
19	Harris	Ken	$176,000	West		
20	Jackson	Robert	$112,000	East		
21	Keller	Janet	$105,000	West		
22	Kennedy	Sandra	$135,000	East		
23	Linn	Vera	$80,000	Midwest		
24	Parker	Greg	$196,000	South		
25	Peterson	Tom	$98,000	Midwest		
26	Stevens	Carla	$110,000	East		
27						
28						
29						

Figure 10.5: Adding a record at the end of the database

> To minimize updating the database range and the need for formatting new fields, add records to the middle of the database instead of the end. You can also use keyboard commands as a shortcut for insertion. Use Command-I to display the Insert box and speed up entry.

new record. It is not necessary to reset the database range or to format data entered to any fields. When new records are inserted in the middle of a database, the database range is updated automatically to include the new record, and the formats are still in effect.

ADDING FIELDS

You can add fields to the database the same way that you add records. To add a field to the right of the current fields, type the field name at the top of the column and then enter the field data for each record. Figure 10.6 shows a new field added to the database. You will then need to redefine the database range to include the new field. You will also need to format the new field.

You can also insert a field by adding a blank column using the Insert command or Command-I. Enter the field name at the top of the new blank column, then enter the data for each record. If you insert a field, the database range definition is updated automatically but you will probably have to format the new field, because fields often have different formats from adjacent fields.

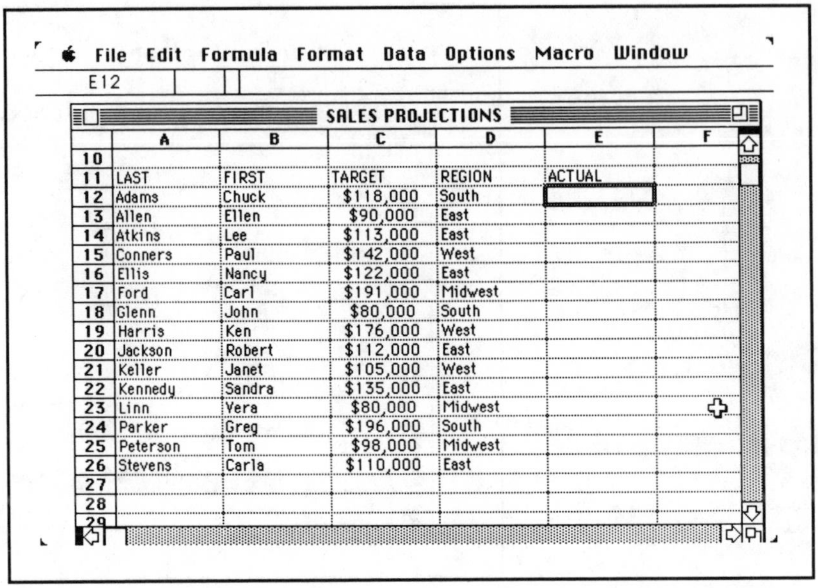

Figure 10.6: Adding a new field

DELETING RECORDS AND FIELDS

To eliminate the necessity of updating the database range, add new fields within the current database range instead of beyond it.

To delete records from a database, click the numbers of the rows you wish to delete. Pull down the Edit menu and choose Delete (or use Command-K). The records will be deleted and the records below the deleted rows will move up to recover the space.

To delete fields, follow the same procedure but click the headers of the columns for the fields to delete. Then use the Delete command or Command-K to delete the field. When either records or fields are deleted, the range definition is adjusted automatically and the database size decreases.

You won't see a warning message or dialog box when you delete records. If necessary, you can recover the delete with the Undo command on the Edit menu.

In the next chapter you will learn how to delete records based on a specified criteria.

MOVING RECORDS

To rearrange the order of the records and fields in your database, select the cells to move. Pull down the Edit menu and choose Cut. Click the new location, then select the Paste command from the Edit menu. The cells you selected will be in their new location.

SAVING THE DATABASE

Before leaving this chapter, be sure the database is saved because you will be using it again in the following chapters. Choose Save As from the File menu and assign a name to the worksheet. Then click OK.

USING DATABASES EFFECTIVELY

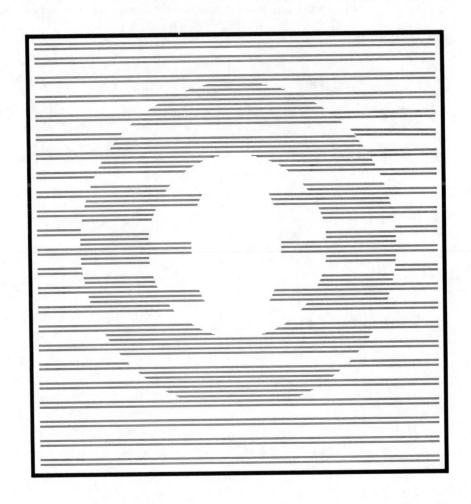

CHAPTER 11

SO FAR YOU'VE LEARNED HOW TO CREATE DATA-
bases and edit them, but database management is far more than this.
In this chapter you will learn how to use your Excel database to find
records that meet specific criteria and how to use the Excel database
statistical functions to calculate statistics using records that match the
criteria you have defined.

USING CRITERIA

Criteria are rules or tests by which records are judged. If a record
meets the rule (or passes the test), it is accepted, or said to match.
Below are some typical applications that use criteria:

- Finding all the addresses with a specified zip code range in a
  database of addresses

- Finding all the members with a membership expiration date
  equal to or earlier than a specified date in an organizational
  membership list

- Finding all the salespeople with sales exceeding a specified
  value in a sales database

- Finding all prospects that match a specified tickle date in a
  prospect list

Notice a single word used in each of these applications: *specified*.
You are defining a specification, and you wish to find all records in the
database that match this specification. The specification is called
the criterion.

You can also create complex test relationships. For example, a
record will be accepted if it passes Criteria A *or* Criteria B, Criteria A
and Criteria B, or Criteria A *and not* Criteria B.

Using criteria is a simple three step process: defining the criteria range, entering the specification, and initiating the action.

DEFINING A CRITERIA RANGE

Before you can define your criteria, you must create a range on the worksheet that can be used to specify the criteria. This is called the criteria range.

Create this range for the worksheet you used in the last chapter:

1. Open the worksheet with the File Open command.

2. Select all of the field names you will use for the criteria by clicking cell A11 and dragging to cell D11.

3. Copy these to a blank area of the worksheet: row 3. Pull down the Edit menu, choose Copy, and click cell A3. Pull down the Edit menu and choose Paste. The field names are now copied to a new area of the worksheet.

4. Select the criteria range. Click cell A3 and drag to cell D4. Notice that you have selected a range that includes *two* rows, as shown in Figure 11.1. You will enter criteria for searches into the second row.

5. Name this range. Pull down the Data menu and choose Set Criteria. This assigns the name Criteria to the worksheet area that you just defined. You can use the name Criteria in formulas and commands.

The criteria range must always include at least two rows. The first row defines the field names and the following rows are used to enter values (or value ranges) for the fields. However, you may need two, three, or even more rows in some cases. Allow as many as are necessary.

In defining the criteria range, it is not necessary to copy all of the field names. Copy only those you will need for your searches. Field names must be identical to those in the database, but case is ignored—you can use upper- or lowercase in specifying the field names.

You can redefine the criteria range at any time. Simply select the new range and issue a new Set Criteria command.

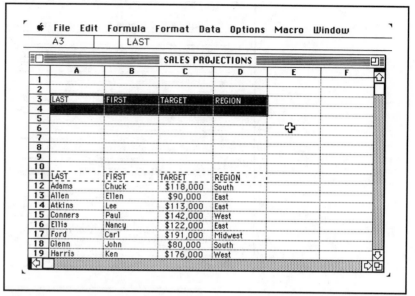

Figure 11.1: Creating a criteria range

ENTERING THE SPECIFICATION

The next step is to enter the desired specification for the criteria. Under the word REGION (in cell D3), enter **West** into cell D4, as shown in Figure 11.2.

When entering criteria, keep the following rules in mind:

- The criteria you enter is not case sensitive. (You can enter WEST or West.)

- You can use numbers, labels, or formulas to define the criteria.

- The criteria must always be positioned directly below the field name to which they correspond in the criteria name row.

- Be sure there are no rows left entirely blank in the criteria range. A blank row is like a wild card and will match any database record; therefore it will cause the search to stop on the first record. As long as at least one cell in the row contains

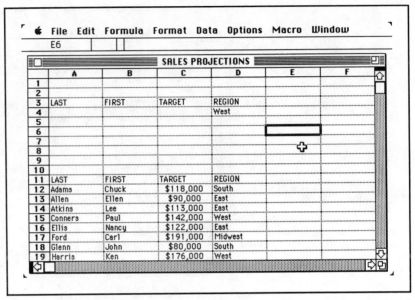

Figure 11.2: Specifying the criteria

a criterion, the search will work, as cells in the same row will combine their criteria specification.

• Use the Clear command on the Edit menu to clear a criteria cell.

INITIATING THE ACTION— THE FIND COMMAND

Once the criteria are specified, you can use them to initiate any of three actions: find, delete, or extract. As an illustration, try the example below.

To find the first record that meets our Region = West specification, pull down the Data menu and choose Find. Excel will then display the first record in the database that meets the specified criterion, as shown in Figure 11.3. Notice that the scroll boxes have changed— they are now striped instead of white. The number of the record in the database is displayed in the upper left where the active-cell designator normally is. The menu has changed and no longer contains the Find option.

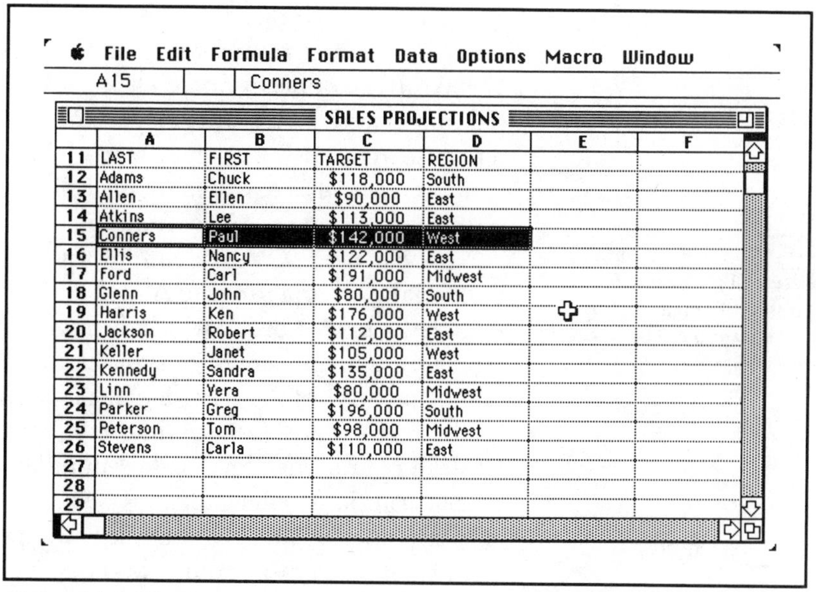

Figure 11.3: Finding the first record that matches the criterion

To find the next match, use the scroll arrows. They permit you to move through the database to the next or previous record that meets the specified criteria. If you move the scroll box at the right all the way to the end of the scroll bar, Excel will display the last record in the database that matches the criterion. While in this search mode, the Edit commands (Copy, Cut, etc.) are still active. This allows you to edit the records once you find them.

To exit the search, pull down the Data menu and choose Exit Find. The scroll boxes return to normal. You can also exit by clicking any cell in the worksheet outside of the database range. You can now specify another criteria and search the database again.

When the Find command is activated, it starts from the beginning of the database if no cell in the database is active. However, if any database cell is active, the search starts from that cell.

COMBINING SEARCH CRITERIA

Now try to combine two search conditions. Enter **176000** in cell C4 under TARGET (leaving West in cell D4) and repeat the Find

To clear a criteria cell always use Clear on the Edit menu. If you try to clear a cell by entering a space, all you do is enter a space as a part of the search criteria.

operation. Notice that the two conditions are combined and Excel looks for the first record where the region is West *and* the target is 176000. It is not necessary to click Set Criteria again. As long as the cell range used for criteria entry is not changed, you can continue to repeat searches using other criteria. When you have more than one entry in a row, Excel will find only cells that fit all the specified criteria. This is called an *AND* condition.

Now clear cell C4 and enter **East** in D5, leaving West in D4. Expand the criteria range to A3 to D5. Initiate a Find, and Excel will stop on the first record in which the region is West *or* East. As you can see, more than one entry in a column tells Excel to find records containing any one of the criteria. This is called an *OR* condition. If you use both AND and OR conditions at once, you can create complex Boolean operations. The next section describes methods of creating special criteria specifications.

Remember, if you use multiple rows specifying criteria, you must include all of them in your criteria range. Issue a new Set Criteria command if necessary. If you clear some criteria rows, reset the criteria to exclude those rows; otherwise, Excel will search for either a blank record *or* the existing criteria, and the search will stop on the first record in the database.

Notice that you now have two areas on the worksheet: the database area and the criteria area. You can use the remainder of the worksheet for normal worksheet applications: formulas, text, or whatever you wish.

COMPLEX CRITERIA SPECIFICATION

If you have a large database or a large criteria range, use two windows for simple access: one window for the database, another for the criteria range.

Excel criteria specifications can be divided into three broad categories: simple, comparison, and computed. In any given single search, you can mix these as necessary. You have already seen an example of simple criteria where a single value is entered in the criteria range to match records in the database. Now let's look at comparison and computed criteria.

COMPARISON CRITERIA

There are two types of comparison criteria: numeric and text.

NUMERIC COMPARISON CRITERIA You can use any of the following relational operators to specify a numeric comparison criteria:

> \>   Greater than
>
> \<   Less than
>
> \> =   Greater than or equal to
>
> \< =   Less than or equal to
>
> \<\>   Not equal to

For example, enter **>150000** in cell C4 under TARGET, clear D5, and be sure D4 still contains West. Reset the criteria range to A3 through D4. Initiate a Find, and Excel will stop on the first salesperson in the Western region with a target greater than 150,000.

    You can tell Excel to search for records with a value within a range of numbers by setting up two columns in the criteria name row with the same field name. Put one limit under one and the second limit under the other. For example, the criteria shown in Figure 11.4 would find all salespeople with a target sales value between $100,000 and $150,000.

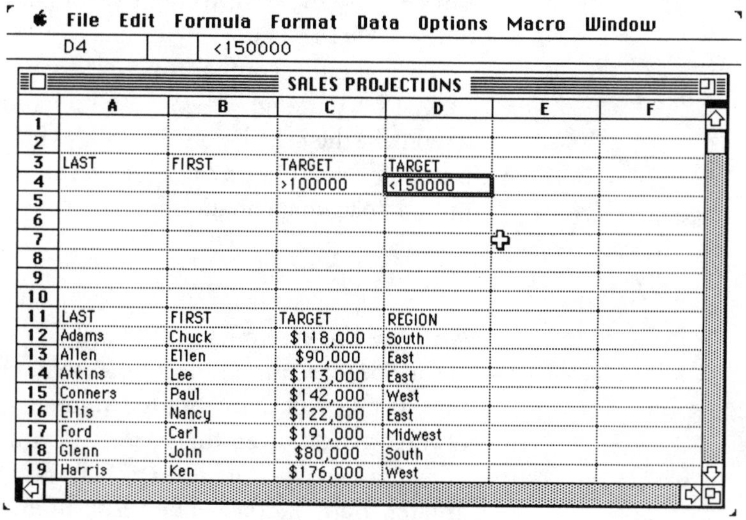

Figure 11.4: Searching for a range of numbers

TEXT COMPARISONS You can use the relational operators to compare text fields as well. A is less than B and F is less than m. Upper- and lowercase letters are considered equivalent.

You can also use a question mark (?) to match a single character or an asterisk (*) to match a group of characters. For example, J?dy will match Judy and Jody, and rob* will match Robert Jackson.

In finding exact text matches, use extra care with Excel. Both Rob and = "Rob" in B4 would match Robert Jackson. In both cases B4 would show only Rob. If you wanted to find only people with the first name Rob and not Robert, you would have to use an equal sign with the text inside a quotation as below:

    = " = Rob"

This would put = Rob in B4 and would match only a first name of Rob.

USING FORMULAS IN CRITERIA

You can also use formulas to create criteria. There are, however, some precautions you must be aware of. Suppose we use the formula **>E3** in C4 and put a value of **120,000** in E3. Now you might suppose this would match any record with a target greater than 120,000, but actually the trick will not work because Excel will look for a text entry >E3 in a cell.

To make this comparison work, you must first expand the criteria range to A3 through E4. Always remember to extend the criteria range to contain the calculation. Leave the heading for E3 blank (there is no header for the column for a calculated criteria in the criteria range) and put the following equation in E4:

    = C12 > $E$7

Note the absolute reference to cell E7. Any reference to a cell outside of the database range must be absolute because it will always refer to that specific cell. Now put the value for comparison, 120,000, in E7. If you have followed this correctly, you should see the word FALSE in E4, as shown in Figure 11.5, because the value in C12 is not greater than 120,000. The result of any computed criteria (a condition) is always displayed as TRUE or FALSE. You have now created

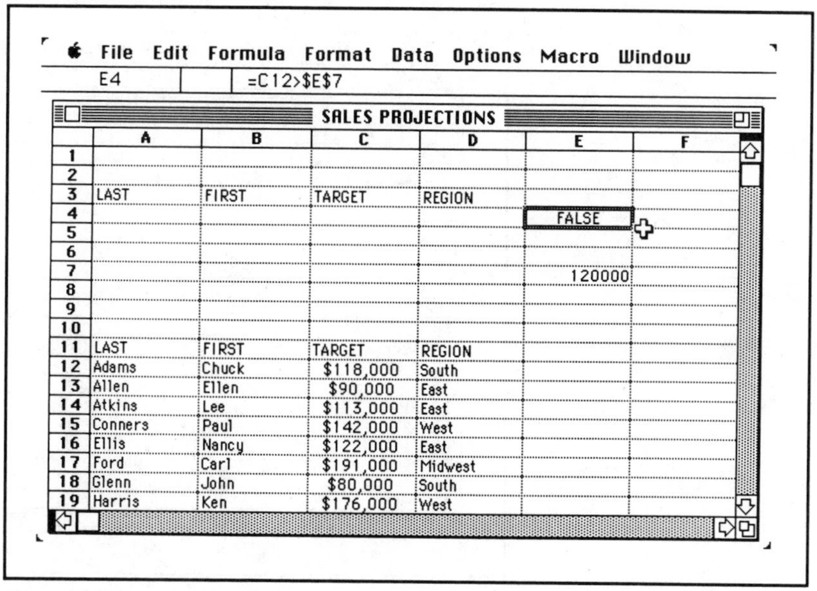

Figure 11.5: A criteria calculation

a computed criterion in E4 in which the target value (C12 in the first record) is compared with the value in E7. Initiate the Find, and it should stop on the first target greater than 120,000.

Figure 11.6 shows another example. A few actual sales figures have been added to compare with the targets. The criteria area includes the formula **= (E12/C12) > = 1** as a criterion in the criteria name row. The criteria range is A1 to A2. This is requesting a match if the actual sales equal or exceed the target value.

You can also use functions in computed criteria. For example, you could compare the square root of a list of fields to a fixed value:

```
= SQRT(C12) > $E$7
```

USING DATABASE
STATISTICAL FUNCTIONS

You use database functions in the same way that you use worksheet functions. Let's experiment with your original Sales Projections

	A	B	C	D	E	F
1						
2	FALSE					
3						
4						
5						
6						
7						
8						
9						
10						
11	LAST	FIRST	TARGET	REGION	ACTUAL	
12	Adams	Chuck	$118,000	South	$80,000	
13	Allen	Ellen	$90,000	East	$120,000	
14	Atkins	Lee	$113,000	East	$110,000	
15	Conners	Paul	$142,000	West	$140,000	
16	Ellis	Nancy	$122,000	East		
17	Ford	Carl	$191,000	Midwest		
18	Glenn	John	$80,000	South		
19	Harris	Ken	$176,000	West		

A2   =(E12/C12)>=1

SALES PROJECTIONS

🍎 File Edit Formula Format Data Options Macro Window

Figure 11.6: Using a formula in a criterion

database. As a goal, assume you wish to find the sum of the eastern sales targets:

1. In the criteria area, enter **East** into cell D4. Be sure that cells A4, B4, and C4 are clear.

2. Click cell E6 to select it. This will be our working cell for the answer.

3. Pull down the Formula menu and choose Paste Function.

4. The Paste Function dialog box shown in Figure 11.7 appears. Scroll this dialog box until DSUM( ) is displayed, then double-click this function. The function name is now entered into the formula bar with an equal sign before it, as shown in Figure 11.8. The cursor is in the formula bar, ready for you to enter the first argument.

5. Pull down the Formula menu and choose Paste Name. When the Paste Name dialog box shown in Figure 11.9 appears, double-click Database (the name of your database). It is now entered into the formula bar.

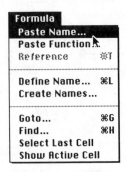

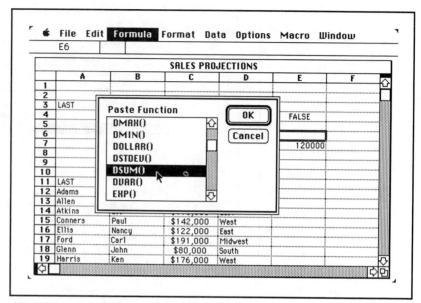

Figure 11.7: Pasting a function name

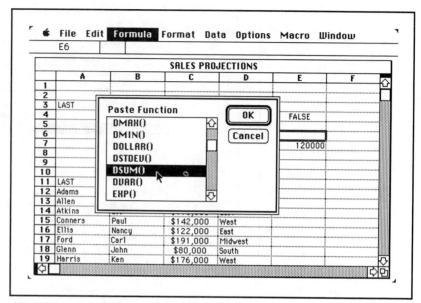

Figure 11.8: Starting the formula entry

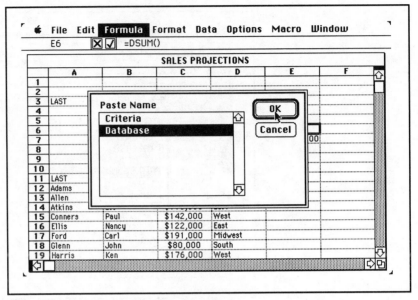

Figure 11.9: Completing the formula entry

6. Type a comma, **"Target"** (with quotation marks), and another comma from the keyboard.

7. Pull down the Formula menu again and choose Paste Name.

8. Double-click Criteria, and it is entered into the formula bar.

9. Click the enter box to complete the entry.

You now have a complete formula:

= DSUM(Database,"Target",Criteria)

This matches the general form for the DSUM function previously defined in Chapter 8 as **DSUM(database,field name,criteria)**. The sum of the eastern sales targets is now displayed in cell E6: 682,000. Enter **West** into cell D4, and the sum changes to 423,000: the sum of the western sales targets. You can specify any region, and cell E6 will automatically change to reflect those target totals. Although you created the formula by pasting the function and name, you could have entered the entire formula from the keyboard. If you need to review the database functions, turn back to Chapter 8.

DATABASE MANAGEMENT TIPS

Database functions are a valuable asset in building your worksheets. Below are a few tips.

- Use the CHOOSE and MATCH functions with your databases. For example, for the database in this chapter you had to enter the full region name for each region. To simplify entry and to eliminate misspellings, you could have created a new field in column F called REGION CODE. Then you could put the equation **CHOOSE(F12,"South","East", "Midwest","West")** in D12 and copy it down the column. Then you could enter a region code for each REGION CODE field, and the corresponding region would be entered in the REGION field.

- You can use functions on any continuous range of cells in the worksheet. Enter the continuous range as the database in the function and the range for the criteria. It is not necessary to define any database or criteria. For example, if you have a set of grades and want to do some statistical calculations, you can use the statistical database functions, entering the database range for the database argument in the function. You still need a criteria range, but you don't have to define it with Set Criteria; just enter the cell names in the database function.

- You can set up multiple criteria on the worksheet. Although only one can be active at a time, you can have several set up ready to use. Just use Set Criteria to select the one you wish to use, leaving the others still on the worksheet.

- You can use the field index number instead of the field name in the database function's second argument. For example, in the DSUM example of the previous section you could have used the number 3 (to refer to the third field) instead of the word "Target" as the second argument. You can also use a reference to the field header in the database. Just click on the field name to enter it into the database function.

OTHER OPERATIONS USING CRITERIA

You have already seen how you can find records based on a specified criteria. You can also extract or delete records based on a criteria.

EXTRACTING RECORDS

You can extract the part of your database that matches specified criteria and place it in another area of the worksheet or in another worksheet. For example, suppose you have a large database of many addresses, and you want to extract only those with local zip copes for mailing. As an example, use the database in Figure 10.1 and assume you want only the people from New York.

Extraction is a three-step process: defining the criteria, defining the extraction destination range, and initiating the extraction.

DEFINING THE CRITERIA   You define criteria for extraction just as you would define it for a search. Select any criteria you desire. For this example, select the New York zip codes, as shown in Figure 11.10.

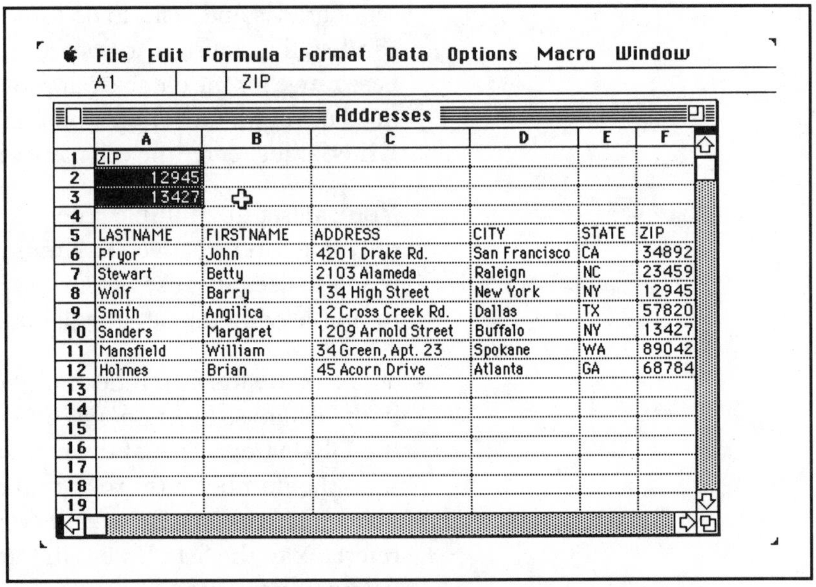

Figure 11.10: Selecting the criteria for extraction

DEFINING THE EXTRACTION RANGE To define the extraction range, copy the cells that contain the field names into a new area of the worksheet or into another worksheet as shown in Figure 11.11. Be sure there is sufficient room for the extracted database. You may delete any field names that are not needed in the extracted database.

Next, select all of the field names for the area in which you want to copy the extracted records. If you want to copy all of the matching records, select all of the field names of the destination range. If you want only a partial extraction, select one or more rows of the destination range. Only those rows will be filled. This is useful if you don't know how many records will match the criteria and you are afraid the extraction might destroy some other data.

THE EXTRACTION Pull down the Data menu and choose Extract. You will then see the Extract dialog box shown in Figure 11.12. You can select Unique Records Only if you don't want the extracted file to contain any duplicates. Click OK. The extracted records will be copied into the new worksheet area, as shown in Figure 11.13.

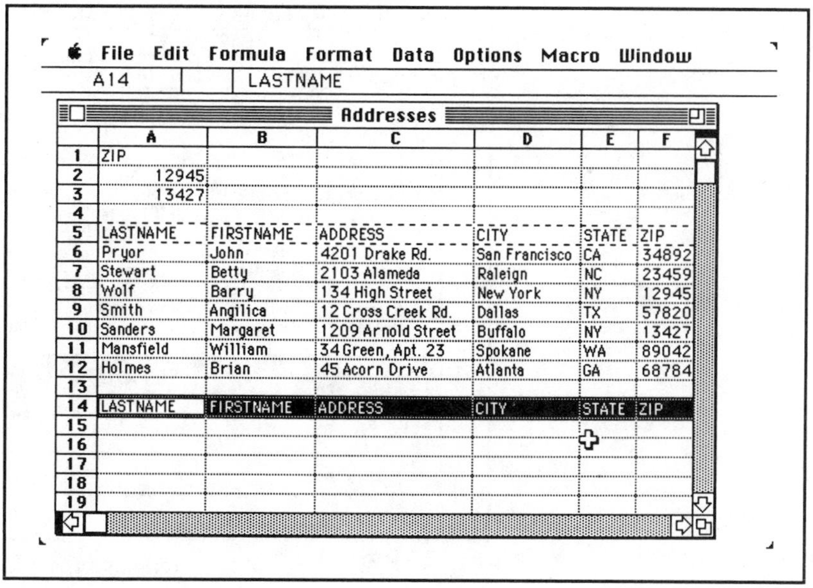

Figure 11.11: The destination database

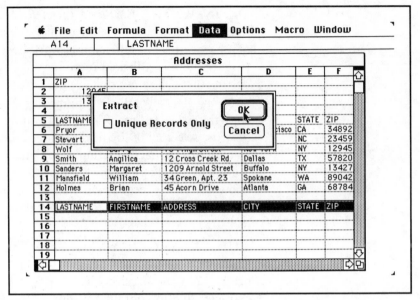

Figure 11.12: The Extract dialog box

	A	B	C	D	E	F
1	ZIP					
2	12945					
3	13427					
4						
5	LASTNAME	FIRSTNAME	ADDRESS	CITY	STATE	ZIP
6	Pryor	John	4201 Drake Rd.	San Francisco	CA	34892
7	Stewart	Betty	2103 Alameda	Raleign	NC	23459
8	Wolf	Barry	134 High Street	New York	NY	12945
9	Smith	Angilica	12 Cross Creek Rd.	Dallas	TX	57820
10	Sanders	Margaret	1209 Arnold Street	Buffalo	NY	13427
11	Mansfield	William	34 Green, Apt. 23	Spokane	WA	89042
12	Holmes	Brian	45 Acorn Drive	Atlanta	GA	68784
13						
14	LASTNAME	FIRSTNAME	ADDRESS	CITY	STATE	ZIP
15	Wolf	Barry	134 High Street	New York	NY	12945
16	Sanders	Margaret	1209 Arnold Street	Buffalo	NY	13427
17						
18						
19						

Figure 11.13: The new extracted database

The following precautions should be observed when performing extractions:

- The extracted database will contain only values. Formulas are extracted as values, not formulas.

- The extracted database is not linked to the master. If the master is updated, the extracted database is not updated.

- If the destination range is defined by selecting one or more fields, all records in the original database that match the desired criteria will be transferred. Transferred records can overwrite existing cell data without any precautionary message given. Select a cell range for the destination range, or be sure any cells under the destination field headers are cleared of data.

Before continuing, save the worksheet. You will need this original worksheet in the next section.

DELETING RECORDS

To delete records from a database, first select the criteria for the deletion. Next, pull down the Data menu and choose Delete, then click OK. Excel automatically deletes the selected records and moves up the remaining records to close the space.

You will see an alert box when you delete records. Be sure that the database is saved before you delete any part of it because a database deletion cannot be undone.

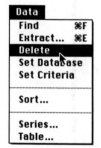

Use the Find command to preview records to be deleted before deletion.

SUMMARY

You have now created an on-screen database and used the database to calculate the totals for the worksheet part of the same document. Save this worksheet—you will use it in many examples while you are exploring the more advanced features of Excel.

SORTING
DATABASES

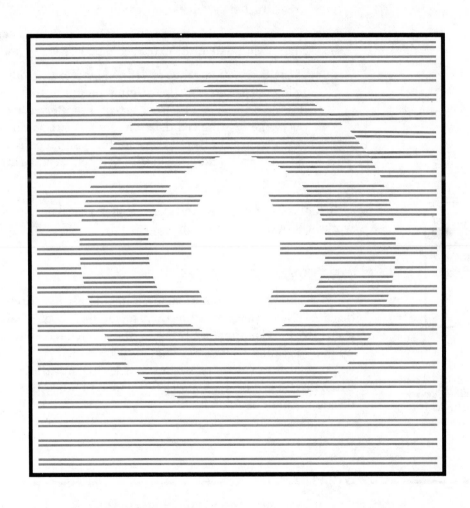

CHAPTER 12

WITH EXCEL, YOU CAN QUICKLY SORT YOUR DATA-
base in any desired sequence. Sorting is useful for many types of
databases: you can sort a mailing list in either name or zip code
order; an inventory file in part number order; and a prospect list in
name or date order.

Usually, when you enter records in a database, you do so in a random order. When you finish entering the data, you can sort the
records in whatever order you want. If you enter new records at a
later time, you can either add them in the correct position (using the
Insert command), or add them to the end of the database and resort
the database.

You can sort a database by rows or columns, with any number of
fields, called *keys*, controlling the sort. Each field can be sorted in
ascending or descending order. In most cases you will want to sort by
rows. A columnar sort will rearrange the field order.

SORTING ON A SINGLE FIELD

As an example, try sorting the Sales Projections database by the
region field:

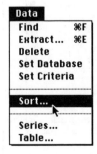

1. Be sure that you have saved a copy of the worksheet and that
   it is open. Select A12 through D26 as the range of cells to
   sort. (Notice that you do not include the row containing the
   field names.)

2. Pull down the Data menu and choose Sort. The Sort window
   shown in Figure 12.1 appears. This is actually a window, not
   just a dialog box, and it can be moved but not resized.

3. Click the title bar and move the window so that you can see cell D12. If necessary, scroll the underlying worksheet to make D12 available.

4. Click cell D12 (to sort by region), and this cell reference will be entered into the Sort window as the first key. Click OK. Alternately, you could manually enter $D$12 as the first key in the Sort window. The items are now sorted alphabetically by region, as shown in Figure 12.2.

Below are some tips on sorting:

- After selecting the sort range, use the mouse to select the cell in the sort column for the key. Then, when you initiate the Sort command, the cell name will already be entered and you will not have to click any cell. If you prefer clicking, note that you can click any cell in the column to define the sort key, including the field name. However, the range of the sort must be defined explicitly. Therefore, always define the range carefully, then select the key by clicking any cell

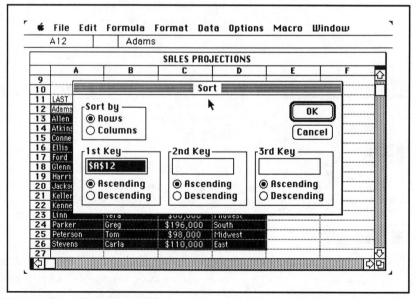

Figure 12.1: The Sort window

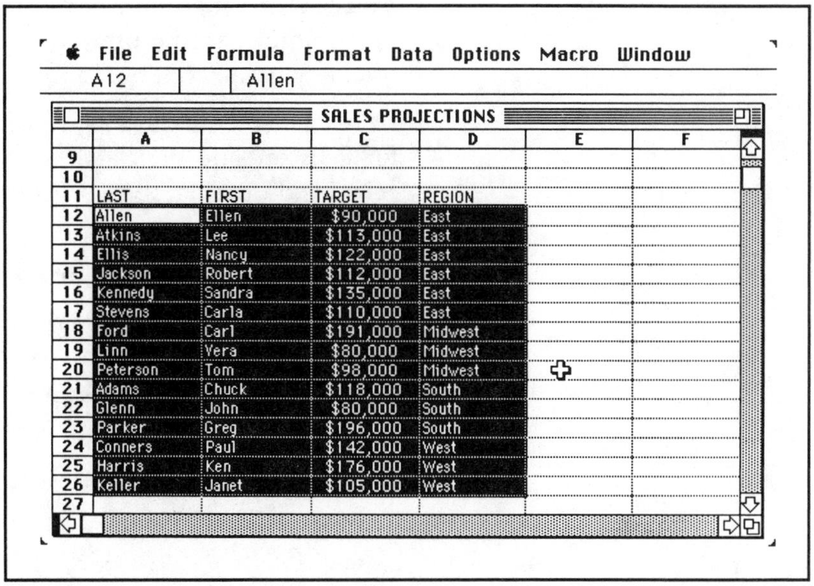

Figure 12.2: The database after sorting

in the column to sort—even if it is outside the range or the column designator. In the above example with the Sort window displayed, you could have clicked any cell in column D.

- You cannot undo a sort. If you think you might need to recover a sort, add a new field (column) that contains the database's record (row) numbers before you sort the database. Use the Series command to assign a sequential number to each record (Chapter 14). After you've sorted the database, you can easily recover the previous order by sorting the database using the record-number field as the key.

- When defining the sort range, be sure all fields of all records are selected; i.e., the entire database range excluding the field names. Do not select the row with the field names. You cannot use the Goto command with the Database name to select the database range for sorting, because it will include the field names.

- If you plan to sort the database often, name the sort range with the Formula Define Name command. Then you can use the Goto command to select this range.

- You can use range names or formulas to define the sort keys. For example, in the previous sort exercise you could have used any named cell in column D as the key.

- Be sure, if you use calculated fields, to use absolute references for cells outside the database and relative references for cells inside the database. Otherwise, a sort will scramble the formulas.

- Numeric characters are sorted before alphabetic characters.

- Sorting a database will lose the order of entry. If necessary, include a field that indicates a date (and perhaps time) of entry.

- You can use macros (Section 7) to time stamp, ID, and sort entries.

- You can sort on any type of range. It does not need to be defined as a database.

SORTING ON TWO OR THREE FIELDS

Using the same technique, you can easily sort on two or three fields. Suppose, in the previous example, you want the database sorted by region, by last name within the region, and by first name if the last name is the same (there are no duplicate last names here, but we will assume this could happen).

1. Select the range to sort.

2. Select Sort from the Data menu. The Sort window will be displayed.

3. Click anywhere in column D to define the first key. Do not press Return or click OK yet.

4. Click in the second key field for the second key.

5. Click anywhere in column A, the column for the last name.

6. Click in the third key field for the third key.

7. Click anywhere in column B, the column for the first name.

8. Click OK or press Return.

The database will be sorted by region, and by name within the region.

Keep in mind that sorting using multiple keys in this way is not the same as doing multiple sorts. If you try multiple sorts, each sort will rearrange the order of the previous sort. For example, if you sort the above database by region and then by last name, the region order will be completely lost. Using multiple keys insures that the second sort does not invalidate the first sort; i.e., the database remains sorted by region after the sort on the last name is completed. Last names are only sorted within the same region.

SORTING BY MORE THAN THREE FIELDS

In some cases you may wish to sort on more than three keys. This can be done easily if you use the following procedure. The sorting makes the assumption that the most important keys are nonunique. For example, in a database of addresses you could sort by last name and first name, then by zip and last name to get a database in zip, last name, and first name order. Assume the database is to be sorted by six fields:

1. Initiate the sort using the three least important keys; that is, key 4 (key 1), 5 (key 2) and 6 (key 3).

2. Initiate another sort using the three most important keys: 1 (key 1), 2 (key 2),and 3 (key 3).

This method will work with any number of keys. Start from the least important keys, using the most important of these as the first key in the Sort window. If the number of fields is not divisible by three, use a two or one-key sort the first time with the two least or single least important key.

FINDING SALES TOTALS BY REGION

You can use the sorting techniques to find the sales totals for each region in the Sales Projections database. Sort the database by region and add a small worksheet area under the criteria area. In cell B6, enter the sum of the eastern regions as **= SUM(C12:C17)**. Continue with the other sums:

REGION	*CELL*	*FORMULA*
East	B6	= SUM(C12:C17)
Midwest	B7	= SUM(C18:C20)
South	B8	= SUM(C21:C23)
West	B9	= SUM(C24:C26)

Add the row titles **East**, **Midwest**, **South**, and **West** in cells A6 through A9 and the worksheet title **Sales Projections**, as shown in Figure 12.3. In Chapter 15, you will learn a better way to create this same worksheet. For now, save the Sales Projections worksheet for exercises in other chapters.

SPECIAL SORTING TECHNIQUES

The Sort command does not require any defined database or criteria. It can be used on any worksheet range. For example, Figure 12.4 shows a worksheet (not a database) that indicates the sales of various salespeople over a four year period. The sales are shown here in descending year order. Assume that for presentation purposes you need to rearrange this to an increasing year order.

To accomplish this, use a columnar sort rather than a row sort. Select B3 to E7 as the range to sort. Select a column sort, and for the first key click anywhere in row 3. Figure 12.5 shows the resulting worksheet, sorted in increasing year order.

A columnar sort is seldom used for a database. Sorting by columns is generally not even useful for rearranging the field order, because the sort command can sort the columns with the field names only in ascending or descending order. To rearrange fields, you generally use the edit commands, inserting a blank column and then moving the desired field column to the new column.

	A	B	C	D	E
1			SALES PROJECTIONS		
2					
3	LAST	FIRST	TARGET	REGION	
4				West	
5					
6	East	$682,000			423000
7	Midwest	$369,000			
8	South	$394,000			
9	West	$423,000			
10					
11	LAST	FIRST	TARGET	REGION	
12	Allen	Ellen	$90,000	East	
13	Atkins	Lee	$113,000	East	
14	Ellis	Nancy	$122,000	East	
15	Jackson	Robert	$112,000	East	
16	Kennedy	Sandra	$135,000	East	
17	Stevens	Carla	$110,000	East	
18	Ford	Carl	$191,000	Midwest	
19	Linn	Vera	$80,000	Midwest	
20	Peterson	Tom	$98,000	Midwest	
21	Adams	Chuck	$118,000	South	
22	Glenn	John	$80,000	South	
23	Parker	Greg	$196,000	South	
24	Conners	Paul	$142,000	West	
25	Harris	Ken	$176,000	West	
26	Keller	Janet	$105,000	West	

Figure 12.3: Adding the regional sums

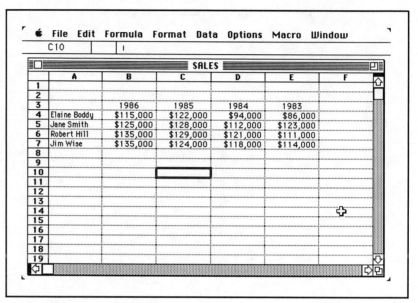

Figure 12.4: Preparing for a columnar sort

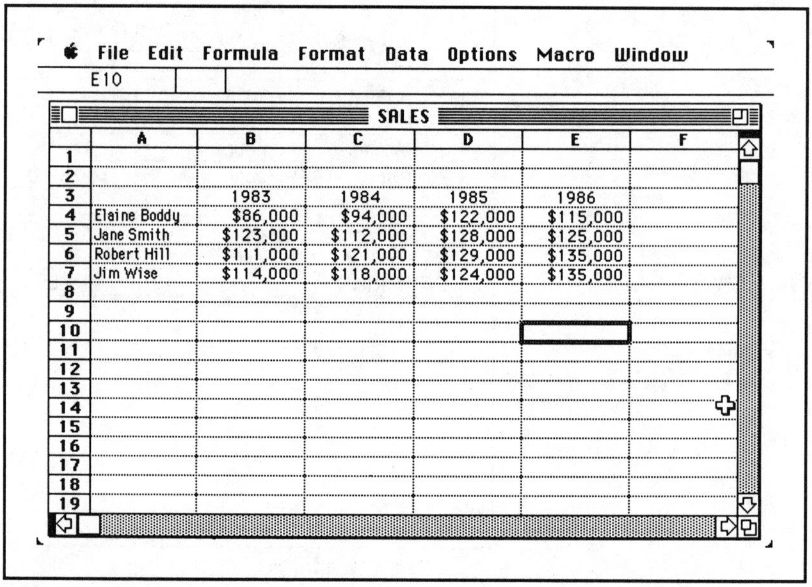

Figure 12.5: After a columnar sort

PART 4

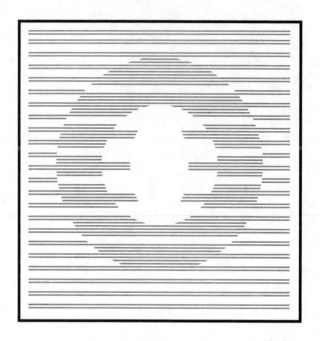

USING SPECIAL TECHNIQUES

EXCEL PROVIDES MANY SPECIAL TECHNIQUES THAT are not supported by competing worksheets. Part 4 will introduce you to many of these techniques with application examples that you can use with your own work. You will learn how to use arrays, tables, how to link documents, and how to use the special printing features of Excel.

USING TABLES

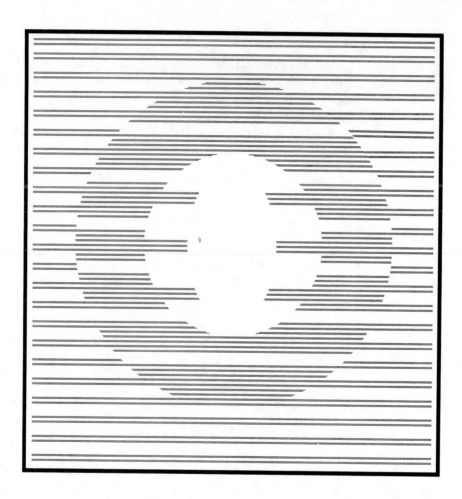

CHAPTER 13 ⸻

THERE MAY BE TIMES WHEN YOU WANT TO CHANGE
certain values on the worksheet to see how the rest of the worksheet
changes as a result. For example, in Chapters 10 through 12, you created a database of sales targets. You then searched this database
using a criterion. You could only use one criterion at a time, which is
somewhat cumbersome if you want to use a series of criteria and then
create a table or chart showing the results of each analysis. You
did create a short worksheet portion showing the totals for each region,
which were calculated using the SUM function. However, the calculations were only correct if the database was sorted by region.

In this chapter, you will learn how to use the Table command to
avoid these problems. You will take the same example (the Sales Projections database and worksheet) and use the Table command to
search the database based on a series of criteria. You will see that
tables are useful for what-if analyses with worksheets because they
allow you to perform multiple analyses with a series of input values.

You will also learn how to use look-up tables. These types of tables
work with the LOOKUP, VLOOKUP, and HLOOKUP functions,
rather than with the Table command. They provide a quick way to
find certain values in your worksheets.

USING THE TABLE COMMAND

The Table command should be used whenever you need to apply a
series of input values to one or two cells in a worksheet to create a series
of output values in one or more columns or rows.

ONE-INPUT TABLES

You use a *one-input table* to see how changes in one cell affect the
values calculated by one or more formulas.

DESIGNING A ONE-INPUT TABLE To design a one-input table, you need three things:

- A single-input cell containing the value that you wish to change.

- A column or row containing the values that will be applied successively to the input cell.

- One or more columns or rows that contain cells for the resulting values, with the formulas used as headings for each column or row. You can use formulas that refer directly to the input cell or to other cells on the worksheet. The formulas do not show on the worksheet.

If you have defined the three areas listed above, you can use a one-input table. First, select the range containing the input values for the input cell and the columns or rows, with the formula headings, for the output values. Pull down the Data menu and choose Table. The Table window shown in Figure 13.1 is displayed. Like the Define Name window, the Table window can be moved, but it cannot be resized, and it does not have a close box. If the input values are in a row, enter the

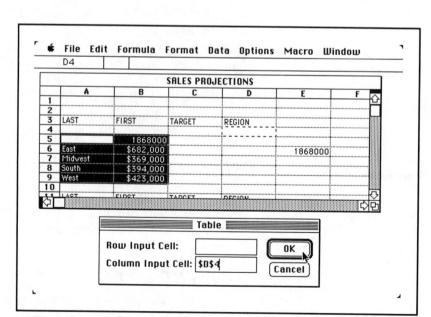

Figure 13.1: The Table window

input cell reference in the Row Input Cell box. If the input values are in a column, enter the input cell reference in the Column Input Cell box. After you've entered the input cell, click OK.

The input cell for the formula must be a *single cell*. The *Column* and *Row* next to the input cell box in the Table window refers to the column or row that contains the values for this input cell, not to the location of the input cell.

CREATING A ONE-INPUT TABLE   So that you can understand the basics of how a one-input table is used, let's experiment with the Sales Projections database that you created in Chapters 10 through 12. You'll set up a one-input table to search the database based on a series of criteria.

First, open the Sales Projections database and worksheet, shown in Figure 13.2. Our particular area of interest is the worksheet

	A	B	C	D	E
1			SALES PROJECTIONS		
2					
3	LAST	FIRST	TARGET	REGION	
4				West	
5					
6	East	$682,000			423000
7	Midwest	$369,000			
8	South	$394,000			
9	West	$423,000			
10					
11	LAST	FIRST	TARGET	REGION	
12	Allen	Ellen	$90,000	East	
13	Atkins	Lee	$113,000	East	
14	Ellis	Nancy	$122,000	East	
15	Jackson	Robert	$112,000	East	
16	Kennedy	Sandra	$135,000	East	
17	Stevens	Carla	$110,000	East	
18	Ford	Carl	$191,000	Midwest	
19	Linn	Vera	$80,000	Midwest	
20	Peterson	Tom	$98,000	Midwest	
21	Adams	Chuck	$118,000	South	
22	Glenn	John	$80,000	South	
23	Parker	Greg	$196,000	South	
24	Conners	Paul	$142,000	West	
25	Harris	Ken	$176,000	West	
26	Keller	Janet	$105,000	West	

Figure 13.2: The Sales Projections database and worksheet

portion—rows 6 through 9—which contain the sales totals by region. These totals were obtained previously using the SUM function, which required the database to be sorted by region.

See how the SUM function works by using the Edit Insert command to add a row to the database portion (rows 12 through 26), then delete the database row. You will notice that, if you do it carefully (that is, keeping the database in region order), the formulas for the totals in rows 6 through 9 will change to reflect your additions and deletions.

Now, sort the database in name order (refer to Chapter 12 if you need help) so that the database is alphabetized by name. The totals in the worksheet cells B6 through B9 have also changed, and now they

	A	B	C	D	E
1					
2					
3	LAST	FIRST	TARGET	REGION	
4				West	
5					
6	East	$776,000			423000
7	Midwest	$368,000			
8	South	$320,000			
9	West	$404,000			
10					
11	LAST	FIRST	TARGET	REGION	
12	Adams	Chuck	$118,000	South	
13	Allen	Ellen	$90,000	East	
14	Atkins	Lee	$113,000	East	
15	Conners	Paul	$142,000	West	
16	Ellis	Nancy	$122,000	East	
17	Ford	Carl	$191,000	Midwest	
18	Glenn	John	$80,000	South	
19	Harris	Ken	$176,000	West	
20	Jackson	Robert	$112,000	East	
21	Keller	Janet	$105,000	West	
22	Kennedy	Sandra	$135,000	East	
23	Linn	Vera	$80,000	Midwest	
24	Parker	Greg	$196,000	South	
25	Peterson	Tom	$98,000	Midwest	
26	Stevens	Carla	$110,000	East	

Figure 13.3: Database after sorting, with incorrect worksheet totals

are incorrect, as shown in Figure 13.3. This is because the formulas for these cells did not change to reflect the new order.

Notice, however, that the total in cell E6 did not change when you sorted the database. This is because the total was calculated using the DSUM function (see Chapter 11). Examine the formula for this cell, and you will see that the total is based on a criterion:

= DSUM(Database,"Target",Criteria)

Although the DSUM function gives the correct value, you can only use a single criterion at a time. With a table, however, you can use multiple criteria.

Now, let's change the formulas for cells B6 and B9 so that the values are calculated using a table and the DSUM function. Follow these steps:

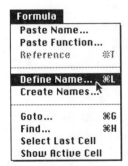

1. Close the current worksheet without saving the changes and reopen the Sales Projections database and worksheet so that the data are correct. Clear cell D4. Add two rows after row 10 to give yourself some working space. The field names should now be in row 13.

2. Be sure that the database is defined as well as the criteria range. Pull down the Formula menu and choose Define Names. You should see both Database and Criteria listed in the window. (If they are not, refer to Chapter 10.) Click Cancel to close the Define Names window.

3. Create a row containing the formula that will be used for the table by copying cell E6 into cell B5. The formula must be in the first row of the table. B5 is the heading cell for the column that will contain the results of the formula in B5. The resulting worksheet is shown in Figure 13.4.

4. Select the table area with the formula in the first row by clicking cell A5 and dragging to cell B9.

5. Pull down the Data menu and select Table. The Table window (Figure 13.1) should be displayed. Move the window so that cell D4 is visible.

6. Click Column Input Cell on the Table window because the criteria will be from the **Region** column.

	A	B	C	D	E	F
1						
2						
3	LAST	FIRST	TARGET	REGION		
4				West		
5		423000				
6	East	$776,000			423000	
7	Midwest	$368,000				
8	South	$320,000				
9	West	$404,000				
10						
11						
12						
13	LAST	FIRST	TARGET	REGION		
14	Adams	Chuck	$118,000	South		
15	Allen	Ellen	$90,000	East		
16	Atkins	Lee	$113,000	East		
17	Conners	Paul	$142,000	West		
18	Ellis	Nancy	$122,000	East		
19	Ford	Carl	$191,000	Midwest		

B5 =DSUM(Database,"Target",Criteria)

SALES PROJECTIONS

File Edit Formula Format Data Options Macro Window

Figure 13.4: Worksheet after copying the formula

7. Click cell D4. This indicates that the selected values in column A (cells A6 through A9) will be applied sequentially as the value of cell D4. The value of $D$4 is now displayed in the Table window.

8. Click OK.

The totals for cells B6 through B9 remain the same, but the formula for each cell is now different. Examine their formulas shown in Figure 13.5. What has happened? Each title in cells A6 through A9 is applied successively to cell D4. The formula in the first row of column B of the selected range is then used to evaluate the cell in column B that corresponds with the name in column A. Figure 13.6 shows the results. Compare this figure with Figure 13.2 and the erroneous Figure 13.3.

Now sort your database again by name:

1. Select rows 14 through 28. Be careful not to select row 11, which contains the database field names.

2. Pull down the Data menu and select Sort.

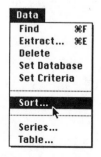

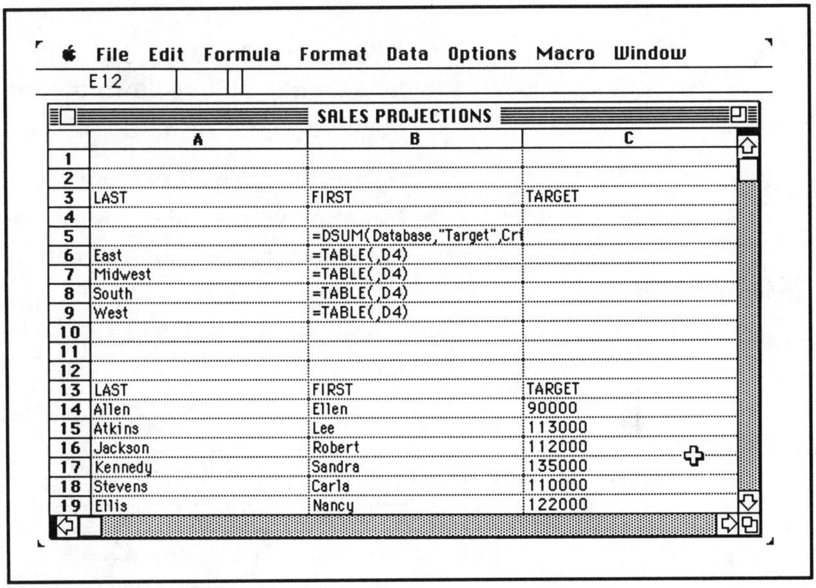

Figure 13.5: The formulas

3. The Sort window shown in Figure 13.7 is displayed. It can be moved, but it doesn't have a close box, a resizing box, or scroll bars. Move the window so that you can see the totals in column B easily, click on any cell in column D, and then click OK.

This time, the totals did not change. You can edit, resort, or otherwise modify the database, and the worksheet totals will always remain accurate.

CALCULATING TWO COLUMNS   Using the Table command, you can use multiple formulas and calculate the values for more than one column or row. For example, save the Sales Projections worksheet and then try the following experiment. Assume that you now have a few actual sales figures, and you want to create a separate field for them in your database. Then, you want to recalculate the worksheet total values using the Table command. Follow these steps:

1. Add a new field to your database titled **ACTUAL**, as shown in Figure 13.8.

If you add or insert rows within the database range, your entries will be formatted correctly, and the database totals will be updated to reflect the changes. If you add data to the end of the database, you will need to redefine the database area in order for the totals to be correct. You will also need to format the new entries at the end of the database (by pulling down the Format menu and choosing Number).

2. Enter the values shown in Figure 13.8 into this field.

3. Redefine your database area by selecting the range with the field names, pulling down the Data menu, and choosing Set Database.

4. Add the new field to your criteria area, as shown in Figure 13.9.

5. Redefine your criteria area by selecting the range, pulling down the Data menu, and choosing Set Criteria.

6. Copy the formula in cell B5 into cell C5, then edit the word TARGET to **ACTUAL** in C5. Figure 13.10 shows the formulas.

	A	B	C	D	E
1					
2					
3	LAST	FIRST	TARGET	REGION	
4					
5		1868000			
6	East	$682,000			1868000
7	Midwest	$369,000			
8	South	$394,000			
9	West	$423,000			
10					
11					
12					
13	LAST	FIRST	TARGET	REGION	
14	Allen	Ellen	$90,000	East	
15	Atkins	Lee	$113,000	East	
16	Jackson	Robert	$112,000	East	
17	Kennedy	Sandra	$135,000	East	
18	Stevens	Carla	$110,000	East	
19	Ellis	Nancy	$122,000	East	
20	Ford	Carl	$191,000	Midwest	
21	Linn	Vera	$80,000	Midwest	
22	Peterson	Tom	$98,000	Midwest	
23	Adams	Chuck	$118,000	South	
24	Glenn	John	$80,000	South	
25	Parker	Greg	$196,000	South	
26	Conners	Paul	$142,000	West	
27	Harris	Ken	$176,000	West	
28	Keller	Janet	$105,000	West	

Figure 13.6: The worksheet values calculated with the Table command

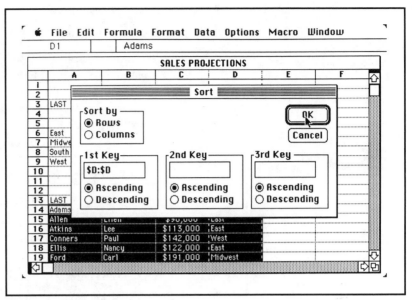

Figure 13.7: The Sort window

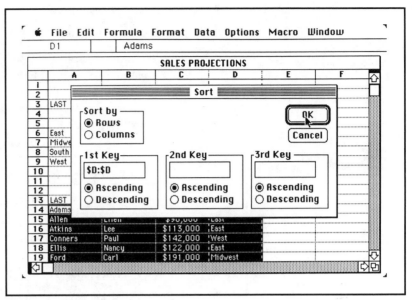

Figure 13.8: The new actual sales field

7. Select cells A5 through C9, including your new field.

8. Pull down the Data menu and choose Table.

9. Click the Column Input Cell box in the Table window, and click cell D4 just as you did before, then click OK.

Now both columns will be calculated, and the results will be displayed, as shown in Figure 13.9.

	A	B	C	D	E
1					
2					
3	LAST	FIRST	TARGET	REGION	ACTUAL
4					
5		$1,868,000	$1,893,000		
6	East	$682,000	$645,000		1868000
7	Midwest	$369,000	$365,000		
8	South	$394,000	$418,000		
9	West	$423,000	$465,000		
10					
11					
12					
13	LAST	FIRST	TARGET	REGION	ACTUAL
14	Adams	Chuck	$118,000	South	$110,000
15	Allen	Ellen	$90,000	East	$95,000
16	Atkins	Lee	$113,000	East	$80,000
17	Conners	Paul	$142,000	West	$165,000
18	Ellis	Nancy	$122,000	East	$115,000
19	Ford	Carl	$191,000	Midwest	$185,000
20	Glenn	John	$80,000	South	$95,000
21	Harris	Ken	$176,000	West	$190,000
22	Jackson	Robert	$112,000	East	$110,000
23	Keller	Janet	$105,000	West	$110,000
24	Kennedy	Sandra	$135,000	East	$125,000
25	Linn	Vera	$80,000	Midwest	$85,000
26	Parker	Greg	$196,000	South	$213,000
27	Peterson	Tom	$98,000	Midwest	$95,000
28	Stevens	Carla	$110,000	East	$120,000

Figure 13.9: The worksheet showing actual sales results by region

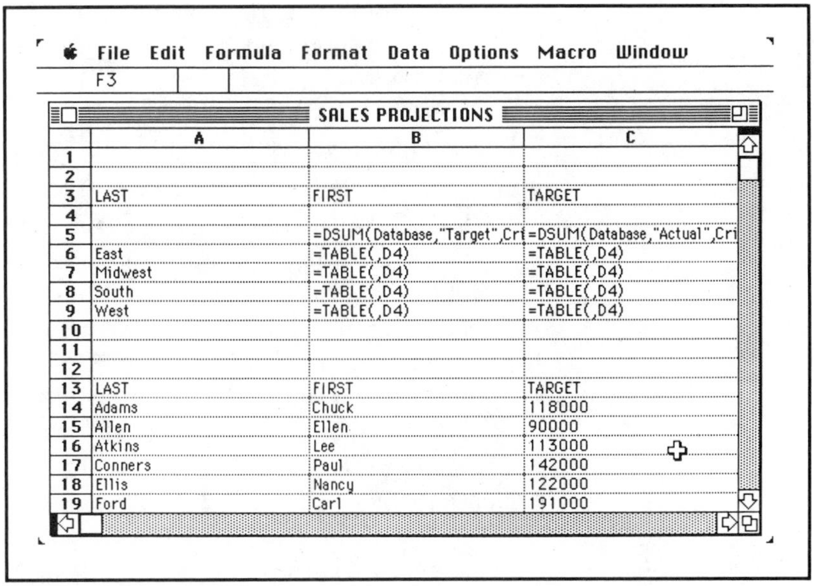

Figure 13.10: Formulas for two-column one-input table

TWO-INPUT TABLES

In a one-input table, a single input cell is used to calculate the values for one or more columns or rows. In a two- input table—as its name implies—two input cells are used to calculate the values for one or more columns or rows.

DESIGNING A TWO-INPUT TABLE To design a two-input table, you need to define the following four areas on your worksheet:

- Two input cells to contain the values that you wish to change.

- A row containing the values that will be applied successively to one of the input cells.

- A column containing the values that will be applied successively to the other input cell.

- One or more columns or rows that contain cells for the resulting values, with the formulas used as headings for each column or row. You can use formulas that refer directly to the input cell or to other cells on the worksheet.

Once you have set up these areas on your worksheet, you can use a two-input table, as described below.

CREATING A TWO-INPUT TABLE   You create a two-input table by following the same procedure that you used to create a one-input table, except that you will have both a row input cell and a column input cell. First, select the range of cells containing the input rows or columns and the output rows or columns with the formulas. Then, pull down the Data menu and select Table. In the Row Input Cell box, enter the reference to the input cell for which you wish the row to be calculated. In the Column Input Cell box, enter the reference to the input cell for which you wish the column to be calculated. Then click OK. Excel will then calculate the values for both input cells.

Figure 13.11 shows an example using a two-input table to calculate monthly payments for a variety of interest rates and time periods for an $8000 loan. The interest rates are placed in one column and the period values (in months) in a row. Two input cells must be defined, one for the interest values (B3) and one for the periods (C3). The following formula is placed at the intersection of the row and column:

= PMT(B3/12,C3, − 8000)

Don't worry about the #DIV/0! in B6. It is there because the two input cells are empty. Select B6 to F12. Click the Table menu and for the Row Input Cell click C3. For the Column Input Cell click B3. Excel should then create the table shown in Figure 13.11.

EDITING TABLES

You can edit the values used for input cells or the formulas of a table by using the commands on the Edit menu. After you make any changes, the table will be automatically updated using the new input values or formulas. However, you *cannot* edit the output columns or rows of a table (such as cells B6 through B9 in the Sales Projections database and worksheet example). For example, try changing Midwest to Europe on your worksheet—select cell A7 and enter **Europe**.

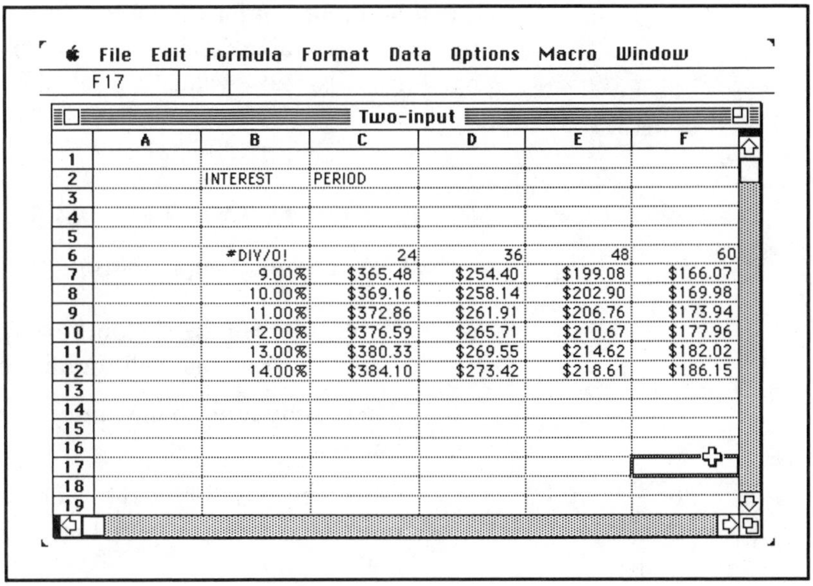

	A	B	C	D	E	F
1						
2		INTEREST	PERIOD			
3						
4						
5						
6		#DIV/0!	24	36	48	60
7		9.00%	$365.48	$254.40	$199.08	$166.07
8		10.00%	$369.16	$258.14	$202.90	$169.98
9		11.00%	$372.86	$261.91	$206.76	$173.94
10		12.00%	$376.59	$265.71	$210.67	$177.96
11		13.00%	$380.33	$269.55	$214.62	$182.02
12		14.00%	$384.10	$273.42	$218.61	$186.15
13						
14						
15						
16						
17						
18						
19						

Figure 13.11: A two-input table

Because there are no records that match this criterion, the value in cell B7 becomes zero. You will not be able to edit the individual cells B6 through B9 or even to clear them. You cannot clear a portion of a table; you must clear the entire table.

If you wish to use the Cut and Paste commands to move a table or the Copy and Paste commands to copy a table, you must first select the *entire* table. You cannot move or copy a portion of a table. (The *table,* in this case, refers to the output rows and columns. You can copy or move the input values for the table.) To select an entire table, double-click anywhere within the table.

If you copy a value from an output row or column into another cell of the worksheet, the new cell will contain only the value, not the formula.

When you select cells in the output columns or rows, the formula bar will display the table reference. The braces indicate that the cell is one of a series of cells. For example, the formula bar for cells B6, B7, B8, and B9 shows:

{ =TABLE(,D4)}

(D4 is the input cell for the table.) The braces indicate that the formula is part of a table. The same formula will appear when you select any of the cells whose values are calculated by the table.

NOTES FOR USING THE TABLE COMMAND

The following notes apply to using the Table command:

- You enter the formula for the output into the first cell in each column or row that will contain the output values.

- There is no limit to how many tables you can have active at one time.

- Once you have defined a range as a table, the entire range must be cleared or edited as a unit—tables cannot be partially cleared.

USING TABLES FOR LOOKUP ACCESS

Another application for tables is to use them as a substitute for formulas to produce an output value from an input value. In this case you are using table functions, not the Data Table command. Such tables are called *lookup tables*. You can create lookup tables anywhere on a worksheet. Here are some typical applications for lookup tables:

- Looking up the number of days in a month

- Looking up a tax rate for a particular income

- Looking up a category value for a product or employee

- Looking up a price for a particular category value

This should give you some idea of the value of the lookup table. In each case there is no easy formula to get the desired value. The table is used instead.

THE CHOOSE FUNCTION

The simplest type of lookup table uses the CHOOSE function. In fact, it is so simple it is seldom used; yet its simplicity makes it easy to use when it is applicable.

The CHOOSE function has the following form:

= CHOOSE(index,value1,value2,....value*n*)

The table, in this case, is the linear list of arguments within the function call. The value of *index* determines which item of the list the CHOOSE function chooses and returns.

For example, the command below will return the current name of the day of the week:

= CHOOSE(WEEKDAY(NOW( )),"Sun","Mon","Tue","Wed", "Thu","Fri","Sat")

THE MATCH FUNCTION

The MATCH function is used to return the position of an item in a list that most closely matches a lookup value. The general form is

= MATCH(lookup value,lookup range,type)

For example, assume the following cell values are in row 1: A1 = 22, B1 = 43, and C1 = 54. The function

= MATCH(43,A1:C1)

returns the value 2.

The third argument is optional, but if used it defines the rules for the search. A value of 1 indicates the function should return the largest value in the range equal to or less than *lookup value*. A value of 0 indicates only an exact match is accepted. If *type* is – 1, the function returns the smallest value in the range that is greater than or equal to *lookup value*. If the argument is omitted, a default value of 1 is assumed. If nothing in the range matches the test condition, the error value #N/A is returned.

In order to specify the type as 1, the table must be in ascending order. If you want the type to be – 1, the table must be in descending order.

THE INDEX FUNCTION

The general form of the INDEX function is as follows:

= INDEX(index range,row,column,area)

This function returns the address of a cell, not the value of the cell. The cell containing the function, however, displays the value from the specified cell in the table. An example will make this clearer.

To use the function, you must first create a table in a separate area of the worksheet. The table must be a rectangular range that includes at least four cells. The *index range* argument is used to define the range of the table. The next two arguments define the *row* and *column* for the retrieval. For example, assume the following

A1   = INDEX(C1:E3,A5,A6)

A5   = 2

A6   = 3

returns the address of E2 to A1; that is, row 2 and column 3 in the table. A1 would display the contents of E2.

As an example, Figure 13.12 shows a worksheet for determining the percentage a bank might charge for a loan based on the credit risk. The risk categories are 1, 2, and 3 in column B. Row 5 shows the years for the loan. The formula in B11 to calculate the percentage is

= INDEX(C6:F8,D1,D2)

The row and column headings are not used in the formula and are for labeling only. D1 and D2 contains the actual table displacements.

You can also use multiple areas, using the third argument to tell Excel which area to use:

= INDEX((C1:E3,F1:H3),2,3,2)

In this case the third argument value of 2 forces the use of the second table range, or F1:H3.

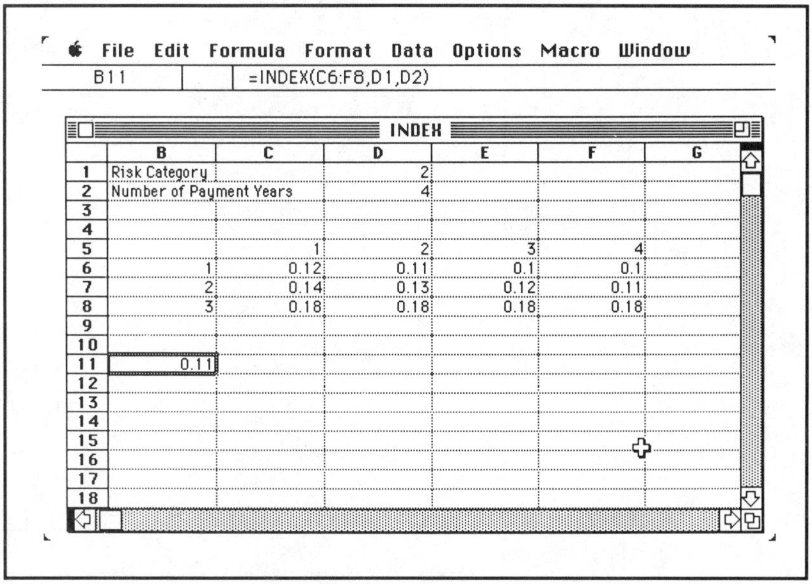

Figure 13.12: An example using the INDEX function

THE LOOKUP FUNCTIONS

You can also access lookup tables in a separate area of the worksheet using the LOOKUP, VLOOKUP, and HLOOKUP functions (see Chapter 8). These functions permit you to locate a value in a table based on the value of a test variable. The first argument in each function is called the test variable. The second argument defines the lookup table as an array (see Chapter 15).

The LOOKUP, VLOOKUP, and HLOOKUP functions search the first row or column of the table and return the largest value that is equal to or less than the test value. The table values must be in ascending order. For example, suppose cells D1 through D3 contain a table with the values 10,000, 20,000, and 40,000, and cells F1 through F3 contain the values 5%, 6%, and 7% (see Figure 13.13). If you used the function LOOKUP(25000,D1:F3) it would return 6%. The general form of LOOKUP is

= LOOKUP(*value,array*)

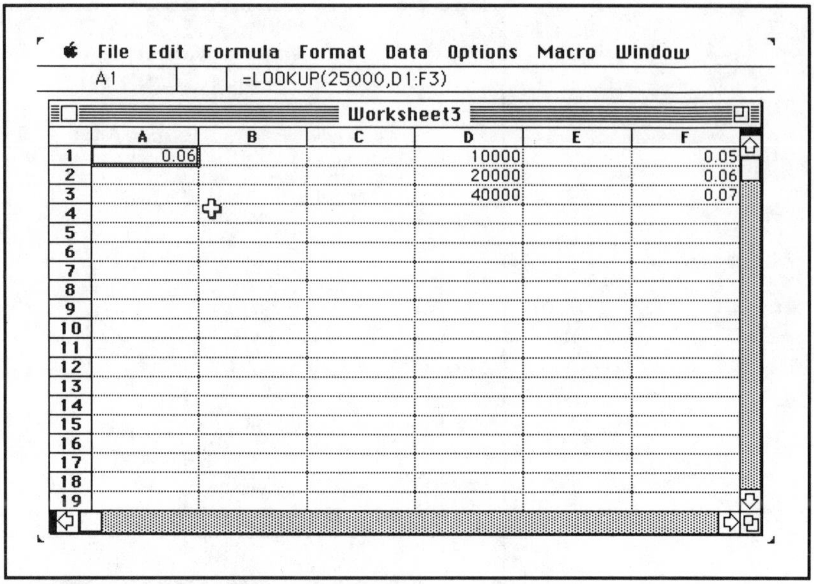

Figure 13.13: The LOOKUP function

The function searches the first row or column of *array* for *value* and returns the value of the corresponding cell of the last column or row. The LOOKUP function is identical to that of other worksheet programs.

The HLOOKUP and VLOOKUP functions contain a third argument. HLOOKUP defines how far to move into the column, and VLOOKUP defines how far to move in the row. For example, using the lookup table described in the previous example, the function VLOOKUP(25000,D1:F3,3) returns 6%, and the function VLOOKUP(25000,D1:F3,1) returns 25000, as the first column is 1, and the value is returned from that column.

Lookup tables are useful for obtaining a value that cannot be directly calculated from other cells on the worksheet using a formula such as a risk rating on a loan based on two specified variables.

The third argument is used the same way, but has a different value than in many competing worksheet programs. Excel counts the first column as column 1, many others count it as column 0. Table values must be in ascending order in order to work.

SUMMARY

In this chapter, you have learned how to create two types of tables: what-if tables (using the Table command) and lookup tables (using the LOOKUP functions). What-if tables are used to apply a series of input values to one or more cells to create a series of output values. Lookup tables are used as substitutes for formulas for certain types of worksheet calculations.

USING SPECIAL FEATURES

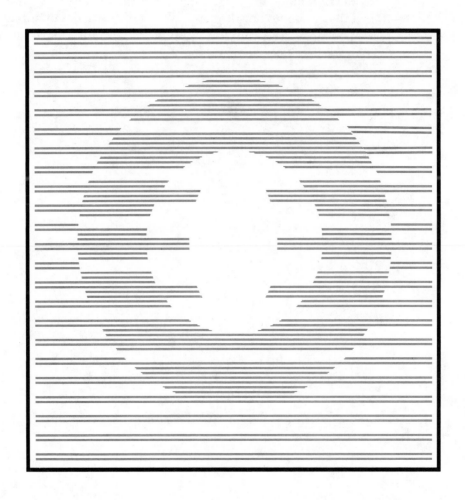

CHAPTER 14

ALTHOUGH YOU HAVE SUCCESSFULLY CREATED
several worksheets by now, you have mainly used the standard features that are necessary for working with most worksheets: moving,
copying, using functions, and formatting.

In this chapter, you will be introduced to some of Excel's special
features that make it even easier to create your worksheets. These
include copying and clearing only specific information, entering a
series of values, controlling when calculations are done, protecting
cells, and using iterations.

Excel's more advanced special features are covered in later chapters. These include linking worksheets, using arrays, and creating
and executing macros.

SELECTIVE CLEARING AND COPYING

Excel stores two types of data for each cell: the value or formula
and the format. Excel's Clear and Paste Special commands allow you
to selectively work with only the values, formulas, or formats of the
selected cells.

SPECIAL CLEARING

Edit	
Can't Undo	⌘Z
Cut	⌘H
Copy	⌘C
Paste	⌘U
Clear...	⌘B
Paste Special...	
Delete...	⌘K
Insert...	⌘I
Fill Right	⌘R
Fill Down	⌘D

The Clear command on the Edit menu can be used to delete only
the formulas or formats of the selected cells, as well as to delete all the
data. As Figure 14.1 shows, Excel's default selection in the Clear dialog box is Formulas, which clears the values of the selected cells, but
retains the formatting. If you click All, the values, formulas, and formats in the selected cells will be cleared. If you click Formats, the
selected cells will revert to the General template format. If you enter
new values or formulas, they will be displayed in the previous format.

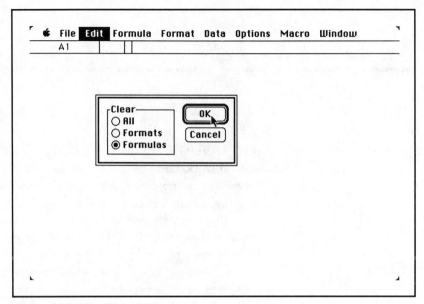

Figure 14.1: The Clear dialog box

As an example, open your Sales Projections database and select a few target values in column C. Pull down the Edit menu, choose Clear, click Formats, and then click OK. The format of the cells that you cleared return to the General template format— the dollar signs and commas are gone. Reformat the cells to their previous format before you continue.

SPECIAL COPYING

The Paste Special command on the Edit menu lets you control what you copy into another cell. You can copy just values, formulas, or formats instead of copying all the data from one cell or cell range to another.

Excel's default selection in the Paste Special dialog box, shown in Figure 14.2, is All. The Operation part of the dialog box permits you to perform operations between cells as part of the copy process. The Operation options are particularly useful for combining data from several worksheets into a single summary worksheet. For example, a sales manager may receive worksheets from several sales areas. She

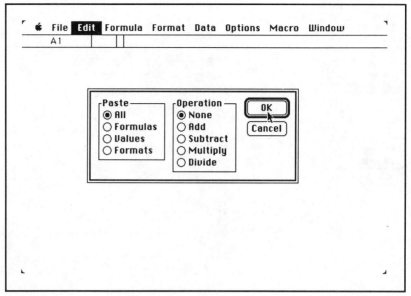

Figure 14.2: The Paste Special dialog box

could use the Add option in the Operation part of the Paste Special dialog box to combine the totals when she copies them into a summary worksheet.

Let's see how the Paste Special command works. First, add a name to the end of your Sales Projections database. Notice that the value for TARGET is not formatted correctly. You could use the Format command to reformat the entry, but it is easier to use the Paste Special command to copy only the format. Follow these steps:

1. Enter the values for the new salesperson in row 29, as shown in Figure 14.3

2. Click cell C28 to select the cell format to copy

3. Pull down the Edit menu and choose Copy

4. Click cell C29, which is the destination cell

5. Pull down the Edit menu and choose Paste Special

6. When the Paste Special dialog box appears (Figure 14.2), click Formats, then click OK

Edit	
Can't Undo	⌘Z
Cut	⌘H
Copy	⌘C
Paste	⌘V
Clear...	⌘B
Paste Special	
Delete...	⌘K
Insert...	⌘I
Fill Right	⌘R
Fill Down	⌘D

⌘ File Edit Formula Format Data Options Macro Window

E29

SALES PROJECTIONS

	A	B	C	D	E	F
19	Ford	Carl	$191,000	Midwest		
20	Glenn	John	$80,000	South		
21	Harris	Ken	$176,000	West		
22	Jackson	Robert	$112,000	East		
23	Keller	Janet	$105,000	West		
24	Kennedy	Sandra	$135,000	East		
25	Linn	Vera	$80,000	Midwest		
26	Parker	Greg	$196,000	South		
27	Peterson	Tom	$98,000	Midwest		
28	Stevens	Carla	$110,000	East		
29	Albertson	George	100000	South		
30						
31						
32						
33						
34						
35						
36						
37						

Figure 14.3: Adding a new salesperson

> Use the Copy and Paste commands whenever possible to enter data into new columns and rows in a worksheet. This saves entry time and helps prevent mistakes.

The new entry in cell C29 in now formatted correctly, as shown in Figure 14.4.

To see how an Operation option works, repeat steps 3 through 6 above. Then, when the Paste Special dialog box appears, leave All selected and click Add in the Operation box. The contents of cell C28 are added to the contents of cell C29 in the copy process, and your worksheet should contain the result shown in Figure 14.5.

SPECIAL EDITING TECHNIQUES

Here are some helpful editing tricks to keep in mind:

- You can use the Edit menu to edit a formula in the formula bar as well as to move or copy cell contents. The Cut and Copy commands enable you to delete a portion of a formula or copy a portion to another part of the formula.

- Typing Command-' copies a cell formula to the cell immediately below.

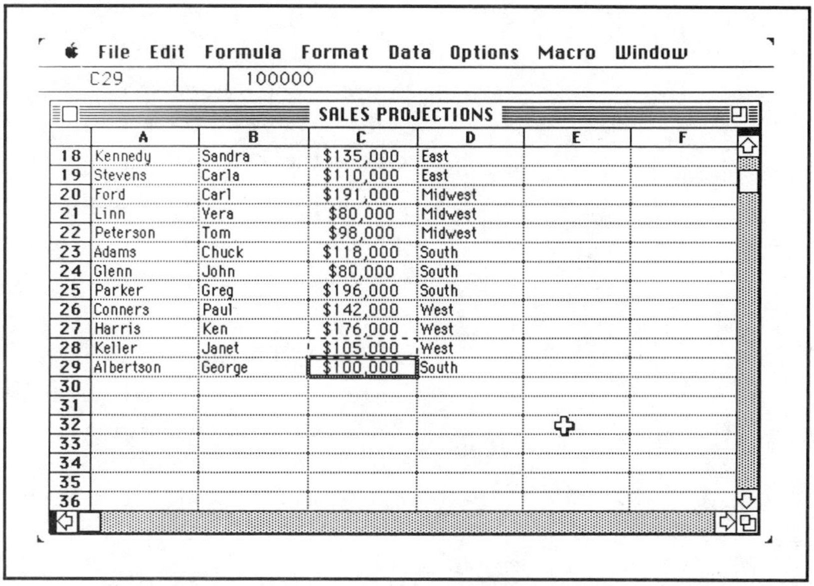

```
  ⬛ File  Edit  Formula  Format  Data  Options  Macro  Window
     C29              100000
  ┌─────────────────────── SALES PROJECTIONS ───────────────────┐
  │         A          B          C          D          E        F
  │ 18 │Kennedy   │Sandra   │$135,000 │East      │        │      │
  │ 19 │Stevens   │Carla    │$110,000 │East      │        │      │
  │ 20 │Ford      │Carl     │$191,000 │Midwest   │        │      │
  │ 21 │Linn      │Vera     │$80,000  │Midwest   │        │      │
  │ 22 │Peterson  │Tom      │$98,000  │Midwest   │        │      │
  │ 23 │Adams     │Chuck    │$118,000 │South     │        │      │
  │ 24 │Glenn     │John     │$80,000  │South     │        │      │
  │ 25 │Parker    │Greg     │$196,000 │South     │        │      │
  │ 26 │Conners   │Paul     │$142,000 │West      │        │      │
  │ 27 │Harris    │Ken      │$176,000 │West      │        │      │
  │ 28 │Keller    │Janet    │$105,000 │West      │        │      │
  │ 29 │Albertson │George   │$100,000 │South     │        │      │
  │ 30 │          │         │         │          │        │      │
  │ 31 │          │         │         │          │        │      │
  │ 32 │          │         │         │          │   ✛    │      │
  │ 33 │          │         │         │          │        │      │
  │ 34 │          │         │         │          │        │      │
  │ 35 │          │         │         │          │        │      │
  │ 36 │          │         │         │          │        │      │
  └───────────────────────────────────────────────────────────┘
```

Figure 14.4: The result of the Paste Special command

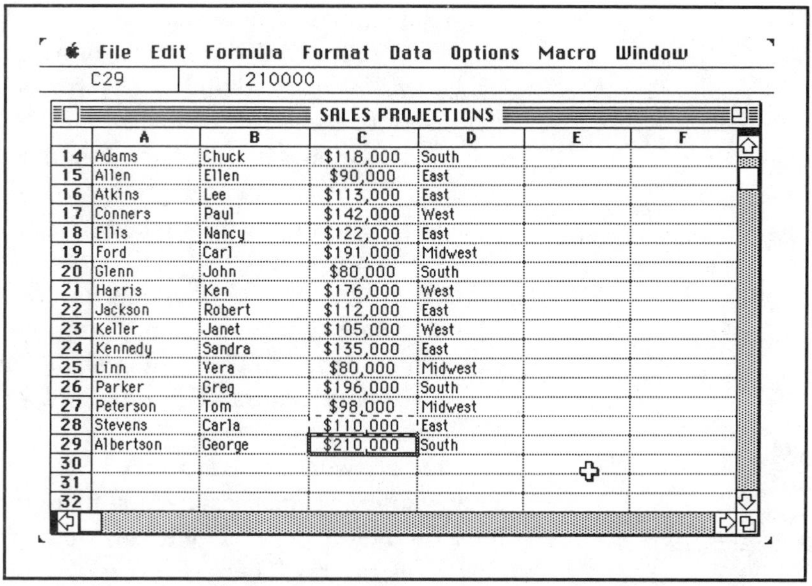

```
  ⬛ File  Edit  Formula  Format  Data  Options  Macro  Window
     C29              210000
  ┌─────────────────────── SALES PROJECTIONS ───────────────────┐
  │         A          B          C          D          E        F
  │ 14 │Adams     │Chuck    │$118,000 │South     │        │      │
  │ 15 │Allen     │Ellen    │$90,000  │East      │        │      │
  │ 16 │Atkins    │Lee      │$113,000 │East      │        │      │
  │ 17 │Conners   │Paul     │$142,000 │West      │        │      │
  │ 18 │Ellis     │Nancy    │$122,000 │East      │        │      │
  │ 19 │Ford      │Carl     │$191,000 │Midwest   │        │      │
  │ 20 │Glenn     │John     │$80,000  │South     │        │      │
  │ 21 │Harris    │Ken      │$176,000 │West      │        │      │
  │ 22 │Jackson   │Robert   │$112,000 │East      │        │      │
  │ 23 │Keller    │Janet    │$105,000 │West      │        │      │
  │ 24 │Kennedy   │Sandra   │$135,000 │East      │        │      │
  │ 25 │Linn      │Vera     │$80,000  │Midwest   │        │      │
  │ 26 │Parker    │Greg     │$196,000 │South     │        │      │
  │ 27 │Peterson  │Tom      │$98,000  │Midwest   │        │      │
  │ 28 │Stevens   │Carla    │$110,000 │East      │        │      │
  │ 29 │Albertson │George   │$210,000 │South     │        │      │
  │ 30 │          │         │         │          │        │      │
  │ 31 │          │         │         │          │   ✛    │      │
  │ 32 │          │         │         │          │        │      │
  └───────────────────────────────────────────────────────────┘
```

Figure 14.5: The result of the Paste Special command with an Operation option

- Typing Command – enters the system date in the current cell. Use it as a date stamp.

- You can copy a cell range without changing relative references by clicking the cell range, dragging through the contents in the formula bar, copying, and then pasting.

- To enter a formula into a range of cells, select the first cell, enter the formula, select the rest of the range, and then press Option-Return (instead of just Return).

- Use caution with the Paste Special command. If the Add option is selected, the new values will replace the old in the range selected. You have no audit trail. It would be better to create a new range, keeping the values in the new range that was added. The command is very useful, however, for adding a constant in one cell to a range of cells.

THE UNDO COMMAND

If you make a mistake in editing, you can quickly recover the original worksheet by using the Undo Command on the Edit menu. For example, suppose you accidentally erase a range of cells. To recover the range, simply pull down the Edit menu and choose Undo. In the same way, if you are editing in the formula bar, you can use the Undo command to restore the original contents of the cell.

Once an Undo is initiated, the Edit menu changes to show a Redo command. You can use this command, if desired, to return to your edited worksheet before the Undo.

In most cases you can undo a command only if no other command has been issued; i.e., you can only undo the last command issued. In addition, only commands issued from the Edit menu (Copy, Cut, etc.) can be undone. These are really the only commands that need undoing. Some commands (Goto, Find, etc.) do not affect the ability to undo an edit command.

You cannot undo a Delete on the File menu, or the Delete and Sort commands on the Data menu.

If you are working with a very large worksheet and try a move or copy, you may get a message that there is insufficient room and you must choose whether to Continue, Stop, or Undo. If you get this box, always select Stop. Then select a smaller range to move or copy. This protects you in case an Undo is necessary later.

DELETION AND INSERTION OF PARTIAL ROWS AND COLUMNS

Unlike most competing programs, Excel permits you to delete a partial row or column. Select the range to delete and choose the Delete command from the Edit menu. A dialog box will then ask you how you want the space to be filled: by shifting cells left or up. Select the desired option and then click OK.

Deletion of partial rows and columns is generally safer than deleting an entire row or column. If you delete an entire row or column, check the rest of the row or column to be sure no important data will be deleted. Even in deleting partial rows and columns, check to the right or below (depending upon the direction of the adjustment) before deletion.

You can use the Insert command in the same way to insert partial rows and columns. Excel displays the same dialog box, which asks which way to shift cells in order to fill the space.

CHANGING FORMULAS TO VALUES

There may be times when you want the value of a cell that was calculated by a formula to remain at a particular value; that is, you want to change a formula value to a constant value. You can do this by using the Values option in the Paste Special dialog box (see Figure 14.2).

For example, you might want to employ this option after you've used the NOW function to date a worksheet. By using this function and the desired template, you can put the date and time on a worksheet, as you did earlier in your Amortization worksheet (see Figure 14.6). The problem is that each time you load the worksheet, the NOW function immediately recalculates and stores the new date and time in the cell, making it impossible for you to see the original date and time of the saved worksheet. To resolve this problem, just before you save the worksheet, change the cells containing the date and time from formulas to values.

To change formulas to values, use the following procedure:

1. Select the cell or cell range that contains the calculated values that you wish to change to constant values

2. Pull down the Edit menu and choose Copy, then Paste Special

3. Click Values in the Paste Special dialog box (see Figure 14.2), then click OK

The easiest way to reenter the date is to type Command

If you update the worksheet, reenter the date if it has been switched to a constant.

CREATING A SERIES OF VALUES

Excel's Series command gives you a quick and easy way to enter sequential numbers into columns or rows. For example, the Series command would have been quite useful when you created the Amortization worksheet in Chapter 8. Column A of that worksheet contains a series of numbers, as shown in Figure 14.6. When you created the worksheet, you had to enter each number into column A sequentially, a laborious job since there were 48 payments in the example.

To use the Series command, you simply enter the starting value into the first cell of the row or column, select the cell range for the

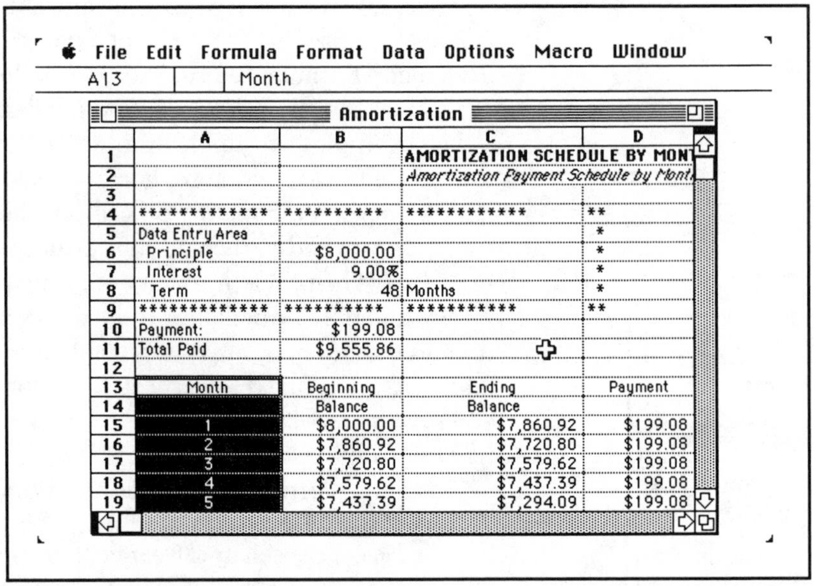

Figure 14.6: The Amortization worksheet

series (including the starting cell), pull down the Data menu, and choose Series. When you see the Series dialog box shown in Figure 14.7, select whether you want the series in a row or column and choose the series type (as explained below). Then, enter a step value for each increment of the series (the default value is 1). After you've made your selections, click OK, and Excel will automatically enter the Series values.

As Figure 14.7 shows, you have a choice of three types of series:

- A linear series, in which each entry is increased by a constant amount.

- A growth series, in which each entry is multiplied by the step value. For example, a linear series with a starting value of 1 and a step value of 2 would increase 1, 3, 5, and so on. A growth series with the same starting value and step value would increase 1, 2, 4, 8, 16, and so on. The growth type of series is useful for calculating compounded interest or growth rates.

- A date series, in which the date is increased by the unit (day, weekday, month, or year) that you select in the Date unit box in

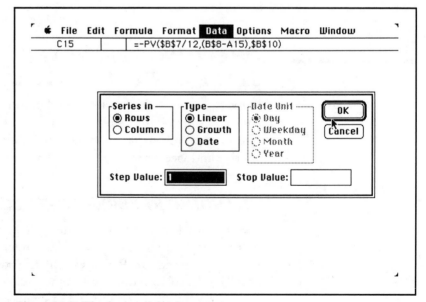

Figure 14.7: The Series dialog box

the Series dialog box. For example, to create columnar headings for the months of the year, enter the first month, select the row for the column titles, click Date, and then click Month.

You can also choose a stop value for a series. For example, if you did not know how many rows or columns your series would require, you could select a larger range than you needed and enter a specific stop value in the Series dialog box. The series would then terminate at that specified value.

Now, you can try the easy way of entering the data into column A of your Amortization worksheet. After you clear column A from row 15 down, follow these steps:

1. Enter the starting value of 1 into cell A15

2. Select the range of cells A15 through A62

3. Pull down the Data menu and select Series

4. When the Series dialog box appears, (Figure 14.7) leave the default Columns and Linear options selected and click OK

With just a few clicks, the series is now entered into column A.

CHANGING REFERENCE STYLES AND TYPES

Excel gives you the flexibility to change both the style of cell referencing (from column letter and row number to numbers for both columns and rows) and the type of cell referencing (from absolute to relative and vice versa).

CHANGING REFERENCE STYLES

Some worksheet programs designate rows and columns in a different style than Excel uses. They reference a cell's location in R1C1 style—with an R followed by the row number and a C followed by the column number—rather than using Excel's column letter and row number (A1) style. For example, Figure 14.8 shows the

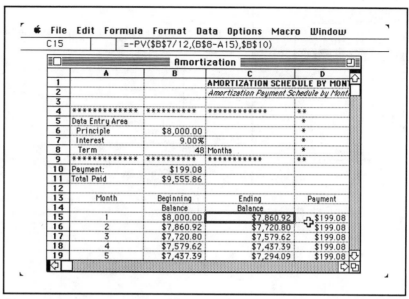

Figure 14.8: A formula in Excel's reference style

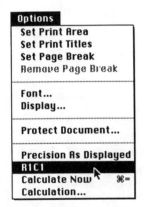

formula for cell C15 of the Amortization worksheet in Excel's reference style. Figure 14.9 shows the same formula in R1C1 style. Notice the difference in both absolute and relative addressing.

If you are more familiar with the R1C1 style and would rather have Excel use it, you can change to that style by using the R1C1 command on the Options menu. The worksheet's column letters will change into numbers, so that both the rows and columns are referenced by numbers, as shown in Figure 14.10.

To change the worksheet back to Excel's normal referencing style, pull down the Options menu and click A1.

CHANGING REFERENCE TYPES

There may be times when you need to change the type of cell reference in a formula. For example, when you click a referenced cell to enter it into a formula, it is automatically entered as a relative cell address. You can easily change the reference with a single mouse click: pull down the Formula menu and choose Reference. This will toggle the reference between absolute, mixed, and relative.

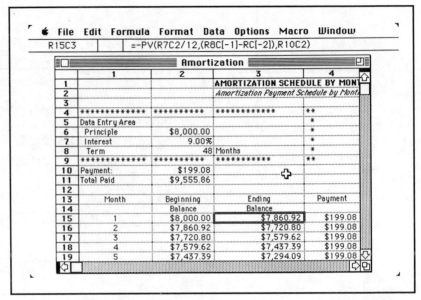

Figure 14.9: A formula in R1C1 style

Figure 14.10: The Amortization worksheet in R1C1 style

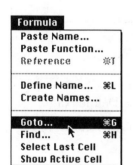 Another quick way to change the type of reference is to type Command-T instead of pulling down the Formula menu and selecting Reference.

There are only two points to note before you use the Reference command:

- The formula bar must be active (click the cursor in the formula bar).

- The command changes only the reference to the left of the insertion point in the formula bar, unless you have selected several references by dragging the cursor in the formula bar.

MOVING TO AND FINDING CELLS

The Formula menu lists several commands that let you move quickly to particular cells and find cells that contain specific data.

MOVING TO SPECIFIC CELLS

If you are using a large worksheet, you will occasionally need to move quickly to a particular cell on the worksheet. The Goto command on the Formula menu allows you to jump to any specified cell. When you use this command, you will see the dialog box shown in Figure 14.11. Simply enter the reference to the cell that you want to make active in the Reference box and click OK.

There is even an easier way to move to a particular cell. If there is a cell or cell range on your worksheet that you use often, assign it a name using the Define Name command on the Formula menu (see Chapter 9). Then, when you click Goto, you will see that name in the dialog box's list of active names. Double-click the name, and you'll move to that cell or cell range.

The Goto command actually has more uses than just getting you to a particular cell quickly—you can use it for range selection, formula entry, or viewing. Let's try a few simple experiments so that you can see for yourself.

First, open your Amortization worksheet and define a name for cell C18:

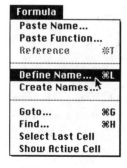

1. Select cell C18 (be sure that you have Excel's normal A1 display)

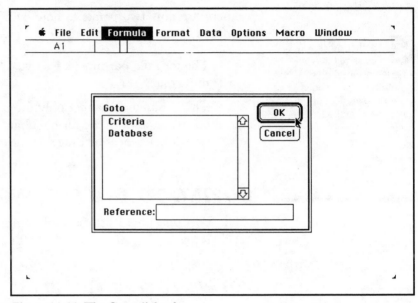

Figure 14.11: The Goto dialog box

Formula
Paste Name...	
Paste Function...	
Reference	⌘T
Define Name...	⌘L
Create Names...	
Goto...	⌘G
Find...	⌘H
Select Last Cell	
Show Active Cell	

2. Pull down the Formula menu and choose Define Name

3. Enter **Test** into the Define Name window, as shown in Figure 14.12, and click OK

Now, use the Goto command to select a range:

1. Select cell C15

2. Pull down the Formula menu and select Goto

3. Hold down the Shift key and double-click Test in the Goto dialog box, as shown in Figure 14.13

As described in Chapter 4, pressing the Shift key while clicking allows you to select a range without dragging, and pressing the Command key while clicking permits you to select several discontinuous cells.

You have now selected the entire cell range from C15 to C18. The result is shown in Figure 14.14. You can use both the Shift and Command keys to select a range for the Goto command, just as with any other type of cell range selection.

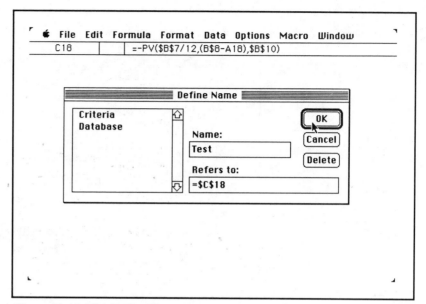

Figure 14.12: The Define Name window

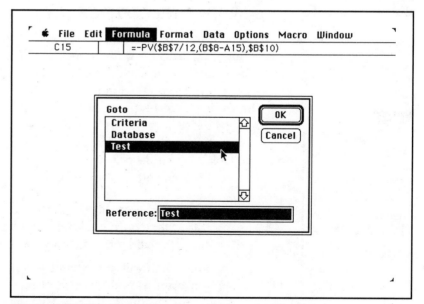

Figure 14.13: The Goto dialog box with the name Test listed

	1	2	3	4
			AMORTIZATION SCHEDULE BY MON	
2			*Amortization Payment Schedule by Mont*	
3				
4	************	**********	************	**
5	Data Entry Area			*
6	Principle	$8,000.00		*
7	Interest	9.00%		*
8	Term	48	Months	*
9	************	**********	************	**
10	Payment:	$199.08		
11	Total Paid	$9,555.86		
12				
13	Month	Beginning	Ending	Payment
14		Balance	Balance	
15	1	$8,000.00	$7,860.92	$199.08
16	2	$7,860.92	$7,720.80	$199.08
17	3	$7,720.80	$7,579.62	$199.08
18	4	$7,579.62	$7,437.39	$199.08
19	5	$7,437.39	$7,294.09	$199.08

R15C3   =-PV(R7C2/12,(R8C[-1]-RC[-2]),R10C2)

Figure 14.14: Selecting a range with the Goto command

If there is a cell range that you use often, select the entire range and assign a name to it. You can then use the Goto command to quickly select that range.

Formula
Paste Name...
Paste Function...
Reference   ⌘T

Define Name...   ⌘L
Create Names...

Goto...   ⌘G
Find...   ⌘H
Select Last Cell
Show Active Cell

FINDING SPECIFIC CELLS

There may be times when you need to find the specific cell that contains a particular value or formula. You can do this by using the Find command on the Formula menu.

When you select the Find command, you'll see the Find dialog box shown in Figure 14.15. Once you've entered what you want to find in the Find What box, you can have Excel look in formulas or in values, look for the entry as a whole unit or as part of other entries, and look by columns or by rows.

Here are some other features of the Find command:

- If you have a single cell selected when you use the Find command, the entire worksheet will be searched. If you have a range selected, only the range will be searched.

- The search will stop when Excel finds the first occurrence. If you want to find the next occurrence, press Command-H. (This skips the dialog box.) To find the previous occurrence,

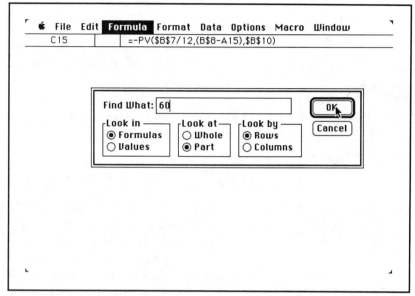

Figure 14.15: The Find dialog box

type Shift-Command-H. (This is different than the Data menu, where Command-F finds the next occurrence.)

- In entering the search string into the Find What box, you can use the wild-card characters * and ?, where ? represents a single character and * represents a group of characters. You can also use any of the relational operators to specify the search string (see Chapter 4).

- The Look By box is used to specify the direction of the search—either by rows or columns. If you know the approximate location of the cell on a large worksheet, specifying the correct direction here can speed up the search.

When you've finished editing a worksheet, use the Find command to locate all unresolved references by searching for #REF.

As an example, you can use the Find command to locate the cell on your Amortization worksheet that contains the final payment. Follow these steps:

1. Pull down the Formula menu and choose Find

2. When the dialog box is displayed (see Figure 14.15), enter **48**

3. Click Values to indicate that you wish to search in values instead of in formulas

4. Click Whole to indicate that you want to skip cells (such as cell C14) in which the value is a part of the cell's contents

5. Click OK

The cursor should be on cell A62—the month cell in the last payment row.

SELECTING THE LAST CELL

The Select Last Cell command on the Formula menu allows you to move quickly to the last cell of the worksheet. This cell is one of the most important cells in the worksheet because it determines the amount of memory needed for the worksheet. Occasionally, a cell in the remote regions of a worksheet can get "trashed" if you inadvertently select it and enter data. This command is also useful if you simply want to move quickly to the last cell, but you do not remember its location.

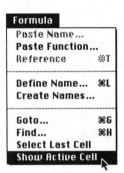

DISPLAYING THE ACTIVE CELL

You can use the Show Active Cell command on the Formula menu to quickly return to the worksheet's active cell. This is particularly useful when you select a cell or cell range, then scroll away to view something else on the worksheet.

CALCULATION OPTIONS

The Calculation command on the Options menu allows you to tell Excel when to recalculate values and when to use iteration.

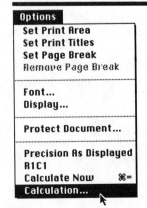

CONTROLLING RECALCULATIONS

Normally, each time that you change a value, formula, or name, Excel will automatically recalculate all cells that are dependent on the changed cells. The time required for Excel to recalculate a worksheet depends upon the size of the worksheet and the number of open documents. If you are entering data on a large worksheet, recalculations can be quite time-consuming. You can speed up the process by using the Calculation command on the Options menu to turn off the calculations until you've entered all the data.

When you use the Calculation command, you will see the Calculation dialog box shown in Figure 14.16. Click Manual to turn off calculations, then click OK.

Tables are very time-consuming to recalculate, as the worksheet must be recalculated for each input value. For some worksheets, you may want Excel to automatically recalculate all values except for the tables. If you select this option on the Calculation dialog box, the tables will only be recalculated when you use the Table command on the Data menu.

The Iteration part of the Calculation dialog box controls iterations (see the next section). The Iteration option must be turned on if you plan to use iterations.

To calculate the worksheet after you have entered all the data, first be sure that the formula bar is not selected, then pull down the Options menu and choose Calculate Now.

If the formula bar is active when you select the Calculate Now command, Excel will evaluate the formula and enter the result

When working with large worksheets, if the recalculation speed seems slow, turn off the calculation during data entry or worksheet editing. When you are ready for calculating, use Options Calculate Now.

Figure 14.16: The Calculation dialog box

(*not* the formula) into the active cell. You can also select part of a formula and use the Calculate Now command to evaluate only that part.

Remember, you only need to use the Calculate Now command when you have set Excel in the manual calculation mode. When it is in the automatic calculation mode, the Calculate Now command will do nothing, unless the formula bar is active, as described above.

USING ITERATIONS

There may be times when your calculations require you to use formulas that depend upon each other in a circular manner. Excel allows you to perform these calculations by using *iterations*. Let's try an example so that you can get an idea of how this works.

Acme Manufacturing had a good year, and the Board decided to pay the employees a bonus. The amount allocated for the bonus payments was 5 percent of the net profit after the bonuses were subtracted from the gross profit. Create the worksheet shown in Figure 14.17 to help the Board calculate the bonus:

1. Enter the row titles **Gross Profit**, **Bonus**, and **Net Profit** in cells A3, A4, and A6, respectively, and enter **23500** as the value for Gross Profit

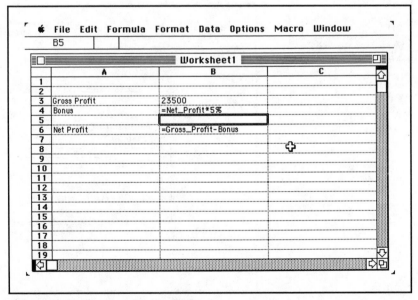

Figure 14.17: The Iteration worksheet

2. Create the names by selecting rows 3 through 6 (entire rows), pulling down the Formula menu, and choosing Create Names

3. Click Left Column, then click OK, as shown in Figure 14.18

4. Enter the formula for Net Profit as **Gross_Profit-Bonus**.

5. Enter the value of the Bonus as **Net_Profit*5%**

What happens? You will quickly get the circular reference error message shown in Figure 14.19.

This message indicates that you have created formulas that depend on each other in a circular manner. In this case, Net Profit is the Gross Profit minus the Bonus, but you need to know the Net Profit before the Bonus can be calculated. You need to use iterations in order to make your calculation.

Continue with the worksheet:

6. Pull down the Options menu and choose Calculation

7. When the Calculation dialog box appears, click Iteration, then click OK, as shown in Figure 14.20

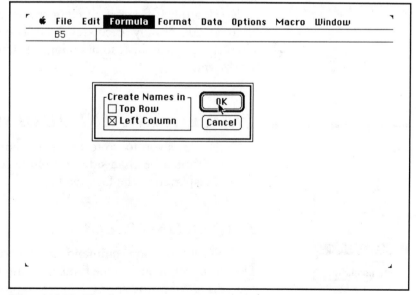

Figure 14.18: The Create Names dialog box

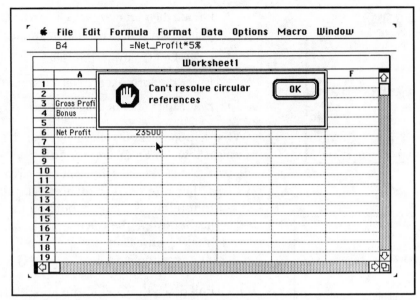

If you see the "Can't resolve circular references" error message and you didn't intend to use a circular calculation, check your equations. The alert box is warning you that you have an error in an equation.

In this case, the resulting values change less and less with each iteration. The iterations are said to converge to a solution. In some examples, the resulting values may change more and more with each iteration. In this case, the iterations diverge, and no real solution is possible. Both the design of the model and the starting values determine whether the solution converges or diverges.

Figure 14.19: The circular reference error message

Excel will repeat the calculations until the Net Profit and Bonus change by 0.001 or less or a maximum of 100 iterations has occurred. As shown in Figure 14.20, these limits are set in the Calculation dialog box. The final Iteration worksheet is shown in Figure 14.21.

Excel is much faster than competitors at doing iterative calculations because it only calculates the cells necessary for resolving the circular reference, instead of taking the time to recalculate the entire worksheet.

PROTECTING AND HIDING CELLS

Excel allows you to protect cells on your worksheets so that their contents cannot be changed and to hide cells so that their formulas are not displayed in the formula bar.

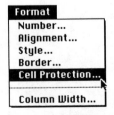

PROTECTING CELLS

The Cell Protection command on the Format menu and the Protect Document command on the Options menu together allow you to protect cells on your worksheets. When you protect cells, you *lock* them so

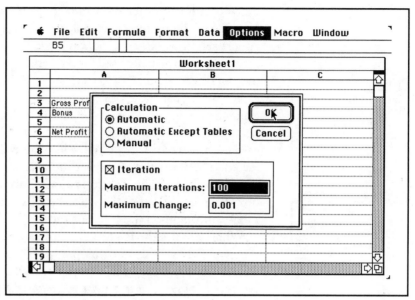

Figure 14.20: The Calculation dialog box

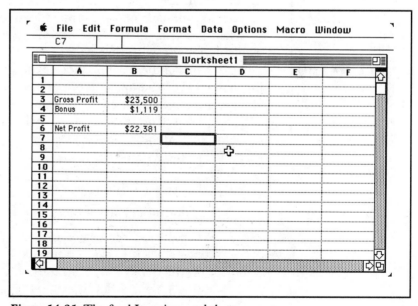

Figure 14.21: The final Iteration worksheet

that no one can enter data into them or alter their contents. One example of the usefulness of cell protection is for a worksheet like the Amortization worksheet that you created in Chapter 8, in which only three cells were actually used for data entry. All of the remaining cells in the worksheet could be protected to prevent them from being altered.

When you use the Cell Protection command on the Format menu, unless you tell Excel otherwise, *all* the cells of the document are, by default, locked. So, the general procedure for protecting some of the cells on a worksheet is to first select the cells that should *not* be protected. Then, use the Cell Protection command on the Format menu to unlock these cells by clicking Locked in the Cell Protection dialog box. Protect the rest of the worksheet by selecting the Protect Document command on the Options menu.

When you use the Protect Document command, you must enter a password. If you forget this password, you will never be able to unlock the protected cells. For this reason *always check the password that you enter to be sure that it is what you intended before you click OK.* Keep a record of your passwords. Exactly the same word must be entered to unprotect the document.

When you need to unlock a protected cell, the procedure is just the reverse. First, use the Unprotect Document command on the Options menu. Then, select the cells that you want to unlock and use the Cell Protection command on the Format menu to unlock them.

When a document is protected, many commands are no longer available for use with that worksheet. The menus will change to reflect the loss of these commands—many commands are no longer highlighted. For example, all of the commands on the Format and Data menus, except the Find command, are inactive.

To see how cell protection works, try locking all but the data-entry cells on your Amortization worksheet. After you open that worksheet, follow these steps:

1. Select cells B6 through B9 (the data-entry cells)

2. Pull down the Format menu and choose Cell Protection

3. When the Cell Protection dialog box shown in Figure 14.22 appears, click Locked to unlock the cells that you selected (you will remove the X next to Locked to turn off this toggle option.), then click OK

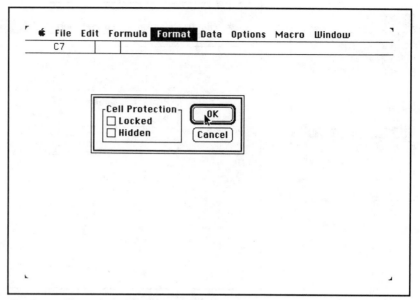

Figure 14.22: The Cell Protection dialog box

4. Pull down the Options menu and choose Protect Document

5. When the Protect Document dialog box shown in Figure 14.23 appears, enter the password **Secret**, then press Return or click OK

Your Amortization worksheet is now protected. You can enter a new interest rate, principle, or term, but you cannot alter the contents of any other cells. Try to edit the other cells just to see what happens. You will get an alert box with the message

Cell is locked

If it is ever necessary to alter the formulas or otherwise change the protected areas of your Amortization worksheet, follow the reverse procedure:

1. Pull down the Options menu and select Unprotect Document

2. Enter **Secret** as the password in the Unprotect Document dialog box, as shown in Figure 14.24, then click OK

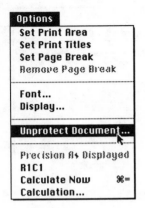
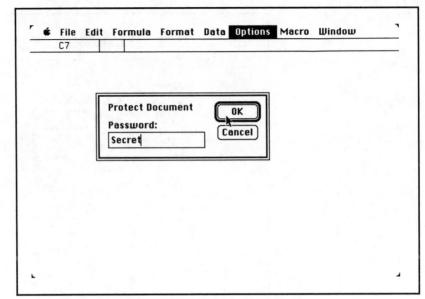

Figure 14.23: The Protect Document dialog box

Protect as many cells as possible in your document, leaving unprotected only the cells that depend upon input data. This prevents someone from accidentally changing a formula or constant data in a worksheet that may be the basis of important decisions.

3. Select the cells that you want to unlock

4. Pull down the Formula menu and click Cell Protection

5. Click Locked in the Cell Protection dialog box (Figure 14.22) to remove the X and unlock the selected cells

If you forget which cells are protected, use the Display command on the Options menu to turn off the grid lines. The *unprotected* cells will be underlined, as shown in Figure 14.25.

HIDING CELLS

You may wish to prevent a user from seeing the formula used in a particular calculation. You can do this by hiding a cell, using a procedure similar to the one that you use to protect cells. First, select the cell or cell range that you want to hide. Then, pull down the Format menu and choose Cell Protection. When the Cell Protection dialog box appears (see Figure 14.22), click Hidden (the default mode is locked, not hidden). Then click OK. Next, pull down the Options

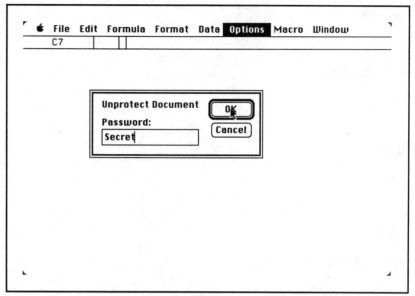

Figure 14.24: Turning off the protection

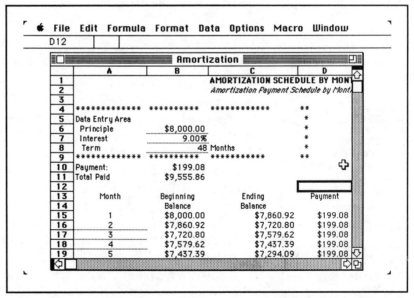

Figure 14.25: Underlines indicate the unprotected cells on the Amortization worksheet

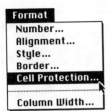

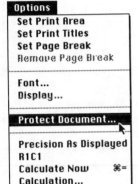

menu and click Protect Document. When the Protect Document dialog box (see Figure 14.23) appears, enter your password and click OK. Then, when the hidden cell is selected, its formula will not appear in the formula bar.

To recover hidden cells, use the Unprotect Document command on the Options menu. Enter your password in the Unprotect dialog box. As with protected cells, you must remember your password or you will never see the formulas again.

Another way to hide a column of cells is to set the column width to zero. It is very easy, however, for any user to recover a column that was hidden by this method. What is more, the column headers will indicate there is a missing column. The advantage, however, is that the actual value of the cell is hidden from the user. Cell protection hides only the formula used to calculate the result, not the result. A column width of zero hides the result.

Setting a column width to zero is easy—just drag or use the Column Width command (entering 0). Recovering the column is more difficult, as you can't select it. To recover, select columns to the left and right, then change all three widths to a larger value. Then change the other two columns back to their original value.

CONTROLLING THE PRECISION

Excel stores all the numbers that you enter into your worksheets with a full 14-digit precision. (*Precision* refers to the number of decimal places to which a value is carried when it is stored or displayed.) It performs all calculations with this full precision, without regard to how the number is displayed. In some cases, you may wish to switch this so that Excel stores the numbers and performs calculations only with the precision displayed. For example, you may want to switch the precision when the results of formulas do not seem to match the numbers used to calculate them. You can change the precision for all templates except the General template, which always stores numbers with full precision.

To switch from full precision to the displayed precision, pull down the Options menu and click Precision as Displayed. To switch back, pull down the Options menu and click Full Precision.

USING ARRAYS

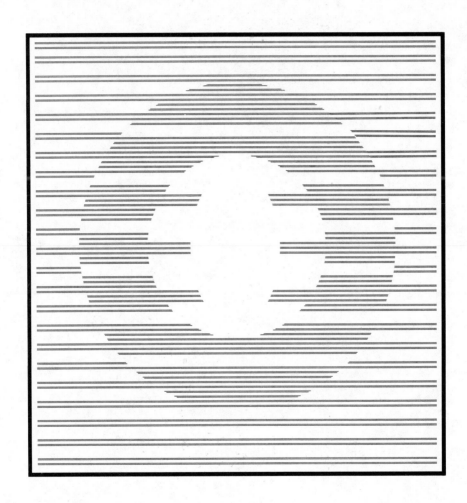

CHAPTER 15

IN SOME APPLICATIONS, YOU MAY WANT TO USE MUL-
tiple values as arguments for a function, or you may want a function to
produce multiple values. Such a list of multiple values is called an *array*.

In all of the examples in the previous chapters, you used function
arguments with only a single value. In this chapter, you will learn
how to use multiple-value arguments, or arrays. The basic concept of
using arrays will be illustrated with a simple example. Then, you will
work through a more complex example that clearly shows how arrays
can make your worksheet calculations much easier.

USING ARRAYS

In a simple function, the arguments each refer to a single value—a
single cell or a single cell range. For example, the result of the formula **= SUM(A1:A11)** is the sum of the values from cells A1
through A11—a single cell range. You can use an array or list in a
function call just as you use individual values.

ENTERING AN ARRAY

Suppose that you have an Inventory worksheet that lists four products with a quantity on hand and a cost for each one, as shown in Figure 15.1. The extended cost for each product equals the quantity on
hand multiplied by the cost. The total inventory value, then, is the
sum of the extended costs for each product. Enter the data for the Inventory worksheet, using the formulas shown in Figure 15.2.

Notice that you entered the same formula four times in the
Ext. Cost row. It would be easier to calculate the total value of

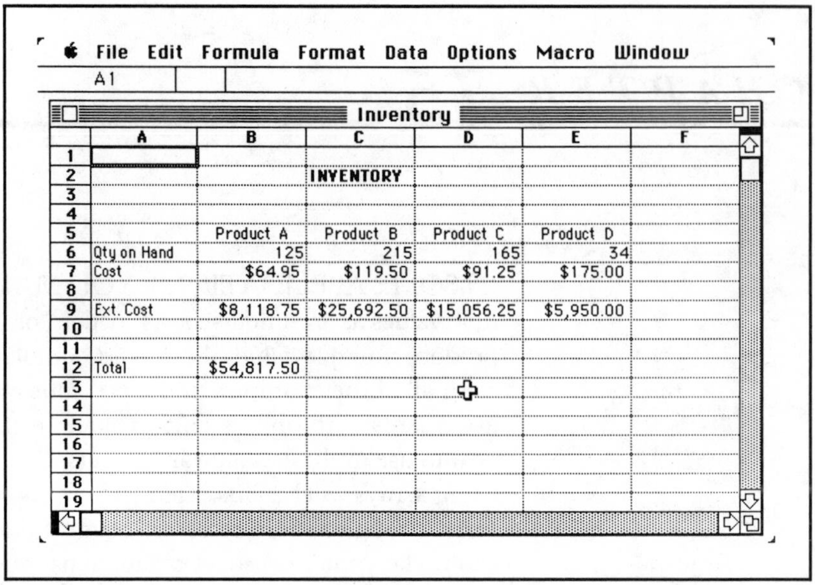

Figure 15.1: The Inventory worksheet

the inventory using arrays. To do so, type in the following formula for the total in cell B14:

    = SUM(B6:E6*B7:E7)

After you have entered the formula from the keyboard, *hold down the Command key while you press Return or click the enter box.* This will force Excel to accept the arguments as arrays. As shown in Figure 15.3, the displayed total in cell B14 is still the same as what was in B12 before, but the formula used to calculate that total is different.

Notice also that you can now change any quantity on hand amount or cost in row 6 or 7 and the total in B14 will change to reflect the new quantity on hand or cost. Row 9 is not used at all; in fact, if you clear row 9, the total in B12 will be zero, as you can see in Figure 15.3. The total in B14 will still be correct.

Examine the formula in B14. Notice that it is exactly as you entered it, except that when you used the Command key, Excel enclosed the formula in braces:

    { = SUM(B6:E6*B7:E7)}

	A	B	C	D	E
1					
2			INVENTORY		
3					
4					
5		Product A	Product B	Product C	Product D
6	Qty on Hand	125	215	165	34
7	Cost	64.95	119.5	91.25	175
8					
9	Ext. Cost	=Qty_on_Hand*Cost	=Qty_on_Hand*Cost	=Qty_on_Hand*Cost	=Qty_on_Hand*Cost
10					
11					
12	Total	=SUM(B9:E9)			

Figure 15.2: The Inventory worksheet formulas

Use arrays to speed up data entry. In this example, the use of the array eliminated the necessity of naming the rows, entering the first formula, and then filling right. Instead, only the final total formula was entered. Arrays can also save worksheet space, as with the elimination of a row in this example. However, arrays can make your worksheet more difficult to interpret and check.

The values for the cell ranges B6 through E6 and B7 through E7 are treated as an array. The SUM function multiplies the corresponding values in each list and then sums the products to get the final total. Using the formula is the same as typing

$$B14 = B6*B7 + C6*C7 + D6*D7 + E6*E7$$

You can also use range names in an array formula. Using the last example, you can name row 6 and 7 using the Define Names command. You can then enter the formula in B14 as follows:

$$\{ = SUM(Qty\_on\_Hand*Cost)\}$$

As you just learned, there is a simple technique for using arrays with Excel: After you enter a function with an array, hold down the Command key while you press the Return key or click the enter box. Excel will add braces to indicate that the function contains an array.

Many of the functions listed in Chapter 8 *require* array arguments. With these functions, it is not necessary to use the Command key, as Excel assumes the argument is an array.

CALCULATING MULTIPLE OUTPUT VALUES

In the previous example, multiple values were used to obtain a single output value. In some cases, you may have multiple output values; that

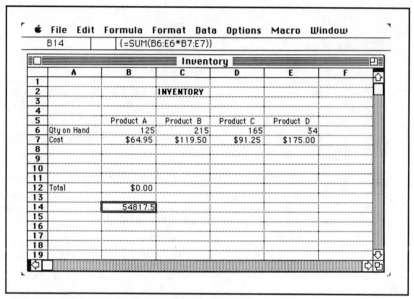

Figure 15.3: Using arrays to calculate the total

is, the output of the function is an array. To understand how to use multiple outputs, look at the following linear-regression example.

Linear regression is often used to project a future trend from known data about the past. This technique is used by manufacturing operations to project data on future productivity based on changes in the number of employees, working conditions, and other factors. It can also be used by a sales department to plan warehousing, marketing, and sales representation.

Suppose, for example, that your company discovered there was a relationship between the disposable income per person in various areas and the sale of its product. You have information about the disposable income in future years, and you wish to project your sales for these future years. This would enable you to plan how much warehouse space is needed, the number of sales representatives to employ, your marketing costs, and other factors. You'll use linear regression to make this projection. In the following example, you'll first do the linear regression using conventional worksheet techniques. Then, you'll do the same linear regression using arrays. This way you will see the advantage of using arrays.

Figure 15.4 shows how the linear regression would be done without arrays. The formulas are shown in Figure 15.5, and the values

LINEAR REGRESSION EXAMPLE

Year	Disposable Income ($K)	Projected Disp. Income ($K)	Sales ($)	Disp. Income X Sales	Disp. Income Squared	Projected Sales
1978	$200		$2,350	470,000	40,000	
1979	$260		$2,500	650,000	67,600	
1980	$270		$2,400	648,000	72,900	
1981	$190		$2,390	454,100	36,100	
1982	$119		$2,360	280,840	14,161	
1983	$115		$2,260	259,900	13,225	
1984	$325		$2,575	836,875	105,625	
1985	$350		$2,550	892,500	122,500	
1986	$302		$2,503	755,906	91,204	
1987	$212		$2,475	524,700	44,944	
1988		$250				2,453.40
1989		$275				2,480.62
1990		$325				2,535.07
Sum	2,343.00		24,363.00	5,772,821	608,259	
Average	234.30		2,436.30	577,282	60,826	

Value of a = 1.08898019
Value of b = 2181.15194

Figure 15.4: Doing a linear regression the hard way

are plotted in Figure 15.6 (the x axis is the disposable income, and the y axis is the sales). As the graph shows, there seems to be a correlation that could be used to plan future sales.

The data for the disposable income and sales are used to calculate the constants for the linear regression. This calculation is done in cells C16 and C17 using the following formula:

$$b = \frac{\Sigma xy - x\Sigma y}{\Sigma x2 - x\Sigma x}$$

$$a = \bar{y} - b\bar{x}$$

$$y_n = a + bx_n$$

	A	B	C	D	E	F	G
3			LINEAR REGRESSION EXAMPLE				
7	Year	Disposable	Projected	Sales	Disp. Income	Disp. Income	Projected
8		Income	Disp. Income	($)	X Sales	Squared	Sales
9		($K)	($K)				
11	1978	200		2350	=B11*D11	=B11*B11	
12	1979	260		2500	=B12*D12	=B12*B12	
13	1980	270		2400	=B13*D13	=B13*B13	
14	1981	190		2390	=B14*D14	=B14*B14	
15	1982	119		2360	=B15*D15	=B15*B15	
16	1983	115		2260	=B16*D16	=B16*B16	
17	1984	325		2575	=B17*D17	=B17*B17	
18	1985	350		2550	=B18*D18	=B18*B18	
19	1986	302		2503	=B19*D19	=B19*B19	
20	1987	212		2475	=B20*D20	=B20*B20	
21	1988		250				=$C$30+($C$29*C21)
22	1989		275				=$C$30+($C$29*C22)
23	1990		325				=$C$30+($C$29*C23)
25	Sum	=SUM(B11:B20)		=SUM(D11:D20)	=SUM(E11:E20)	=SUM(F11:F20)	
27	Average	=B25/10		=(D25/10)	=(E25/10)	=(F25/10)	
29		Value of a=	=((E25-(B27*D25))/(F25-(B27*B25)))				
30		Value of b=	=(D27-(C29*B27))				

Figure 15.5: The formulas for the linear regression example

Enter the data for the entire worksheet, as shown in Figure 15.5. You can use the Fill Down command to enter much of the data, but you will still find it cumbersome to use this approach to obtain your projections.

Now try the same thing using arrays:

1. Copy the Projected Disposable. Income values in column C into the Disposable Income column (column B) for a single Income array.

2. Combine the Sales and Projected Sales columns into a single column.

3. Delete all but the three columns that contain the data for the two input arrays, which are labeled Disp. Income and Sales. Sales will also be the output array. Your worksheet should now look like Figure 15.7.

4. Enter the first array formula. You will need to use two functions: SUM and LINEST. The LINEST function has two

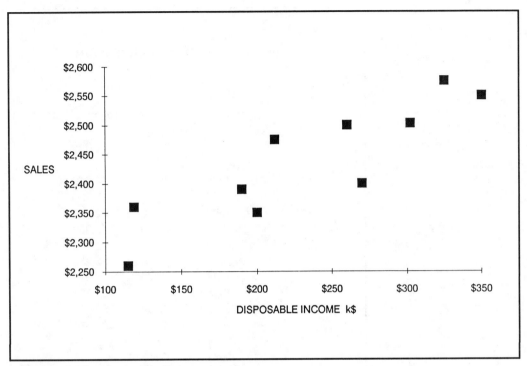

Figure 15.6: The chart of the linear regression

arrays for an input and one array for an output (see Chapter 8). Enter the following formula into cell C21:

= SUM(LINEST($C$11:$C$20,$B$11:$B$20)*{250,1})

In this case, you should also enter the braces from the keyboard.

5. Copy the formula in cell C21 into cells C22 and C23, then use the commands on the Edit menu to paste the proper sales value into each formula. Your final formulas should look like those shown in Figure 15.8.

6. Format the worksheet as shown in Figure 15.9, then print it out.

The final projected values are the same as those that you obtained the hard way, but your work is much, much less.

```
                    LINEAR REGRESSION
                       Using Arrays


           YEAR        DISP.        SALES
                       INCOME         $
                        $K

           1978        $200        $2,350
           1979        $260        $2,500
           1980        $270        $2,400
           1981        $190        $2,390
           1982        $119        $2,360
           1983        $115        $2,260
           1984        $325        $2,575
           1985        $350        $2,550
           1986        $302        $2,503
           1987        $212        $2,475
           1988        $250
           1989        $275
           1990        $325
```

Figure 15.7: The linear regression input data

Let's review the array formula that you just used. The LINEST function will return an array of two values: the slope (m) and the intercept (b) of the line of regression, represented by $y = b + mx$. These are the same constants that you calculated earlier using multiple columns, squares, sums, and averages. Excel does it all with a single LINEST function.

The general form of the LINEST function is

LINEST(y-array,x-array)

The y-array is the known and projected sales (C11:C23). The x-array is the known and projected disposable income. The LINEST

	A	B	C
1			
2			
3		LINEAR REGRESSION	
4		Using Arrays	
5			
6			
7	YEAR	DISP.	SALES
8		INCOME	$
9		$K	
10			
11	1978	200	2350
12	1979	260	2500
13	1980	270	2400
14	1981	190	2390
15	1982	119	2360
16	1983	115	2260
17	1984	325	2575
18	1985	350	2550
19	1986	302	2503
20	1987	212	2475
21	1988	250	=SUM(LINEST($C$11:$C$20,$B$11:$B$20)*{250,1})
22	1989	275	=SUM(LINEST($C$11:$C$20,$B$11:$B$20)*{275,1})
23	1990	325	=SUM(LINEST($C$11:$C$20,$B$11:$B$20)*{325,1})

Figure 15.8: The final linear regression formulas using arrays

function returns an array of two values: The slope of a regression line that fits the points and the y intercept of the line. This returned array is then used with the SUM function (as in the previous example) to calculate the x value for a known y value. The formula multiplies the first argument of the LINEST function (the slope) by an x value (250) and adds the second part of the LINEST function (the y intercept) multiplied by 1:

$$y \text{ value} = (x \text{ value})* \text{ slope} + (y \text{ intercept})*1$$

The 1 is really a dummy constant, and is only necessary to keep both arrays the same size.

You could also try an exponential regression using the LOGEST function. The other functions that require arrays are GROWTH,

LINEAR REGRESSION
Using Arrays

YEAR	DISP. INCOME $K	SALES K	
1978	$200	$2,350	
1979	$260	$2,500	
1980	$270	$2,400	
1981	$190	$2,390	
1982	$119	$2,360	
1983	$115	$2,260	
1984	$325	$2,575	
1985	$350	$2,550	
1986	$302	$2,503	
1987	$212	$2,475	
1988	$250	$2,453	*
1989	$275	$2,481	*
1990	$325	$2,535	*

*Projected

Figure 15.9: The final printout using arrays

TREND, COLUMNS, ROWS, and TRANSPOSE. The LOOKUP functions and others (such as MIRR) also can use arrays. Even functions that normally use single-value arguments, such as SUM, can also work with array arguments (as with the examples in this chapter).

Chapter 23 contains more examples of linear regression and explains how to do a more complex quadratic regression.

CREATING THE REGRESSION CHART

The creation of charts is described later in Part 5, but you can take the time now to make the regression graph shown in Figure 15.6 if you want. Start with the worksheet of Figure 15.7 and follow these steps:

1. Select All to C20. Pull down the Edit menu and choose Copy. This puts the series data in the Clipboard.

2. Open a new chart. Pull down the Edit menu and choose New. Select Chart on the dialog box. An empty chart will be displayed.

3. Now pull down the Edit menu and choose Paste Special. On this dialog box click Categories in First Column. This will map the first column to the category axis and the second column to the value axis.

4. Pull down the Chart Gallery menu and click Scatter. Click the first option for the scatter chart.

5. Add any axis labels or titles desired.

ARRAY CONSTANTS

In Chapter 7, you created a Cash-Flow Analysis worksheet that had a parameter file with several constants. These constants could then serve as inputs for formulas used elsewhere in the worksheet. In the same way, you could store an array as a single constant and use it in formulas, just as you would an array.

To enter an array of values into any cell, type in the values separated by commas and enclose the array in braces. Use the equal sign and the Command key.

For example, enter = {1,2,3} as an array into a cell range of three cells in the same row. The cell range will contain an array with the values 1, 2, and 3. You can enter arrays with multiple rows by separating the rows with semicolons. For example, the array = {2,4,5;1,2,6} represents an array of five columns and two rows.

When entering array constants, separate rows with commas, and column designations with semicolons. The range will be treated as a single unit. You will not be able to clear or cut individual cells in the array range. You can, however, format and copy individual cells.

RULES FOR USING ARRAYS

Here are some general rules for using arrays:

- The values of an array must be constant values and not formulas. An array can contain numeric, text, logical, or error values (such as #VALUE!). Text values must be enclosed in quotation marks.

- You can use an array with almost any function.

- When an array is used with a function, the type of values must be consistent with what is required by the function.

- When an array formula is entered into a range of cells, the formulas should produce an array that is the same size as the selected cell range.

- Relative cell addresses in an array are considered relative to the cell in the upper-left corner of the range. If you copy an array, the relative references are adjusted.

- You cannot enter arrays that have a mixed number of columns in the rows. For example, {4,9,1;3,4} is an illegal array.

- If an array is used as an argument in a function, all other arguments in the same function should be arrays of the same size. For example, SUM(A7:C7 + A8:C8) is normal. If you use SUM(A7:C7 + B8:C8), Excel will expand the second array to the same size.

- You cannot edit the individual cells or a constant array.

- You can select an array by double-clicking any cell in the array.

EDITING AN ARRAY FORMULA

You can enter an array formula in a range of cells in the same way that you enter any formula in a range of cells: hold down the Command key while you press the Return key. There is a difference, however, when you are editing a formula that has been entered into a range of cells. After an array formula is entered into a range, you

Edit	
Undo Cut	⌘Z
Cut	⌘H
Copy	⌘C
Paste	⌘U
Clear...	⌘B
Paste Special...	
Delete...	⌘K
Insert...	⌘I
Fill Right	⌘R
Fill Down	⌘D

cannot edit or clear an individual cell or delete rows or columns within that range. The entire cell range must be treated as a single unit. You must select and edit or clear the entire range.

You can edit an array formula by using the commands on the Edit menu. If you click the cursor on any point in the formula bar, whatever you type will be entered at the cursor location. You can also drag the cursor in the formula bar to mark a range of characters, then use the Cut command to delete the marked characters. Once you have finished editing the formula, clicking the enter box or pressing the Return key will complete the entry. (Remember, if you enter a constant array to a range of cells, the individual cells of the array cannot be edited.)

LINKING
DOCUMENTS

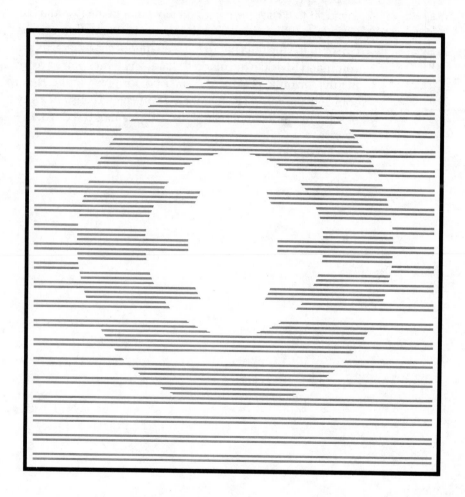

LINKING DOCUMENTS CREATES A RELATIONSHIP IN which a change in one document will automatically affect a cell or cells in the other. In Chapter 3, for example, you created a chart that was linked to a worksheet. If you tried to make any changes in the worksheet, they were immediately reflected in the chart.

You can link cells or cell ranges in two or more documents. This allows you to set up a hierarchical structure of worksheets that will always reflect your most current data.

In this chapter, you will learn some of the basic concepts of linking documents. You will be guided through a simple example, then you will use this example to study the more complex aspects of linking documents.

LINKING WORKSHEETS

When you link cells in different worksheets, the values in one will change whenever you change the values in the other. This is an easy way to be sure that your associated worksheets are up to date without having to enter new data into each one. You can link individual cells of worksheets or whole cell ranges.

LINKING SINGLE CELLS

In this and the more complex examples in the next few chapters, I'll assume that you know the basic procedures. Although you'll be told what to do, I won't include all the steps on how to do it. If you need help, refer to the chapters in the first part of the book.

Let's link two worksheets together to see how linking works. In the following example, you'll link one cell in the Sales Projections worksheet that you created in Chapters 10 through 12 to a cell in a new Cash-Flow Analysis worksheet.

Assume that your Sales Projections worksheet was prepared by the Sales Department manager of a company. She needs to copy the sales totals for all the regions into a new worksheet that will be used by another department in the company for a cash-flow analysis. The projected sales totals will change as the year progresses, and the company's managers want to have the Cash-Flow Analysis worksheet updated automatically to reflect each change.

After you open your Sales Projections worksheet, follow the steps below to create two linked documents:

1. Insert two new rows after row 10 and make cell B11 the sum of cells B6 through B9, as shown in Figure 16.1. Add the hyphens in cell B10, then save this worksheet as **Sales Projections3**.

2. Use the New command on the File menu to open a new worksheet. Move and resize both worksheets so that you can see columns A and B in rows 5 through 11 and some of the first entries under TARGET in the database, as shown in Figure 16.2.

3. Enter the title **Acme Manufacturing** in cell B2 on the second worksheet and **Sales** and **Cost of Goods** in cells A6 and A7, respectively, as the first two row headings.

Figure 16.1: Adding a total

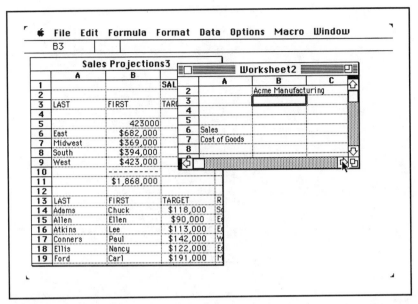

Figure 16.2: Opening the second worksheet

4. Click cell B6 on the new worksheet to indicate that the sales total will be placed in this cell.

5. Enter an equal sign into the formula bar.

6. Click cell B11 in the Sales Projections3 worksheet twice. The first click will make this worksheet partially active, and the second click will enter the formula for cell B11 into cell B6 of the new worksheet.

7. Click the enter box in the formula bar of the new worksheet to complete the entry.

8. The sales total from cell B11 of the Sales Projections3 worksheet is now in cell B6 of the new worksheet, as shown in Figure 16.3.

9. Format the total in the new worksheet by using the Number command on the Format menu.

Now, take a few minutes to examine your worksheets. Look at the formula for cell B6 in the new worksheet (see Figure 16.3). It consists of

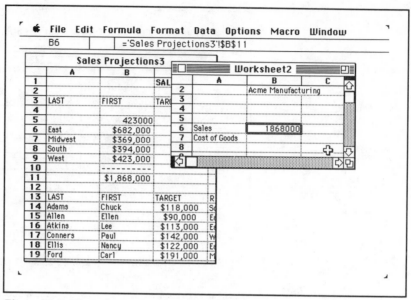

Figure 16.3: The sales total on the second worksheet

the linked worksheet's name in single quotation marks, an exclamation point, and an absolute reference to cell B11 of the linked worksheet. You could have entered the same formula from the keyboard.

In summary, here's how to link a cell in a worksheet to a cell in another worksheet: use the mouse or the keyboard to enter the name of the referenced worksheet, add an exclamation point, and then add cell references or names.

Now, experiment with the linked worksheets to see what happens when you make changes. Change one of the target figures for a name in the Sales Projections database. You will see the total in cell B11 change, as well as the total in cell B6 of the new worksheet.

DEPENDENT AND SUPPORTING DOCUMENTS

Whenever the values of targets in the Sales Projections3 worksheet change, the values in the new worksheet also will change. The new worksheet is called the *dependent document* because the value in at least one of its cells depends on values in another worksheet. The Sales

Projections worksheet, which contains the value for the dependent worksheet, is called the *supporting document.* The dependent worksheet contains an *external reference formula*—a formula that refers to a cell or cell range on the supporting document.

You can create complex and interlinked hierarchical documents that depend on each other at several levels. You can also link several supporting documents to a single dependent document. For example, our theoretical company could have sales worksheets for several regions and use these as supporting documents for a single company-wide Sales Projections worksheet.

Before leaving this section, continue to experiment with the link that you created. What happens, for example, if you save the dependent worksheet, change the values for a target in the supporting worksheet, and then open the dependent worksheet again? Have the values in the dependent worksheet been updated to reflect your change? The next few sections will explain some of the basic rules for linking documents and give you some tips on making the links effective.

LINKING CELL RANGES

In the previous example, you linked a single cell in one worksheet to a single cell in another worksheet. You can also link a range of cells in one worksheet to a range of cells in another worksheet using the same basic procedure.

To link cell ranges, first select the range of cells on the dependent worksheet that you want to contain the formulas. Type in or copy the formula, referencing the appropriate cell range on the supporting worksheet. Then, hold down the Command key and press Return or click the enter box.

USING NAMES TO LINK WORKSHEETS

If you create linked worksheets and then use the Copy or Cut commands to move cells in the supporting worksheet, the relative cell addresses in the formulas will not be adjusted properly. To avoid this problem, use names instead of cell references for the linked cells.

Let's try an example to see how using names can help. With your linked Sales Projections3 and new worksheets open, follow these steps:

1. Select cell B11 on your Sales Projections3 worksheet

2. Pull down the Edit menu and select Cut

3. Select cell C11 on the Sales Projections3 worksheet

4. Pull down the Edit menu and select Paste

You'll see that the total on the dependent worksheet is now incorrect. In other words, the dependent worksheet has not been adjusted to refer to the new location of the sales total cell in the supporting worksheet. If you assign a name to that cell, the dependent worksheet will always be correct, even if you move the referenced cell on the supporting worksheet. Let's do this now:

1. Be sure Total is A11. Select A11:B11

2. Pull down the Formula menu and choose Create Names

3. When the Create Names dialog box shown in Figure 16.4 appears, click Left Column, then click OK (you've given row 11 the name Total)

4. Click cell B6 on the dependent worksheet, type an equal sign, and click cell B11 on the Sales Projections3 worksheet once

5. Pull down the Formula menu, choose Paste Names, and double-click Total in the Paste Names dialog box

6. Click the enter box

Now, repeat the four steps at the beginning of this section. This time, the dependent worksheet will follow your changes in the supporting worksheet.

When you create linked documents, use names as much as possible so that you can freely move and copy cells.

SAVING LINKED DOCUMENTS

Saving linked documents is the same as saving documents that are not linked. Use the Save As command on the File menu to save each of the open documents.

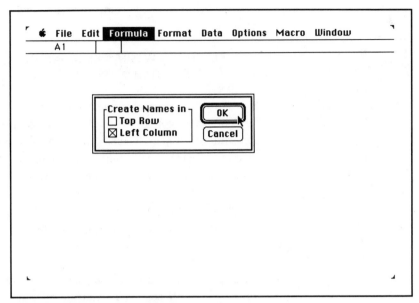

Figure 16.4: Defining the name

USING CLOSED DEPENDENT DOCUMENTS

If the dependent and supporting documents are both open and either active or partially active, changes in the supporting document are always reflected in the dependent document. There may be times, however, when you have the supporting document closed (stored on the disk) while the dependent worksheet is open. To understand what happens in this case, you must distinguish between a simple external reference formula and a complex external reference formula.

A *simple* external reference formula references one of the following:

- A cell or cell range
- A named cell or cell range
- A named constant value

In the previous examples, you used a cell reference and then a named cell, which are simple external references. The following are other examples of simple external references:

```
Sales!East
'Cash Flow Analysis'!$B$3
```

If you want to open the dependent worksheet, but you don't want the dependent cells to be recalculated, use the Calculations command on the Options menu before you open the dependent worksheet. Click Manual in the Calculation dialog box (see Figure 16.6), then click OK. Then, when you open the dependent worksheet, the values will remain as they were when you last closed it.

Any other type of reference is a *complex* external reference. For example,

East!Total + West!Total + Midwest!Total + South!Total
'Cash Flow Analysis'!SUM(A3:A5)

are complex external reference formulas.

Whenever you open or create a document that contains simple external references, Excel will try to calculate the formula. If the supporting worksheet is open, Excel can get the information from the computer memory, as in the last example. If the supporting worksheet is closed, Excel will search for the worksheet on the disk and try to find the values it needs. If Excel can't find the supporting worksheet on the disk, it will display a message and the dialog box shown in Figure 16.5. You can then switch to the disk that contains the supporting worksheet.

Unlike documents with simple external references, when you open a document with complex external reference formulas, the supporting worksheets *must be open*. Excel will not look for any supporting data for complex external references that are not already in the computer memory. If you forget to open all your supporting worksheets, you will get the error message #REF! in the cells that cannot be calculated.

VIEWING AND OPENING LINKS

Each time that you save a dependent document, Excel also saves the names of all the associated supporting worksheets. If you want to see a list of the names of all the worksheets used to support a currently active document, pull down the File menu and choose Open Links. The Open Linked Documents dialog box shown in Figure 16.7 will appear. This dialog box lists the names of all the supporting worksheets.

If you want to open one of these documents, select it and click Open. If you only need to view the list, click Cancel when you're done.

If you selected a worksheet and clicked Open, Excel will open it. You can select more than one worksheet by dragging or selecting the names while pressing the Command key. If Excel cannot find a supporting worksheet specified by the dependent document, it will permit you to change disks.

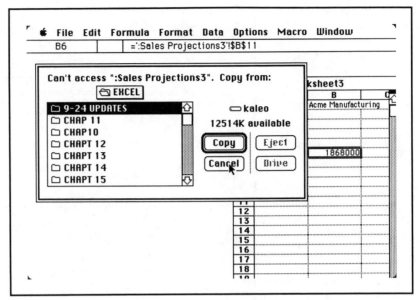

Figure 16.5: Excel tries to find the supporting document

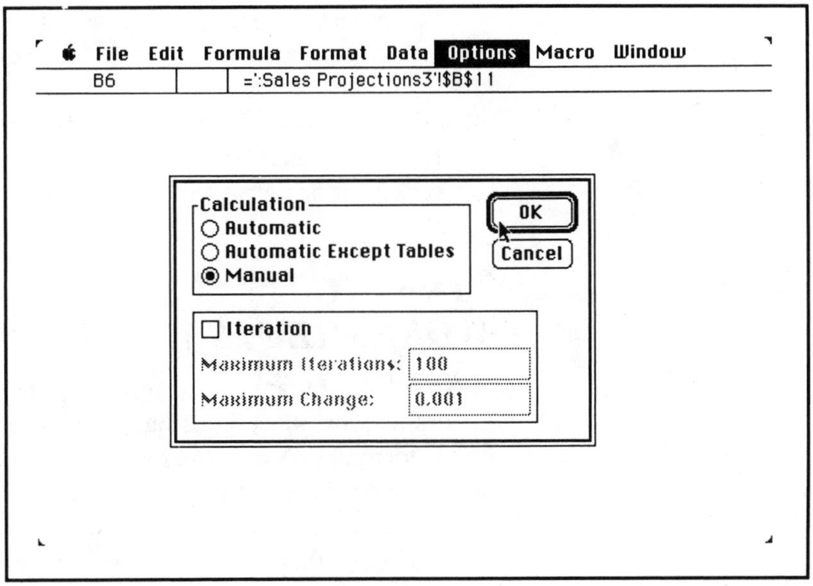

Figure 16.6: Turning off the calculations

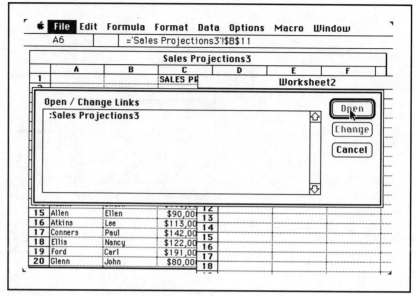

Figure 16.7: Opening the links

REMOVING DOCUMENT LINKS

To remove the links in a dependent worksheet to any supporting document, you only need to remove the references to the supporting document. If you wish to scan a document and be sure that all the links are removed, use the Find command on the Formula menu (not the one on the Data menu). Search for the name of the supporting worksheet or for an exclamation point.

LINKING WORKSHEETS WITH ARRAYS

A worksheet that uses array formulas and references can be linked to another worksheet by using external references, just like any other linked formulas. A cell on a dependent worksheet can reference a cell on a supporting worksheet by using the worksheet name, an exclamation point, and the worksheet cell reference.

Remember that if cells on the supporting worksheet are moved, corresponding references on the dependent worksheet will not follow the move. For this reason, you should use names to define cells or cell ranges. You can assign a name to a cell range within a row or column and use the name as an array on a dependent worksheet. When you use a name as an array, the only additional step that you need to take is to hold down the Command key while you click the enter box or press Return to complete the formula entry. To see how this works, let's link a cell in a new worksheet to the cell that contains the total value in the Inventory worksheet that you created at the beginning of Chapter 15. Follow these steps:

1. Open the Inventory worksheet and define the row titles on it as names (see Chapter 9)

2. Open up a new worksheet window and display both windows on the screen, as shown in Figure 16.8

3. Enter the title Inventory Summary in cell B1 of the new worksheet

4. Select cell B3 as the cell for the total, pull down the Formula menu, and choose Paste Function (you'll see the Paste Function dialog box shown in Figure 16.9)

5. Scroll to SUM and double-click it

6. Click anywhere in the Inventory worksheet to partially select the window, pull down the Formula menu, and select Paste Name (you'll see the Paste Name dialog box shown in Figure 16.10)

7. Double-click Qty_on_Hand

8. Enter * from the keyboard

9. Pull down the Formula menu, choose Paste Name, and double-click Cost in the Paste Name dialog box

Now note this difference:

10. Hold down the Command key and click the enter box or press Return

The correct total is now in cell B3 on the new worksheet, and the formula is in its formula bar, as shown in Figure 16.11.

Formula

Paste Name...
Paste Function...
Reference   ⌘`

Define Name...   ⌘L
Create Names...

Goto...   ⌘G
Find...   ⌘H
Select Last Cell
Show Active Cell

Formula

Paste Name...
Paste Function.
Reference   ⌘`

Define Name...   ⌘L
Create Names...

Goto...   ⌘G
Find...   ⌘H
Select Last Cell
Show Active Cell

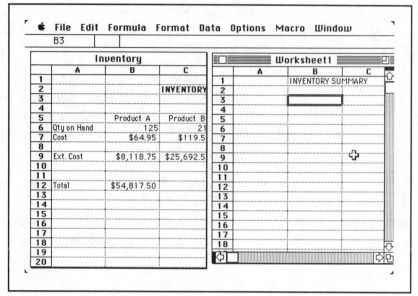

Figure 16.8: Displaying the two worksheets

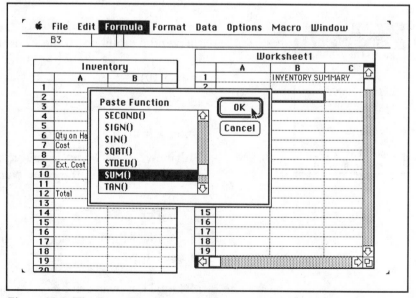

Figure 16.9: The Paste Function dialog box

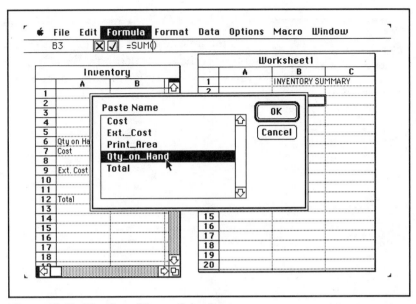

Figure 16.10: The Paste Name dialog box

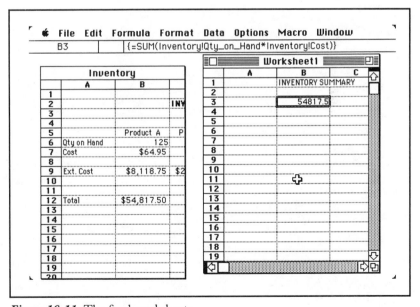

Figure 16.11: The final worksheets

SUMMARY

Using linked worksheets is easier than creating large worksheets that are cumbersome to scroll and update.

You have now had some experience in creating linked worksheets. You also have learned how Excel uses external references to create links between supporting and dependent worksheets. For information on linking charts, refer to Chapter 19.

PRINTING WORKSHEETS

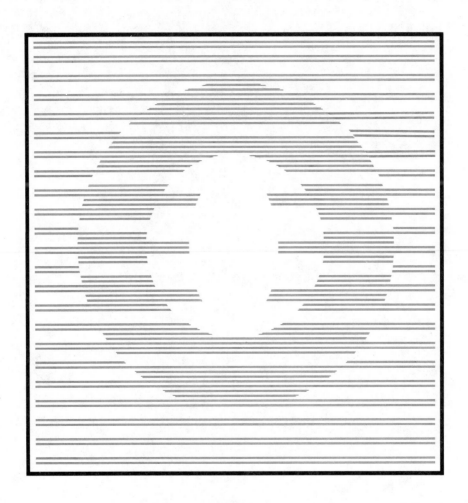

EXCEL INCLUDES MANY FEATURES THAT MAKE IT easy to create presentation quality reports from your worksheet. You can add headers and footers, define your own page breaks, print specific worksheet ranges, print a report sideways or on special paper, control the margins, turn grid lines on and off, and activate several other special features. In this chapter you will learn to use all the printing features of Excel.

THE FILE MENU OPTIONS

There are three options on the File menu that control printing: Printer Setup, Print, and Page Setup.

The Printer Setup option must be used the first time you use Excel, but you won't have to use it again unless you change printers. It selects the printer type and baud rate.

The Print command, however, must be used before every printing cycle. It displays the Print dialog box, which controls the quality of the print, the amount of pages that are printed, the number of copies, and the type of paper feed.

The third file menu command, Page Setup, allows you to add special effects to your printout such as reduction, orientation, headers, footers, margins, and row/column headings or gridline printing.

THE PRINTER SETUP DIALOG BOX

The Printer Setup dialog box permits you to choose the output port for printing the worksheets. You can choose between the normal printer output port or the serial port. The default is the standard printer output port.

THE PRINT DIALOG BOX

The actual printing action for a worksheet or chart is initiated from the File menu with the Print command or by typing Command-P. This displays the Print dialog box shown in Figure 17.1. Excel remembers the selections you make on this dialog box and applies them to the next print cycle unless you change them in between. The Print selections are discussed individually below.

The contents of the dialog boxes shown in this chapter will vary with the type of printer and the version of the print driver that you are using. The figures in this chapter apply to the ImageWriter printer with driver version 2.6.

PRINTING OPTIONS The Print dialog box offers you a variety of ways that you can print your document. The options will vary with your printer, but if you have an ImageWriter you have the options listed below.

Quality You can choose from three levels of quality for your printed output: Draft, Faster, or Best. On the ImageWriter, Best produces the highest quality output, but the printing is only 45 characters a

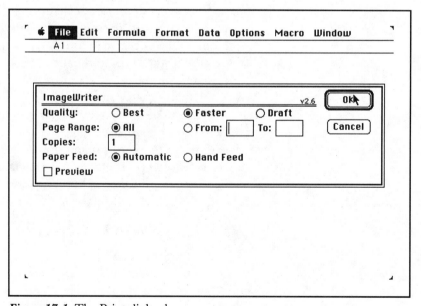

Figure 17.1: The Print dialog box

second. Faster prints a worksheet much faster at 180 characters a second, but the quality is not as good. Draft is the fastest (250 characters per second), but is poor quality and the gridlines are omitted.

Page Range   The default of the Page Range option is All. However, if you made minor changes to your worksheet and want to print only a part of it, or if the printer jams on a page and you need only that page printed, select the From box and fill in the pages you want to print.

Copies   This option determines how many copies of the worksheet are printed. The default is one.

Paper Feed   The Paper Feed option controls whether automatic (continuous) or hand feed is used with the printer. If you select Hand Feed, printing will stop between each page so you can insert a new page.

PREVIEWING A PRINT   Use the Preview option in the Print dialog box if you want to see a screen display showing what a particular worksheet will look like when it is printed. Excel will display an entire printed page on the screen. You cannot print the preview image so you must turn off the Preview mode before you can actually print the worksheet.

THE PAGE SETUP DIALOG BOX

Use the Page Setup command on the File menu to bring up the dialog box shown in Figure 17.2. The options in this dialog box will vary with the printer and driver version you use. The screen is created by the operating system, not Excel.

HEADERS AND FOOTERS   A *header* is a line of text that prints on the top of every page. A *footer* is a line of text that prints at the bottom of every page. By default, Excel will print the file name of the document as a header and the page number as a footer.

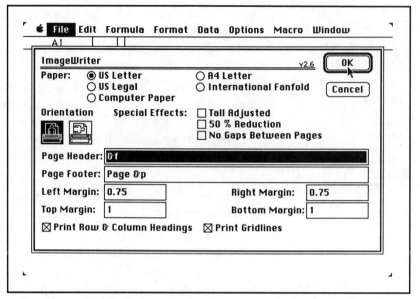

Figure 17.2: The Page Setup dialog box

To set a different header or footer, you must first clear the defaults. Select Page Header or Page Footer, drag the cursor until the entire text area is dark, then press Delete. Then enter the new text in the Page Header or Page Footer box and click OK.

You can justify headers and footers and include a date, time, and page number. You can also control the style of headers and footers. The control codes that you can use in creating headers and footers are listed in Table 17.1.

Try turning off the default headers and footers on your Balance worksheet. Load the worksheet, then pull down the File menu and click Page Setup. When the Page Setup dialog box appears, the cursor will be on the Page Header entry. Press the Delete key, and the Page Header box will clear. Drag the cursor over the Page Footer box until it turns dark, then press the Delete key again to clear the current footer entry. Click OK and your worksheet will be printed without a file name or page number.

PRINTING SIDEWAYS   With the ImageWriter printer, you can use the Page Setup command on the File menu to print a worksheet

SYMBOL	FUNCTION
&L	Left-justify following characters
&C	Center following characters
&R	Right-justify following characters
&P	Print page number
&D	Print current date
&T	Print current time
&F	Print the name of the document
&B	Print in boldface
&I	Print in italics
&&	Print an ampersand

Note: You can combine two or more of these in a header or footer.

Table 17.1: Header and Footer Control Codes

vertically or horizontally. Select Page Setup from the File menu, then click the alternate orientation. If you then print your file, it will be printed sideways. Use this option if your worksheet has many columns but very few rows.

REDUCING A WORKSHEET AND OTHER EFFECTS In some cases your worksheet may be too large for a page, but you can fit it on a page by reducing it. The special effects option on this menu allows you to print your worksheet at a 50 percent reduction.

You can use this same menu to select two other paging options:

- No Gaps Between Pages: Choosing this option tells Excel to print over the perforation. This can be useful when you are printing a large worksheet that extends over a page.

- Paper: Excel offers five different paper sizes to choose from.

THE OPTIONS MENU

The Options menu controls the printing of ranges, titles, break settings, font selection, and the printing of formulas or values. Remember that the Format menu controls individual cells while the Options menu controls the entire worksheet.

PRINTING A RANGE

You can choose to print just part of a worksheet. This is particularly useful when you're working with only a portion of a very large worksheet.

To print part of a worksheet, first select the range to be printed. Pull down the Options menu and choose Set Print Area. Then, pull down the File menu and select Print. Excel names the area that you selected Print_Area. You can refer to this area in other commands by using this name (see Chapter 9).

Subsequent printings will again print this same range. To turn off the printing of a range and print the entire worksheet, use the Define Names command on the Formula menu and delete the Print_Area name.

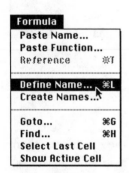

As an example, follow these steps:

1. Select the cell range that you want to print

2. Pull down the Options menu and choose Set Print Area

3. Pull down the File menu and choose Print

4. When the Print dialog box appears, click OK

Your printout will contain only the area of the worksheet that you selected. Another example of this procedure is included in the Printing Formulas section later in this chapter.

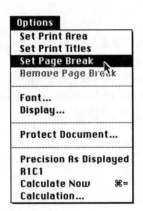

SETTING A PAGE BREAK

You can force a page break at any point in the worksheet. First select any cell in the row that you want the page break to come *before*. Pull down the Options menu and choose Set Page Break. The row with the selected cell will be the first row of the next page.

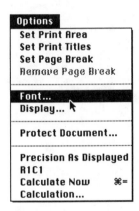

To remove a page break, first select a cell in the row below the page break. Pull down the Options menu and choose Remove Page Break.

PRINTING PAGE TITLES

You can select certain rows or columns to be printed on each page. This is particularly useful for printing column or row titles on each page of a worksheet.

To print a particular row at the top of each page, select the row, pull down the Options menu, and choose Set Print Titles. When you print the worksheet, the selected row will be at the top of each page. If you want to print a column at the left edge of each page, first select the column, then follow the same procedure. Excel names the area that you selected Print_Titles. You can refer to this area in other commands by using this name (see Chapter 9).

PRINTING FORMULAS

Sometimes it is helpful to have a printout of the formulas that were used for a worksheet. A printout with formulas is useful for documenting a worksheet so that you have a record of the equations used. The basic procedure for printing formulas is simple: display the formulas, then print the worksheet. For example, let's print the formulas for the two columns of your Cash-Flow Analysis worksheet. Open that worksheet and follow these steps:

1. Pull down the Options menu and choose Display.

2. When the Display dialog box shown in Figure 17.3 appears, click Formulas, then click OK. The formulas are now displayed in each column. Notice that the columns are twice as wide as your regular column setting so that the formulas will fit.

3. Pull down the Options menu and select Font. Set the Font size to **9** so that three columns are displayed.

4. Pull down the File menu and choose Page Setup. The Page Setup dialog box (Figure 17.2) appears. Be sure that the setup is Tall and not 50% reduced, then click OK.

Figure 17.3: The Display dialog box

5. Select columns A through C, pull down the Options menu, and choose Set Print Area.

6. Pull down the File menu and choose Print.

7. When the Print dialog box (Figure 17.1) is displayed, click OK.

You should now have a printout showing the formulas in the selected area. The final printout is shown in Figure 17.4.

SUMMARY

Now you've seen how Excel makes it possible for you to create presentation quality spreadsheets that can be used for reports, slides, or overheads, Chapter 6 introduced fonts, borders, and styles you can use to emphasize your conclusions. This chapter has extended these techniques to include options to control the printing of gridlines, column and row headings, and formulas. This chapter also introduced the techniques for printing headers and footers.

	A	B	C
1			
2			
3			
4			
5			
6			
7		29586	29617
8			
9	CASH ON HAND	43000	=B37
10			
11	INCOME		
12	Sale of Goods	83394	110237
13	Sale of Services	6432	10234
14	Total Sales	=B12+B13	=C12+C13
15	Interest Income	=($L$3/12)*B9	=($L$3/12)*C9
16		----------	----------
17	Total Income	=B14+B15	=C14+C15
18			
19	EXPENSES		
20	Cost of Goods	=$L$4*B12	=$L$4*C12
21	Rent	11543	8923
22	Salaries	19894	15234
23	Taxes	1204	1094
24	Supplies	2050	2050
25	Repairs	2873	2873
26	Advertising	=$L$5*B12	=0.1*C14
27	Insurance	734	734
28	Utilties	2345	2345
29	Emp. Benefits	1234	1234
30	Dues, Subscriptions	254	254
31	Travel	1432	1432
32	Miscellaneous	500	500
33		----------	----------
34	Total Expenses	=SUM(B20:B32)	=SUM(C20:C32)
35			
36	Net Income	=B17-B34	=C17-C34
37	Net Cash on Hand	=B9+B36	=C9+C36

Do not use the Options Display command to turn off row and column headings or the gridlines for printing. These options refer only to the display. Use File Page Setup to turn these off while printing.

Figure 17.4: The printout with formulas

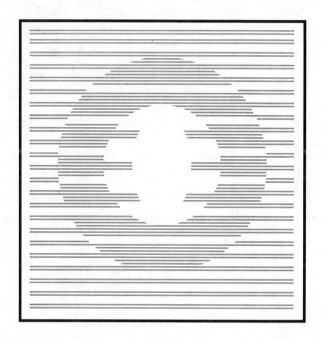

GRAPHICS

EXCEL'S CHARTING CAPABILITIES GIVE YOU AN easy and effective way to illustrate the results of your worksheet and database analyses. Graphs convey the full significance of what you are presenting in a concise and persuasive manner. You can use them to show relationships, comparisons, and trends.

Using Excel, you can create a graphic representation of your data with only a few clicks of the mouse. The graphs will be dynamically linked to your data—whenever the data change, your graphs will change too. With Excel, you also have a wide choice of formats and features to use with your graphs. You can choose from 42 different types of graphs to present your data. You can alter fonts on any part of the graph, add arrows, and include comments to add clarity.

USING GRAPHICS AND CHARTS

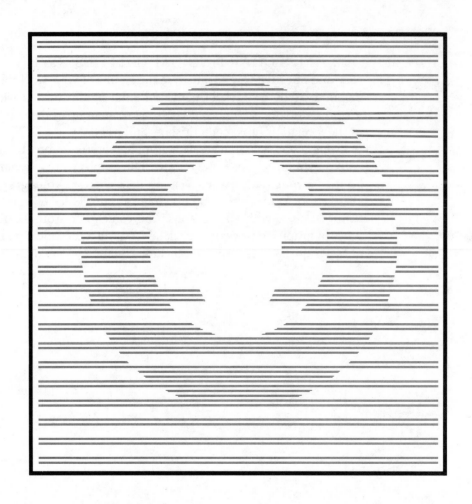

IN THIS CHAPTER, YOU WILL PRODUCE A SIMPLE graph from a worksheet that you created earlier. While you're working with this simple graph, you will quickly see the advantages of adding graphic presentations to your reports.

GRAPHS AND CHARTS

Graphs and charts show visual relationships. They are especially useful for relaying information to busy people who don't have the time to pore over tables of numbers. Although the Excel documentation uses *chart* and *graph* interchangeably, I make a distinction between the two terms. A graph is a visual presentation of one or more sets of data. A chart is a single document that displays graphics. You could create one chart from several graphs.

Figure 18.1 shows the various components of a chart. These components are described below:

- Axes: The straight lines used on the graph for measurement and reference. A pie chart has no real axis; all other types have two: the x axis (the horizontal line) and the y axis (the vertical line). The x axis shows the data classification, and the y axis shows the quantity or unit of measure.

- Markers: The Type of indicator used on the graph to represent the data. A column graph uses vertical bars filled with a pattern for markers. A line graph uses small symbols.

- Tick marks: The small vertical lines that divide the axes. They are used to indicate categories (e.g., quantities or regions) and scales (e.g., dollars or another type of measurement).

- Plot area: The area bounded by the axes or, in the case of a pie chart, the area within the circle.

- Scale: The range of values covered by the y axis of the chart.
- Legend: The symbols and labels used to identify the different types of data on the chart.
- X-axis label: The title for the x axis.
- Y-axis label: The title for the y axis.
- Chart title: The text that is the title of the graph or chart.
- Grid Lines: Optional horizontal or vertical lines in the plot area that help the viewer determine the value of a marker.

Each marker on a graph represents a data point. A set of related markers is a data series. With the exception of the pie chart, you can plot several data series on a single graph by using different types of markers, as shown in Figure 18.1. In a pie chart, you can represent only a single data series.

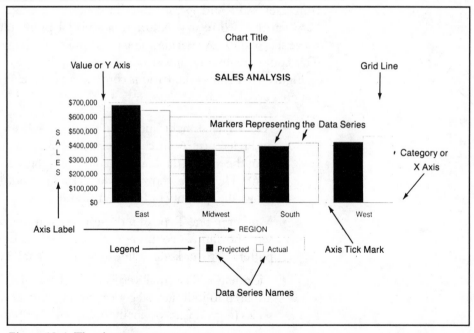

Figure 18.1: The chart components

TYPES OF GRAPHS

The type of graph that you should use for a particular presentation depends upon what you are trying to communicate. With Excel, you can create any of 42 different types of graphs. These can be divided into six general types:

- Column graphs: Useful for representing quantitative information, particularly for making comparisons between groups of data. Figure 18.1 is an example of a column graph.

- Bar graphs: The same as column graphs, except that they are rotated 90 degrees. The categories are on the vertical axis and the values are on the horizontal axis. Figure 18.2 shows a bar graph that is used to compare sales-forecast figures with actual sales.

- Line graphs: Useful for describing and comparing numerical information, especially for showing trends or changes over time. Figure 18.3 shows a line graph that is used to indicate the growth in sales of a product over a period of time.

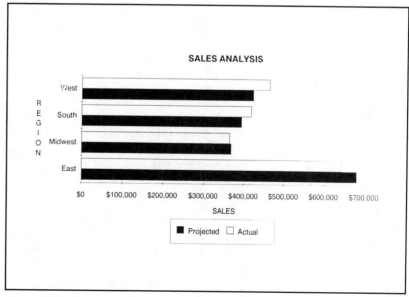

Figure 18.2: A bar graph

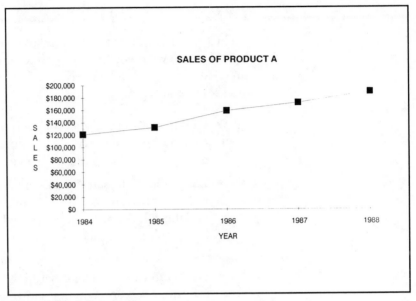

Figure 18.3: A line graph

- Pie charts: Useful for showing the relationship of quantitative data as they relate to the whole. Figure 18.4 shows a pie chart created from the same data that was used for the bar chart in Figure 18.1.

- Area graphs: Useful for showing the relative importance of different data. Figure 18.5 shows an area graph that compares the sales of two products.

- Scatter graphs: Useful for showing the relationship between two variables. The individual data points are marked, but the relationship between these points is left to the observer. Figure 18.6 shows a scatter graph with points representing income and sales figures.

You may create a chart and then decide that the type of graph that you selected does not suit the chart's purpose. This is not a problem – you will find it very easy to convert one type of Excel graph to another with only a few clicks of the mouse. You should feel free to experiment with the different types until you've created a chart that communicates what you intended.

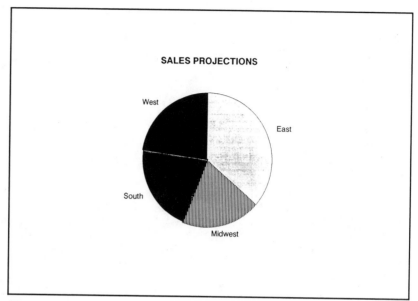

Figure 18.4: A pie chart

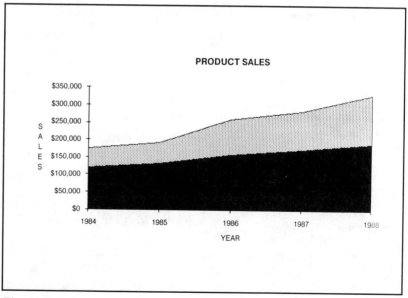

Figure 18.5: An area graph

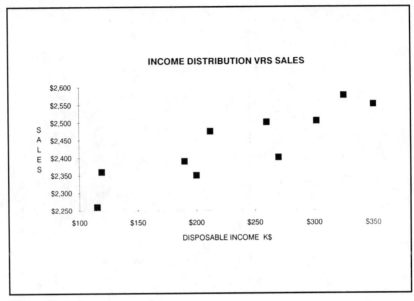

Figure 18.6: A scatter graph

CREATING A CHART

Now you can create a chart. Start Excel with the Sales Projections worksheet that you created in Chapter 12 by double-clicking the Sales Projections icon. You should see the worksheet shown in Figure 18.7. To chart the regional sales as a column graph follow these steps:

1. Identify the data series that you want to show on the graph by clicking cell A6 and dragging to cell B9

2. Pull down the File menu and choose New

3. When the New dialog box shown in Figure 18.8 is displayed, click Chart, then click OK

You should now see the chart shown in Figure 18.9. Notice that Excel automatically scales the y axis, creates the column categories, and labels the columns. You also will see a new menu bar at the top of the screen.

SALES PROJECTIONS				
LAST	FIRST	TARGET	REGION	ACTUAL
			West	
	423000	465000		
East	$682,000	645000		423000
Midwest	$369,000	365000		
South	$394,000	418000		
West	$423,000	465000		
LAST	FIRST	TARGET	REGION	ACTUAL
Adams	Chuck	$118,000	South	$110,000
Allen	Ellen	$90,000	East	$95,000
Atkins	Lee	$113,000	East	$80,000
Conners	Paul	$142,000	West	$165,000
Ellis	Nancy	$122,000	East	$115,000
Ford	Carl	$191,000	Midwest	$185,000
Glenn	John	$80,000	South	$95,000
Harris	Ken	$176,000	West	$190,000
Jackson	Robert	$112,000	East	$110,000
Keller	Janet	$105,000	West	$110,000
Kennedy	Sandra	$135,000	East	$125,000
Linn	Vera	$80,000	Midwest	$85,000
Parker	Greg	$196,000	South	$213,000
Peterson	Tom	$98,000	Midwest	$95,000
Stevens	Carla	$110,000	East	$120,000

Figure 18.7: The Sales Projection worksheet

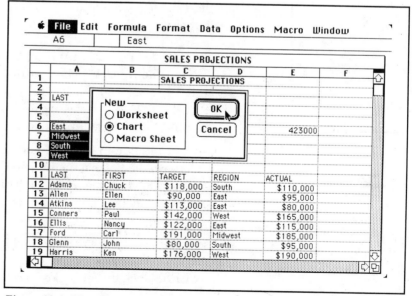

Figure 18.8: The New dialog Box

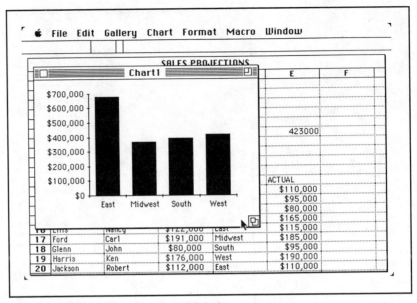

Figure 18.9: The chart after the initial plot

The chart still needs a title and axes labels. You can create these by following the steps below:

1. Add a title. Pull down the Chart menu and choose Attach Text. When the Attach Text dialog box shown in Figure 18.10 is displayed, click OK. Enter the title 1988 SALES PROJECTIONS to the title area that is now marked on the graph. Click the enter box to complete the entry.

2. To put the title in boldface and larger print, click the title, pull down the Format menu, and select Text. When the dialog box shown in Figure 18.11 is displayed, click Bold in the Style box, click 12 for the font size, and then click OK.

3. Add a label for the y axis. Pull down the Chart menu and select Attach Text. When the dialog box appears, click Value Axis, then click OK, as shown in Figure 18.12. Enter SALES. Click the enter box to complete the entry.

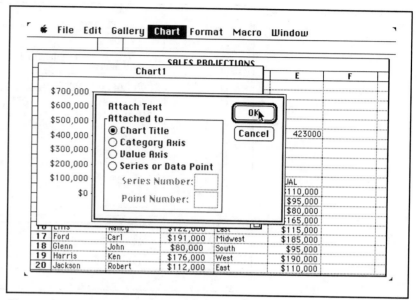

Figure 18.10: Adding the title

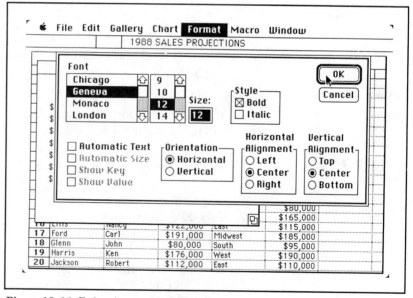

Figure 18.11: Enlarging and boldfacing the title

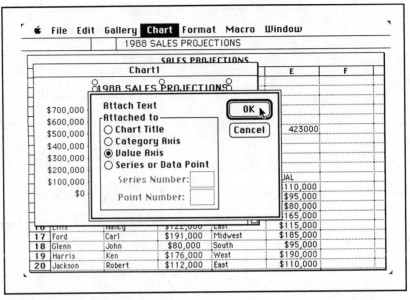

Figure 18.12: Labeling the y axis

4. Format the y-axis label so that it appears vertically. Click the y-axis label. Pull down the Format menu and select Text. Click Vertical in the Orientation box when the dialog box appears (see Figure 18.11), then click OK.

5. Add a label for the x axis. Pull down the Chart menu and choose Attach Text. Click Category Axis in the dialog box (see Figure 18.12), then click OK. Enter the title **REGION**. Click the enter box to complete the entry.

When you've finished creating the chart, you can print it. Pull down the File menu, choose Print, then click OK in the dialog box (see Figure 18.13). The final printout is shown in Figure 18.14. You should also save the chart. Select the chart, pull down the File menu, and click Save As. In the dialog box shown in Figure 18.15, enter 1988 SALES CHART, then click OK.

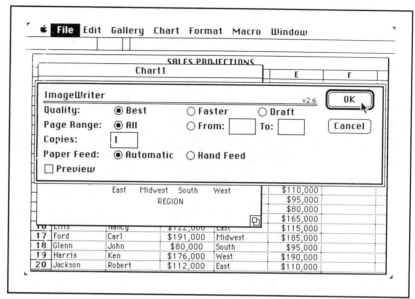

Figure 18.13: The Print dialog box

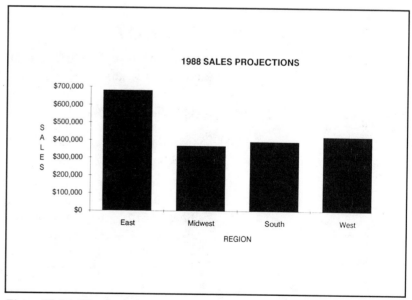

Figure 18.14: The final chart

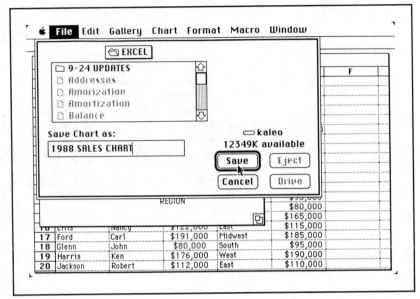

Figure 18.15: Saving the chart

WORKING WITH CHARTS

Once you have created a chart, you can change its size, data-point values, and category names. After you use the sizing box to make the window smaller, you can try the following experiments to see how these changes affect your chart:

1. Select the worksheet, then the chart. What happens to the menu bar?

2. Change the width of the chart, then the height using the sizing window. What happens? The scaling automatically adjusts, and the category labels take two lines if necessary. Adjust the windows so that you can see the target value for the second person in the eastern region on the database, as well as the chart. Figure 18.16 shows the windows now.

3. Change a data-point value. Select cell C13 and change the value to zero. What happens this time? The scaling on the chart changes, and the columns are redrawn, as shown in Figure 18.17.

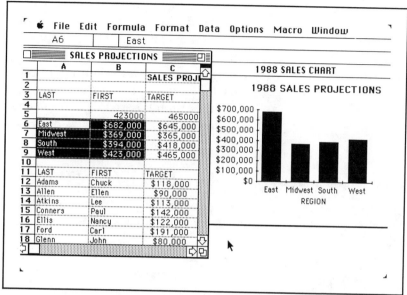

Figure 18.16: Displaying both windows

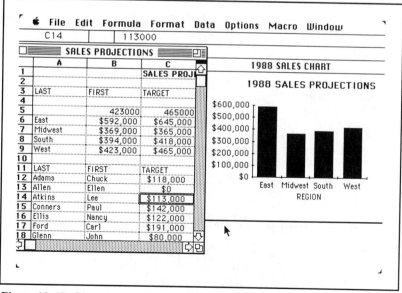

Figure 18.17: Changing the data-point value

4. Change a category name. Select cell A6 and change the value to **Europe.** What happens to the chart? The category labels change, and the chart is redrawn, as shown in Figure 18.18.

As you can see, Excel quickly responds to any changes that you make to the chart or to the worksheet cells that contain the data on which the graph is based. It also can change the chart to an entirely different type just as quickly, as described below.

CHANGING CHART TYPES

Before continuing, create the chart shown in Figure 18.9. You can do this by closing the existing windows, opening the Sales Projections worksheet, selecting cells A6 to B9, and clicking Open on the File menu.

Once you've recreated the chart, you can practice changing the type, legend, and other features. This is how you would change it into a pie chart:

Gallery

Area...
Bar...
✓Column...
Line...
Pie...
Scatter...
Combination...

Preferred

1. Select the chart window, then pull down the Gallery menu and select Pie. The Pie dialog box shown in Figure 18.19 is displayed.

2. Double-click box 5 in the lower left of the dialog box (or click the box and then click OK). Excel displays a pie chart, as shown in Figure 18.20, using the same data that were plotted on your original bar chart.

It is very easy to change a chart type. In creating charts, experiment with different chart types using the Chart Gallery menu to explore different presentation possibilities. Choose the type that best communicates what you want to say.

Before going on, you may wish to experiment with other options on the various menus on the chart menu bar. Try creating other types of graphs. Be sure when you have finished that you close all windows, but do not save the chart or worksheet again.

SUMMARY

In this chapter, you have created a simple chart and experimented with a few of Excel's chart features. Chapter 19 provides information about advanced charting techniques.

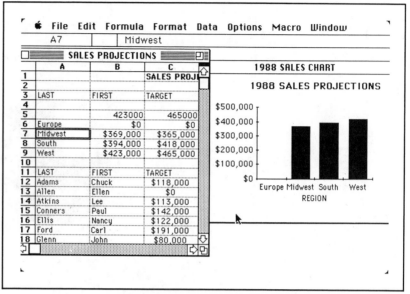

Figure 18.18: Changing a category name

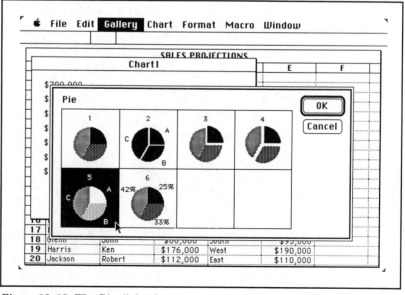

Figure 18.19: The Pie dialog box

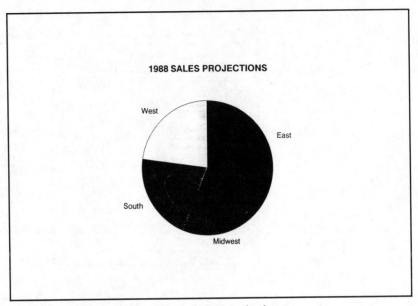

Figure 18.20: The bar chart changed into a pie chart

ADVANCED CHARTING TECHNIQUES

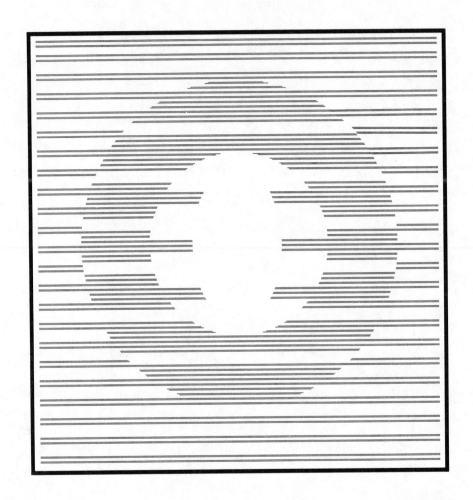

CHAPTER 19

IN CHAPTER 18, YOU WERE INTRODUCED TO EXCEL'S charting capabilities and you learned the basic concepts of charting. This chapter explains how Excel treats the data series that you chart and how it uses the SERIES function to control what is graphed. You will also learn more about formatting the chart and the details of adding text, legends, and grid lines.

You will see that Excel's charting features are extremely flexible. Unlike the worksheet, you can control the font and style of every area of the chart. You can use overlays and copy and paste data series from one chart or worksheet to another chart. You can design presentation-quality charts that communicate quickly and effectively.

THE DATA SERIES

Charts are created from one or more data series. A data series is a collection of data points, each related to the other by some aspect. A data series could also be considered a series of values and a corresponding set of categories. In Figure 19.1, for example, the data series has four data points. The categories are the four regions, and the values for the categories are the sales projections.

A data series is always made up of numeric values. Categories can be either text or numeric values. If you do not specify the categories, Excel will assume that they are sequential numbers (1, 2, 3 . . .). Charting a data series is very easy. You simply select the data series on the worksheet that you wish to chart, pull down the File menu, choose New, and click Chart in the New dialog box.

DATA SERIES ASSUMPTIONS

Understanding how Excel defines the data series is very important. Figure 19.2 shows some examples of how the data series,

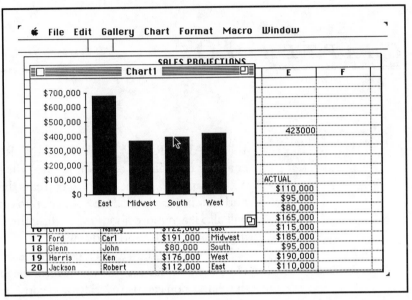

Figure 19.1: The data series

names, and categories are defined. When you create a new chart or copy an existing one, Excel makes the following assumptions about the data series:

- If a data series is longer than it is wide, the text in the left column is used to define the categories, and each column after the first is used as a data series. The column heading, if selected, is used as the data series name.

- If the data series is wider than it is long, the column headings are used to define the categories, and each row of values becomes a data series. The row heading is used as the data-series name.

- If the data series is square or the category headings are numeric, Excel does not define any categories for the chart, and each row of values is used as a data series.

CHANGING DATA SERIES DEFINITIONS

You can change the way that Excel defines the data series by using Copy on the worksheet Edit menu, then the Paste Special command

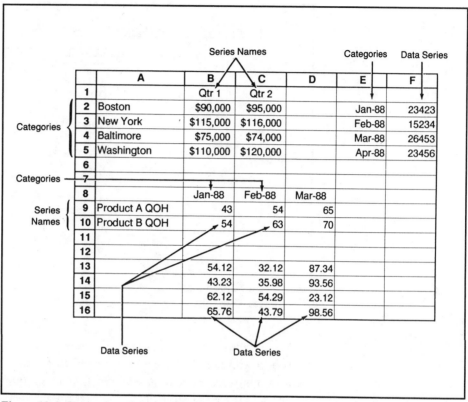

Figure 19.2: Examples of data series, series names, and categories

on the Chart Edit menu. When you click the Paste Special command, the dialog box shown in Figure 19.3 will appear. The options in this dialog box allow you to define a series of numeric values as your category headings or to switch Excel's normal definitions (see Figure 19.2) so that the chart has more data series than categories.

ADDING A DATA SERIES

After you've created a chart, you can easily add another data series to it. First, select the values for the new data series on the worksheet. Pull down the Edit menu on the worksheet menu bar and choose Copy. Click anywhere on the chart once, to select it. Then, use either the Paste or Paste Special command (as described above) on the Edit menu of the chart menu bar to paste the data series onto the chart.

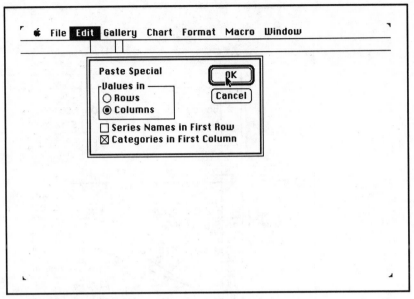

Figure 19.3: Using the Paste Special command

As an example, let's first create a chart from a single data series, then add another data series to the existing chart. Open the Sales Projections worksheet that you created in Chapter 13 (see Figure 19.4) and create the chart from the first data series:

1. Select cells A6 through B9

2. Pull down the File menu and choose New

3. Double-click Chart and you will see the chart shown in Figure 19.5

Now, copy and paste the second data series onto this same chart:

1. Select cells C6 through C9 on the Actual Sales worksheet

2. Pull down the Edit menu and select Copy

3. Select the chart

4. Pull down the Edit menu and choose Paste

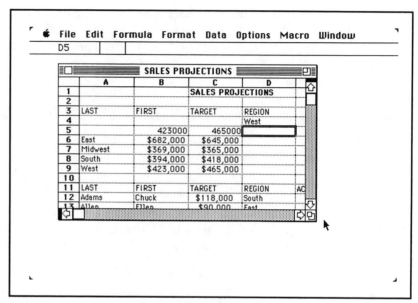

Figure 19.4: The Sales Projections worksheet

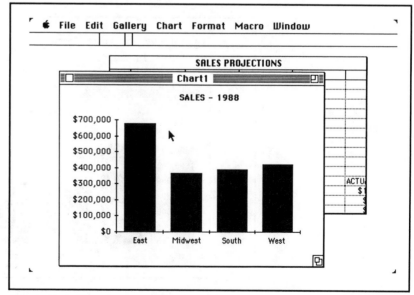

Figure 19.5: Charting a single data series

The final chart is shown in Figure 19.6.

Using this method, you can continue to copy and paste additional data series onto the chart. The new data series can be from the same worksheet or from another worksheet.

THE SERIES FUNCTION

Excel uses the SERIES function to create graphs. This function has four arguments:

1. The data-series title, if one exists, in quotation marks

2. The category titles, which include the external reference to the linked worksheet

3. The data-series definition, which also includes a reference to the linked worksheet

4. The plot-order value

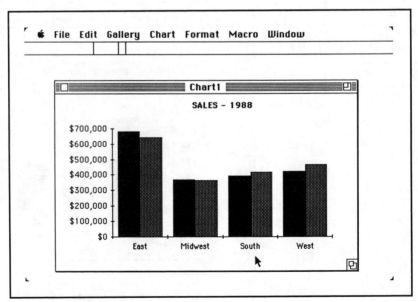

Figure 19.6: The final chart

If you include a row or column title when you select the worksheet area to be graphed, Excel will automatically make that the data-series title argument. The category titles and data- series definition arguments are actually arrays, and they follow the rules for using arrays (see Chapter 15).

You can enter all of the SERIES arguments by pointing and clicking or by typing them in from the keyboard. The function can be edited in the formula bar, just like any other formula. For example, you can enter your own data-series title and then point and click to enter the next two arguments.

You can see an example of the SERIES function by clicking any one of the black columns on the graph that you just created (Figure 19.6). The formula bar will display the SERIES function used to create that graph, as shown in Figure 19.7. In this example, the first argument is missing because a data-series title did not exist. The second argument defines the cells with the categories, and the third argument defines the cells with the values for the data series. The

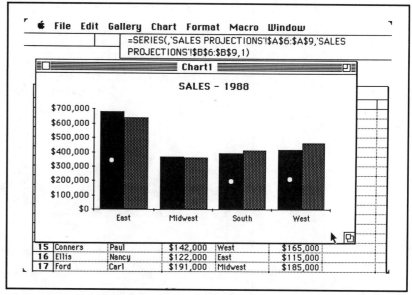

Figure 19.7: The SERIES function for the first data series

fourth argument defines the plot order, which is a value of 1 because this data series is the first one plotted on the graph. The white dots indicate the selected series.

Now, click any patterned column on the same graph, and the formula bar will display the function shown in Figure 19.8. The first argument, the data-series title, is omitted. The second argument defines the same categories used for the first plot, the third argument defines the cells with the values for the second data series, and the plot-order argument has a value of 2, indicating that this is the second plot on the graph.

Notice also how the chart is linked to the Sales Projections worksheet—the worksheet title and exclamation point are a part of the second and third arguments. This means that any time that the worksheet values change, the chart will also change to show a graph of the updated data series.

Now close the chart (without saving it) and create a new chart with the values of cells A5 through B9 on the Sales Projections worksheet. Click any column on the graph and examine the formula bar. This

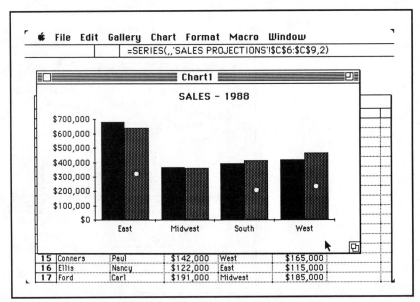

Figure 19.8: The SERIES function for the second data series

time, the first argument is the same as the column title on the worksheet (423000), and it becomes the title on the chart, as shown in Figure 19.9. In the function, the title is enclosed in quotation marks.

You can copy and paste the second data series from the worksheet onto the graph, but be sure to select only cells C6 through C9. If you copy and paste cells C5 through C9, the column title will be used in the first argument of the SERIES function as the data-series title, and it will be the chart title unless you change it using the Attach Text command on the Chart menu, as described below.

The next two sections explain how you can edit a graph's SERIES function to change the data-series titles, the legend titles, and the plot order.

EDITING TITLES AND LEGENDS

Excel automatically makes a graph's legend titles the same as the data-series titles in the first argument of the SERIES function. You can edit the legend by editing the data-series title in the formula bar.

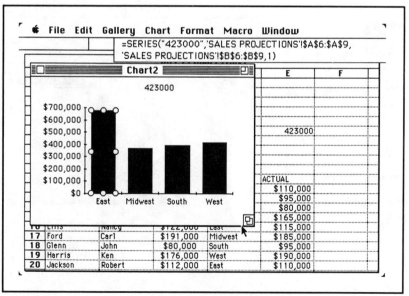

Figure 19.9: Using the data series title as a chart title

Now, let's create another chart from the Sales Projections worksheet. This time, you'll edit the data-series titles and add a legend. Follow these steps:

1. Create a new chart showing the projected sales values by selecting cells A5 through B9 and using the New command on the File menu. The chart will be created, but the title will be wrong.

2. Copy and paste the range of cells C6 through C9 onto this same chart to show the actual sales values.

3. Select one of the black columns on the chart and edit the formula bar so that the current title, "423000", becomes **"Projected Sales"**. To do this, pull down the Edit menu and use the Cut command to remove the current title. Then, type in the new title from the keyboard, as shown in Figure 19.10. Click the enter box when you're done.

4. Click a patterned column. This data series has no title. Add the new title **"Sales Projections"** into the formula bar by typing it in from the keyboard, as shown in Figure 19.11.

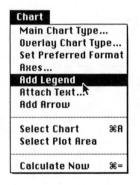

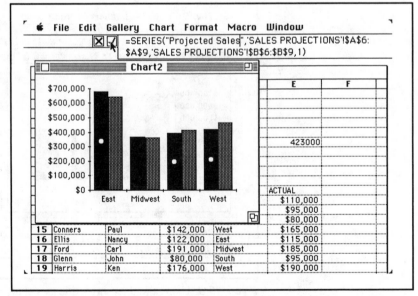

Figure 19.10: Entering a title for the first data series

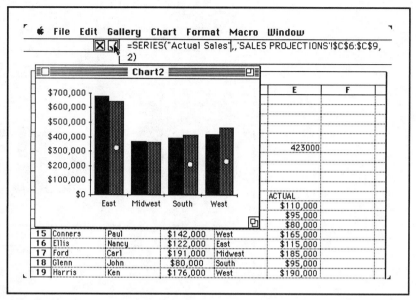

Figure 19.11: Entering the second data series title

5. Pull down the Chart menu and choose Add Legend.

The final chart should look like Figure 19.12. Save the chart (pull down the File menu and select Save As)—you will need it later.

ALTERING THE PLOT ORDER

Excel automatically plots the various data series in the order that you select them. You can alter the plot order by editing the fourth argument in the SERIES function, which is the one that controls the plot order. If you change the plot number to the number of another data series, the other series will be renumbered appropriately. For example, if you changed the plot order value for the first plot in a three-plot graph to 2, Excel would automatically change the plot order value of the current second plot to 1. If you omit the plot number when you enter a formula, the data series will be entered using the next available plot number. After you edit the function and click the enter box, Excel will redraw the chart and change the legend.

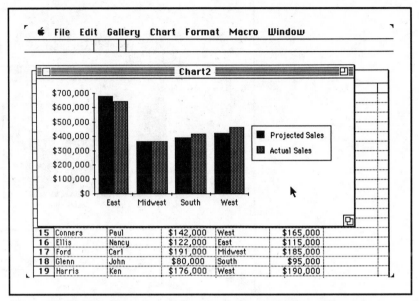

Figure 19.12: The chart after adding the data series titles and legend

Try changing the plot order on your example chart. Select the first data series and change the last argument of its formula to 2. Click the enter box, and Excel will redraw the chart. Click the second data series and notice it is now assigned a plot order of 1. Edit the formula for the first data series again so that it is the first series plotted.

DELETING A DATA SERIES

If you wish to remove a data series from a chart, use the following procedure:

1. On the chart, click the data series that you want to delete. Its formula will appear in the formula bar.

2. Erase the formula by using the Backspace key or by using the Cut command on the Edit menu.

3. Press the Return key or click the enter box.

The chart will be redrawn without that data series.

You can clear all the data series in a chart by using the following procedure:

1. Pull down the Chart menu and choose Select Chart. Markers will appear to show that the entire chart is selected.

2. Pull down the Edit menu and select Clear.

3. When the Clear dialog box appears (see Figure 19.13), click Formulas, then click OK.

The entire chart will clear, but the formats (chart types) remain. If you copy and paste other data series into the chart, they will be in the format of the previous graphs.

COPYING A DATA SERIES

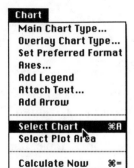

As with worksheets, you can easily copy data from one chart to another chart. To copy a data series and insert it on another chart, follow these steps:

1. Be sure that the source chart (the one with the data series that you are going to copy) is active.

2. Pull down the Chart menu and choose Select Chart. The entire chart will be marked.

3. Pull down the Edit menu and choose Copy. The chart will be marked with dotted lines, as with any other copy operation.

4. Make the destination chart active by clicking it, or pull down the File menu and choose New to create a new chart.

5. Pull down the Edit menu and select Paste Special.

6. When the Paste Special dialog box appears (see Figure 19.14), click Formulas, then click OK.

The data series will be copied to the second chart, but the format information (chart type) is not copied. This means that if you copy a data series that was displayed as a column graph into a line graph, the copied data series will also be plotted as a line graph.

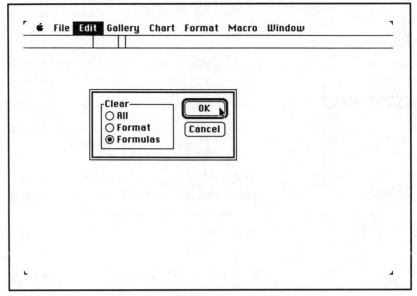

Figure 19.13: The Clear dialog box

CHOOSING THE CHART TYPE

The Gallery menu can be used to quickly change from one chart type to another. There are six basic chart types on the menu: area, column, bar, line, pie, and scatter. Each menu selection displays a dialog box from which you can select a subset of the basic type. For example, the dialog box for the column chart type is shown in Figure 19.15.

CHANGING CHART TYPES

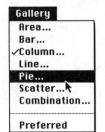

To change the type of a displayed chart, pull down the Gallery menu and choose the new chart type. When the dialog box for that type appears, click the format that you want to replace the existing type, then click OK. Excel will redraw the chart in the new type.

Another way to quickly change the graph type is to pull down the Chart menu and choose Main Chart Type. When the dialog box shown in Figure 19.16 is displayed, click the desired type of chart.

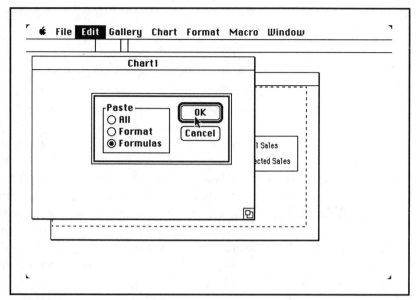

Figure 19.14: The Paste Special dialog box

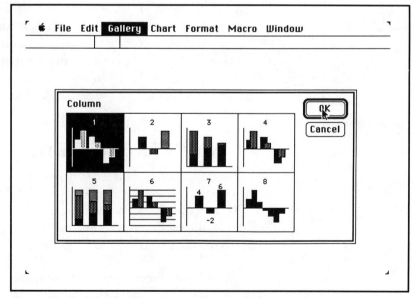

Figure 19.15: Selecting the column chart type

When you change the chart type using either of these methods, *all* the data series plotted on the chart will change to the new type. If you want to change the type of only one data series on the chart, use the overlay method described later in this chapter.

SETTING A PREFERRED TYPE

You can also set a preferred chart type that will be used each time that you create a chart unless it is altered. In the default mode, Excel automatically draws a column chart. In all of our examples, the first graph defaulted to a column type. To change the preferred format type, first set the active chart to the desired preferred format. Then, pull down the Chart menu and choose Set Preferred Format.

After you've selected a chart type as your preferred format, you can still select that type from the Gallery menu, just like any other type. You may find it useful to set a preferred format if you are going to alter your chart but you may want to switch back to the earlier format. Before you change the format, save the current format as the preferred format. Then, if you need to switch back, select the preferred format from the Gallery menu. This way, you won't have to remember which of the 42 chart formats was used for the original chart.

MOVING PIE WEDGES

A pie chart is different from other chart types in that it uses only a single data series. If you select more than one data series on a worksheet and try to create a pie chart, only the first series will be plotted. The legend lists categories instead of data-series titles.

When you "explode" a wedge in a pie chart, you separate it from the rest of the pie, as shown in Figure 19.17. To do this, simply select the wedge and drag it to the desired location.

USING OVERLAY CHARTS

You can plot two data series in different graph types by overlaying the charts. The overlays can even have different value axes.

As an example, let's use the Sales Projections worksheet values and plot the projected sales as a column graph and the actual sales as an overlay line graph. Follow these steps:

1. On the Sales Projections worksheet, select cells A6 through C9

2. Open a new chart, plotting both data series as a column graph

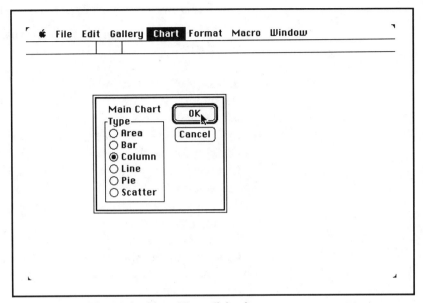

Figure 19.16: The Main Chart Type dialog box

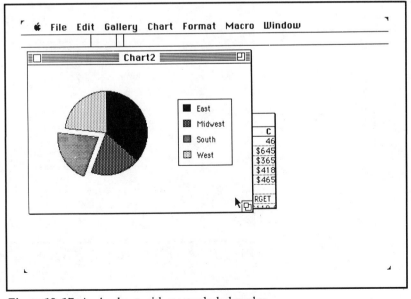

Figure 19.17: A pie chart with an exploded wedge

3. Pull down the Chart menu and select Overlay Chart Type

4. When the Overlay Chart Type dialog box shown in Figure 19.18 appears, double-click Line

The chart will be redrawn with the actual sales values as an overlay, as shown in Figure 19.19. Notice that you did not select which data series was the overlay. Excel assumes that the first data series is the main chart type and the second data series is the overlay. You can alter this by editing the plot order in the SERIES function or by using the Overlay Chart command on the Format menu. If there are more than two data series, they will be divided equally between the main and overlay type. If there is an odd number of data series, the main chart will contain the extra data series.

To switch a chart with an overlay back to a single chart, pull down the Chart menu and choose Overlay Chart Type. Double-click None in the dialog box, as shown in Figure 19.20.

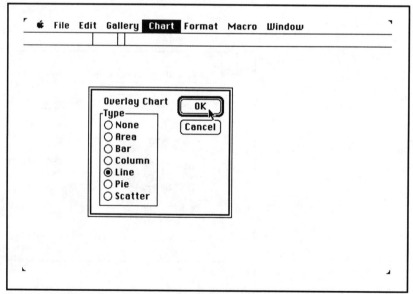

Figure 19.18: The Overlay Chart Type dialog box

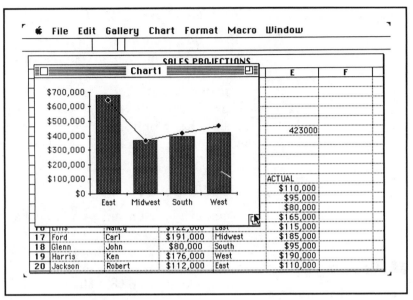

Figure 19.19: Using an overlay chart

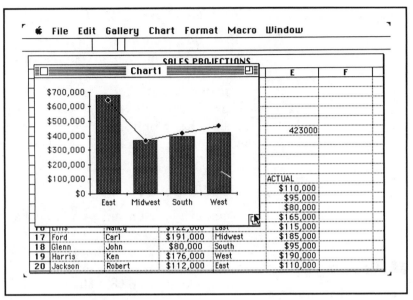

Figure 19.20: Turning off the overlay

CHART PRESENTATION FEATURES

Excel offers you many options that you can use to improve the appearance of your charts. You can add text at any point in the chart, control the font and size of the text and values, add arrows to emphasize parts of a chart, add titles to axes, change the legend position, or add grid lines. In this section, you'll practice using each of these features on the column chart showing the projected and actual sales values from the Sales Projections worksheet (see Figure 19.10).

ADDING TEXT

You can add text to any part of the graph. If text is added to a predefined area of the graph (axis, data series, data point, or title) it is called *attached text,* as it is attached to that specific area. Text that is not associated with any particular part of the graph is called *unattached text.*

Now, add a title to your chart as attached text:

1. Pull down the Chart menu and choose Attach Text

2. When the Attach Text dialog box shown in Figure 19.21 appears, select the area to which the text is to be attached and

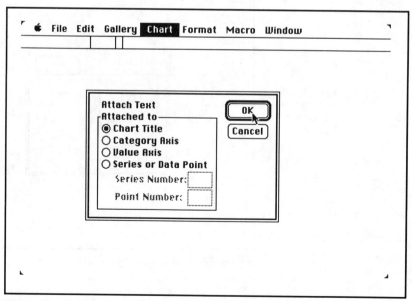

Figure 19.21: Selecting the area to which the text is to be attached

click OK. There will now be a marker on the chart where the text will be entered.

3. Enter the text from the keyboard. It will be entered into the formula bar, and you can edit it just as you edit a formula. Enter **SALES ANALYSIS.**

4. Click the enter box. The title will now be displayed on the chart, as shown in Figure 19.22.

Now, add a date to the chart as unattached text:

1. Type the date **7/31/88** on the keyboard. It appears in the formula bar and can be edited.

2. Click the enter box. The date will be entered into approximately the center of the chart with little boxes around it, as shown in Figure 19.23.

3. Click the text and drag it to the upper right of the chart, below the title. The chart now looks like Figure 19.24.

To remove attached and unattached text, select the text and backspace over it.

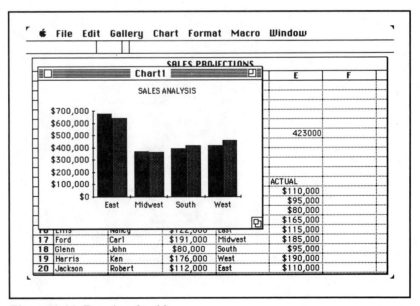

Figure 19.22: Entering the title

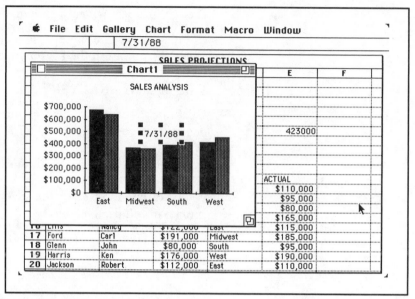

Figure 19.23: Entering unattached text

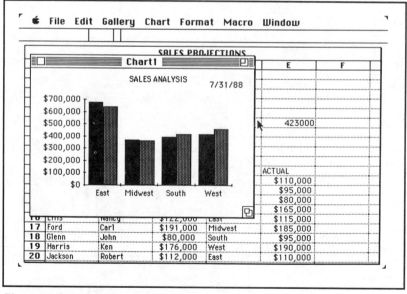

Figure 19.24: Adding unattached text

FORMATTING TEXT

Excel lets you change the font, size, and style of any text on your chart. You can also change its orientation, making it vertical or horizontal.

To format both attached and unattached text, first enter the text and position it, then use the Text command on the Format menu. Follow these steps to boldface the title of your Sales Analysis chart:

1. Click the title, which is the text to be formatted

2. Pull down the Format menu and choose Text

3. When the dialog box shown in Figure 19.25 is displayed, click Monaco, 12, bold, and OK

Your chart should now look like Figure 19.26.

You can use the same basic procedure to add a title to either or both axes, as you did in Chapter 18. Figure 18.15 in that chapter shows how axes titles appear on a graph. To add these titles, pull

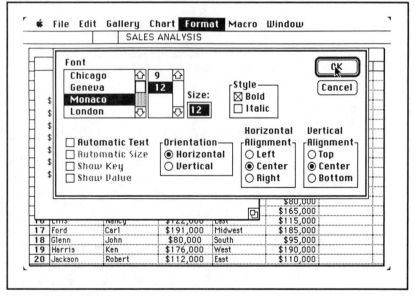

Figure 19.25: The Text dialog box

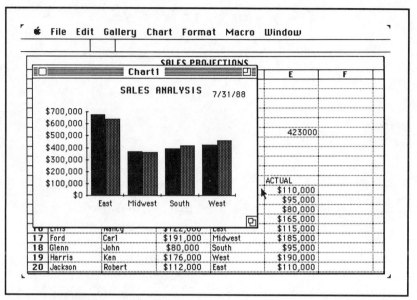

Figure 19.26: Boldfacing the title

down the Chart menu and choose Attach Text. When the dialog box
(see Figure 19.21) appears, select the axis that will be titled. Then,
enter the title from the keyboard and click the enter box. To format
the title, select the title and choose the Text command on the Format
menu. Select the font, size, and orientation in the Text dialog box
(see Figure 19.25), and click OK.

ADDING AND MOVING LEGENDS

A legend is used to define the symbols and labels in the chart. On a
pie chart, it defines the categories. On other charts, it defines the data
series. Once you've added a legend to a chart, you can move it and
reformat it.

To add a legend to a chart, simply pull down the Chart menu and
select Add Legend. Excel will place the legend at the right of the plot
area, and it will resize the graph to make room for the legend. You
can readjust the window size if necessary. Add a legend to your Sales
Analysis chart. It should look like Figure 19.27.

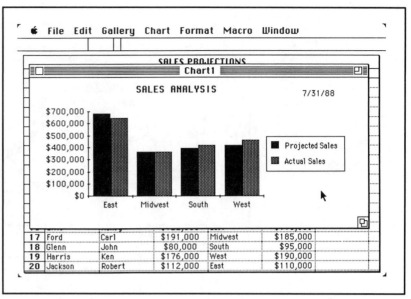

Figure 19.27: Adding a legend

Now, let's move the legend to the bottom of the chart:

1. Pull down the Format menu and select Legend
2. When the Legend dialog box shown in Figure 19.28 is displayed, click Bottom to move the legend to the bottom of the chart, then click OK

The last thing you should do with your legend is format it:

1. Click the legend area on the chart
2. Pull down the Format menu and select Text
3. When the Text dialog box appears (see Figure 19.29), select any formatting option you want, then click OK

Your chart should now look like Figure 19.30.

If you want to delete a displayed legend, pull down the Chart menu and select Delete Legend.

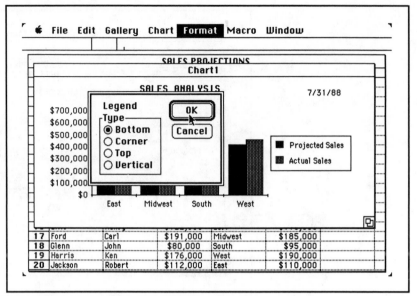

Figure 19.28: Positioning the legend

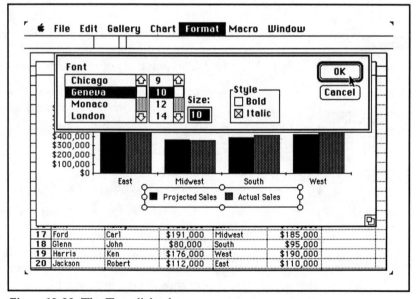

Figure 19.29: The Text dialog box

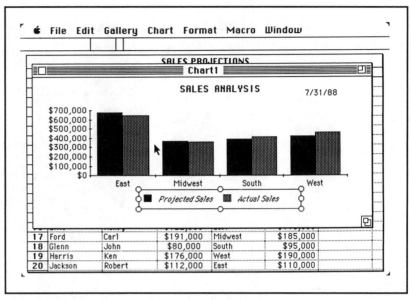

Figure 19.30: Moving and formatting the legend

In the next few sections, experiment with your Sales Analysis chart to see how each of the features described affects it.

FORMATTING GRID LINES

Grid lines appear on a chart as horizontal and vertical lines at regular intervals in the plot area. They help you to determine the value of a data point. You can add major grid lines (at tick marks), or minor grid lines (between tick marks), or both, and make the lines heavier.

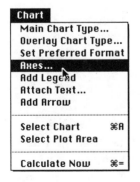

To add grid lines to a chart, follow these steps:

1. Pull down the Chart menu and choose Axes

2. When the Axes dialog box shown in Figure 19.31 is displayed, click the type of grid lines that you want, then click OK

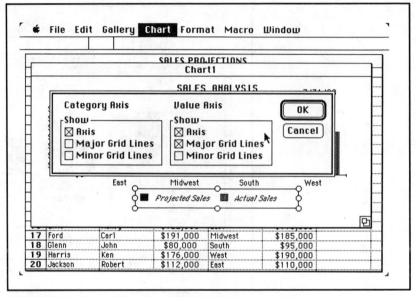

Figure 19.31: Controlling the grid lines display

To control the weight of the lines, follow these steps:

1. Click a horizontal or vertical grid-line set

2. Pull down the Format menu and choose Patterns

3. Select the line weight (in the Border Weight box) in the Pattern dialog box, shown in Figure 19.32, then click OK

The weight selection in the Pattern dialog box applies to the grid lines, axis, or arrow selected before you used the Patterns command. Figure 19.33 shows a chart with grid lines for the value axis.

FORMATTING AXES

You can also control the formatting of either axis. The Axis command on the Format menu lets you control the tick marks, order of the categories, number of categories, scaling, and zero crossing of an axis. To use it, select the axis, pull down the Format menu, and choose Axis. You will see the dialog box shown in Figure 19.34. See Appendix C for an explanation of the options in this dialog box.

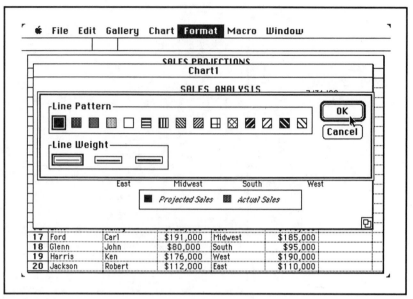

Figure 19.32: Selecting the line weight and marker pattern

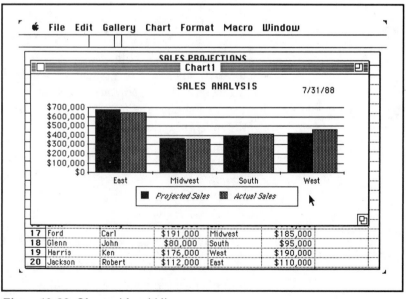

Figure 19.33: Chart with grid lines

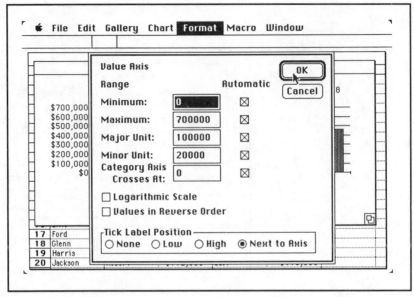

Figure 19.34: Formatting the axis

You can also change the line weight of an axis. First, click the axis, then pull down the Format menu and click Patterns. When the Patterns dialog box (see Figure 19.32) appears, click the line weight that you want in the Border Weight box.

The Text command on the Format menu allows you to change the font, size, or style of the tick-mark labels on the axes. After you select the axis, pull down the Format menu and choose Text. When the dialog box (Figure 19.29) appears, select the desired format options, then click OK. To change the format of an axis label, click the label, then follow the same procedure.

To turn off the axis display (but leave the category and value headings) pull down the Chart menu and choose Axes. When you see the Axes dialog box (Figure 19.31), click Axis under the appropriate heading (Category Axis or Value Axis) to remove it from the chart.

FORMATTING A DATA SERIES

You can select a new pattern for a data series, stack two data series, and overlap bar and column charts.

To change the data-series marker pattern, select the data series, pull down the Format menu, and choose Patterns. You'll see the dialog box shown in Figure 19.32, which gives you your choices for patterns. Select the new pattern and click OK.

To stack or overlap data series, pull down the Format menu and choose Main chart or Overlay chart. The dialog box shown in Figure 19.35 appears. The options in this dialog box control the relationship of the main chart to the overlay chart, as described below:

- Stacked: The second data series is added as a stacked graph to the first data series.

- 100%: The category values are normalized to 100%. The absolute values do not appear on the chart.

- Vary by Categories: The pattern for each data point is varied (for a single data series only).

- Drop lines: Lines extend from the highest value in each category to the axis.

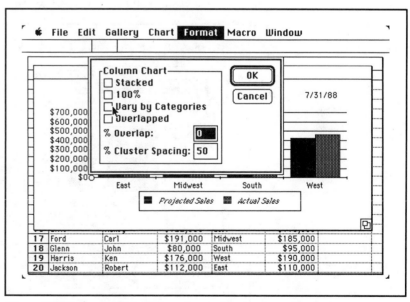

Figure 19.35: Controlling data-series stacking and overlap

- Hi-Lo Lines: Lines extend from the highest point in each category to the lowest.

- Overlapped: Bar and column charts are overlapped.

- % Overlap: Controls the amount of overlap.

- % Cluster Spacing: Controls spacing between bars.

- Angle of First Slice: Controls the angle of the first edge of the first slice from the vertical (for a pie chart).

Keep in mind that you must enter a negative percent of overlap. A positive number will space the series farther apart.

ADDING ARROWS

Another one of Excel's presentation features is the capability to add arrows. If you want to add an arrow to emphasize any part of a chart, follow these steps:

1. Pull down the Chart menu and choose Add Arrow. An arrow then appears on the chart, as shown in Figure 19.36.

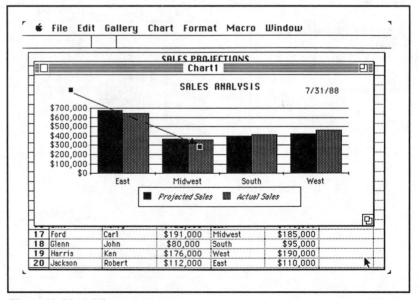

Figure 19.36: Adding an arrow

2. Click the arrow and drag it where you want it to appear on the chart, as shown in Figure 19.37. You can move either end by dragging the black box at that end.

3. Use the Patterns command on the Format menu to change the width of the arrow line and the type of arrowhead.

You can repeat this procedure and add as many arrows as you want to any chart.

To delete an arrow, click the arrow, pull down the Chart menu, and choose Delete Arrow.

USING ARRAYS WITH CHARTS

Excel uses the SERIES function to create charts. Two of the arguments of this function—categories and values—are always arrays. You can edit any chart's SERIES function to convert the array references to constants. For more details, refer to Chapter 15.

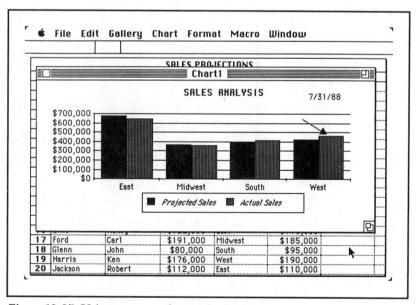

Figure 19.37: Using an arrow for emphasis

LINKING CHARTS

Whenever you create a chart, it is automatically linked to a supporting worksheet. Whenever the supporting worksheet is changed, the chart is updated to reflect the new values.

The procedure for linking charts follows the same rules as the one for linking worksheets:

- When you copy and paste a chart, Excel automatically creates the data-series formulas and external references.

- If you move supporting cells, Excel does not adjust external references to that cell. Use names to avoid this problem.

- You can block recalculation of a chart by choosing the Manual option in the Calculation dialog box.

- External references in a data-series formula must be absolute cell addresses or named references.

You can see how a chart and a supporting worksheet are linked by opening the Actual Sales database that you created in Chapter 12.

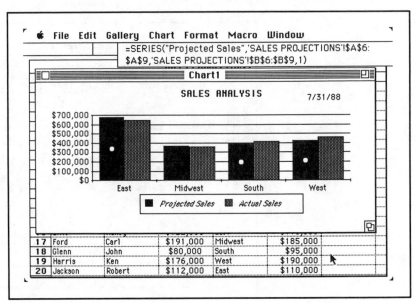

Figure 19.38: The chart data-series formula showing the link

Use the one with some actual sales figures. If you created a chart from these data, open that, too. If not, select cells A6 through C9 on the database and draw a chart. Then, click either of the columns on the chart. You will see the data-series formula in the formula bar, with the reference to the worksheet that created the chart, as shown in Figure 19.38. The formula uses a simple external reference. This means that you can open the chart without opening the worksheet, and Excel will get the values it needs from the disk.

SUMMARY

This chapter has given you a complete overview of Excel's extensive charting capabilities. The chart is always drawn from one or more data series that you defined. After the basic chart is created, you can alter the type of chart, label the chart or axes, add a legend, arrows, or unattached text, and control the format of any part of the chart. You can use these charting features to create high-quality graphics, suitable for reports and presentations.

P A R T 6

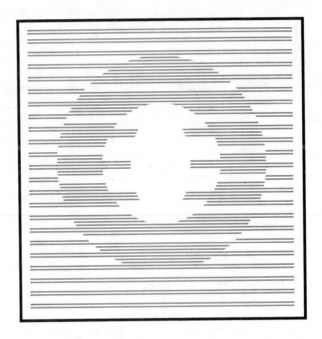

USING EXCEL PRODUCTIVELY

NOW THAT YOU'VE GAINED SOME BASIC EXPERIENCE with Excel's features, you are probably interested in using it to solve problems. Although the application possibilities for Excel are far too numerous for this book, three of the most common applications are inventory control, financial managment, and trend analysis. Part 6 will look at each of these, as well as teach you how to use Excel with other application sortware. In addition, you will gain some knowledge of basic application principles you can use for other problems.

USING EXCEL WITH
OTHER SOFTWARE

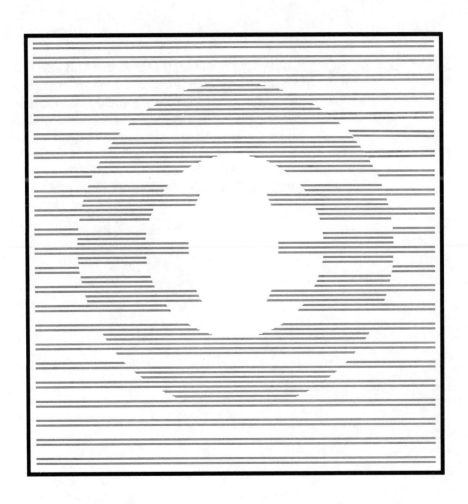

NOW THAT YOU'VE MASTERED EXCEL, YOU MAY want to use it with other software products, such as spreadsheet programs, word processors, and database managers. You can transfer data from most of these programs to Excel, and you can also transfer Excel data to most of these programs. Here are some typical reasons for using Excel with other software:

- You want to insert a worksheet or chart that was created with Excel into a word-processed document created with MacWrite or Microsoft Word.

- You have several worksheets that were created on an IBM-PC with Lotus 1-2-3. You want to transfer them to your Macintosh and print them using Excel's presentation features.

- You have a database file that was created with Microsoft File, and you want to use it on an Excel worksheet to do some special analyses.

- You created an Excel worksheet at home on your Macintosh. You need to transfer it to Lotus 1-2-3, which you are using at work on an IBM-PC.

You can also use the Switcher with Excel and either Microsoft Word or MacWrite. The Switcher permits you to keep both your word-processing program and Excel in the Macintosh memory at the same time and copy and paste data quickly between the two. This, in effect, gives you an integrated program capability.

EXCEL WITH MACWRITE AND MICROSOFT WORD

There is two-way transfer capability between Excel and MacWrite and Microsoft Word—you can transfer data from Excel to these programs or from them to Excel. If you plan to transfer much data

between Excel and a word processor, you should use the Switcher, as described in the following section. Otherwise, you can use one of the methods described below.

TRANSFERRING DATA TO A WORD PROCESSOR

If you need to copy a worksheet or chart from Excel into a word-processed document, there are two methods you can use. The first is generally the preferred method.

THE COPY PICTURE AND COPY CHART COMMANDS The easiest way to transfer Excel worksheet data to a word processor is to use a special form of the Copy command on the Edit menu. First, select the cells or cell range that you wish to copy. Then, hold down the Shift key, pull down the Edit menu, and choose Copy Picture. (When you hold down the Shift key, the Copy command on the Edit menu changes to Copy Picture if a worksheet is active.)

To copy a chart, first select the chart, then choose Copy Chart on the Chart Edit menu (it is not necessary to use the Shift key). When you choose the Copy Chart command, the dialog box shown in Figure 20.1

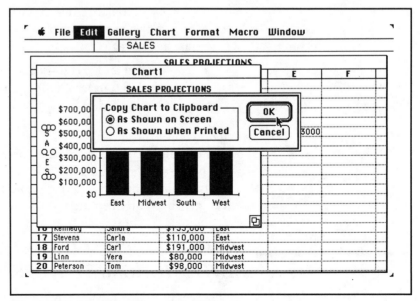

Figure 20.1: The Copy Chart dialog box

will be displayed. This dialog box is used to select whether you wish the copy to be like the screen display or like the printed version.

The above procedure will copy the selected range into the Clipboard (you can use the Show Clipboard command on the Window menu to see the size of the range you have copied). Next, exit Excel and start the word processor. Open your word-processed document and select the area for the copied worksheet or chart. Use the Paste command on the word processor's Edit menu to paste the Clipboard contents into the document.

TRANSFERRING DATA IN TEXT FORM   The second method for transferring data from Excel to a word processor is a little more complex. You must save the worksheet data in text form and then use this text in your word-processed document. This requires the following steps:

1. Use the Save As command on the File menu. When the dialog box appears, click Text to save your document in text form, as shown in Figure 20.2.

2. Click Save in the dialog box.

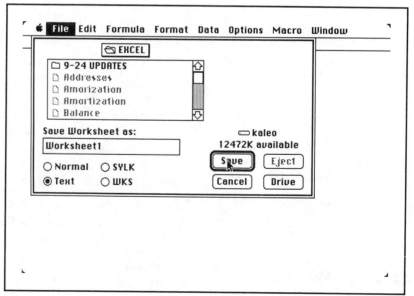

Figure 20.2: Saving the worksheet in text form

When the worksheet is saved in text form, each row becomes a line with the columns separated by tabs. This is one method for transferring data to special word processors, desktop publishers, and similar software when the normal transfer methods don't seem to work. You'll lose the formatting information, but at least you will have your data.

TRANSFERRING DATA
FROM A WORD PROCESSOR

Before you transfer data *from* MacWrite or Microsoft *to* Excel, the word-processed file must be in the correct format: each line should end with a carriage return and columns should be separated by tabs. Save the word-processed data as text, using the Text Only option.

Then, start Excel. Use the Open command on the File menu to load the document. Each tab-separated value will be in a separate cell in the row, and each carriage return will start a new row. Be sure to start with a new worksheet. The data will load starting in A1. Once the data is loaded, you can add empty rows or columns to move the starting location of the data you loaded.

USING THE SWITCHER

Using the Switcher will save you considerable time if you are planning to transfer a lot of data between Excel and another application program. It prevents starting and stopping programs and speeds up the transfer. Both of the programs and the data for each remain in the Macintosh's memory. As a result, you can switch quickly from one application to another. Refer to Appendix F to learn how to install the Switcher.

Here are some general rules for using the Switcher with Excel and other programs:

1. Use the Options command on the Switcher's Switcher menu to set up a common Clipboard for Excel and the word processor.

2. Initially install Excel with 256K of RAM or more. Install the other program with whatever memory it requires. The

amount of memory required by Excel depends on the size of the worksheet.

You can also use Microsoft's Quick Switch to transfer data between Excel and Word. Using Quick Switch, you can effectively link worksheets to a Microsoft Word document. For more information, see a Quick Switch manual.

USING THE SCRAPBOOK

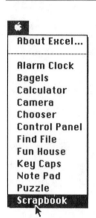

If you need to move many items from one application to another, it is often quicker to use the Scrapbook than to use Switcher. You would begin by following these steps to move the selected Excel data to the Scrapbook:

1. Move the data to the Clipboard using the Copy command on the Edit menu (do not use Copy Picture with the Shift key)

2. Pull down the Apple menu and click Scrapbook

3. Pull down the Edit menu and click Paste

Now that you have the data in the Scrapbook, you can look at it. While the Clipboard will show only the size of the copied area (such as 4R × 1C), the Scrapbook displays the actual worksheet text.

Repeat the above procedure for each item that you want to transfer. Then, use the following procedure to copy the Excel data from the Scrapbook into the second application:

1. Start the application and open the document that will receive the copy of the first item

2. Pull down the Apple menu and choose Scrapbook

3. Scroll through the Scrapbook until you find the item that you need

4. Select Cut or Copy to move the item from the Scrapbook to the Clipboard. You will not be able to select the Clipboard, but if the Scrapbook is active, a cut or copy will transfer the Scrapbook data to the Clipboard.

5. Select an insertion point in your document and use the Paste command to move the item from the Clipboard into your document

6. Repeat steps 1 through 5 for each item you want to transfer

Be sure that the Scrapbook file is on the same disk as your destination application.

You can also use the Scrapbook to transfer data *to* Excel *from* another program. For example, you can set up data in a word processor with the columns separated by rows and the rows separated using carriage returns. Select it, copy it to the Scrapbook (as above), start Excel and copy it from the Scrapbook through the Clipboard to any selected position in the worksheet (or to multiple positions).

USING EXCEL WITH LOTUS 1-2-3

If you already have Lotus 1-2-3 on an IBM-PC, you can move worksheets from Lotus 1-2-3 to Excel or from Excel to Lotus 1-2-3.

To transfer data in either direction, you will need some type of networking or communications software. The transfer is considered a binary-file transfer, so both computers will need software that has binary-file transfer capability and that uses the same protocol. Good examples are Centram's TOPS network (2372 Ellsworth Ave., Berkeley, CA 94704), Peter Mackie's PC to Mac and Back (Seaquest Software, 4200 N.W. Columbia Ave., Portland, OR 97229), and DataViz's MacLink Plus. Follow the directions of the product you plan to use to transfer the files between the computers.

When you transfer in either direction, the cell properties of your worksheet, including values, formulas, format, and protection, and any names that you assigned are converted. However, window properties (such as panes) are not converted. Although the function arguments and their order in Excel are often different from those in Lotus 1-2-3, when you transfer files, Excel automatically converts them. For example, you can take the Amortization worksheet that you created in Chapter 8, which has the PMT and PV functions, and transfer it to Lotus 1-2-3, which uses different arguments. The Lotus 1-2-3 worksheet will be correctly calculated using the proper formulas.

Excel has many functions and features (such as arrays) that are not a part of Lotus 1-2-3. These, of course, cannot be converted correctly. If you plan to do many transfers from Excel to Lotus 1-2-3, avoid using arrays and Excel's other special functions. Appendix E provides more details on how to transfer data between Excel and Lotus 1-2-3.

TRANSFERRING FROM EXCEL TO LOTUS 1-2-3

To transfer an Excel document to Lotus 1-2-3, first save the document as a WKS document. Do this by pulling down the File menu and choosing Save As. When the dialog box appears, enter the document name, using the extension .WKS; for example, TEST.WKS would be a valid name. Then, click the WKS option and click Save, as shown in Figure 20.3. The WKS option saves the document in a special format that is compatible with Lotus 1-2-3. Use your communications program to transfer the WKS document to the IBM-PC. You can then load the document and use it with Lotus 1-2-3.

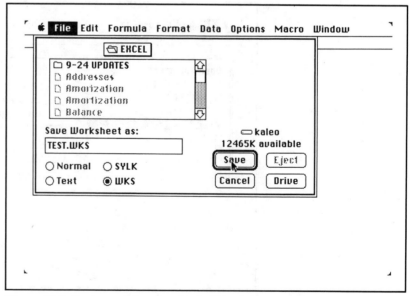

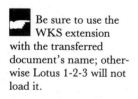 Be sure to use the WKS extension with the transferred document's name; otherwise Lotus 1-2-3 will not load it.

Figure 20.3: Saving a document that will be transferred to Lotus 1-2-3

TRANSFERRING FROM LOTUS 1-2-3 TO EXCEL

Transferring Lotus 1-2-3 worksheets to Excel is very easy. Use your communications programs to transfer the document to Excel. Then, simply start Excel and open the document using the Open command on the File menu. The Open Document dialog box, shown in Figure 20.4, will include the name of the Lotus 1-2-3 document. You do not need to use any special options.

EXCEL AND OTHER SOFTWARE

Excel can be used with Microsoft File for database- management applications, as well as with Microsoft Chart, and with Multiplan.

To move Excel records to Microsoft File, save the records as text from Excel. Before loading the data to Microsoft File, create the Microsoft File database structure. The fields of the database must

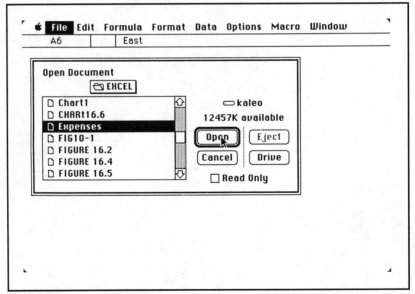

Figure 20.4: Opening a Lotus 1-2-3 document that was transferred to Excel

match your Excel database fields. Excel charts can be moved to Microsoft File to be used as picture fields. To move a chart to a picture field, use the Copy Chart command on the Edit menu.

You can use Microsoft Chart to do more extensive chart formatting. The file format for Microsoft Chart is the same as that of Excel's chart file. You can use the same files with either program. The Gallery and Format menus are also the same in both programs.

Many Microsoft application products (Excel, Multiplan, etc.) support the special SYLK format. This is a standard format that can be used for data transfer to or from Excel. It is particularly useful for transferring worksheets between different versions of Excel. To save a worksheet in this format, select File Save As and click SYLK after entering the file name. Then click OK (see Figure 20.3).

If you are using Multiplan, you can use this SYLK format to transfer worksheets to or from Excel. Formulas recognized by both will be transferred correctly, but formulas specific to either will not be transferred. As with Lotus 1-2-3, data, formulas, formats, and names are transferred within this limitation but window properties (such as panes) are not transferred. Multiplan does not support arrays and cannot support as large a numeric range as Excel. All of the Multiplan functions except DELTA and ITERCNT are supported by Excel. Many Excel functions, however, are not supported by Multiplan.

You can also read a Multiplan worksheet directly with Excel without using the SYLK format. Just open the worksheet with File Open in Excel. Excel recognizes this and converts the worksheet. The converse, though, is not true. Multiplan will only read an Excel worksheet if it is in a SYLK format.

If an old worksheet won't load with a new version of Excel, save the worksheet from the old Excel version in SYLK format. Use your new version to load the SYLK formatted file.

If you experience transfer problems transferring files between Excel and any other Microsoft program or another version of Excel (or Excel on the PC), revert to the SYLK format. For example, save the Excel file as a SYLK file. If the receiving program is a Microsoft program, it can generally detect the SYLK format and load the program correctly.

*INVENTORY CONTROL
AND INVOICING*

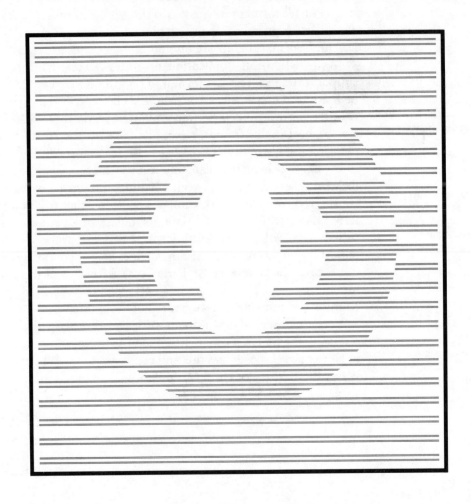

CHAPTER *21*

IF YOU HAVE ANY TYPE OF BUSINESS IN WHICH YOU are creating invoices, you will quickly find that this time-consuming chore would be better delegated to a computer. This chapter will illustrate the basic concepts of creating an invoice with Excel and using an inventory database. The example will show how to get the basic information automatically from the database using multiple price schedules and how to add a tax to the final price based on a tax rate table.

CREATING THE DATABASE

One of your first objectives should be to create the inventory database. For invoicing, the fields in your database should include the part or item number, the description, and a column for each price schedule. For inventory control, you may also wish to add fields for the cost, the current quantity on hand, and the extended cost (quantity on hand multiplied by the cost). This permits you to quickly calculate the current value of the inventory.

An example database is shown in Figure 21.1. The database is started in row 50 to leave room for the invoice, but you can also put it on a separate worksheet and link it to an invoice worksheet if you want. Each inventory item is a record and entered as a separate row. The prices can either be entered as discrete values or as formula-based prices of another column. In some cases you may wish to have separate price categories based on the quantity sold. In this example there are only two price categories. Discrete price values are used and entered in each cell. There should be no blanks in the database, because blanks can cause incorrect data to be entered in the invoice later.

For the invoicing to work properly, the records need to be in order by part number. You can enter them in any order, but after entering them,

	A	B	C	D	E	F
50	PARTNO	DESCRIPTION	Ret Price	Whol Price	QOH	Ext Cost
51	10008	General Purpose Cleaner 1 qt.	$5.00	$4.10	$3.00	$12.30
52	10010	Industrial Cleaner 1 qt	$7.25	$5.25	$3.00	$15.75
53	20014	Lecithin	$9.75	$7.05	$5.00	$35.25
54	20031	Zinc	$5.20	$3.50	$1.00	$3.50
55	20042	Alfalfa Tablets	$8.75	$6.25	$7.00	$43.75
56	20049	Multi-vitamin	$12.50	$8.50	$9.00	$76.50
57	20051	Iron + Vit C	$7.75	$5.10	$3.00	$15.30
58	20061	Beta Carotene	$16.50	$10.75	$1.00	$10.75
59	20081	Vit-E /Sel	$10.10	$7.20	$3.00	$21.60
60	20082	Vitamin C (Chewable)	$6.25	$4.10	$8.00	$32.80
61	20083	Vit-C S/R 500	$6.40	$4.60	$8.00	$36.80
62	20088	Fiber Wafer	$4.50	$3.25	$4.00	$13.00
63	20143	Iron	$8.00	$5.10	$4.00	$20.40
64	20250	Calcium Mag	$6.50	$4.50	$5.00	$22.50
65	20310	B Complex	$10.80	$7.50	$4.00	$30.00
66	20810	EPA	$17.50	$12.75	$1.00	$12.75
67						------------------
68						$402.95

Figure 21.1: The Inventory database

You can use the inventory database without sorting on the part number by creating macros using the Data-.Find macro language function (see Part 7 of this book). This adds another degree of complexity, but the capability is there if you need it.

use the Data Sort command to sort on the first column. Remember, do not include the field name when you define the sort range.

Before leaving this section, you may wish to experiment with the database. You can set up a criteria range and find or extract records based on any criteria.

For the example of this chapter, the invoicing system will not really use this area as a database, but rather as a lookup table so you do not need to name it as a database for the invoicing system to work. However, from the user's perspective it is still a database and naming it as a database is helpful because it permits you to use the Goto command.

CREATING THE INVOICE

A sample output of the invoice system is shown in Figure 21.2. You can store a blank form of this invoice as a template on disk and use it for multiple invoices by filling in the areas that change between invoices. The item descriptions, prices, and the extended price columns are filled

INVOICE

Remit to:

ABC Heatlh Products
48 Midway Lane
Berkeley, CA 94702

Date: 6/25/88
Invoice #   4023
Tax Code   B
Terms   A

Sold to: John Albert
             34 Shady Lane
             Berkeley, CA 94702

Ship to: John Albert
             34 Shady Lane
             Berkeley, CA 94702

Item #	Description	Price	Qty	Ext Price
20143	Iron	$5.10	1	$5.10
20083	Vit-C S/R 500	$4.60	2	$9.20
20810	EPA	$12.75	1	$12.75
			Subtotal	$27.05
			Tax	$1.89
			Grand Total	$28.94

Figure 21.2: The invoice

in automatically. The user enters only the item number and the quantity to ship. The totals are also calculated automatically.

Begin creating the invoice by filling in the text areas using Figure 21.3 as a guide. Fill in the item numbers in cells A15 to A17.

Now add the following formula in cell B15:

    = LOOKUP(A15,$A$50:$A$66,$B$50:$B$66)

	A	B	C	D	E
1		INVOICE			
2					
3	Remit to:				
4	ABC Health Products			Date:	6/25/88
5	48 Midway Lane			Invoice #	4023
6	Berkeley, CA 94702			Tax Code	B
7				Terms	A
8					
9	Sold to:	John Albert	Ship to:	John Albert	
10		34 Shady Lane		34 Shady Lane	
11		Berkeley, CA 94702		Berkeley, CA 94702	
12					
13					
14	Item #	Description	Price	Qty	Ext Price
15	20143			1	
16	20083			2	
17	20810			1	
18					
19					
20					
21					
22					
23					
24					
25					
26				Subtotal	
27				Tax	
28				Grand Total	

Figure 21.3: The starting invoice worksheet

This tells Excel to use the value in A15 (the item number) as a value to look up in the range $A$50:$A$66. The corresponding value (the description) in $B$50:$B$66 is returned. Excel assumes that the table is sorted. In this case the table is our inventory database. Now use the Edit Fill Down command to copy the formula to B16 through B25. You should now see the item descriptions in column B.

You will have one problem at this point. For each row with a blank item number, you will have a = N/A for the description (see Figure 21.4). To eliminate these, modify the formula in B15 to include an IF function using an ISNA function to test for the N/A as follows:

= IF(A15 = 0,'''',LOOKUP(A15,$A$50:$A:$A$66,$B$50:$B$66))

Copy the formula from B15 to cells B16 to B25.

This may be somewhat confusing, but let's look at the basic form of the IF function:

= IF(*condition,value-if-true,value-if-false*)

The program uses A15 = 0 as a condition test for a value in A15. If no value is found in A15, the first expression is used to evaluate the cell value, leaving cell B15 blank. If a value is found, the second expression is used to find the cell value. This should eliminate the = N/A cell values.

	A	B
14	Item #	Description
15	20143	Iron
16	20083	Vit-C S/R 500
17	20810	EPA
18		#N/A
19		#N/A
20		#N/A
21		#N/A
22		#N/A
23		#N/A
24		#N/A
25		#N/A

Figure 21.4: Initial formula entry

The next thing you have to do is fill in the price formula. It is a bit more complicated because the price depends not only on the item number, but also on the Terms code entered in E7. The Terms code tells Excel whether to use the retail price or the wholesale price when calculating the extended cost. Be sure the values for E4 to E7 are entered, then enter the following formula in C15:

IF(A15<>0,(IF($E$7="A",LOOKUP(A15,$A$51:$A$66, $D$51:$D$66),
IF($E$7="B",LOOKUP(A15,$A51$A66,$C$51:$C$66)))),"")

If an item number is entered on a line, Excel will then evaluate the $E$7="A" expression. If this condition is TRUE, the next LOOKUP function is used to find the price from the table using column D. If FALSE, the next IF function is evaluated. This tries another condition, activating another LOOKUP function if TRUE. This time column C will be used for the prices.

Before entering a formula for the extended price, name the Qty and Price columns with their row headers using Formula Create Names. Now enter the extended price formula in E15:

IF(AND(A15<>0,Qty<>0),Price*Qty,"")

Copy this down through E25.

Now add the tax table (Figure 21.5) to the worksheet. This is used as a lookup table by E6 to calculate the tax in E27. The final formulas are listed below:

CELL	FORMULA
E26	= SUM(E15:E25)
E27	= LOOKUP($E$6,$B$47:$B$48,$C$47:$C$48)*E26
E28	= E26 + E27

Now set the alignment, style, and formats for the cells as desired. You should see the worksheet shown in Figure 21.6.

Now use the Format menu to set the borders. (You can see the borders more easily if you use the Options Display command to turn off the gridlines.) Finally, use the File Page Setup to turn off the row and column headings and gridlines on the printed invoice and initiate a print. The resulting invoice should look like Figure 21.2.

	B	C
46	TAX TABLE	
47	A	6.50%
48	B	7.00%

Figure 21.5: The tax table

	A	B	C	D	E
1		INVOICE			
2					
3	Remit to:				
4	ABC Heatlh Products			Date:	6/25/88
5	48 Midway Lane			Invoice #	4023
6	Berkeley, CA 94702			Tax Code	B
7				Terms	A
8					
9	Sold to:	John Albert	Ship to:	John Albert	
10		34 Shady Lane		34 Shady Lane	
11		Berkeley, CA 94702		Berkeley, CA 94702	
12					
13					
14	Item #	Description	Price	Qty	Ext Price
15	20143	Iron	$5.10	1	$5.10
16	20083	Vit-C S/R 500	$4.60	2	$9.20
17	20810	EPA	$12.75	1	$12.75
18					
19					
20					
21					
22					
23					
24					
25					
26				Subtotal	$27.05
27				Tax	$1.89
28				Grand Total	$28.94

Figure 21.6: The final invoice worksheet

IMPROVING THE INVOICING SYSTEM —

This invoicing system is just a nucleus that you can use as a starting point for designing any type of invoice system to meet your needs. A few examples of possible enhancements are listed below:

- You could could add a backorder system, checking the quantity ordered against the quantity in inventory and setting up a backorder if necessary.

- You could add features to modify the inventory on shipping, automatically keeping the quantities in inventory updated.

- You could use the database as a true database, using macros to fill in the invoice cells (see Part 7) and eliminating the need to keep the database records sorted.

FINANCIAL
MANAGEMENT

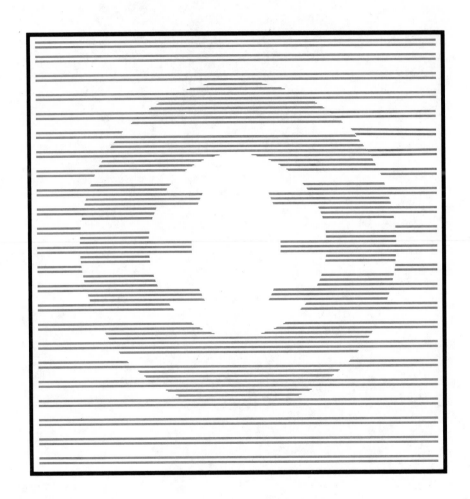

CHAPTER 22

ONE OF THE MOST IMPORTANT APPLICATIONS OF ANY worksheet program is the area of financial management. Using Excel, you can calculate loan payments, make decisions about purchasing or selling investments, and compare investment returns. This chapter will introduce you to the use of Excel's eight basic financial functions: NPV, PV, FV, PMT, NPER, RATE, IRR, and MIRR. In almost any business environment today, the knowledge of how to use these types of financial calculations is almost essential for the success of the business.

THE PRESENT VALUE FUNCTION (PV)

The present value function is used to calculate the present value of an investment that you will be purchasing over a period of time.

As an example, suppose someone offered to give you $1500 in a year if you would give him $1500 today. Would you do it? Probably not. You're probably smart enough to realize that if a money market account at the bank was paying 6 percent, you could at least earn 6 percent on your year's investment by investing it at the bank. You would have $1590 in the bank by the end of the year. If you took your friend up on his offer, you would lose 90 dollars.

In real life the decision is more complex. Suppose you have $5000 to invest. Your friend offers you an investment for $5000 that will pay $1500 a year for the next five years. Now would you take it?

To figure out whether this is a worthwhile investment, you need to compute the present value of the return your friend will give you. The general formula in Excel for this calculation is:

= PV(rate,number_of_periods,payment,future_value,type)

For the moment let's ignore the last two arguments, as they are not needed for the example. We need to assume an interest rate in order to project the investment back to the present. Let's assume that 9 percent is the current money-market rate at the bank. There are five periods and the payment is $1500, so you need to set up the following equation (see also Figure 22.1):

= PV(9%,5,1500)

This returns a present value of −5834, which means you should be willing to spend up to $5834 to get $1500 a year over the next five years (Figure 22.2). Since you are actually only spending $5000, your friend is offering you a good deal.

The present value of an investment depends on three factors: the interest rate, the number of periods, and the amount of the payment. The number of periods and the payment values are normally fixed. Your friend decided this. The interest rate, however, is a variable

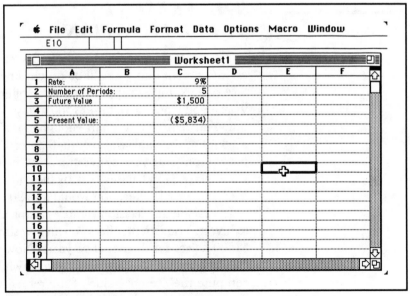

Figure 22.1: The worksheet to calculate the present value

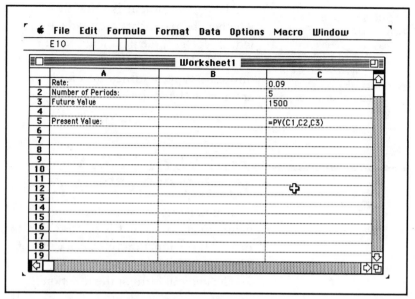

Figure 22.2: Calculating the present value

can assume. It is the hurdle over which the investment must leap before it becomes attractive, and for this reason is often called the hurdle rate. For practical purposes, you would generally use the best rate that you could get at the bank.

Now suppose your friend offers you a different plan. Instead of $1500 for each of five years, you could get $8500 at the end of the five years for the initial $5000 investment. Is it still a good deal? Is it better or worse than the last deal?

Now you don't have a payment, but you do have a future value. The interest and the number of periods is the same:

```
= PV(9%,5,,8500)
```

This time the result is – 5524. This means that at a 9 percent interest, you should be willing to invest $5524 now to get $8500 in five years. Since we only have to invest $5000, it is still a good deal. It is not as good as the last offer, but it is still acceptable. (Note that an extra comma must be inserted to indicate a missing argument.)

Be sure the interest rate corresponds to the payment period. In the previous example we had five payments at one-year intervals. The interest rate, then, should be for the year.

The *type* argument is a handy feature. It is a flag that indicates whether the payments are made at the beginning or end of the period. If type is 1, the payments occur at the beginning of the period. If type is 0, the payments are at the end of the period. If the argument is omitted, type assumes a default value of 0, and payments are assumed to be at the end of the period.

THE NET PRESENT VALUE FUNCTION (NPV)

The net present value function (NPV) is similar to the present value function, except it permits the user to assume unequal payments. If the function returns a value of 0 or greater, the investment is considered a good one.

The general form of the function is

=NPV(rate,inflow1,inflow2,...inflow*n*)

Let's return to the original problem. The initial investment is an outflow, so it must be represented as a negative number. The returns in subsequent years would be inflows, as shown below:

=NPV(9%, −5000,1500,1500,1500,1500,1500)

This returns a value of $766. In using this function, an investment is assumed acceptable if the result is greater than zero. Because this value is greater than zero, the investment is acceptable. Unfortunately, however, this is not the correct answer. The NPV function assumes all payments are evenly distributed and made at the end of the period. The first cash flow—the initial investment—is assumed to occur one time period from today. In this case, the initial inflow (the minus $5000) is made at the beginning of the first period. To adjust for this, subtract the initial investment instead of including it as an inflow as shown below:

=NPV(9%,1500,1500,1500,1500,1500)−5000

This gives a result of $834, which is the correct value (compare this with the −5834 of the last section, remembering that the higher the number for the NPV function, the better the investment). This is the most common way to use the NPV function: using the payback values as the inflow values and subtracting off the initial investment.

Now you can try it with unequal payments. Assume you still invest $5000, but the return is $1000 the first year, $1600 the next two years, $1700 the next year, and $1800 the last year. These can be stored in cells A1 to A5. You can then use the following calculation:

= NPV(9%,A1:A5)

This returns $873, which indicates this is a better investment than the fixed payment schedule, because it is higher than $834. The inflow arguments represent cash coming back, and in this case are positive. You can use positive or negative values for the inflow arguments. For example, if you pay out more cash later, you can use a negative inflow value for that period.

THE FUTURE VALUE FUNCTION (FV)

The future value function, FV, is used to calculate the future value of an investment. It is, therefore, the opposite of PV and NPV. For example, if you are making payments into an IRA or KEOGH account, the FV function will tell you the future value of that account.

The general form of the FV function is

= FV(rate,number_of_periods,payment,present_value,type)

where *rate* is the interest rate, the *number of periods* is the number of payments, and *payment* is how much you pay each time. The last two arguments are optional and will be explained later.

Now let's try an example. Assume you are 48 years old and begin an IRA in which you invest $4000 a year. How much will you have when you are 65? The number of payments is 65 minus 48, or 17.

Assume an interest rate of 11 percent. The equation becomes

$$= FV(11\%, 17, -4000)$$

which returns a value of $178,003.

Because there is no type argument, the above calculation assumed a default value of 0, which means that the payments came at the end of the period. If the payments are at the beginning of the period (you're making your first today), you must set up the equation as follows:

$$= FV(11\%, 17, -4000,, 1)$$

With this kind of a payment schedule, you will have $197,584 if you take it out when you are 65.

You can use the fourth argument (*present value*) to indicate a lump sum investment when two payments are used. For example, if you were creating an IRA with a $5000 investment and you planned no further payments, you would use the following equation:

$$= FV(11\%, 17,, -5000, 1)$$

This IRA account would return $29,475 when you reached age 65.

You can also combine an initial fixed investment with later payments:

$$= FV(11\%, 17, -4000, -5000, 1)$$

This equation returns $227,059.

THE PAYMENT FUNCTION (PMT)

The payment function (PMT) is useful for calculating the payments required to amortize a loan. This is useful when you are borrowing money for a car or house and you want to calculate the payments you can expect. The general form is as follows:

$$= PMT(rate, number\_of\_periods, present\_value, future\_value, type)$$

Be sure that, if monthly periods are used, you convert the interest to monthly interest and convert the years for the payments to months. The second argument is always the number of payments, and the first argument is the interest amount for the payment period.

For example, assume you are purchasing a $12,000 car at 11 percent. Payments are monthly for a five-year period. The resulting formula becomes

    = PMT(11%/12,12*5,12000)

which results in a monthly payment of $261. There are 60 payments (12*5), and the monthly interest for each payment period is 11 percent divided by 12 (11%/12). You can find a more extensive example of this function used in the amortization worksheet in Chapter 8.

Again, the type argument indicates whether the payments are at the beginning or end of the period.

CALCULATING THE RATE OF RETURN

Sometimes you want to do an inversion of the previous formulas; that is, you want to calculate the rate of return and then compare this rate with the rate of return of other investments. Excel provides three functions for calculating the rate of return.

THE RATE FUNCTION

Assume you are back to the initial problem of loaning $5000 with a return of $1500 for the next five years. This time you want to calculate the rate of return for the investment. This would be the percentage for which the NPV is equal to zero. The general form for this function is

    = RATE(number_of_periods,payment,present_value,
    future_value,type,guess)

For this example, the formula would be

    = RATE(5,1500, – 5000)

which returns a value of 15.24 percent, quite a good investment.

The *future value* is used to indicate a lump sum return. For example, if instead of yearly payments, you receive $8500 at the end of five years, the formula would become

```
= RATE(5,, – 5000,8500)
```

yielding a 11.20 percent return. This is not as good as the previous plan.

The *guess* argument is used to define a starting point for calculating the interest. If omitted, a value of zero is assumed.

THE IRR FUNCTION

The IRR, like RATE, is used to calculate the rate of return on an investment. The difference is that it can be used with uneven payments (like the NPV). The general form is as follows:

```
= IRR(values,guess)
```

Notice that there is only one argument for values. The trick, then, is to put the values as a range on the worksheet. If A1 contains – 5000 and each cell from A2 to A6 contains 1500, the formula becomes

```
= IRR(A1:A6)
```

and returns 15.23 percent as before. You can now change any payment value, though, and see the resulting change in the rate of return. You can even make them all zero except the last one, setting the last payment to $8500. That will give you 11.20 percent, the same as in the previous example.

The internal rate of return calculated by RATE or IRR is a commonly used financial statistic. Like the NPV, you can use it to compare financial investments. In the section on the NPV, you learned that an attractive investment is one in which the net present value, discounted at a specified hurdle rate, gives an NPV of zero or greater. The IRR and RATE functions turn this around. In essence, the internal rate of return is that value for which the NPV is zero.

THE MIRR FUNCTION

The MIRR function gives a modified rate of return of a series of cash flows. The general form is

= MIRR(values,safe,risky)

For example, assume you invest $5000 to finance an investment that will return $1400 a year for the next five years. Use the IRR function by entering – 5000 in cell A1 and 1400 in cells A2 through A6. Calculate the IRR as follows:

= IRR(A1:A6)

This results in 12.38 percent. Now assume we borrow the $5000 at 9 percent to make the initial investment. At the end of the five years the true rate of return becomes

= MIRR(A1:A6,9%,12.38%)

or 11.85 percent. The first argument is the range of values. The second is the interest you pay for the money, the third is the interest you will earn. The function does assume that positive cash flows (the $1400 you are receiving each year) is reinvested at the 12.38 percent. The function also works if you borrow more money later and have other years with a negative cash flow. The assumption here is that the new money is borrowed at the same rate at which you initially borrowed it.

ANALYZING TRENDS
AND RELATIONSHIPS

EXCEL CAN BE VERY USEFUL WHEN YOU NEED TO make predictions of future data based on historical trends and when you want to explore the relationships between variables. Below are some examples:

- A company has tracked sales for several years and wishes to use this data to predict sales in future years.

- A city is doing some planning for city roads and wishes to predict future automotive traffic on certain roads based on historical traffic records.

- An environmental agency has obtained some data on the local increase in certain types of cancer and the change in air quality in several areas. The agency wishes to calculate the probable relationship of cancer rates to the various air quality variables.

- Education leaders have tracked the number of local students for several years and wish to use this data to project education resource needs for the future.

Predicting future data from current data is called *regression analysis*. Analyzing the relationship of variables is *correlation analysis*. This chapter will look at how you can do both of these with Excel.

REGRESSION ANALYSIS

The basic goal for any type of regression analysis is to estimate one variable from one or more related variables. Chapter 15 presented a simple regression analysis. Let's now look at more specific aspects of this type of analysis.

LINEAR REGRESSION

One variable is said to be linearly related to another variable if an increase or decrease in one variable causes a proportional increase or decrease in the other. As an example, assume you have accumulated fourteen years of sales data for a company as follows:

YEAR	SALES
1	6.50
2	14.20
3	23.50
4	30.10
5	38.80
6	48.40
7	55.50
8	60.10
9	64.10
10	65.60
11	68.80
12	68.90
13	68.80
14	70.20

For this example the y variable is the sales total, and the x variable is the year. You want to estimate the value of y corresponding to the x values 15, 16, 17, and 18 (the next four years). Once you have estimated these values, you can estimate budget values for employment levels, inventory, and warehousing.

As a start, assume a linear relationship. If this is true, an equation can be found that approximately fits the data of the form:

$$y = a_0 + a_1 x$$

You now need to solve for the values of a_0 and a_1. The resulting curve is said to be the regression curve of y on x, as y is estimated from x; that is, the graph of y as a function of x can be graphed as a straight line.

These constant values can be solved easily with Excel using the LINEST function. The function has two input arguments: the array of y values and the array of x values. It returns an array of two values: a_0 and a_1.

The worksheet for the example is shown in Figure 23.1. Enter the values for A8 to A25 and B8 to B21 as shown. The array function is entered to A31 and B31 as follows:

1. Select A31 and B31

2. Enter the following equation in the formula bar:

   = LINEST(B8:B21,A8:A21)

3. Hold down the Command key and press Return to enter the function as an array

The slope of the line should now be in A31, and the y intercept in B31. Now enter the formula for the first predicted value in C8 as

   = $B$31 + $A$31 * A8

Copy this formula to all cells from C9 to C25. This should give you the array of predicted values in column C.

You now need to calculate an R squared value. This is the number that indicates how well the line fits the data points. The general equation for this value is

$$r^2 = \frac{\Sigma(Yest - Yavg)^2}{\Sigma(Y - Yavg)^2}$$

You can use the worksheet to calculate this by creating a column for each sum and entering the following equation in the first cell for each:

COLUMN	TITLE	EQUATION
D	$(Y - Yavg)^2$	(B8 – $B$28) ^ 2
E	$(Yest - Yavg)^2$	(C8 – $B$28) ^ 2

The average ($B$28) is calculated in column B as the total of that column divided by the number of points in the array (14 in this case). The columnar sums are stored in row 27. The closer the R squared

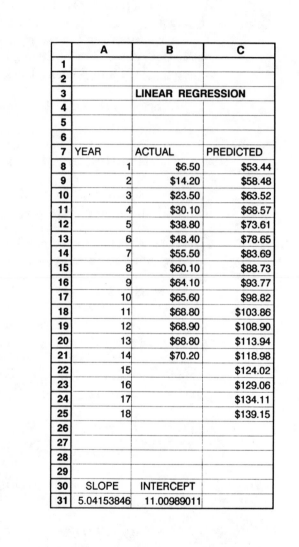

	A	B	C
1			
2			
3		**LINEAR REGRESSION**	
4			
5			
6			
7	YEAR	ACTUAL	PREDICTED
8	1	$6.50	$53.44
9	2	$14.20	$58.48
10	3	$23.50	$63.52
11	4	$30.10	$68.57
12	5	$38.80	$73.61
13	6	$48.40	$78.65
14	7	$55.50	$83.69
15	8	$60.10	$88.73
16	9	$64.10	$93.77
17	10	$65.60	$98.82
18	11	$68.80	$103.86
19	12	$68.90	$108.90
20	13	$68.80	$113.94
21	14	$70.20	$118.98
22	15		$124.02
23	16		$129.06
24	17		$134.11
25	18		$139.15
26			
27			
28			
29			
30	SLOPE	INTERCEPT	
31	5.04153846	11.00989011	

Figure 23.1: The worksheet for the linear regression

value comes to 1 the better the fit of the data to the linear equation represented by the array function. The R squared value is then E27/ D27, or .89966, which represents a good fit (Figure 23.2).

There is another and simpler method of calculating this R squared value. There should also be a linear regression line such that

$$x = b_0 + b_1 y$$

This is the regression curve of x on y. You can use the LINEST function to calculate $b_0 0_1$ and $b_0 1_1$ by simply reversing the arguments in the function used earlier. The R squared value can then be calculated as

$$r^2 = a_0 * b_0$$

Now chart the two data series (Actual and Predicted) using the following technique:

1. Select B8 to B21 on the worksheet

2. Create a new chart (File New) and use the Gallery menu to make it a line chart

3. Select the first option on the Gallery Line dialog box

4. On the worksheet, select C8 to C25

5. Use Edit Copy to copy the series to the Clipboard

6. Select the chart and use Edit Paste to paste the series to the chart

7. Add axis labels and a chart title as desired using Chart Attach Text

You should see the graph shown in Figure 23.3. Notice the points are very close to the line predicted by the linear regression equation, but the scattering of the actual points about the line is not random. Those in the middle are above the line, and those at the end are below the line. The curve of the actual sales line indicates that sales predicted by this linear regression are higher than could realistically be expected from looking at the data for the last few years. This suggests a curved line would probably be a better fit. This alternative will be examined in the next section.

	A	B	C	D	E	F
1						
2						
3		LINEAR REGRESSION				
4						
5						
6						
7	YEAR	ACTUAL	PREDICTED	(Y-Yavg)^2	(Yest-Yavg)^2	
8	1	$6.50	$16.05	1791.10332	1,073.87	
9	2	$14.20	$21.09	1198.64332	768.87	
10	3	$23.50	$26.13	641.174745	514.70	
11	4	$30.10	$31.18	350.491888	311.36	
12	5	$38.80	$36.22	100.429031	158.86	
13	6	$48.40	$41.26	0.17760204	57.19	
14	7	$55.50	$46.30	44.6033163	6.35	
15	8	$60.10	$51.34	127.206173	6.35	
16	9	$64.10	$56.38	233.434745	57.19	
17	10	$65.60	$61.43	281.520459	158.86	
18	11	$68.80	$66.47	399.143316	311.36	
19	12	$68.90	$71.51	403.149031	514.70	
20	13	$68.80	$76.55	399.143316	768.87	
21	14	$70.20	$81.59	457.043316	1,073.87	
22	15		$86.63			
23	16		$91.67			
24	17		$96.72			
25	18		$101.76			
26						
27	SUM	683.5		6427.26357	5782.39254	
28	AVERAGE	48.82142857				
29						
30	SLOPE	INTERCEPT		R squared		
31	5.04153846	11.00989011		0.89966632		

Figure 23.2: Calculating the R squared value

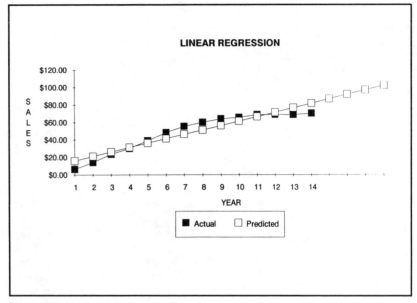

Figure 23.3: The linear regression chart

The TREND function is quite similar to the LINEST function, except that it returns the actual array of values. For example, you could select C8:C21 as an array, then enter **= TREND(B8:B21, A8:A21)** as an array (by holding down the Command key) to this range. You will get the same predicted values.

EXPONENTIAL REGRESSION

The same worksheet can be modified easily to try an exponential regression. The LINEST function in row 31 is changed to a LOGEST function. The arguments remain the same:

= {LOGEST(B8:B21,A8:A21)}

The equation in C8 is changed to

= $B$31 * $A$31 ^ A8

This is then copied down column C. Our predicted sales values are now even higher (Figure 23.4), but are they realistic?

	A	B	C
3		**EXPONENTIAL REGRESSION**	
4			
5			
6			
7	YEAR	ACTUAL	PREDICTED
8	1	$6.50	$15.72
9	2	$14.20	$18.22
10	3	$23.50	$21.13
11	4	$30.10	$24.50
12	5	$38.80	$28.40
13	6	$48.40	$32.93
14	7	$55.50	$38.18
15	8	$60.10	$44.27
16	9	$64.10	$51.32
17	10	$65.60	$59.50
18	11	$68.80	$68.99
19	12	$68.90	$79.99
20	13	$68.80	$92.74
21	14	$70.20	$107.53
22	15		$124.67
23	16		$144.55
24	17		$167.60
25	18		$194.32
26			
27	SUM	683.5	
28	AVERAGE	48.82142857	
29			
30	SLOPE	INTERCEPT	
31	1.15943025	13.55521499	

Figure 23.4: Predicted sales using the LOGEST function

The chart of Figure 23.5 shows the new predictions. The predicted sales look good, but do not match up with what could be expected realistically. The actual sales data is fairly steady over the last few years. The exponential curve predicts a growth that clearly does not fit the true data too well. In some cases, however (such as population growth curves), the exponential regression is quite realistic.

CURVILINEAR REGRESSION

In the real world, you can often accomplish a good fit by extending the linear regression to include additional terms as necessary:

$$y = a_0 + a_1x + a_2x^2 + a_3x^3 + a_ix^i......a_nx^n$$

This is the general form for a curvilinear regression: a regression in which a curved line that fits the data points is calculated. The calculations aren't for the faint of heart, but the rewards are often well worth

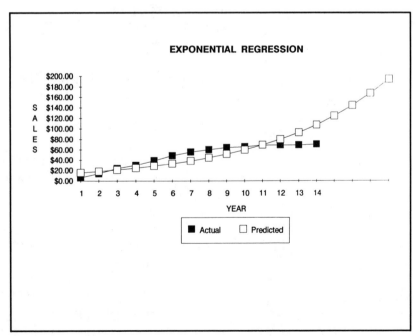

Figure 23.5: The chart of sales using the LOGEST function

it to include at least the a^2 term, giving a quadratic regression. There is no general function to create the constants for the equation, so you must calculate them using the following equations:

$$\Sigma y \quad = a_0 N \quad + a_1 \Sigma x \quad + a_2 \Sigma x^2$$

$$\Sigma xy \quad = a_0 \Sigma x \quad + a_1 \Sigma x^2 \quad + a_2 \Sigma x^3$$

$$\Sigma x^2 y \quad = a_0 \Sigma x^2 \quad + a_1 \Sigma x^3 \quad + a_2 \Sigma x^4$$

The worksheet to calculate the various coefficients and the resulting R squared value is shown in Figure 23.6. This gives the following equations:

$$683.5 \quad = 14 a_0 \quad + 10 a_1 \quad + 1015 a_2$$

$$6273.2 \quad = 105 a_0 \quad + 1015 a_1 \quad + 11025 a_2$$

$$65419.6 \quad = 1015 a_0 \quad + 11025 a_1 \quad + 127687 a_2$$

These can be solved to get the following constants:

$$a_0 = -7.3747253$$
$$a_1 = 11.9357692$$
$$a_2 = -0.4596154$$

The following equation is then used in column C to find the predicted values:

$$y = a_0 + a_1 x + a_2 x^2$$

The R squared value is solved the same way as it is with linear regression. Notice that the R squared value is now close to .995, an extremely good fit.

Here are the column definitions:

COLUMN	TITLE	FIRST CELL EQUATION
A	YEAR	
B	ACTUAL	(entered)
C	PREDICTED	= $E$36 + $E$34*A8 + $E$35*A8*A8

COLUMN	TITLE	FIRST CELL EQUATION
D	X^2	$= A8*A8$
E	X^3	$= A8^3$
F	X^4	$= A8^4$
G	XY	$= A8*B8$
H	X^2*Y	$= A8*A8*B8$
I	$(Y - Yavg)^2$	$= (B8 - \$B\$28)^2$
J	$(Yest - Yavg)^2$	$= (C8 - \$b\$28)^2$

The resulting constants are calculated and stored as follows:

CELL	CONSTANT
E34	a_1
E35	a_2
E36	a_0

Here are some of the formulas to enter in the worksheet. All of the equations will not be listed here. Row 27, as before, contains the following sums:

CELL	FORMULA
D30	$= B27$
F30	$= C5$
G30	$= A27$
H30	$= D27$
D31	$= G27$
F31	$= A27$
G31	$= D27$
H31	$= E27$
D32	$= H27$

	A	B	C	D	E	F	G	H	I	J	K
1											
2											
3		CURVILINEAR	REGRESSION								
4											
5	Number of Years		14								
6											
7	YEAR	ACTUAL	PREDICTED	X^2	X^3	X^4	XY	X^2 * Y	(Y-Yavg)^2	(Yest-Yavg)^2	
8	1	$6.50	$4.10	1	1	1	6.5	6.5	1791.10332	1999.8784	
9	2	$14.20	$14.66	4	8	16	28.4	56.8	1198.64332	1167.11582	
10	3	$23.50	$24.30	9	27	81	70.5	211.5	641.174745	601.494491	
11	4	$30.10	$33.01	16	64	256	120.4	481.6	350.491888	249.858817	
12	5	$38.80	$40.81	25	125	625	194	970	100.429031	64.1231361	
13	6	$48.40	$47.69	36	216	1296	290.4	1742.4	0.17760204	1.27168994	
14	7	$55.50	$53.65	49	343	2401	388.5	2719.5	44.6033163	23.3586325	
15	8	$60.10	$58.70	64	512	4096	480.8	3846.4	127.206173	97.508029	
16	9	$64.10	$62.82	81	729	6561	576.9	5192.1	233.434745	195.913856	
17	10	$65.60	$66.02	100	1000	10000	656	6560	281.520459	295.84	
18	11	$68.80	$68.31	121	1331	14641	756.8	8324.8	399.143316	379.620261	
19	12	$68.90	$69.67	144	1728	20736	826.8	9921.6	403.149031	434.658349	
20	13	$68.80	$70.12	169	2197	28561	894.4	11627.2	399.143316	453.427884	
21	14	$70.20	$69.64	196	2744	38416	982.8	13759.2	457.043316	433.4724	
22	15		$68.25								
23	16		$65.94								
24	17		$62.70								
25	18		$58.55								
26											
27	105	683.5	683.5	1015	11025	127687	6273.2	65419.6	6427.26357	6397.54177	
28		$49									
29											
30	SLOPE	INTERCEPT		683.5 =		14	105	1015			
31	5.04153846	11.00989011		6273.2 =		105	1015	11025			
32				65419.6 =		1015	11025	127687			
33	0.17845075	-1.212220508									
34				a1=	11.9357692		Solve for a0				
35				a2=	-0.4596154		6607.16667	135.333333	1015	9811.66667	
36	0.89966632			a0=	-7.3747253		6273.2	105	1015	11025	
37							----------	----------	----------	----------	
38	R-SQUARED=	0.995375668				#1	333.966667	30.3333333		-1213.3333	
39											
40							68139.931	1140.51724	11025	119754.31	
41							65419.6	1015	11025	127687	
42							----------	----------	----------	----------	
43						#2	2720.33103	125.517241		-7932.6897	
44											
45						Mod of #1	2183.45103	198.317241		-7932.6897	
46							----------	----------	----------	----------	
47							536.88	-72.8			
48											
49							Solve for a2				
50						Mod of #1	1381.93103	125.517241		-5020.6897	
51						#2	2720.33103	125.517241		-7932.6897	
52							----------	----------	----------	----------	
53							-1338.4			2912	

Figure 23.6: The quadratic regression worksheet

CELL	FORMULA
F32	= D27
G32	= E27
H32	= F27

Solving for a_0:

CELL	FORMULA
G35	= D30*G31/G30
H35	= F30*G31/G30
I35	= G30*G31/G30
J35	= H30*G31/G30
G36	= D31
H36	= F31
I36	= G31
J36	= H31
G38	= G35 – G36
H38	= H35 – H36
J38	= J35 – J36

The actual list is much longer than this, but there is nothing unusual in the calculations. You can use normal algebraic methods to solve the quadratic equation.

Figure 23.7 shows the chart of the quadratic regression. Notice that the curve is now a very good fit, but the sales projections are not as good. The projections actually show a dip in sales. This indicates management should begin to take some action to turn things around.

It is a good idea to use cell references instead of numbers when creating the formulas to solve the equations for the constants. This enables the worksheet to be used as a template for other quadratic regressions. For example, the number of samples is stored in C3, permitting it to be used in B28 to calculate the average. This way, you don't have to remember to adjust B28 if rows are inserted or deleted.

In inserting or deleting rows in the input array, insert or delete from the middle to ensure the sum formulas in row 27 remain valid. You can simplify your work in solving for the constants by modifying the x array so that the sum is zero. (For a 15 element array, you would start at -7.) The second equation can then be solved directly for a_1. There are then only two unknowns, and the other two equations can be solved for the other two constants.

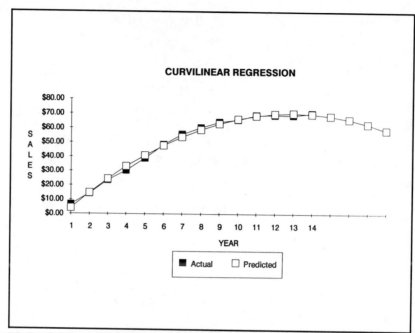

Figure 23.7: Curvilinear regression chart

CORRELATION ANALYSIS

In correlation analysis, you are trying to find how well an equation describes the relationship between two variables. The problem is closely related to regression analysis. In regression analysis, you are trying to find a curve that fits the data. In correlation analysis, you are measuring how well the curve fits the data. Indeed, you have already calculated the R squared value for the examples of this chapter. In correlation analysis, this is called the *coefficient of determination.* The square root of this value is the *coefficient of correlation,* or the measure of the fit of the curve. The value can vary from -1 (negative correlation) to 1 (perfect correlation). A value of zero indicates no correlation. The general equation for R squared (the coefficient of determination) is the same as in the previous sections:

$$r^2 = \frac{\Sigma(Y_{est} - Y_{avg})_2}{\Sigma(Y - Y_{avg})_2}$$

As an example, assume you want to find out how much correlation there is between the height of a father and the height of the oldest son. To simplify our work, assume a sample of 14 father/son relationships. Figure 23.8 shows this sample in a worksheet. The fathers are shown as the x array, the sons as the y array.

The basic worksheet is similar to the earlier examples. The A26:B26 cells contain the array **LINEST(B7:B20,A7:A20)**. The sums are in row 22. The R squared value is calculated as E22/C22. The coefficient of correlation is the square root of this, or .7668.

You can also calculate an error of estimate as follows:

$$s_{y,x} = \text{sqrt}(\Sigma(Y - Yest)^{\wedge}2/N)$$

Before charting, be sure the category column is in ascending order. In this case the data was entered in order. If you must sort, select rows 7 to 20. Then select the Data Sort Command and click OK. The values in column A should now be in ascending order. All the rows should have been sorted.

	A	B	C	D	E	F
1						
2		CORRELATION ANALYSIS				
3						
4	Number of Samples		14			
5						
6	X	Y	(Y-Yavg)^2	PREDICTED	(Yest-Yavg)^2	(Y-Yest)^2
7	62	66	2.93877551	65.08035714	6.937579719	0.845742985
8	63	66	2.93877551	65.60714286	4.44005102	0.154336735
9	64	65	7.367346939	66.13392857	2.497528699	1.285794005
10	65	68	0.081632653	66.66071429	1.110012755	1.793686224
11	66	65	7.367346939	67.1875	0.277503189	4.78515625
12	66	66	2.93877551	67.1875	0.277503189	1.41015625
13	67	68	0.081632653	67.71428571	0	0.081632653
14	67	67	0.510204082	67.71428571	0	0.510204082
15	68	69	1.653061224	68.24107143	0.277503189	0.575972577
16	68	71	10.79591837	68.24107143	0.277503189	7.611686862
17	69	68	0.081632653	68.76785714	1.110012755	0.589604592
18	70	68	0.081632653	69.29464286	2.497528699	1.676100128
19	71	70	5.224489796	69.82142857	4.44005102	0.031887755
20	72	71	10.79591837	70.34821429	6.937579719	0.424824617
21						
22	938	948	52.85714286		31.08035714	
23		67.7142857				
24						
25	SLOPE	INTERCEPT		Err of Est	1.489975003	
26	0.52678571	32.4196429		R SQUARED	0.588006757	
27				R	0.766815986	
28	0.52678571	32.4196429				

Figure 23.8: Correlation analysis of father/son heights

In this case, the error of estimate is 1.4899 inches. If the sample is large enough, 68 percent of the sample will fall within 1.4899 inches of the regression line. You will also find 95 percent of the sample within twice this distance and 99.7 percent within three times this distance.

To chart this, first select A7:B20. Then pull down the Edit menu and choose Copy. Open up a new chart using the File menu. The chart area will be blank. Pull down the Edit menu, choose Paste Special. Click Categories in First Column and OK. This will create the first level graph. Use the gallery menu to change it to a Scatter graph of the default type. Set each data series to start at 61 by selecting each axis in turn and using the Format Axis command.

Now add the second data series. Select D7:D20 on the worksheet, pull down the Edit menu, and choose Copy. Select the Chart and use the Edit Paste command to add it to the chart. Pull down the Chart menu and choose Overlay Chart Type. Click Line. This will give you a regression line that passes through the scattered points. Add labels, and the resulting graph should look like Figure 23.9. The

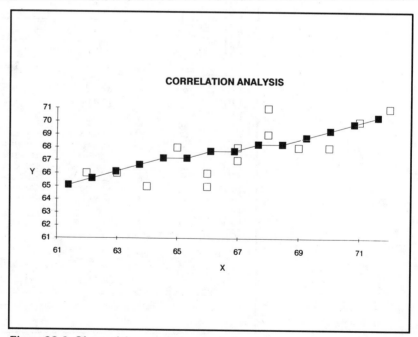

Figure 23.9: Chart of the correlation analysis

results indicate a definite correlation between the height of the fathers and sons.

Keep in mind that statistics should be used for support and not for illumination. The regression analysis only finds a mathematical equation that approximates the existing data. There is no guarantee that future points will fall on the line. The equation defines an observed relationship between two variables. Here are some issues to consider:

- There may really be no relationship between the variables. The observed relationship could be strictly chance.

- The two variables may be two effects of a single cause. There may appear to be a positive relationship between local smog and cancer rates. In reality, they may both be the effects of a single cause if a nearby corporation is producing a pollutant that causes both the smog and cancer.

- There may be other causes to consider. Historical data can be used to predict highway traffic in an area for the future; but if a new shopping center is built nearby, don't expect the same equations to work.

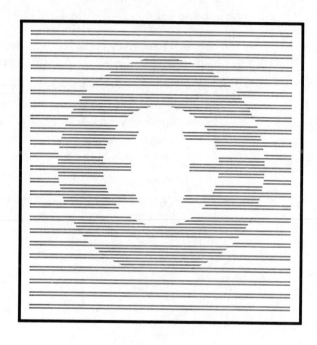

USING MACROS

A MACRO IS A SERIES OF EXCEL COMMANDS THAT perform a specific Excel action. In effect, macros permit you to write and name your own application programs using worksheet commands as well as create your own functions. For this reason, macros are generally considered one of the most important features of any worksheet software package.

Although macros are a part of many worksheet products, Excel's macros have three major distinctions: they are easy to use, they don't take up worksheet room (they're generally saved on separate macro sheets), and they use a special macro language. Remember that Excel can create three types of documents (check your File New command), and you have already explored two of these: the worksheet and chart. The macro worksheet is the third type. (You can save a macro on the worksheet, but keeping it on a separate sheet enables you to use it with many worksheets.)

Excel provides the ability to create two types of macros: *command macros* and *function macros*. In Chapter 24 you will learn when to use command macros and how to create them. Chapter 25 introduces the use of function macros. Chapter 26 provides more advanced macro techniques, and Chapter 27 describes all of the available Excel macro functions.

INTRODUCTION TO MACROS:
THE RECORDER

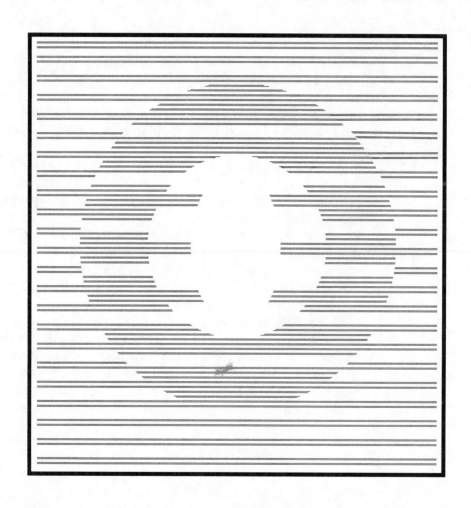

CHAPTER 24

COMMAND MACROS ARE LIKE COMPUTER PROGRAMS, and consist of a series of Excel commands. In this chapter, you will learn when to use command macros and how to create them. You will use Excel's recorder, which makes creating simple command macros very easy.

COMMAND MACRO USES

A command macro is a series of commands that accomplish a desired action. The commands are stored as a single program, which can be executed as many times as necessary.

Command macros are primarily used in two applications: whenever it is necessary to repeat a series of steps two or more times and whenever a complex series of steps must be performed.

If you find yourself repeating certain Excel operations frequently, you should consider using a command macro. Examples of applications that you would use frequently are listed below:

- Putting headings in a worksheet

- Creating schedules for financial calculations

- Formatting and setting up presentation aspects of a frequently-used worksheet

The second use of command macros simplifies and improves the accuracy of a task that must be completed within tight deadlines. For example, suppose that a series of annual reports must be prepared from data that will not be available until a few days before an annual meeting. Weeks before the annual meeting, you could create macros to produce the final report from dummy data. Once the actual data are available, the same macros could be used by almost anyone to create the final reports in a very short time.

As another example, assume a bank sets up a very complex worksheet for working with businesses to make decisions on granting loans. The five-year history of the business is entered, and Excel uses this to make projections for the next five years based on assumptions about several variables, such as interest rates. Two worksheets are created: the history worksheet and the projection worksheet. The worksheets are linked using Excel's linking abilities. Macros are used to set up the linking and prompt the user for the input. These worksheets can then be used at various bank locations by people with little experience with Excel. Macros make this easy.

Just about anything you can do on the worksheet you can also do with a macro. You can write macros that open new worksheets, create charts, create and paste names, display dialog boxes for entry or select, and print worksheets.

Here are some more applications for command macros:

- Creating calendars for the month

- Creating a weekly schedule, with the date and day of the week as headers

- Doing mail merge letters from a database of addresses

- Creating menu structures for a user that has had little Excel experience

- Doing financial schedules

WHAT IS A MACRO?

Turn briefly forward and examine the macro example in Figure 24.7 that you will create later in this chapter. You should recognize many of the commands because they match the menu options you have already used. Don't worry about understanding them now, but keep the following points in mind:

- Although not obvious here, each macro has a name. The first cell in the macro is named by the user.

- The commands are listed in a vertical column. They are executed starting at the named cell and continuing downward until a RETURN, HALT, GOTO or blank cell is reached. A RETURN, HALT or blank cell terminates the macro execution. GOTO causes a branch to the argument of the GOTO function.

COMMAND MACROS VERSUS TEMPLATES

There is a big difference between using a template and a command macro. A template is a blank form with some information and formats already specified. You fill in the blank form to create a worksheet. Templates are useful for many applications and should be used whenever possible. Macros, however, permit automatic execution of Excel commands. An example will clarify this.

Assume you run an advertising agency in which employees are working on jobs for several clients during the day. Each employee needs to track, for each period of the day, the client for which they were working and the job category (different categories are billed at different rates).

You could create a blank time sheet, and it could be saved as a template. The problem with this template, however, is that the employees would still need to fill in their names and the day's date. In addition, they could accidentally enter invalid categories. And they could neglect to fill in certain time slots if they can't remember the category or prefer not to say what they did during that time.

Using a macro permits you to prompt for the employee's code and then the respective input information. The employee's name is then obtained from a lookup table using the employee code. The macro can then look up categories that are entered in a lookup table, reject invalid entries, and calculate totals based on category rates in a table. The macro can be designed to block the possibility of any time slot being left empty. Finally, it can automatically print the time sheet. The user doesn't need to know anything about Excel except to load the worksheet and answer the prompts.

CREATING A COMMAND MACRO

There are two ways to create a command macro with Excel: use the recorder or enter the macro manually. The recorder is the easiest method, but is less flexible than manual entry. In this chapter you will learn the recorder method. For the moment, let's look at using the recorder. The manual entry of command macros is discussed in Chapter 26.

There are essentially three steps to creating a command macro using the recorder:

1. Opening the macro sheet and setting the range

2. Recording the program

3. Naming the macro

Now, suppose that you are one of the managers of Acme Manufacturing. You have created a number of quarterly reports that all use the same heading, as shown in Figure 24.1. You've decided to take advantage of Excel's macro feature and create a macro that will add this heading to any worksheet. The following sections describe how to create this command macro.

OPENING THE MACRO SHEET AND SETTING THE RANGE

The steps that you will take are recorded on a separate macro sheet that looks much like any Excel worksheet. First, open a regular worksheet. Then, follow these steps to open the macro sheet and set the range for the macro:

1. Pull down the File menu and choose New.

2. When the New dialog box shown in Figure 24.2 appears, click Macro Sheet, then click OK.

3. A new document titled Macro1 will open on the screen. The menu bar has not changed. The row and column headings are the same. Notice, however, that the columns are much wider than they are on the typical worksheet document. This permits you to enter formulas and see the entire formula. In this case you are interested in the formula, not the result. (The Options Display command is automatically set to display formulas, but you can switch this back if necessary.)

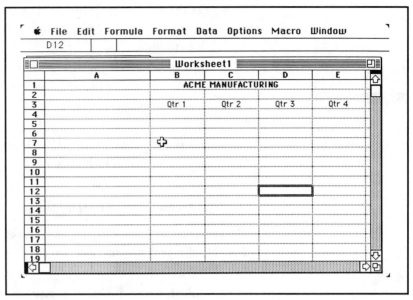

Figure 24.1: The worksheet heading

You can select a range for the macro, but you might run out of space before ending the macro and it is difficult to predict how many cells you will actually need. By selecting the column instead of a single cell in the column, Excel assigns the entire column to the macro. This is generally best.

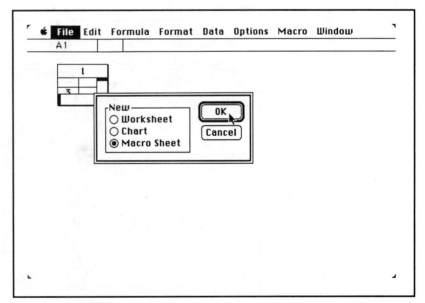

Figure 24.2: The New dialog box

4. Set the macro range by clicking the column A designator on the macro sheet to indicate that you will record your macro in this column.

5. Pull down the Macro menu. If the last item is Absolute Record, click it to change it to Relative Record. Then choose Set Recorder.

6. Size the macro sheet slightly smaller so you can see both sheets and click your original worksheet again to make it active, as shown in Figure 24.3.

RECORDING THE PROGRAM

With your worksheet active, you must turn on the recorder and then actually perform the task that you want the macro to accomplish. Follow these steps:

1. Pull down the Macro menu and choose Start Recorder. Nothing on the macro sheet or worksheet will change.

Figure 24.3: The macro and worksheet windows

2. Carry out the steps that you want the macro to execute:

   a. Select cell C1.

   b. Enter the title ACME MANUFACTURING.

   c. Widen column A by selecting it, pulling down the Format menu, and choosing Column Width. When the dialog box appears, change the width of column A to 20 characters and click OK, as shown in Figure 24.4.

   d. Enter the column titles by selecting cell B3 and dragging the cursor to cell E3. Enter the column titles shown in Figure 24.1.

   e. Center the titles by selecting rows 1 and 3, pulling down the Format menu, choosing Alignment, and double-clicking Center or clicking Center and clicking OK, as shown in Figure 24.5.

   f. Put the title in boldface print by selecting cell C1, pulling down the Format menu, and choosing Style. When the

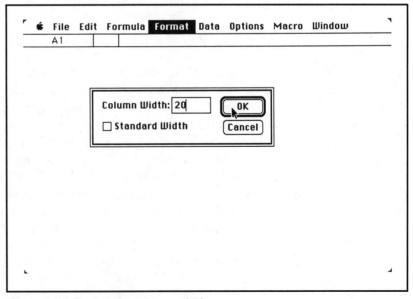

Figure 24.4: Setting the column width

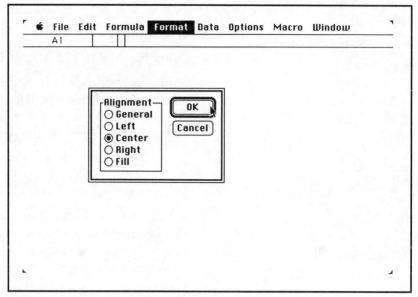

Figure 24.5: Setting the alignment

dialog box appears, click Bold and click OK, as shown in Figure 24.6.

3. Pull down the Macro menu and click Stop Recorder.

Your macro sheet should now look like Figure 24.7. Notice that your commands have been stored in column A using a special language. Column A now contains a series of formulas that are much like the formulas that you use on your worksheets. The formulas contain functions from the Excel macro language. Like any functions, these have arguments. The SELECT function selects the cell or cells specified in the argument, and the FORMULA function is used to enter data into a specified cell or cell range. Compare each function in the column with your actions when you followed the steps above.

In any macro, the statements are any of four types:

- Action statements, which move the cursor, format, or do any menu activities

- Assignment statements, which assign a value to a variable (look forward to Figure 25.2 for an example)

> ✓ If you make a mistake during entry, correct it and your correction will automatically be recorded in the macro. You can also use the Cancel button to clear an entry before it is entered on the macro worksheet.

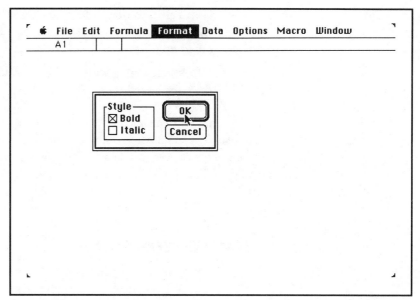

Figure 24.6: Selecting the style

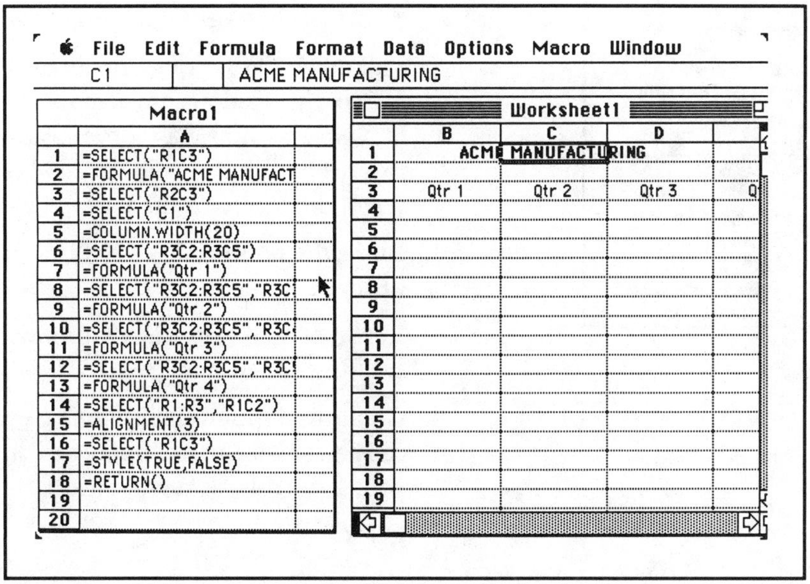

Figure 24.7: The macro worksheet after the command entry

- Control statements, such as those that use the IF command, which control what statements are executed based on a specified condition

- I/O statements, which receive keyboard information from the user based on a prompt or display messages to the user

You may also have comment statements, the macro name, and other features in your macro; but you cannot have a blank cell in the macro. In Chapter 26, you will learn more about how to use Excel's macro language to key in your macros manually.

NAMING THE MACRO

The macro has now been recorded, but it must be assigned a name before you can use it. You can also assign the macro a keystroke sequence that can be used to execute the program.

Follow these steps to name your macro:

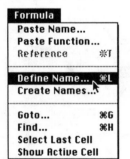

1. Select the macro sheet.

2. Select the first cell in the macro sheet.

3. Pull down the Formula menu and choose Define Name. You will see the window shown in Figure 24.8. Notice that the familiar window now has some new options that apply only to macros and that the Refers To box references $A$1, the first cell of the macro commands. The cursor is in the Name box.

4. Enter the name HEADING in the Name box. Do not click OK yet.

5. In the Macro box, click Command to indicate that you are creating a command macro.

6. Click the Option-Command Key box and enter an uppercase X. (You can use uppercase or lowercase letters to define your keystroke sequence.)

7. Click OK.

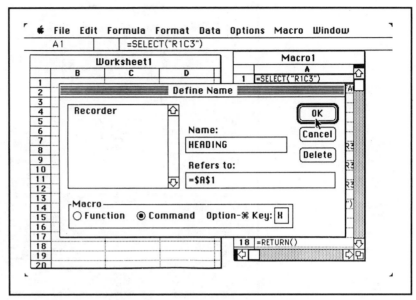

Figure 24.8: The Define Name window for macros

Name macros using the same rules as naming a function: use periods instead of spaces.

You have now named your command macro and defined a keystroke sequence that you can use to execute this macro.

SAVING THE MACRO

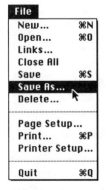

Macros are not associated with any worksheet or chart document; they are stored as separate macro documents. You must save the macro sheet after it is created if you want to use the macro that it contains later or with other worksheets.

Follow these steps to save your command macro:

1. Select the macro sheet

2. Pull down the File menu and choose Save As

3. When the dialog box shown in Figure 24.9 appears, enter the name HEADING, then click OK

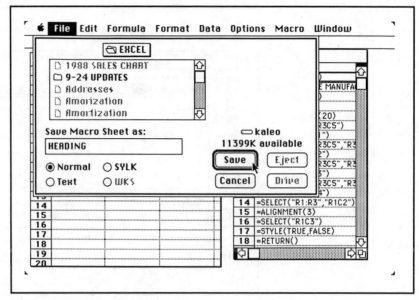

Figure 24.9: Saving the macro sheet

You can store many macros to use with the same document. Then, when you open that one sheet, all the command macros stored on it will be available for your use.

EXECUTING YOUR COMMAND MACRO

To execute your HEADING macro, you can use either of two methods:

- Choose the Run command on the Macro menu
- Press the keyboard sequence

However, before you use either method, the macro sheet that contains the macro must be open. If the macro sheet is not open, you can open it by pulling down the File menu and choosing Open. The dialog box shown in Figure 24.10 will appear. Select the name of the macro sheet, then click OK.

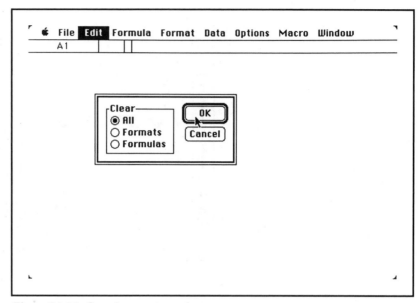

Figure 24.10: Opening a macro sheet

Now, clear your worksheet by selecting the entire worksheet, pulling down the Edit menu, and selecting Clear. When the dialog box shown in Figure 24.11 appears, click All, then click OK.

To execute your command macro using the Macro menu, follow these steps:

1. Be sure that the worksheet is clear and selected

2. Pull down the Macro menu and choose Run

3. When the dialog box shown in Figure 24.12 is displayed, double-click the macro name HEADING

Excel will execute the macro, and the heading will be entered onto the worksheet. Your worksheet should look like Figure 24.1.

To execute a command macro from the keyboard, first clear the worksheet area. Then hold down the Command key, press the Option key, and press the key that you assigned to the macro (an uppercase X for this example). The macro will be executed to create the worksheet heading shown in Figure 24.1.

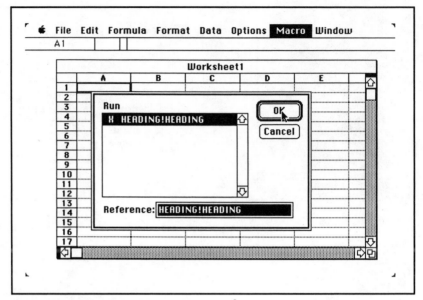

Figure 24.11: Clearing the worksheet

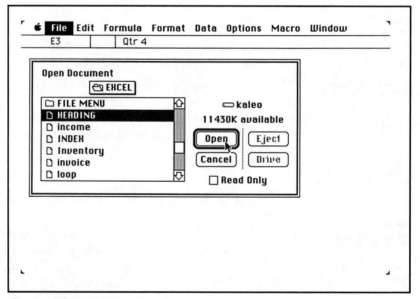

Figure 24.12: The Run dialog box

EDITING A MACRO

You can edit the macro sheet, just like any other Excel document. You can change arguments, delete or insert rows, or even create the entire macro by manually entering it from the keyboard.

You can experiment by making the following changes in your macro sheet:

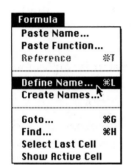

1. Change the column width of column A to 25 characters

2. Put the title in italics instead of boldface

Now, execute your command macro again using the new macro.

You can also edit the macro name. To change the name or key-stroke sequence, follow these steps:

1. Select the macro sheet

2. Select the first cell of the macro

3. Pull down the Formula menu and choose Define Name

4. When the Define Name dialog box appears (refer to Figure 24.8), click the macro's name

5. Edit the name in the Name box or the keyboard code in the Macro box

6. Click OK

Be careful when editing macros that you do not insert a blank cell in other macros on the same worksheet. For example, you may insert a row to add a new line to a macro. At the same time, however, this can open a new blank cell in every macro in other columns. Use the special form of the Insert command that only moves the cells in the single column.

You can easily add new entries to the end of an existing macro. If you turn the recorder on to record on a range that already has entries, the previous entries are not deleted. Instead, Excel temporarily removes the RETURN at the end. The new entries are added at the end, and the RETURN appended again. If this is not what you want, redefine the recorder range first or begin entries after the previous RETURN.

USING COMMAND MACROS

This chapter is intended as only a brief introduction to command macros. Here are some basic rules for using command macros:

- Be sure that you think through what you are trying to accomplish before you enter the commands. You may wish to do a dummy run to test the sequence before you record it. In this way, you can avoid entering errors or unnecessary extra steps into the macro sheet.

- Generally, the first step in recording a macro is to position your cursor at the desired point on the worksheet. Don't forget to start the recorder, *then* position the cursor.

- Don't be bashful about using macros. Anytime that you find yourself planning to repeat a command sequence, save it as a command macro.

- Make the macros as readable as possible. Using presentation features such as style and border control without gridlines helps readability.

- You can put the name of the macro in the first named cell of the macro (see Figure 25.2 in the next chapter).

- You can put many macros on one macro sheet, each with its own name. You can then use the macro sheet as a library, opening it when you open Excel and using it with many worksheets.

- Document your macros. Add comments to clarify what the macro is doing. The best place for comments is in the column to the immediate right of the macro column.

SUMMARY

This chapter is intended only as an introduction to macros. Macros are one of the most powerful features of the Excel spreadsheet program. The next two chapters will explore macros in more depth.

USING FUNCTION
MACROS

CHAPTER 25

EXCEL'S FUNCTION MACRO CAPABILITY PERMITS you to create your own functions, extending the function library that is already a part of Excel. You can decide what arguments are needed in your functions and what results are to be returned in the worksheet cell. Once you create a function macro, you can include it in formulas, just as you would use any other Excel function.

For most standard applications, Excel's extensive built-in functions can be used. However, you may need to define your own functions for special applications, such as civil engineering and financial analyses, in which lengthy, specialized formulas are used frequently.

In this chapter, you will learn how to create function macros and how to use some of Excel's macro language functions. You'll find a complete alphabetical list of the functions in Chapter 27.

FUNCTION MACRO USES

A function macro is essentially a user-defined function. It calculates an output dependent variable from one or more independent input variables. As explained in Chapter 8, a function is an abbreviation for a formula. A function can also be defined as an operator, similar to a symbol operator such as + or −. It contains one or more arguments that are used as input to calculate a result. When you create a function macro, you define the arguments, results (using the RETURN( ) function), and formulas to calculate the results. You should create function macros whenever you need to use special formulas many times in several worksheets. If you use function macros, you don't have to remember the formulas to get your results. You only have to remember the name of the function and the type and order of the arguments.

CREATING A FUNCTION MACRO

Let's create a simple function macro that can be used to convert a temperature from centigrade to Fahrenheit. There are four steps to creating a function macro:

1. Defining the formulas and arguments
2. Entering the function
3. Defining the name
4. Saving the macro

DEFINING FORMULAS AND ARGUMENTS

The formula for the temperature-conversion function is

$$b = (9/5) * a + 32$$

where b equals the temperature in Fahrenheit and a equals the temperature in centigrade. The function will have the name FAHRENHEIT and contain one input argument for the temperature in centigrade.

ENTERING THE FUNCTION MACRO

To create the function macro, first open a macro sheet by pulling down the File menu, choosing New, and double-clicking Macro Sheet on the New dialog box (see Figure 25.1). This will open a blank macro sheet. Function macros must be entered manually—you cannot use the recorder.

Follow these steps to enter the FAHRENHEIT function macro:

1. Enter the function macro title **FAHRENHEIT** into cell A1, as shown in Figure 25.2.

2. In cell A2, define the input argument for the function using the ARGUMENT macro language function. Enter = **ARGUMENT**("centigrade"), including the quotation marks with the argument name.

3. In cell A3, define your formula: = **(9/5)*centigrade + 32**.

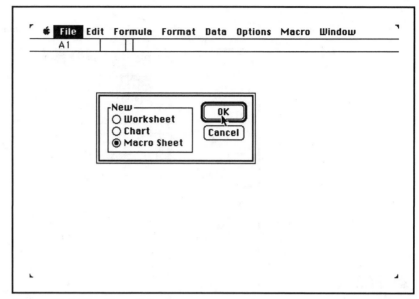

Figure 25.1: The New dialog box

4. In cell A4, use the RETURN macro language function and reference the cell on the macro sheet that contains the result: **RETURN(A3)**.

When entering a function macro, keep in mind the following rules:

- Excel's macro language functions must be preceded by an equal sign, like any other function.
- When using ARGUMENT statements, the names of the input arguments must be enclosed in quotation marks.
- In the formulas, the names of the input arguments are not enclosed in quotation marks.

Include comments in function macros. If the macro is entered to column A, use column B to comment on your macro. Specify the arguments, results, and the calculations.

NAMING THE FUNCTION MACRO

The next step is to assign a name to the function macro. Use the following procedure:

1. Be sure that the first cell of the macro sheet is selected

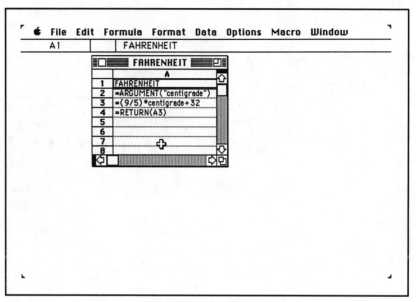

Figure 25.2: Entering the function macro

Formula

Paste Name...	
Paste Function...	
Reference	⌘T
Define Name...	**⌘L**
Create Names...	
Goto...	⌘G
Find...	⌘H
Select Last Cell	
Show Active Cell	

2. Pull down the Formula menu and choose Define Name

3. When the Define Name window appears, the name FAHR-ENHEIT from the first cell is displayed in the Name box, as shown in Figure 25.3

4. Click Function in the Macro box, then click OK

File

New...	⌘N
Open...	⌘O
Links...	
Close All	
Save	⌘S
Save As...	
Delete...	
Page Setup...	
Print...	⌘P
Printer Setup...	
Quit	⌘Q

SAVING THE FUNCTION MACRO

Before you use this function macro, save the macro sheet by following these steps:

1. Select the macro sheet

2. Pull down the File menu and choose Save As

3. When the dialog box shown in Figure 25.4 appears, enter the name **FAHRENHEIT**

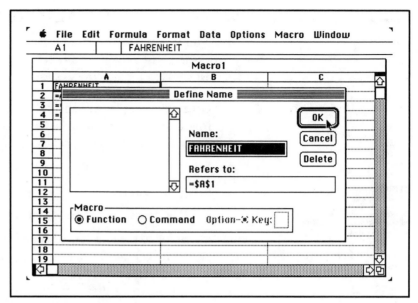

Figure 25.3: The Define Name window

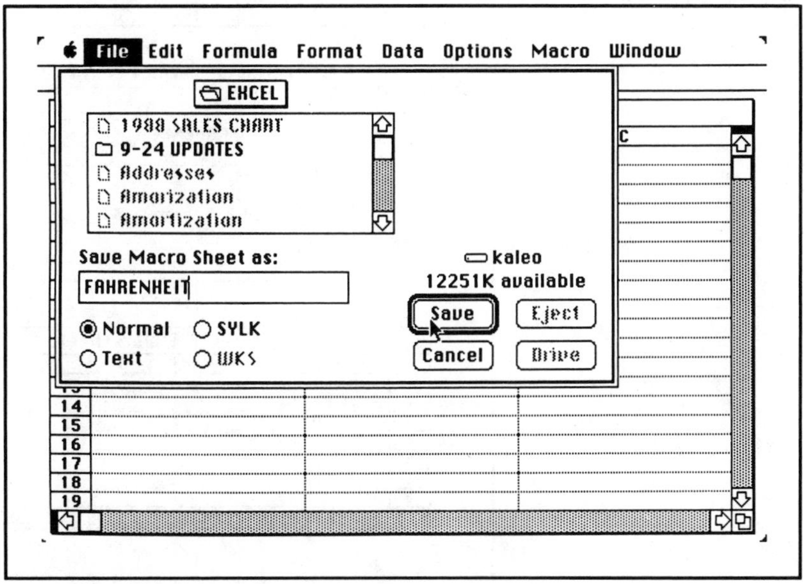

Figure 25.4: Saving the function macro

USING FUNCTION MACROS

Once you've created a function macro, you can use it in formulas on a worksheet just as you would use any other function. Let's use the FAHRENHEIT macro to see how a function macro works:

1. Create the simple worksheet shown in Figure 25.5. Enter the row titles **Centigrade** and **Fahrenheit** in cells A2 and A3. Enter the value of 80 in cell B2.

2. Enter the formula:

   a. Select cell B3.

   b. Pull down the Formula menu and choose Paste Function.

   c. Scroll to the end of the list on the dialog box and click the name of your new function, as shown in Figure 25.6. The formula for cell B3 should now appear in the formula bar, as shown in Figure 25.7.

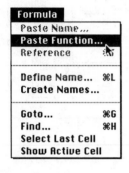

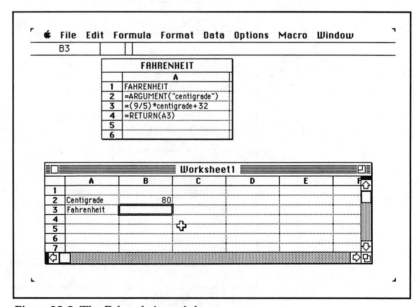

Figure 25.5: The Fahrenheit worksheet

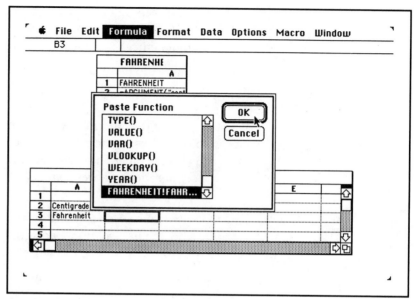

Figure 25.6: The Paste Function dialog box

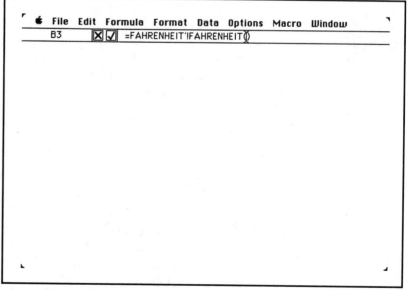

Figure 25.7: Starting the formula

d.   Click cell B2 on the worksheet. This will enter B2 as the argument to the function in B3 and complete the formula entry, as shown in Figure 25.8.

e.   Click the enter box or press Return. The result 176 is displayed in cell B3.

Experiment with your new worksheet—enter a few different values into cell B2 and watch the results change in cell B3.

You can also use function macros in tables. Here is a procedure for creating a centigrade to Fahrenheit conversion table:

1.   Create two columns, A and B, for the temperatures. In row 5, label the first column **Centigrade** and the second column **Fahrenheit**, as shown in Figure 25.9.

2.   In cell A7, enter the first centigrade temperature to be used: 0.

3.   Use the Series command on the Data menu with a step value of 5 to fill in the rest of column A to at least 100 degrees.

4.   Now you must put the formula that references the macro function in cell B6. To do so, select cell B6, pull down the Formula menu, and click Paste Function. When the Paste Function dialog box (Figure 25.6) appears, click your new FAHRENHEIT function, then click OK. Next, click cell C6 to indicate that it is the input cell for the argument, then click the enter box.

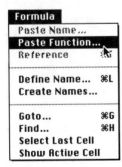

5.   Select the range for the table by clicking cell A6 and dragging to the end of column B.

6.   Now set up the table by pulling down the Data menu and choosing Table. When the Table window appears, click Column Input Cell, click cell C6, and then click OK.

Excel will then apply each input centigrade temperature to cell C6, use this as an input to the FAHRENHEIT formula in cell B6, and then put the results in column B. Figure 25.10 shows the worksheet with the calculated values.

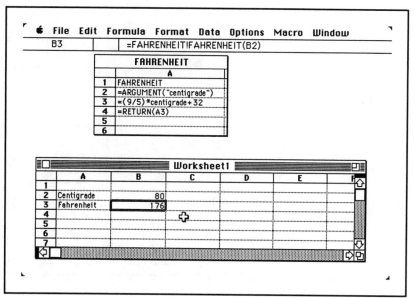

Figure 25.8: Completing the formula

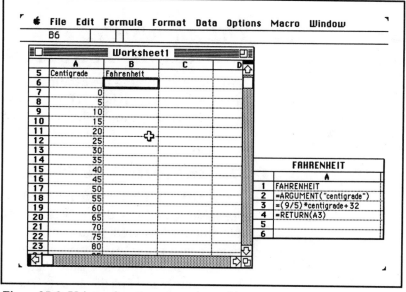

Figure 25.9: Using a function macro in a table

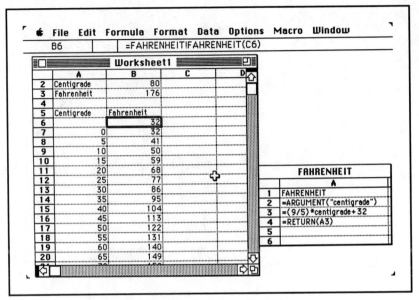

Figure 25.10: The worksheet after the table calculation

THE ARGUMENT AND RESULT FUNCTIONS

As you have seen in the example above, Excel's macro language ARGUMENT and RESULT functions can be used to control the types of input and output values calculated by your function macros.

THE ARGUMENT FUNCTION

The ARGUMENT function is used to pass values from the worksheet to the function. In the previous example, the ARGUMENT function contained a single argument. You can also use an additional argument to control the type of value passed. This optional second argument is primarily used to ensure that the proper type of argument is always included in a function macro. The second argument also permits the use of arrays as input arguments.

The form of the function with the second argument is =ARGU-MENT(name,type), where type is one of the following numbers:

TYPE VALUE	*REQUIRED ARGUMENT*
1	Numeric
2	Text
4	Logical
8	Reference
16	Error
64	Array

If the input value for the function is not of the proper type, Excel will try to convert it. If the value cannot be converted, Excel will return the error value #VALUE! without executing the function. The type argument values can be combined to permit the entry of several data types. If the argument is omitted, Excel uses 7 as a default value, which permits the entry of numeric, text, or logical values.

There is also a third form of the ARGUMENT function: =ARGUMENT(name,type,ref). In this case, ref is used to refer to a specific cell on the macro sheet. You can then use formulas on the macro sheet to refer to the input value by a name or by a cell reference. For example, on your FAHRENHEIT macro sheet, you could change cell A2 to the value

    =ARGUMENT("centigrade",1,A5)

and the formula for cell A3 to

    = (9/5) * A5 + 32

and the formula would still work correctly. The third argument, A5, refers to a cell on the macro sheet. Try this, and you'll see that the centigrade value from the worksheet is entered into cell A5 on the macro sheet, which is used as the input cell for the formula.

When you are defining a function, you can include several arguments. Each is specified in a separate cell of the macro worksheet, using the ARGUMENT function. For example, suppose you want to create your own PMT function and call it PMTX. The built-in function uses five arguments. For example, to use the PMT function to calculate the payments for borrowing $24,000 at 15 percent for 3 years you would use the following equation:

$$= PMT(.015/12,360,24000,,0)$$

Two arguments are not used.

You could, however, write your own function using only three arguments and calculate the interest using the macro shown in Figure 25.11. This macro uses three input values to calculate a single output value.

In a similar way, you can input arrays to a function, or have a function return an array value. It is also possible to create macro functions that use no input arguments, such as a function that prompts for a value and then returns the value to the program.

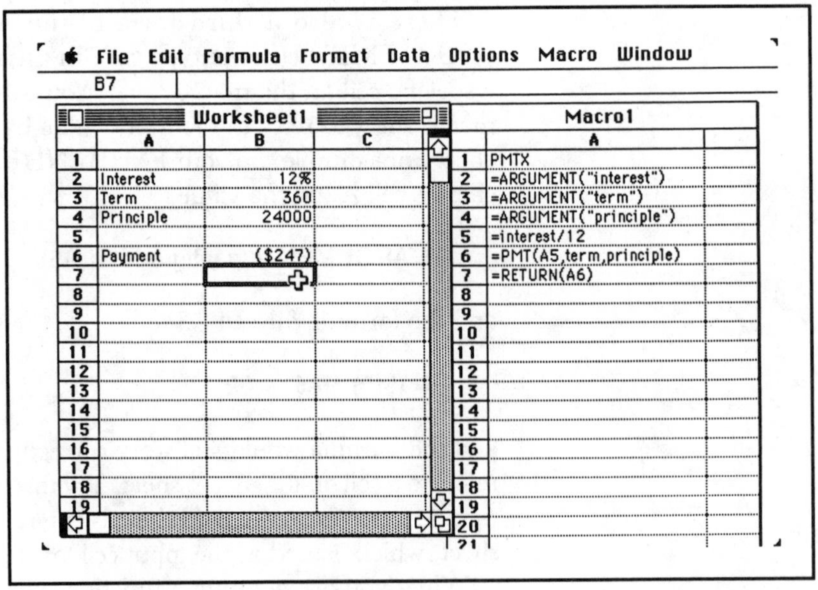

Figure 25.11: Using multiple input values

THE RESULT FUNCTION

You can use the RESULT function to indicate the type of value that you want to be returned, in the same way that you use the ARGU-MENT function to control the input value. The function takes the form = RESULT(*ref,type*).

The numeric values for *type* are the same as those for the ARGU-MENT function. If the result of the function calculation is of a different type, Excel will try to convert it. If Excel cannot do this, it will return the error value *VALUE!.

As with the ARGUMENT function, you can use the second argument of the RESULT function to indicate an array as the output result. Just be sure that you use the proper *type* value for the array. You can also combine values so that your output could be several types of data. For example, a value of 71 would permit numeric, text, or logical values, or even arrays.

The RESULT function is not the same as the RETURN function. RESULT should be used as the first formula on the macro sheet in your function macro.

SUMMARY

You have now seen how to create two types of macros: the command macro and the function macro. When should you use a command macro and when should you use a function macro?

Command macros can be created with the recorder if they are simple, and even the initial development of complex command macros can be simplified using the recorder to test various aspects. You can also initiate the execution of the macro using an Option-Command sequence or use the Macro Run command.

Function macros can't be created with the recorder, but can be assigned a name and used like other Excel built-in functions. They can be called from the worksheet or from another macro. After execution, they return a resulting value to the calling cell.

Whereas command macros are generally used to automate tasks that involve a sequence of commands, function macros have a simpler and more specific role: they supply a value based on a defined procedure.

CREATING PROGRAMS
WITH MACROS

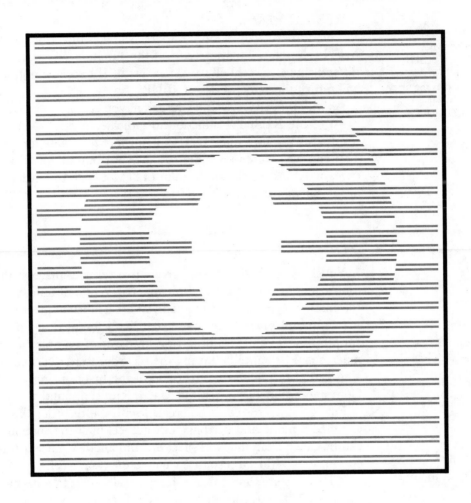

EVEN SOMEONE WITH A MINIMUM OF EXCEL EXPERI -ence can easily create command macros by turning on the recorder. However, you cannot create very complex macros with the recorder. To create more advanced command macros, you can use Excel's macro language. If you are designing an application, you will probably need to use both the recorder and manual macro entry.

This chapter describes how to use Excel's macro language to create interactive macros and macros with decision structures and loops. You will also learn more about using both relative and absolute cell addressing in macro sheets, how to interrupt an executing macro, and how to organize your macro sheets. You will learn when to use the recorder and when to use manual entry. In the next chapter you will find a directory of all the Excel macros.

Before beginning this chapter, be sure that you have already used the recorder to create a few command macros.

RECORDING CELL REFERENCES

You may want to include both relative and absolute cell references in your macros. Excel's recorder can handle both types of cell addressing. In the default mode, the cell references entered in a macro are relative to the cell that was active when you started the recorder.

The recording mode can be set only after the recorder range has been set.

To switch to absolute cell addressing, pull down the Macro menu. Absolute Record should be displayed as one of your choices. This means that the current reference mode is relative. If you click Absolute Record, the references that you record will use absolute cell

addressing. The next time that you pull down the Macro menu, Relative Record will be displayed instead of Absolute Record. Click it to switch back to relative cell addressing.

You can switch from relative to absolute cell addressing and back at any time while you are recording, and the final macro can be a mixture of both types. However, once the macro is recorded, the references cannot be switched by using a command on the Macro menu. You then have to edit the macro sheet to change the reference types.

As an exercise, record a simple command macro that enters the title ACME MANUFACTURING into cell C1 and the value of Test two rows below the title cell, as shown in Figure 26.1. (Be sure that Cell C1 is selected within the macro.) It will be recorded using the relative cell addressing. Then, repeat the exercise, but this time, pull down the Macro menu and select Absolute Record. When you're done recording, run each macro, starting with the cursor on a cell other than C1. With absolute referencing, the titles will be put in C1 and C3, as you originally created them. With relative referencing, the titling will start from the starting active cell.

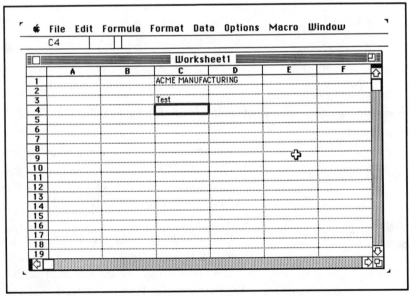

Figure 26.1: Testing relative and absolute cell addressing in macros

RECORDER MESSAGES

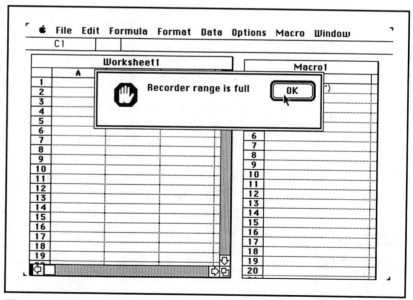

When defining a range, select the entire column to allow plenty of room for your macro.

Occasionally, while you're creating a macro the recorder may stop, and Excel will display the error message "Recorder range is full," as shown in Figure 26.2. This means that you did not choose a large enough macro sheet range when you started recording the macro. If there is room on the macro sheet, select a new macro range that includes the old range and continue. If there is not enough room on the macro sheet, replace the RETURN function on the old macro sheet with a GOTO function that references a cell on a new macro sheet and continue on the new sheet. For example

GOTO (LIBRARY!A1)

would have the macro continue in the first cell of a macro sheet titled LIBRARY. Macro sheets are as large as worksheets, so you'll seldom run out of room. So for more applications, simply specify a larger range.

Figure 26.2: Recorder error message

WRITING MACRO PROGRAMS

You may need to create a command macro with some special features that cannot be added using the recorder. Typical examples include interactive macros and macros that contain branching and loops. To include these features, you will need to write your own macro sheet or alter an existing one. In this section, you will learn more about these programming techniques.

When you create your own macros, in many cases it is better to record a simple version of the macro first, then insert the extra steps without the recorder.

CREATING INTERACTIVE MACROS

There may be times when you want your command macro to stop during execution and obtain an input value from the user, then continue. This is called an *interactive macro*. Interactive macros can be used for very simple tasks, as well as for complex programs, such as creating advanced macro sheets automatically, so the user has to enter only the data needed at the proper steps. Remember, however, that the development of complex macros takes quite a bit of programming development time.

There are three ways to make an Excel macro interactive:

- Using the INPUT function
- Using the question mark form of a command
- Using an ALERT command

Let's try each of these methods.

In the example, you will create a simple macro that will insert a worksheet heading. The heading will contain names of months, but you need to make the macro interactive because you want to specify the starting and ending months. You also want the macro to stop and display a message and wait for you to tell it to continue.

To start, create a macro that will generate the worksheet shown in Figure 26.3. Follow these steps (refer to Chapter 24 if you need help):

1. Clear the worksheet, open a macro sheet, set the recorder, and select the worksheet

2. Start the recorder

3. Select cell C1, enter the title, and put it in boldface print

4. Expand column A to 20 characters by using the Column Width command on the Format menu

5. Enter **Jan-88** in cell B3

6. Use the Series command on the Data menu to enter the remaining months by selecting column B through column M of row 3 and then selecting Month in the Date Unit box in the Series dialog box (see Figure 26.4)

7. Center the data in the first three rows

8. Stop the recorder

The final macro sheet should look like Figure 26.5. Run the macro to be sure that it works.

You will now modify this macro sheet to make the command macro interactive in three different ways.

THE INPUT FUNCTION   You can replace any of the macro sheet's existing function arguments with the INPUT function. Then,

Figure 26.3: The worksheet for the interactive command macro

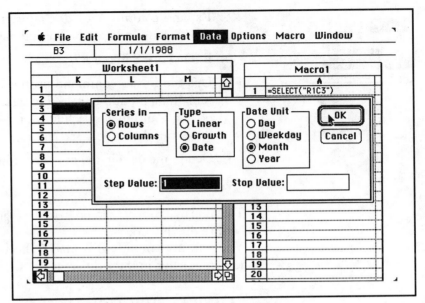

Figure 26.4: The Series dialog box

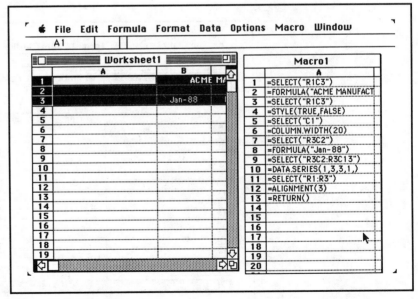

Figure 26.5: The macro sheet

when the macro reaches that function, it will stop and ask for the input value. The form of the input function is INPUT(*prompt, type, title*). Its arguments represent the following:

- *prompt* is the message to be displayed to the user in the window.

- *type* is an integer that represents the type (or types) of input numbers that can be accepted (see Chapter 25).

- *title* is the name of the window. If *title* is omitted, it is assumed to be Input.

Now, edit cell A7 on the macro sheet so that it reads

= FORMULA(INPUT("Enter the starting date ",1))

Repeat the macro execution. The program will stop and display the Input window shown in Figure 26.6. Enter the starting date **Nov-88** and click OK. Column B on the worksheet is now headed Nov-88, and the remaining headings automatically increment from that date, as

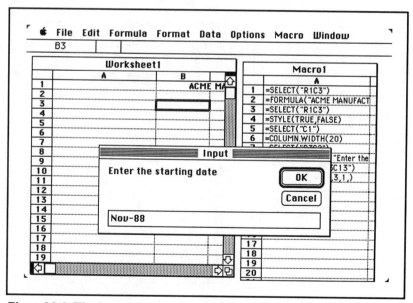

Figure 26.6: The Input window

shown in Figure 26.7. Repeat this exercise again, entering letters that aren't a valid month abbreviation, such as **Apl**. What happens?

THE QUESTION MARK COMMAND FORM Another method for obtaining input is to use the *question mark form* of the command. Most macro language commands that produce a dialog box have a question mark form. If you want your macro to stop and display the command's dialog box, replace the command with its question mark form.

To specify the ending month in the heading that your macro creates, and thus control the number of columns printed when the macro is executed, you need to use the Series dialog box. Cell A10 on the macro sheet contains the DATA SERIES command. Replace this command with

= DATA.SERIES?( )

Now, execute your macro again. After you have filled in the Input window, you will see the Series dialog box, as shown in Figure 26.8.

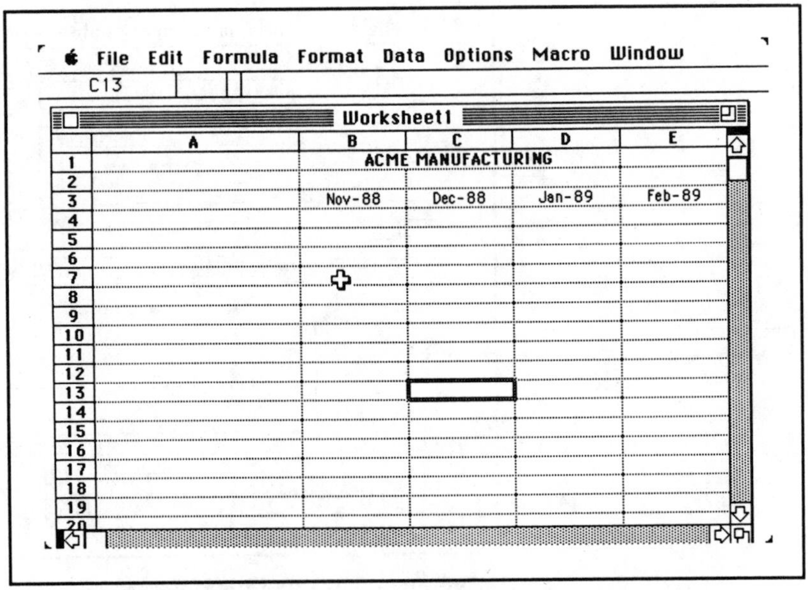

Figure 26.7: The worksheet after entering a date in the Input window

Click Month, enter a stop value of **Jan-89**, and click OK. Your worksheet will be printed with only three columns.

ALERT BOXES   A third way to obtain input during a macro execution is through the use of an alert box. The form of the ALERT function is = ALERT(*text, type*), where *type* is a value for the type of icon and buttons to display, and *text* is the prompt to display in the box. The values available for *type* are listed below:

Type	*Icon*	*Buttons*
1	? (caution)	OK, Cancel
2	* (note)	OK
3	! (stop)	OK

After the DATA.SERIES? command in cell A10 of your macro sheet, insert a new line (select the row, pull down the Edit menu, and select Insert). On this line, add the following command:

= ALERT("Are you having fun? ",1)

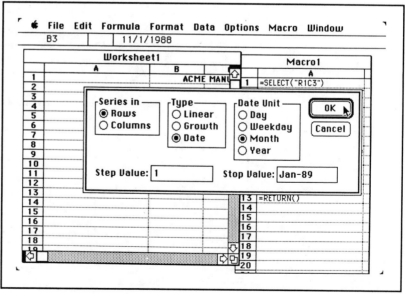

Figure 26.8: Using the question mark form of the command

Now, execute your macro one last time. The program will stop and display an alert box, as shown in Figure 26.9. Click OK, and the macro will continue. If you click Cancel, the function returns a logical value of FALSE, and in this case the macro execution still continues as the return value is not tested.

BRANCHING: MAKING DECISIONS

You can use the IF and GOTO functions in your macros to create program branches, loops, and other controls.

USING THE IF AND GOTO FUNCTIONS   You can use the IF function in a macro to make decisions based on a certain value. For example, you could use the ROWS function in cell A1 of the macro sheet to return the number of rows in a range selection. It would have the following form:

= ROWS(SELECTION( ))

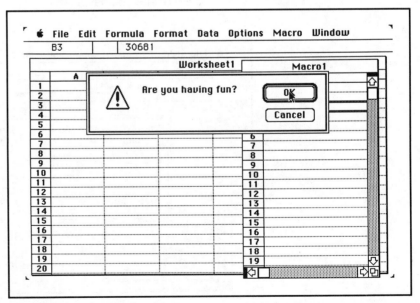

Figure 26.9: Using an alert box

Later in the program, the macro could examine this value and make a decision based on the number of rows. For example, the command

= ALIGNMENT(IF(A2 = 1,3,2))

would adjust the alignment according to the number of rows. If there is one row, the ALIGNMENT function will use 3, and the display will be centered. If not, the ALIGNMENT function will use 2, and the display will be left-justified. The first value applies if the IF function is true, the second if the function is false. (See Chapter 27 for further explanation of the ALIGNMENT function.)

You can combine the IF function with the GOTO function to control the direction of the program execution with the IF statement. For example, the command

= IF(A2 = 1,GOTO(A13))

would have the program go to cell A13 if the value in cell A2 was 1.

You can also use Boolean operators (AND, OR, etc.) to combine conditions before a decision. For example, the command

= IF(AND(A2 = 1,A3 = 1),GOTO(A13))

would have the program go to cell A13 only if both cells A2 and A3 had a value of 1.

The GOTO function can even be used to branch to another macro and, when that macro is completed, return to the calling macro to continue.

Be careful not to confuse IF and GOTO. IF is an Excel function and returns a value based on a condition. GOTO is a macro function, and defines the cell from which the next program statement will be read.

LOOPING You can also use the IF function to control looping in a macro. To use loops, you must first set a variable in a cell to an initial value using the SET.VALUE function. For example, the command

= SET.VALUE(A25,1)

in cell A2 would put the value of 1 in cell A25 on the macro sheet. Inside the loop, the following would be entered:

= SET.VALUE(A25,A25 + 1)

This increments the value in A25 each time it is executed.

When the macro is invoked, each time that the above statement is encountered, the value of that cell would be incremented by 1. You could then have the macro test the condition after cell A25 is incremented and determine if it should remain in the loop by using the following command:

$$= IF(A25 < = 25, GOTO(A3))$$

Be sure that you loop back *after* the SET.VALUE function.

Figure 26.10 shows another example of using a loop in a macro. This macro calculates the greatest common denominator (GCD) of two numbers. Notice two columns are used for the macro, with the Formula Create Names command used to define the cells in column B from column A.

OTHER CONTROL STRUCTURES Using the IF and GOTO functions, you can set up a wide variety of control structures, such as IF-THEN-ELSE and WHILE commands. The techniques are the same as with other languages.

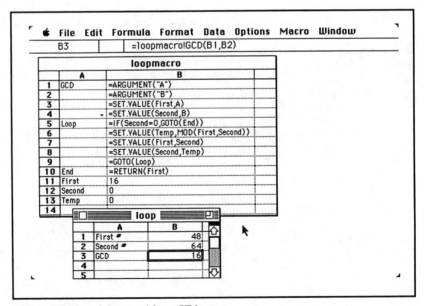

Figure 26.10: A Macro with an IF loop

Figure 26.11 shows a REPEAT-UNTIL loop that calls another menu macro. The user selects from various menu options, and the selected option is invoked. The looping continues until the Quit option is selected.

CALCULATION ORDER

When Excel calculates a worksheet, it does the entire worksheet without regard to the order of the cells. Each time that you edit a cell, all cells that depend on the edited sheet are recalculated. However, the calculation order for a macro sheet is quite different. The macro sheet represents a procedural program, and the order of the statements determines the order of the execution. Calculation begins at the first cell of the macro (the named cell) and proceeds down the column until a RETURN, HALT, blank cell, or GOTO function is encountered. The first three terminate the macro execution. The GOTO function defines the cell from which the next statement will be read.

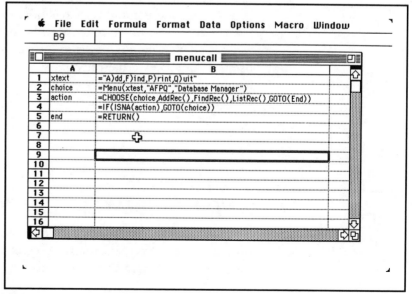

Figure 26.11: A REPEAT-UNTIL loop

INTERRUPTING A MACRO EXECUTION

You can interrupt the execution of a macro, just as you would interrupt a printing, by pressing Command-. (the Command key and a period). The dialog box shown in Figure 26.12 is then displayed. This box shows the current cell to be calculated on the macro sheet and has three buttons: Halt, Step, and Continue. The Halt button terminates the macro execution, the Continue button continues the execution, and the Step button displays the Single-Step window shown in Figure 26.13. You can use this window to go through the macro one step at a time, which is useful if your macro doesn't work the way you want it to and you want to check each step individually.

USING MACRO SHEETS

With many competing products, a macro is stored on the actual worksheet with which it is used, and the macro can only be run with that worksheet unless you copy it into another worksheet. Because macros are entered into a remote area of the worksheet, the worksheet is much larger and requires more computer memory. Excel's macros are stored in separate sheets, and they can be used with any worksheet. You should, however, be careful when creating links and using names as external references on macro sheets, because these features are always identified with specific worksheets. If you use an exclamation point without a worksheet name in a formula, the reference always refers to the active worksheet.

COMMENTING AND LABELING MACROS

If you enter a constant into a cell on a macro sheet, it will be ignored during the execution of the macro. You can use this feature to add comments, create program labels, or to title the program. It is a good idea to

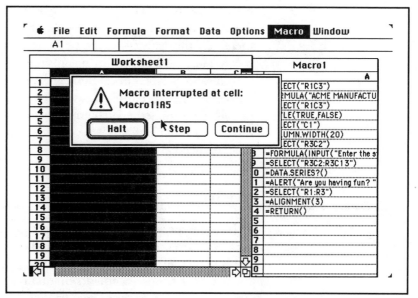

Figure 26.12: The dialog box displayed when you interrupt a macro

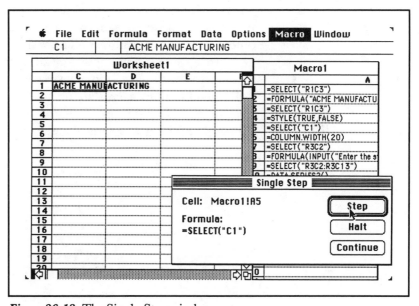

Figure 26.13: The Single-Step window

use comments and labels liberally to document your macros. Include in the comments the definition of each argument, the type of each argument, and the definition and type of result expected. Put the name of the macro in the first cell on the macro sheet.

You can use labels in column A, the macro statements in column B, and comments in column C, as shown previously in Figure 26.10. You can also use this method to name cells that will hold values. You can then use the Formula Define Name command to label all cells in the macro that you need at one time.

DEBUGGING MACROS

If you experience problems in creating a macro, try to simplify what you are doing and then build to the complex. Use the recorder to build the very basic part of the macro, then add the decision controls and other enhancements manually. If you already have a complex macro that has problems, try to break out the troublesome part and test it separately.

To simplify your work, create libraries of common macros that you use. Put the command macros that you use frequently on a single macro sheet, assign the macro sheet a name, and then use this with other programs as a library. This will save you development time and, what's more, you know they already work. You can open several macro sheets with a single worksheet.

Remember that macros are one of the most important features of any spreadsheet program. Take the time to learn how to use them well so that their use is natural and easy.

THE MACRO
LANGUAGE
FUNCTION DIRECTORY

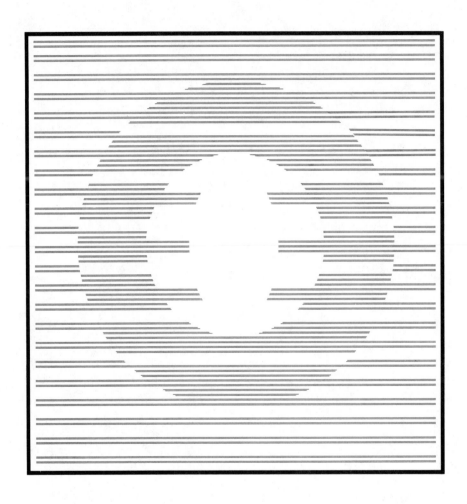

THIS CHAPTER DEFINES EACH OF THE MACROS THAT are available for the Excel user. The macros are in alphabetical order, with each listing giving the arguments, menu equivalent, action definition, and one or more examples. Macro arguments are the same types as those defined by other functions: text, numeric, logical, reference, error, or array.

For each listing, the question-mark equivalent (if available) forces the display of the command-equivalent dialog box, from which the user can choose the desired options.

A1.R1C1(*logical*)

Menu Equivalent

Option, A1/Options, R1C1

Action

Switches display mode to A1 if *logical* is TRUE. Switches display mode to R1C1 if *logical* is FALSE.

Example

= A1.R1C1(TRUE)

switches display mode to A1.

ABSREF(*ref-text, ref*)

Menu Equivalent

(none)

Action

Returns reference of cells that have a relative relationship to *ref* as specified by *ref-text*. *Ref-text* must be an R1C1-style relative reference.

Example

=ABSREF("R[-1]C[-2]",C4)

equals A3.

ACTIVATE(*window*)

Menu Equivalent

Window, XXXXX

Action

Activates the window defined by *window*.

Example

=WINDOW(Worksheet1)

activates Worksheet1.

ACTIVATE.NEXT( )

ACTIVATE.PREV( )

Menu Equivalent

Equal to typing Command-M and Command-Shift-M

Action

Activates the next or previous window.

Example

=ACTIVATE.NEXT( )

ACTIVATE.CELL( )

Menu Equivalent

(none)

Action

Returns reference to active cell in the selection.

Note

The SELECTION command returns the selected range, ACTIVATE.CELL returns the active cell in that range.

Example

On a new worksheet

    = ACTIVE.CELL( )

equals Worksheet1!A1.

ALERT(*text, type*)

Menu Equivalent

(none)

Action

Displays an alert box with the message *text* (see Figure 27.1). The box can be one of the three following types:

TYPE VALUE	*ACTION*
1	Caution alert with a ? icon and both the OK and Cancel buttons
2	Note alert with a * icon and OK button
3	Stop alert with a ! icon and OK button

Example

    = ALERT("Number must be less than 10",2)

ALIGNMENT(*type*)

ALIGNMENT?( )

Menu Equivalent

Format, Alignment

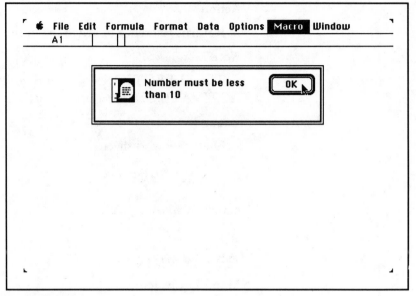

Figure 27.1: Alert box

Action

Aligns the selected cells to the *type* format:

TYPE VALUE	FORMAT
1	General
2	Left
3	Center
4	Right
5	Fill

Example

= ALIGNMENT(3)

centers the selected cells.

ARGUMENT(*name, type*)

ARGUMENT?(*name, type, ref*)

Menu Equivalent

(none)

Action

Permits passing arguments to a macro. For each argument of a macro, there must be one ARGUMENT function in the macro. ARGUMENT functions must come before any other formulas in the macro except the RESULT function. If you use the form ARGUMENT(*name, type*), *name* refers to the value passed in the macro. If you use the form ARGUMENT(*name, type, ref*), the value is passed to *ref* (on the macro sheet), and *name* refers to the cell where the value is stored. The first form must be used if the value passed is a reference.

The value of *type* determines what types of values Excel will accept for the argument. If the value passed is not the correct type, Excel will attempt to convert it. If it cannot be converted, Excel returns an error value #VALUE!.

TYPE VALUE	*ARGUMENT TYPE ACCEPTED*
1	Number
2	Text
4	Logical
8	Reference
16	Error
64	Array

You can combine these for multiple types. For example, a value of 3 for *type* would permit a number or text to be accepted. If *type* is omitted, a default value of 7 is assumed, which permits numbers, text, or logical values. *Type* must be specified to use arrays or references.

Example

(See Chapter 25.)

BEEP( )

Menu Equivalent

(none)

Action

Sounds the Macintosh bell. The volume can be controlled from the control panel. Useful for alerting the user after a specified action is completed.

Example

= BEEP( )

BORDER(*outline, left, right, top, bottom*)

BORDER?( )

Menu Equivalent

Format, Border

Action

Creates the specified border on the currently selected cells. Each argument indicates whether the specified option is checked (TRUE) or not (FALSE).

Example

= BORDER(TRUE,FALSE,FALSE,FALSE,FALSE)

draws an outline around the currently selected cells.

CALCULATE.NOW( )

Menu Equivalent

Options, Calculate Now

Action

Initiates a calculation on the current worksheet.

Example

    = CALCULATE.NOW( )

CALCULATION(*type, iteration, number-of, change*)

CALCULATION?( )

Menu Equivalent

Options, Calculation

Action

Specifies the type of calculation to use. There are three types:

TYPE VALUE	*CALCULATION TYPE*
1	Automatic
2	Automatic except tables
3	Manual

Iteration is a logical value where TRUE indicates checked, FALSE indicates not checked.

Number-of and *change* are numbers representing the maximum number of iterations and the maximum amount of change respectively.

Example

    = CALCULATION(2,FALSE)

sets the calculation type to automatic except for tables.

CALLER( )

Menu Equivalent

(none)

Action

Gives the reference of the cell containing the function that called the current macro. If the function was part of an array formula in an array of cells, CALLER( ) gives the reference of the range. Useful in a macro if the calculation depends on the location or size of the calling reference.

Example

= ROWS(CALLER( ))

returns the number of rows in the calling reference.

CANCEL.COPY

Menu Equivalent

(none)

Action

Cancels border around a range after a cut or copy operation.

Example

= CANCEL.COPY

CELL.PROTECTION(*locked, hidden*)

CELL.PROTECTION?( )

Menu Equivalent

Format, Cell Protection

Action

Specifies cell protection or hiding on the selected range. Locked and hidden are logical values where TRUE is checked and FALSE is not checked.

Example

= CELL.PROTECTION(TRUE,FALSE)

CLEAR(*parts***)**

CLEAR?( )

Menu Equivalent

Edit, Clear

Action

Clears the specified cell range. There are three types of *parts:*

PARTS	CLEARS
Parts	Clears
1	All
2	Formats
3	Formulas

Example

= CLEAR(1)

CLOSE( )

Menu Equivalent

(None: same as clicking close box on active window)

Action

Closes currently active window.

Example

= CLOSE( )

COLUMN.WIDTH(*width***)**

COLUMN.WIDTH(*width, ref***)**

COLUMN.WIDTH?( )

Menu Equivalent

Format, Column Width

Action

The first form changes the width of currently selected columns. The new width will be *width*. The second form changes the width of the columns containing *ref* to *width*. If *ref* is specified, it should be an external reference to the current worksheet or an R1C1 reference in a text style (in quotation marks).

Examples

=COLUMN.WIDTH(16)

changes the currently selected columns to a width of 16.

=COLUMN.WIDTH(16,!$B:$C)

changes the width of columns B and C to 16.

COMBINATION(*type*)

COMBINATION?( )

Menu Equivalent

(Chart) Gallery, Combination

Action

Selects the combination chart type from the menu. *Type* is a number that corresponds to a format in the gallery.

Example

=COMBINATION(2)

COPY( )

Menu Equivalent

Edit, Copy

Action

Copies the selected cells or data series to the Clipboard.

Example

    = COPY( )

COPY.CHART(*as-shown*)

COPY.CHART?( )

Menu Equivalent

(Chart) Edit, Copy Chart

Action

Copies the selected chart to the Clipboard. *As-shown* must be the number 1 or 2 with the following meanings:

1   Copy as shown on the screen

2   Copy as when it will be printed

Example

    = COPY.CHART(1)

COPY.PICTURE( )

Menu Equivalent

Edit, Copy (while holding down Shift key)

Action

Copies selection to the Clipboard as a picture.

Example

    = COPY.PICTURE( )

CREATE.NAMES(*top-row, left-column*)

CREATE.NAMES?( )

Menu Equivalent

Formula, Create Names

Action

Creates names using row or column headings. Arguments must be logical values, with TRUE indicating checked and FALSE indicating not checked.

Example

= CREATE.NAMES(TRUE,FALSE)

creates names in the top row.

CUT( )

Menu Equivalent

Edit, Cut

Action

Deletes the selected range from the worksheet.

Example

= CUT( )

DATA.DELETE( )

DATA.DELETE?

Menu Equivalent

Data, Delete

Action

Deletes the records from the database that meet the specified criteria.

Example

= DATA.DELETE( )

DATA.FIND(*logical*)

Menu Equivalent

Data, Find /Data, Exit Find

Action

The value of *logical* determines the action. If *logical* is TRUE, Excel attempts to find a record that meets the specified criteria. If *logical* is FALSE, Excel attempts an Exit Find.

Example

= DATA.FIND(TRUE)

DATA.FIND.NEXT( )

DATA.FIND.PREV( )

Menu Equivalent

Equal to typing Command-F and Command-Shift-F

Action

Finds the next and previous records in the database that match the specified criteria.

Example

= DATA.FIND.NEXT( )

DATA.SERIES(*series-in, type, unit, step, stop*)

DATA.SERIES?( )

Menu Equivalent

Data, Series

Action

Creates a data series in the selected range. There are two choices for the *series-in* argument:

1   Rows

2   Columns

The three choices for the *type* argument are as follows:

1   Linear

2   Growth

3   Date

And the four choices for the *unit* argument are below:

1   Day

2   Weekday

3   Month

4   Year

Step and *stop* are numbers that indicate the starting and stopping points for the series.

Example

=DATA.SERIES(2,1,,1,)

creates a linear series in the selected column.

DEFINE.NAME(*name, refers-to, type, key*)

DEFINE.NAME?( )

Menu Equivalent

Formula, Define Name

Action

Defines a name for a cell range. The arguments are defined as follows:

name	Text value for name
refers-to	If an external reference, refers to cells named. If omitted, the selected range is assumed. If a number, text, or logical value, Excel assigns the name to the value.
type	Defines the macro type. 1 is a function, 2 is a command. (Macro sheet only.)

key   Defines the letter to activate the command. It must be in quotation marks, as ''Z''. (Macro sheet only.)

Examples

= DEFINE.NAME(''TEST'','' = R1C2'')

assigns the name TEST to cell B1.

= DEFINE.NAME(''INCOME'',SELECTION( ))

assigns the name INCOME to the current selected range.

= DEFINE.NAME(''QTY'','' = R1C2:R6:C2'')

assigns the name QTY to the range B1:B6.

DELETE.FORMAT(*format*)

Menu Equivalent

Format, Number (Delete)

Action

Deletes *format* from the format list. *Format* must be text.

Example

= DELETE.FORMAT(''#,##0.00'')

DELETE.NAME(*name*)

Menu Equivalent

Formula, Define Name (Delete)

Action

Deletes *name* from the name list. *Name* must be text.

Example

= DELETE.NAME(''QTY'')

deletes the name QTY from the current list.

DEREF(*ref*)

Menu Equivalent

(none)

Action

Gives the value of the cells in *ref*. If *ref* is a single cell, it gives the value in that cell. If *ref* is a range, an array of values is returned.

Note

In the SET.NAME function and others, references are not automatically converted to values. In these cases, this function must be used.

Example

= SET.NAME("QTY",DEREF(B2))

sets QTY to the value in B2.

DISPLAY(*formulas, gridlines, headings*)

DISPLAY?( )

Menu Equivalent

Options, Display

Action

Changes the display form. The arguments refer to the checkboxes in the dialog box with TRUE indicating checked, FALSE indicating not checked.

Example

= DISPLAY(TRUE,TRUE,FALSE)

turns on formulas and grid lines with no row or column headings.

DOCUMENTS( )

Menu Equivalent

(none)

Action

Gives an array of the currently opened documents in text values in alphabetical order. Using the INDEX function, you can then select a document name from the array to use as an argument in another function.

Example

= DOCUMENTS( )

might equal {"Worksheet1","Worksheet2"}

ECHO(*logical*)

Menu Equivalent

(none)

Action

Turns screen updating off (*logical* = FALSE) or on (*logical* = TRUE) during macro execution. Macros run faster if updating is off.

Example

= ECHO(FALSE)

EDIT.DELETE(*direction*)

EDIT.DELETE?( )

Menu Equivalent

Edit, Delete

Action

Deletes the selected range from the worksheet. *Direction* must be a number: 1 shifts cells left to adjust, 2 shifts cells up.

Example

= EDIT.DELETE(1)

deletes the range and shifts cells left. The same command will delete the current row if the row heading is selected.

ERROR(*logical, ref*)

Menu Equivalent

(none)

Action

Turns macro error checking on or off. If *logical* is TRUE, error checking is turned on. If an error is encountered during the macro execution, control branches to *ref*. If *ref* is omitted, a dialog box (Figure 27.2) is displayed for user action. If *logical* is FALSE, errors in the macro are automatically ignored and execution continues.

Example

= ERROR(TRUE)

EXTRACT(*unique*)

EXTRACT?( )

Menu Equivalent

Data, Extract

Action

Extracts records from the database based on the specified criteria. If *unique* is TRUE, only unique values are extracted.

Example

= EXTRACT(TRUE)

FILE.DELETE(*document*)

FILE.DELETE?( )

Menu Equivalent

File, Delete

Action

Deletes *document* from the disk. If *document* is not on the disk, user will be prompted to insert a disk with *document*.

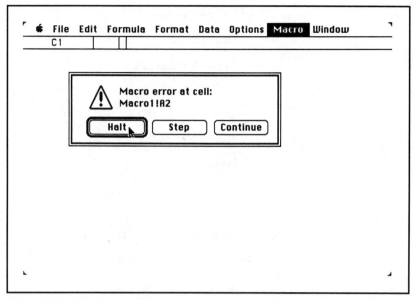

Figure 27.2: The Error dialog box

Example

    = FILE.DELETE("TEST")

FILL.DOWN( )

FILL.RIGHT( )

Menu Equivalent

Edit, Fill Down and Edit, Fill Right

Action

Fills the range with the value in the first cell of the range.

Example

    = FILL.RIGHT( )

FONT(*name, size*)

FONT?( )

Menu Equivalent

Options, Font

Action

Sets the worksheet text display to font *name* and size *size*.

Example

= FONT("Geneva",10)

FORMAT.NUMBER(*format*)

FORMAT.NUMBER?( )

Menu Equivalent

Format, Number

Action

Formats the selected cells to *format*.

Example

= FORMAT.NUMBER("#,##0.00")

FORMULA(*formula-text*)

Menu Equivalent

(none)

Action

Inserts *formula-text* in the active cell.

Examples

= FORMULA(5)

enters 5 into the active cell.

=FORMULA(INPUT("Enter: ",0))

prompts for a formula that will be entered into the active cell.

FORMULA.ARRAY(*formula-text*)

Menu Equivalent

(none)

Action

Inserts *formula-text* as an array to the selection. It is the equivalent to entering an array formula while pressing Command.

Example

If B1:B6 is selected,

=FORMULA.ARRAY(5)

enters an array of { =5} in the range.

FORMULA.FILL(*formula-text*)

Menu Equivalent

(none)

Action

Inserts *formula-text* in each cell of the currently selected range. It is the equivalent of entering a formula while pressing the Option key.

Example

If B1:B6 is selected,

=FORMULA.FILL(4)

enters 4 in each cell of the range.

FORMULA.FIND(*find-text, look-in, look-at, look-by***)**

FORMULA.FIND?( )

Menu Equivalent

Formula, Find

Action

Searches for a formula or value in the current worksheet. The *find-text* argument is the text for which to search. The *look-in* argument has two choices:

1   Formulas

2   Values

The *look-at* argument also has two choices:

1   Whole cell

2   Part of cell

And the *look-by* argument has the following two choices:

1   Rows

2   Columns

Example

    = FORMULA.FIND("6",2,1,1)

searches the worksheet for the first cell with the value of 6 and makes the cell active if found.

FORMULA.FIND.NEXT( )

FORMULA.FIND.PREV( )

Menu Equivalent

Equivalent to typing Command-H and Command-Shift-H

Action

Finds the next or previous cells on the worksheet that matches the search criteria.

Example

    = FORMULA.FIND.NEXT( )

FORMULA.GOTO(*ref*)

FORMULA.GOTO?( )

Menu Equivalent

Formula, Goto

Action

Goes to the cell referenced as *ref*. *Ref* can be a name or external reference (using A1 or R1C1 references).

Example

If A2 is INCOME, the following are all equivalent:

    = FORMULA.GOTO(!$A$2)
    = FORMULA.GOTO("R2C1")
    = FORMULA.GOTO("INCOME")
    = FORMULA.GOTO(!INCOME)

FULL(*logical*)

Menu Equivalent

Equal to double-clicking the title bar of a window

Action

Controls the size of the displayed window. If *logical* is TRUE, Excel makes the displayed window full-size. If *logical* is FALSE, Excel returns the active window to its previous smaller size.

Example

    = FULL(TRUE)

GALLERY.AREA(*type*)

GALLERY.AREA?( )

Menu Equivalent

(Chart) Gallery, Area

Action

Converts the currently displayed chart to Area form. *Type* is a number that must correspond to a valid format in the gallery.

Example

= GALLERY.AREA(1)

GALLERY.BAR(*type*)

GALLERY.BAR?( )

Menu Equivalent

(Chart) Gallery, Bar

Action

Converts the currently displayed chart to Bar form. *Type* is a number that must correspond to a valid format in the gallery.

Example

= GALLERY.BAR(1)

GALLERY.COLUMN(*type*)

GALLERY.COLUMN?( )

Menu Equivalent

(Chart) Gallery, Column

Action

Converts the currently displayed chart to Column form. *Type* is a number that must correspond to a valid format in the gallery.

Example

= GALLERY.COLUMN(1)

GALLERY.LINE(*type*)

GALLERY.LINE?( )

Menu Equivalent

(Chart) Gallery, Line

Action

Converts the currently displayed chart to Line form. *Type* is a number that must correspond to a valid format in the gallery.

Example

= GALLERY.LINE(1)

GALLERY.PIE(*type*)

GALLERY.PIE?( )

Menu Equivalent

(Chart) Gallery, Pie

Action

Converts the currently displayed chart to Pie form. *Type* is a number that must correspond to a valid format in the gallery.

Example

= GALLERY.PIE(1)

GALLERY.SCATTER(*type*)

GALLERY.SCATTER?( )

Menu Equivalent

(Chart) Gallery, Scatter

Action

Converts the currently displayed chart to Scatter form. *Type* is a number that must correspond to a valid format in the gallery.

Example

    = GALLERY.SCATTER

GET.FORMULA(*ref*)

Menu Equivalent

(none)

Action

Gives the contents of the upper-left cell of *ref* as it would appear in the formula bar. Formulas will be returned in R1C1 format.

Example

    = GET.FORMULA(!A1)

returns 5 if A1 contains 5.

GET.NAME(*name*)

Menu Equivalent

(none)

Action

Returns the definition of *name* as it would appear in the Refers To box of the Define Name command. The definition is in text form. If the name contains references, they are returned in R1C1 style.

Example

If NET is defined as SALES-COST, then

    = GET.NAME("!NET")

returns "SALES-COST".

GOTO(*ref*)

Menu Equivalent

(none)

Action

Macro execution branches to upper-left cell of *ref. Ref* can be an external reference to another macro sheet.

Example

= GOTO(C4)

HALT( )

Menu Equivalent

(none)

Action

Terminates execution of current macro. If macro was called by another macro, that macro is also terminated.

Example

= HALT( )

HLINE(*number*)

VLINE(*number*)

Menu Equivalent

(none)

Action

Scrolls the active window *number* rows (VLINE) or columns (HLINE). *Number* can be positive (forward scroll) or negative (backward scroll). *Number* should be an integer.

Example

= VLINE(9)

scrolls the active window down nine rows.

HPAGE(*number*)

VPAGE(*number*)

Menu Equivalent

(none)

Action

Scrolls the active window *number* window-fulls horizontally (HPAGE) or vertically (VPAGE). *Number* must be an integer, but can be positive (scroll forward) or negative (scroll backward).

Example

= HPAGE(1)

HSCROLL(*column-number*)

VSCROLL(*row-number*)

Menu Equivalent

(none)

Action

Scrolls the active window horizontally or vertically to the specified column or row. It is the equivalent of dragging the scroll box. *Column-number* and *row-number* should be percentages less than 100 or fractions.

Examples

= HSCROLL(64/256)

scrolls to column BL.

= VSCROLL(25%)

scrolls to row 4096.

INPUT(*prompt, type, title*)

Menu Equivalent

(none)

Action

Displays a dialog box with title *title* and prompt *prompt* to which the user can enter input (Figure 27.3). The box contains an OK and a Cancel button. When the OK button is clicked or Return pressed, the function gives the value entered by the user. If you click Cancel or press Command-., the function gives the logical value FALSE. If you omit *title*, the title INPUT is assumed. *Type* defines the type of value the function returns:

0   Formula

1   Number

2   Text

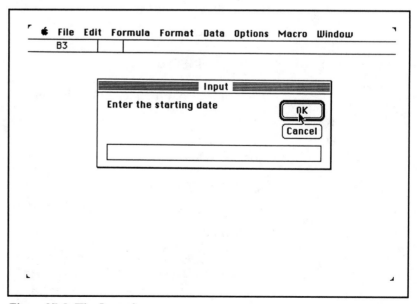

Figure 27.3: The Input box

4   Logical

8   Reference (Absolute)

16   Error

64   Array

Example

= INPUT("Enter the current interest rate: ",1)

INSERT(*direction*)

INSERT?( )

Menu Equivalent

Edit, Insert

Action

Inserts rows or columns in the worksheet. *Direction* must be a number: 1 shifts cells right to adjust, 2 shifts cells down.

Example

= INSERT(1)

inserts a column and shifts cells right.

LEGEND(*logical*)

Menu Equivalent

(Chart) Chart, Add Legend and (Chart) Chart, Delete Legend

Action

If *logical* is TRUE, a legend is added to the chart. If *logical* is FALSE, the current legend is deleted.

Example

= LEGEND(TRUE)

LINKS(*document*)

Menu Equivalent

(none)

Action

Returns an array of the names of all worksheets referred to by external references in *document* as text values. You can then select individual names from the array for other functions using the INDEX function.

Example

If the chart SALES PROJECTION is open and refers to a worksheet SALES, this function opens the worksheet:

= OPEN.LINKS(LINKS("SALES PROJECTION"))

MAIN.CHART.TYPE(*type*)

MAIN.CHART.TYPE?( )

Menu Equivalent

(Chart) Chart, Main Chart Type

Action

Changes the basic type of the main chart. *Type* is a number that defines the new type:

1   Area

2   Bar

3   Column

4   Line

5   Pie

6   Scatter

Example

= MAIN.CHART.TYPE(1)

MESSAGE(*logical, text*)

Menu Equivalent

(none)

Action

Displays the message *text* if *logical* is TRUE. If *logical* is FALSE, the message is taken down. This macro function is useful for displaying a message to the user about what a macro is doing.

Example

= MESSAGE(TRUE,"Sorting the database..")

MOVE(*x-number, y-number, window*)

Menu Equivalent

Equal to moving a window by dragging its title bar

Action

Moves *window* to *x-number, y-number*. The horizontal range is from 1 to 512. The vertical range is from 1 to 342. The origin is in the upper left of the screen. *Window* must be a window name in the form of text. If *window* is omitted, the active window is moved. You can also specify the Clipboard for moving.

Example

= MOVE(256,171)

moves the active window to the lower-right quarter of the screen.

NEW(*type*)
NEW?( )

Menu Equivalent

File, New

Action

Opens a new worksheet, chart or macro sheet. *Type* must be a number that indicates the type to open:

1   Worksheet

2   Chart

3   Macro Sheet

Example

= NEW(1)

opens a new worksheet.

NEW.WINDOW( )

Menu Equivalent

Window, New Window

Action

Opens a new window on the current document

Example

= NEW.WINDOW( )

OFFSET(*ref, row-offset, column-offset*)

Menu Equivalent

(none)

Action

Gives a reference of the same size and shape as *ref*, but shifted by *row-offset* and *column-offset*. *Row-offset* and *column-offset* must be numbers, and positive or negative integers can be used. If an offset is in error, an error value #REF is returned.

Example

> = OFFSET(D4,2,3)

gives G6.

OPEN(*document, update*)

OPEN?( )

Menu Equivalent

File, Open

Action

Opens *document*. *Document* must be a text name. If not found on the current disk, Excel will prompt to insert the disk. *Update* is used to control the updating of external references. If TRUE, external references are updated. If FALSE, external references are not updated. If omitted, no external references are assumed.

Example

> = OPEN("SALES")

OPEN.LINKS(*documents-1, documents-2,...*)

OPEN.LINKS?( )

Menu Equivalent

File, Links

Action

Opens the documents specified that are linked to the current document. The document names can be generated with the LINKS function.

Example

If the chart SALES PROJECTION is open and refers to a worksheet SALES, this function opens the worksheet:

> = OPEN.LINKS(LINKS("SALES PROJECTION"))

OVERLAY.CHART.TYPE(*type*)

OVERLAY.CHART.TYPE?( )

Menu Equivalent

(Chart) Chart, Overlay Chart Type

Action

Changes the type of the overlay chart to the type specified as *type:*

1	None
2	Area
3	Bar
4	Column
5	Line
6	Pie
7	Scatter

Example

= OVERLAY.CHART.TYPE(3)

PAGE.SETUP(*header, footer, left, width, top, length, headings, message*)

PAGE.SETUP(*header, footer, left, right, top, bottom, headings, gridlines*)

PAGE.SETUP(*header, footer, left, width, top, height, size*)

PAGE.SETUP?( )

Menu Equivalent

File, Page Setup

Action

Sets up the current worksheet page. *Header* and *footer* must be text. *Left, right, top, bottom, width, length,* and *height* are numbers. *Headings* and *gridlines* are logical values for TRUE if checked, FALSE if not checked. *Message* is text. *Size* is a number where 1 is screen size, 2 is fit to page.

Example

> = PAGE.SETUP("Sales - 1988",Page &p,
> 0.75,0,0.75,1,1,TRUE,TRUE)

PASTE( )

Menu Equivalent

Edit, Paste

Action

Pastes from the Clipboard to the current location.

Example

> = PASTE( )

PASTE.SPECIAL(*parts, operation*)

PASTE.SPECIAL?( )

Menu Equivalent

Edit, Paste Special (copying from worksheet to worksheet)

Action

Pastes from the Clipboard to the current location with the following *parts* options:

1 All
2 Formulas
3 Values
4 Formats

and the following *operation* options:

1 None
2 Add

3   Subtract

4   Multiply

5   Divide

Example

    = PASTE.SPECIAL(1,1)

pastes formulas, values, and formats to the destination worksheet.

PASTE.SPECIAL(*values-in, series-names, categories*)

PASTE.SPECIAL?( )

Menu Equivalent

(Chart) Edit, Paste Special (copying from worksheet to chart)

Action

Pastes a series from a worksheet to a chart. The *values-in* options are as follows:

1   Rows

2   Categories

Series-names and *categories* are logical values, with TRUE for checked and FALSE for not checked.

Example

    = PASTE.SPECIAL(1,TRUE,FALSE)

PASTE.SPECIAL(*parts*)

PASTE.SPECIAL?( )

Menu Equivalent

(Chart) Edit, Paste Special (pasting from chart to chart)

Action

Copies from a chart to another chart. *Parts* is a number:

1   All

2   Formats

3   Formulas

Example

   = PASTE.SPECIAL(1)

PRECISION(*logical*)

Menu Equivalent

Options, Precision As Displayed

Action

Sets the precision of the calculation. If *logical* is TRUE, calculations are made to full precision. If FALSE, calculations are made to the displayed precision only.

Example

   = PRECISION(TRUE)

PREFERRED( )

Menu Equivalent

(Chart) Gallery, Preferred

Action

Changes displayed chart to default, or preferred format.

Example

   = PREFERRED( )

PRINT(*range, from, to, copies, feed*)

PRINT( )

PRINT?( )

Menu Equivalent

File, Print

Action

Prints the worksheet, chart, or macro sheet. The arguments correspond to the same arguments on the dialog box. *Range* is a number where 1 is print all, 2 is print a range. *From* and *to* specify the range limits. *Copies* is a number. For *feed*, 1 is continuous and 2 is cut sheets.

Example

= PRINT(1,,,1,1)

prints one copy of the entire worksheet in a continuous manner.

PRINTER.SETUP(*printer, port, baud*)

PRINTER.SETUP?( )

Menu Equivalent

File, Printer Setup

Action

Sets up the printer for printing. *Printer* is a number where 1 is the Macintosh, 2 is the TTY. *Port* is a number where 1 is the printer port, 2 is the modem (serial) port. *Baud* specifies the baud rate as follows:

NUMBER	BAUD RATE
1	300
2	600
3	1200
4	2400

| 5 | 4800 |
| 6 | 9600 |

Example

= PRINTER.SETUP(1)

PROTECT.DOCUMENT(*logical*)

PROTECT.DOCUMENT?( )

Menu Equivalent

Options, Protect and Options, Unprotect

Action

Turns document protection on (if *logical* is TRUE) or off (if *logical* is FALSE). To control with a password, use the PROTECT-.DOCUMENT?( ) form of the command.

Example

= PROTECT.DOCUMENT?( )

ref(argument-1,argument-2)

ref( )

Menu Equivalent

(none)

Action

If a reference is specified in a reference cell, Excel branches to the upper-left cell of the specified reference. Ref can be a reference or a name of another reference. Using this method, one macro can call another macro on the same or another macro sheet. Arguments are values passed to the called macro.

Example

= TESTVALUE(!$R$3)

RELREF(*ref-1, ref-2*)

Menu Equivalent

(none)

Action

Gives the reference of *ref-1* relative to the upper-left cell of *ref-2*. The reference is returned in text as an R1C1-style reference.

Example

= RELREF(A1,D4)

gives "R[-3]C[-3]".

REMOVE.PAGE.BREAK( )

SET.PAGE.BREAK( )

Menu Equivalent

Options, Set Page Break and Options, Remove Page Break

Action

Sets or removes a page break at the indicated cell.

Example

= SET.PAGE.BREAK( )

RESULT(*type*)

Menu Equivalent

(none)

Action

Defines the type of value that is to be returned by the function. The RESULT function is optional except when references or arrays are returned. If used, it must be the first function in the macro. *Type* defines the type of value returned:

TYPE VALUE	MEANING
1	Number
2	Text
4	Logical
8	Reference
16	Error
64	Array

Example

= RESULT(64)

RETURN(*values*)

RETURN( )

Menu Equivalent

(none)

Action

Terminates the macro execution and, optionally, returns value(s) to the calling program or macro. If *values* is returned, the type is specified by the RESULT function, which (if used) must be the first function in the macro.

Example

= RETURN( )

RUN(*ref*)

RUN?( )

Menu Equivalent

Macro, Run

Action

Initiates a macro execution defined by *ref*. *Ref* should be an external reference to a macro on a macro sheet or an R1C1-style external reference on a macro sheet.

Example

= RUN(MACROS!Heading)

SAVE( )

Menu Equivalent

File, Save

Action

Saves the current worksheet under its current name.

Example

= SAVE( )

SAVE.AS(*document, type*)

SAVE.AS?( )

Menu Equivalent

File, Save As

Action

Saves the worksheet using the name *document*. *Type* is a number that defines the saved format as follows:

1   Normal
2   SYLK
3   Text
4   WKS

The document is saved to the default disk drive. To save to another drive, use the SAVE.AS?( ) form.

Example

   = SAVE.AS("Sales",1)

SELECT(*selection-ref, active-cell-ref*)

Menu Equivalent

Equal to selecting cells with the mouse

Action

Selects the cells referenced by *selection-ref* and makes *active-cell-ref* the active cell. *Selection-ref* should be either a reference to the active worksheets (such as !B1B3 or !Income) or an R1C1-style reference in text form (such as "R[-2]C[-1]:R[2]C[3]"). If you omit *selection-ref*, the selection is not changed. *Active-cell-ref* should be a reference to a single cell inside of *selection-ref* either on the current worksheet or as an R1C1-style reference. If *active-cell-ref* is relative, it is assumed to be relative to the currently active cell. If *active-cell-ref* is omitted, it is assumed to be the upper-left cell of *selection-ref*.

Example

   = SELECT(!Sales,!A5)

SELECT.CHART( )

Menu Equivalent

(Chart) Chart, Select Chart

Action

Selects the entire chart.

Example

   = SELECT.CHART( )

SELECT.LAST.CELL( )

Menu Equivalent

Formula, Select Last Cell

Action

Makes the last cell of the worksheet the active cell.

Example

= SELECT.LAST.CELL( )

SELECTION( )

Menu Equivalent

(none)

Action

Gives the currently selected cells as an external reference.

Example

If the current worksheet is SALES PROJECTIONS and the cells B1 to B3 are selected:

= SELECTION( )

gives 'SALES PROJECTIONS'!B1:B3.

SET.CRITERIA( )

Menu Equivalent

Data, Set Criteria

Action

Assigns the name Criteria to the currently selected range.

Example

= SET.CRITERIA( )

SET.DATABASE( )

Menu Equivalent

Data, Set Database

Action

Assigns the name Database to the currently selected range.

Example

= SET.DATABASE( )

SET.NAME(*name, value*)

Menu Equivalent

(none)

Action

Defines a name on the macro sheet as a specified value. *Name* must be a text value for the name to be assigned. *Value* can be a number, text, logical, error value, array, or a reference.

Note

If *value* is to be the value of a referenced cell, you must use the DEREF function.

Example

= SET.NAME("One",1)

assigns the name ''One'' to the value 1.

= SET.NAME("Qty",DEREF(A3))

assigns the name ''Qty'' to the value in A3 on the macro sheet.

SET.PAGE.BREAK( )

(See REMOVE.PAGE.BREAK( ))

SET.PRINT.AREA( )

Menu Equivalent

Options, Set Print Area

Action

Defines the current selection as the worksheet area to be printed with the File Print command.

Example

$$= SET.PRINT.AREA()$$

SET.PRINT.TITLES()

Menu Equivalent

Options, Set Print Titles

Action

Defines current selection as the text that will be used as page titles when the worksheet is printed.

Example

$$= SET.PRINT.TITLES()$$

SET.VALUE(*ref, values*)

Menu Equivalent

(none)

Action

Changes the value of the cells specified by *ref* to *values*. Formulas are not changed. Used for loop control during macro execution. *Ref* must be a reference to cells on the macro sheet. If *ref* is a range, *values* should be an array of the same size.

Example

$$= SET.VALUE(D5,3)$$

sets the value in D5 of the macro sheet to 3.

SHOW.ACTIVE.CELL()

Menu Equivalent

Formula, Show Active Cell

Action

Scrolls worksheet until active cell is visible.

Example

= SHOW.ACTIVE.CELL( )

SHOW.CLIPBOARD( )

Menu Equivalent

Window, Show Clipboard

Action

Opens a window to the Clipboard.

Example

= SHOW.CLIPBOARD( )

SIZE(*x-number, y-number, window*)

Menu Equivalent

Equal to changing the size of a window by dragging the size box

Action

Changes the size of the specified window. The lower-right-hand corner is moved until window is the size defined by *x-number* and *y-number*. The maximum screen width is 512, the maximum height is 303 (the maximum screen height is really 342, but space must be left for the formula bar). If you omit window, the currently active window is assumed.

Example

= SIZE(256,151)

changes the window so that it is contained in the upper-left quarter of the screen.

SORT(*sort-by, 1st-key, 2nd-key, 3rd-key, order*)

Menu Equivalent

Data, Sort

Action

Sorts the specified range in the order defined by the arguments. There are two *sort-by* options:

1   Rows

2   Columns

and two *order* options:

1   Ascending

2   Descending

1st-key, 2nd-key, and *3rd-key* are external references to the current worksheet or R1C1-style references in text. You may also wish to use the DEREF function to define a key.

Examples

= SORT(1,"R12C1",1)

sorts the selected rows, using R12C1 as a key, in ascending order.

If C11 on the worksheet contains the text ''Target'', this function sorts the worksheet using Target as a key:

= SORT(1,DEREF(!$C$11),1)

STEP( )

Menu Equivalent

(none)

Action

Permits calculating a macro one step at a time, and is useful for debugging. When the step function is encountered in a macro execution, the calculation stops and displays a box that defines the next cell to calculate and the formula in that cell (Figure 27.4). The box contains the following buttons: Step, Halt, and Continue. Step executes the next macro cell and stops again. Halt terminates the macro execution. Continue resumes normal macro execution.

Example

    = STEP( )

STYLE(*bold, italic*)

STYLE?( )

Menu Equivalent

Format, Style

Action

Changes the style of the selected cells to that specified by the arguments. *Bold* and *italic* are logical values defined as TRUE (checked) or FALSE (not checked).

Example

    = STYLE(TRUE,FALSE)

sets the selected range to boldface.

TABLE(*row-input, column-input*)

Menu Equivalent

Data, Table

Action

Creates a table in the selected range. *Row-input* and *column-input* should be external references to single cells on the active worksheet or R1C1-type references in text form.

Note

You can use the DEREF function to define cells.

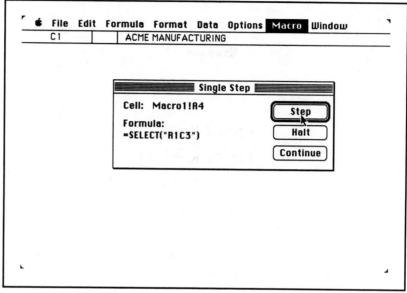

Figure 27.4: The Step dialog box

Example

In the Sales Projection example of this book, cell D4 was used as a column input to define a table. This could also be done as follows:

= TABLE(,"R4C4")

If D3 contains the heading "Criteria" as the name for D4, you could also use the following:

= TABLE(,DEREF(!D$3))

UNDO( )

Menu Equivalent

Edit, Undo

Action

Undoes the previous command.

Example

= UNDO( )

UNLOCK.NEXT( )

UNLOCK.PREV( )

Menu Equivalent

Equal to pressing Tab or Shift-Tab

Action

Moves the active cell to the next or previous unlocked cell in a protected worksheet.

Example

= UNLOCKED.NEXT( )

VLINE(*number*)

(See HLINE.)

VPAGE(*number*))

(See HPAGE.)

VSCROLL(*row-number*)

(See HSCROLL.)

WINDOWS( )

Menu Equivalent

(none)

Action

Returns an array of text values that are the names of all active windows on the screen. You can then use the INDEX function to select from the array.

Example

```
= WINDOWS( )
returns {"Worksheet1","Worksheet2"}
```

APPENDICES

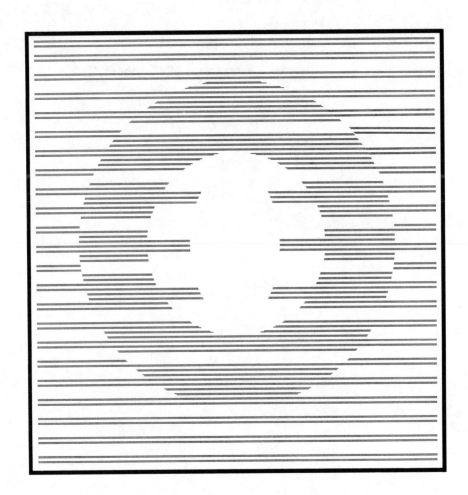

APPENDIX *A* GLOSSARY

TERM	DEFINITION
A1 format	A type of worksheet cell designation in which the columns are represented by letters and the rows by numbers. For example, in A1 format, C4 represents the cell at the intersection of the third column and the fourth row.
absolute cell reference	A reference to a specific cell or group of cells on a worksheet. An absolute cell reference does not change with moving or copying. In Excel's format (A1), an absolute reference is designated with a dollar sign before the column and row (for example, $A$5).
active cell	The cell in which any current keyboard entry is stored. The active cell is always marked by a heavy border. The formula bar shows the contents of the active cell.
active window	The window that is currently selected.
alert box	A type of interrupt dialog box that can be created with Excel's macro language to give the user the option of canceling the program or continuing.
alignment	The position of text or a value in a cell. Alignment can be left, right, or centered.

argument	Values used as input for a function to calculate its output value.
array	A two-dimensional collection of values, normally arranged in rows and columns.
attached text	Text that is attached to a specific object on a chart, such as the chart title, axes labels, and legend. It is created with the Attach Text command on the Chart menu.
axes	The straight lines used on the graph for measurement and reference. A pie chart has no real axis, other types have two.
border	The line around an area on a worksheet or chart.
cancel box	The small box in the formula bar that contains an X. Clicking this box discards any changes you have made in the formula bar.
category	A name associated with a numeric value in a data series. Each data point in a series has a category name and a value.
cell	The intersection of a row and column. It is the basic unit of the worksheet used for storing values, formulas, and text.
chart	One or more graphs displayed in a single document.
chart format	The basic information that defines how a data series is plotted. Excel has 42 chart formats.
chart object	Any part of the chart: axes, markers, lines, legend, plot area, chart, etc.

chart style	The basic type of chart used in a document. Excel has six chart types: area, bar, column, line, pie, and scatter.
circular references	Two or more formulas that depend upon each other for results.
click	To select something on the screen by pointing with the mouse, pressing, and then releasing the mouse button.
close box	The small square box in the upper left of each window that can be clicked to close the window. Clicking the box releases the document from the computer's memory and, optionally, saves it to the disk.
cluster	On a chart, a group of bars or columns in the same category.
column	On a worksheet, a vertical range of cells.
command macro	A series of actions to accomplish a desired result, which is stored as a single program for execution one or more times.
complex external reference	Any reference to a cell on another worksheet that is not a simple external reference (see external reference and simple external reference).
constant value	Anything entered into a cell that is not a formula.
criteria area	The cells on the worksheet that are used to define which records Excel finds, extracts, or deletes in the database. The area is defined with the Set Criteria command on the Data menu.
criteria name row	The cells in the criteria area that contain the criteria names. It is always the first row in the criteria area.

criterion	A test used to find, extract, or delete records in a database.
data point	A category with a corresponding numeric value.
data series	A collection of data points, each related to the other by some aspect.
database	An organized collection of data about one or more items. Each item is represented by a row in the database, and each piece of data about the item is stored as a field in the record. In an Excel database, the records are represented by rows and the fields by columns.
database area	The worksheet cells that contain the field names and the records on which the Find, Delete, and Extract commands operate. The area is defined with the Set Database command on the Data menu.
dependent document	Any document in which one or more cells have a formula that contains a reference to another worksheet.
designators	The indicators at the top and left of the display area that designate the rows and columns. At the left of the worksheet are the row designators, and at the top are the column designators.
document	Any worksheet, chart, or macro sheet either active or saved to the disk.
double-click	To select something on the screen by pointing with the mouse, pressing, and then releasing the mouse button twice in quick succession.

drag

To hold the mouse button down while moving the mouse. Used to select a range of cells.

enter box

The small box in the formula bar that contains a check mark. Clicking this box completes a formula bar entry or edit.

Excel macro language

A special group of functions that can be used to write Excel command macros.

external reference

A reference to a specific cell or group of cells, normally on another worksheet. The reference consists of the worksheet name, an exclamation point, and the cell reference. You can also refer to the currently active worksheet as an external reference by using an exclamation point and the cell reference. This is useful in macros that must refer to cells in several worksheets generically.

extract

To copy records from a database that meet specific criteria.

field

Each piece of data stored about an item in a database. Each cell in a database is one field. Fields are represented as columns in a database, and records are represented as rows.

font

The specific design for the characters used to represent text. You can change the font of an entire worksheet, and, in a chart, you can change the font of individual objects. You can add fonts to Excel by using the DA/Font Mover program external to Excel.

footer
A line of text that appears at the bottom of each printed page of a worksheet or chart; for example, the page number is a footer.

format
Information that controls how the contents of the cell will be displayed. It consists of a template, style, alignment, font, and font size.

formula
One or more values, cell references, names, functions, and operators that are stored in a cell to produce a value.

formula bar
An area below the menu bar that is used for displaying and editing the contents of the active cell.

function
An abbreviation of a formula. A function produces an output value (or values) from a specified input. (Some functions, such as NOW, do not require an input value.)

function macro
A user-defined function. The user defines the arguments, results, and formulas to calculate the results.

graph
A visual representation of one or more data series. It includes the plotted area, labels, legends, and comments.

grid lines
The grid lines on a worksheet are the dotted horizontal and vertical lines between adjacent cells. Grid lines on a chart are the horizontal and vertical lines that extend from the axis across the plot area. Major grid lines extend from the tick marks; minor grid lines extend from the axes between the tick marks.

header	A line of text that appears at the top of each printed page of a worksheet or chart.
input cell	The cell used with a table to hold each of a series of input values.
insertion point	A blinking vertical line that determines the entry point for text typed in from the keyboard. It can be created by clicking in the formula bar or in a text-entry area of a dialog box.
key	A row or column that contains the values that control a sort. To sort rows, the key must be a column. To sort columns, the key must be a row.
label	Text in a chart used to identify that part of the chart.
legend	The symbols with labels used to identify the different types of data on the chart.
link	A defined relationship between two documents caused by formulas in a dependent document referencing cells in a supporting document.
lock	To protect a cell so that its contents cannot be altered.
look-up table	A table that can be used, like a function, to produce an output value from one or more input values.
macro	A collection of functions that can be executed as a procedure to produce some specified result.
macro sheet	A worksheet used to store macros.
main chart	The primary graph on a chart.
marker	A type of indicator used on a graph to indicate the data. For example,

	in a column chart, each column is a marker.
menu bar	The bar at the top of the screen that contains the available menus. The mouse is used to pull the menus down from the menu bar.
mixed cell reference	A reference that consists of both absolute and relative cell addresses (for example, $A5).
overlay chart	A second graph that is plotted in the chart window, which is identical in size and position to the main chart.
pane	A subdivision of a worksheet window.
plot area	The area bounded by the axes, or, in the case of the pie chart, the area within the circle.
point	To move the mouse pointer to an area of the screen.
pointer	The small cursor on the screen that tracks the movement of the mouse.
precision	The number of decimal places with which a value is stored or used in calculations.
print area	That part of the worksheet that will be printed with a Print command.
protect	To make active the protection that has been defined. One or more cells or cell ranges are unlocked or hidden with the Cell Protection command on the Format menu, then the Protect Document command on the Options menu is used to activate the protection for the entire worksheet.
R1C1 format	A type of worksheet cell designation in which the columns and rows are designated by numbers. For example, in

	R1C1 format, R4C3 represents the cell at the intersection of the fourth row and the third column.
range	One or more cells that have been designated to be acted upon by a command.
record	Any row within a database range. A record consists of one or more fields.
the recorder	An Excel mode in which actions taken by the user are recorded on a separate sheet as a program. The program can then be executed again at a later time to repeat the procedure.
row	A horizontal line of cells.
scale	The range of values covered by the y axis on the chart.
select	To specify a worksheet, chart area or a command.
simple external reference	A reference to a cell or cell range on another worksheet that is absolute and refers only to a single cell or cell range or a named cell or cell range. Linked dependent documents with only simple external references will be updated automatically, even if the supporting document is not open. (See external reference.)
split bar	The small black rectangle at the top of the vertical scroll bar and at the left of the horizontal scroll bar. It is used to separate the window into panes.
style	The appearance of the font on the worksheet. Excel has four styles: normal, boldface, italic, and boldface italic.
supporting worksheet	Any worksheet containing a cell referenced by a dependent worksheet.

Switcher	A program that permits two application programs to reside in the Macintosh memory simultaneously. The user can move from one program to the other quickly, without having to reload the program and data from the disk.
table	A range of cells containing the results of applying a series of values to an input cell.
template	One or more characters used to identify how a value is to be displayed. For a number, the template controls the number of digits to be displayed to the right of the decimal and whether a dollar sign or commas are displayed.
tick-mark label	Labels identifying the tick marks on a chart.
tick marks	The axes divisions. Used to indicate categories or scale. The marks are short lines perpendicular to the axes at regular intervals.
toggle	To switch between one of two modes. For example, in the Display dialog box, you can toggle on or off the display of formulas, row and column designators, and grid lines.
unattached text	Text on a chart that is not attached to any object and can be moved.
wild card	Special characters used to stand for any other characters in text. A question mark (?) is used to represent any single character; an asterisk (*) represents a group of characters.

window	An area on the screen that displays a portion of a worksheet or chart.
worksheet	A grid of cells 256 columns wide by 16,384 cells long into which you can enter formulas and values.
x axis	The horizontal (or category) chart axis.
y axis	The vertical (or value) chart axis.

APPENDIX *B* *THE WORKSHEET COMMANDS*

EXCEL HAS NINE WORKSHEET AND DATABASE MENUS: Apple, File, Edit, Formula, Format, Data, Options, Macro, and Window. This appendix describes the functions available with each of these menus.

THE APPLE MENU

This menu is similar to the Apple menu in other applications, except that it includes an About Microsoft Excel command. This command displays a window (Figure B.1) that describes memory usage and lists help topics. To get help on any topic, click the topic, then click the Help button. The information is then displayed. When you have finished reading about the topic, select your next alternative from the four buttons displayed:

- **Topics** means go back to the list of help topics.
- **Next** means go to the next help topic.
- **Previous** means go to the previous help topic.
- **Cancel** means cancel the About Microsoft Excel command.

THE FILE MENU

The File menu is used to manage documents. The commands on this menu allow you to open, close, delete, or print a document. This menu is also used to end an Excel session.

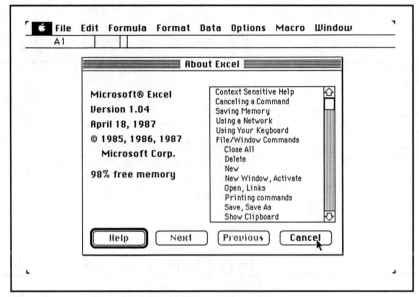

Figure B.1: The About Microsoft Excel window

NEW

The New command creates an empty worksheet or macro sheet or creates a chart from a displayed document. When the dialog box (Figure B.2) is displayed, select the desired alternative:

- **Worksheet** creates an empty worksheet.
- **Chart** plots a chart from an active worksheet.
- **Macro Sheet** creates an empty macro sheet.

OPEN

The Open command opens a document that is already on the disk and displays it as a window. When the command is selected, a dialog box (Figure B.3) that lists the documents on the disk is displayed. Click the desired document name and then click Open. The following options are available:

- **Open** opens the selected document.
- **Eject** ejects the indicated disk. You can then insert another disk, and the contents of that disk will be displayed.

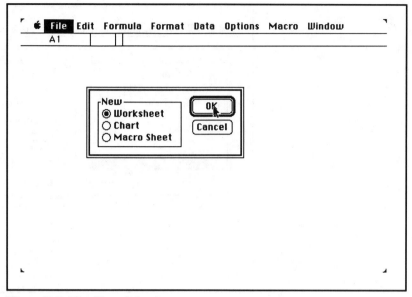

Figure B.2: The New dialog box

- **Drive** selects the alternative drive.
- **Cancel** cancels the command.
- **Read Only** permits reading the document only; changes cannot be saved.

Excel can open a document in the following formats: Excel, WKS, SYLK, Text, or Multiplan. The format is automatically recognized, and the document is opened.

LINKS

The Links command is used to open documents that are linked to the currently active document. If a dependent document is active and you wish to load one or more of the supporting worksheets, use the Links command. The currently linked documents will be displayed in a dialog box (Figure B.4). Click the supporting documents that you want to open. You can make more than one document active at a time by dragging across several names in a range while pressing the

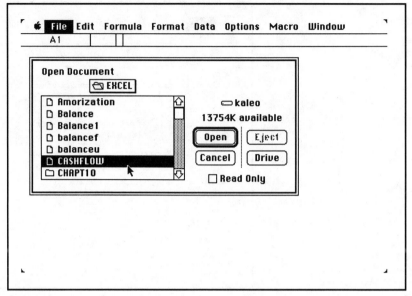

Figure B.3: The Open dialog box

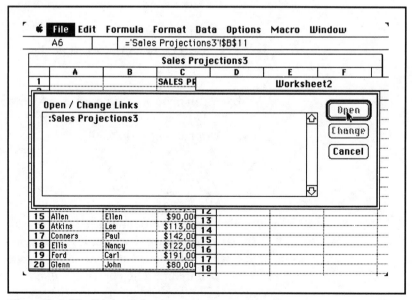

Figure B.4: The Links dialog box

Shift key or by pressing the Command key while clicking to add documents to a selected group (just as you select cells on a worksheet).

CLOSE ALL

The Close All command closes all active windows on the screen. For each window that contains a document with unsaved changes, a dialog box (Figure B.5) will be displayed, asking if you want to save the current changes. Click **Yes** to save changes, **No** to omit changes, or **Cancel** to stop the Close All command. You can also close single windows by clicking their close boxes.

SAVE

The Save command is used to save a document under the name with which it was opened or assigned when you last used the Save As command. The Save command can be used only with worksheets opened in

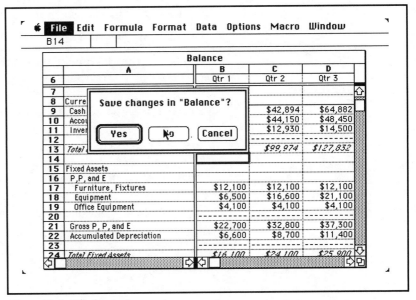

Figure B.5: Closing a document

normal Excel format or the SYLK format. No backup copy is created. The document remains on the screen for further editing.

As you create or edit documents, it is a good idea to save it with this command periodically. The first time that the document is saved, use the Save As command and specify the new name of the document. Successive saves can be done using the Save command.

SAVE AS

The Save As command is used to save a document under a name that you assign in a format that you define. When the command is selected, the dialog box (Figure B.6) suggests the name of the currently active document and displays the name of the disk on which the document will be saved. To save the document under this name in normal Excel format on the specified disk, click the Save button. If you will overwrite an existing file with the same name, Excel will prompt you with this information and permit you to abort the save. The following buttons are available in the Save As dialog box:

- **Drive** changes the drive on which the document will be saved.
- **Eject** ejects the disk with the displayed disk name. You can then insert another disk on which the document can be stored.
- **Cancel** terminates the command without saving the document.
- **Save** saves the document under the specified name on the specified disk.

You can use this same command to save the document in any of four formats. Unless specified, the document is saved in normal Excel format. The following formats are available for selection:

- **Normal** is the normal format for a saved Excel document. Use it if worksheets are to be linked or used with other Microsoft worksheet programs on the Macintosh computer.
- **SYLK** is the format to select if you plan to use the document on another type of computer with other Microsoft products that support this format.

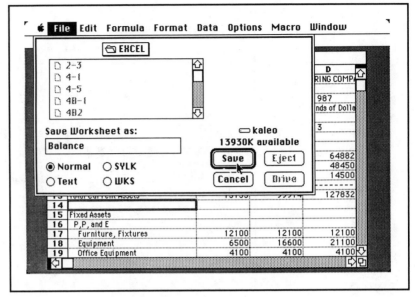

Figure B.6: The Save As dialog box

- **Text** is the format to use to save the worksheet in a text format, with columns separated by tabs and rows delimited by carriage returns. Formatting information is lost.

- **WKS** is the format to use if you plan to use the document with Lotus 1-2-3 on the IBM-PC.

DELETE

The Delete command is used to delete a document on the currently selected disk. When the command is selected, the Delete dialog box (Figure B.7) is displayed. Select the document that you want to delete (you may have to scroll) and click the Delete button. More than one document can be deleted during a single use of the command. To return to the worksheet, click Cancel. The following buttons are available in the dialog box:

You cannot undo a Delete command. Check your entry carefully before clicking Delete.

- **Drive** changes the drive from which the document will be deleted.

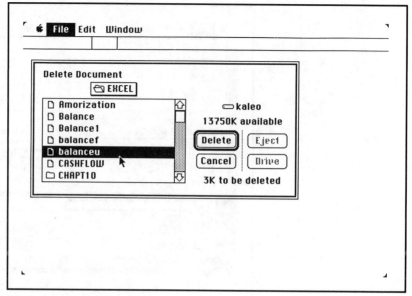

Figure B.7: The Delete dialog box

- **Eject** ejects the disk with the displayed disk name. You can then insert another disk on which the document can be deleted.

- **Cancel** terminates the command without further deleting.

- **Delete** deletes the document under the specified name on the specified disk.

PAGE SETUP

The Page Setup command controls the appearance of the printed document. Each time that you save a document, the current values of the Page Setup command are saved with the document. Two different dialog boxes are available, depending upon the type of printer selected with the Printer Setup command. Figure B.8 shows the dialog box for the Macintosh ImageWriter printer. The following options are available:

- **Paper** controls the paper setting. US Letter is the normal paper setting. You can also select Legal, Computer (15-inch Image-Writer), A4 (European letter size), or International Fanfold.

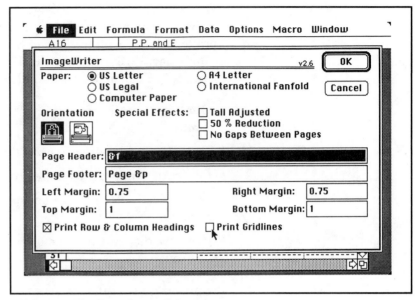

Figure B.8: The Page Setup dialog box

- **Orientation** controls the orientation of the document, allowing you to print vertically or horizontally.

- **Special Effects** controls special options such as tall adjusted (adjusts pictures for proportion), reduction (50%), and no gaps (prints over perforations).

- **Page Header** controls the header on the page (see Chapter 6).

- **Page Footer** controls the footer on the page (see Chapter 6).

- **Left Margin** controls the size of the left margin.

- **Top Margin** controls the size of the top margin.

- **Print Row & Column Headings** controls whether the designators are printed.

- **Print Gridlines** controls whether the grid lines are printed.

PRINT

The Print command prints all or part of the active worksheet. If no area of the worksheet is selected with the Set Print Area command on the Options menu, the entire worksheet is printed. The form of the printout is determined by the Page Setup command. As with the Page Setup command, there are two dialog boxes, depending on the printer selected with the Printer Setup command. The dialog box for the ImageWriter is shown in Figure B.9. With a normal printout (no 50% reduction) all of the following options are available:

- **Quality** selects the resolution of the printout (best, faster, or draft).

- **Page Range** selects the pages of the worksheet to print.

- **Copies** determines the number of copies to print.

- **Paper Feed** selects continuous or single-sheet (cut sheet) printing.

- **Preview** displays the document on the screen as it will be printed.

In the preview mode, the cursor changes to a magnifying glass. You can click any part of the page to see it full size. The Option key changes the pointer to a hand, which can drag the document. To cancel, click the Cancel button.

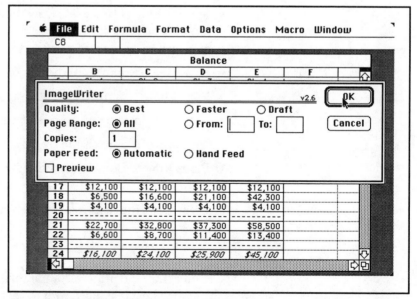

Figure B.9: The ImageWriter Printer dialog box

PRINTER SETUP

The Printer Setup command is used to define the type of printer or modem that you are using. When the command is selected, the dialog box shown in Figure B.10 appears. Click the options to indicate how you want to direct the printer output:

Port and Baud can only be selected if the TTY printer option is used. The default setting is the ImageWriter printer.

- **Printer Setup** selects the driver to be used with your printer. Normally, select the driver that is the same type as your printer.

- **Port** selects the output connector to which the output will be directed.

- **Baud** selects the speed of the output.

QUIT

The current worksheet cannot be displayed or edited again using the Resume Excel icon. Only the arrangement of the windows is saved.

The Quit command is used to terminate an Excel session. All files are closed and the current status (size and position of the windows) is saved in a Resume Excel document. If you have saved information on the Clipboard, it is also saved.

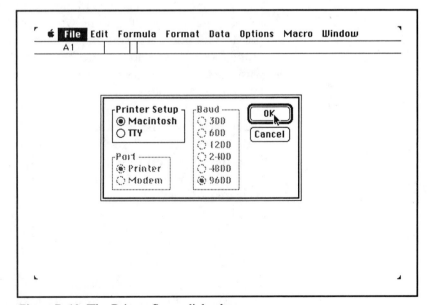

Figure B.10: The Printer Setup dialog box

Whenever you quit Excel, the program will prompt you for each document that has not been saved with the latest changes and permit you to save the document (see Figure B.5).

THE EDIT MENU

The Edit menu is used to edit a worksheet, and it contains commands that are similar to Macintosh editing commands in other application programs.

UNDO

You cannot undo a Delete command on the File menu or a Sort command on the Data menu.

The Undo command is used to undo Edit menu commands. Any Edit menu command can be undone until another command is selected. The menu displays the type of undo available. You can also undo formula-bar entries.

CUT

The Cut command is used to move information on a worksheet or to move information from one worksheet to another. You can also use the Cut and Paste commands in the formula bar to move a part of the formula to another place in the formula bar. Moves are done with the Cut and Paste commands. Copies are done with the Copy and Paste commands.

When the Cut command is used, the contents of the selected area are moved from the worksheet to the Clipboard. The destination area is then selected. The Paste command is used to move the data from the Clipboard to the destination area, and the source area is then cleared. With the Cut and Paste commands, the Clipboard area is cleared—to use the Paste command again, you must select another area to cut.

COPY

The Copy command is used with the Paste command to copy a cell's contents from one cell to another cell on the same worksheet or another worksheet. You can also use the Copy and Paste commands to copy a portion of a formula in the formula bar into another place in the formula bar. Unlike with the Cut and Paste commands, the original cell contents are not cleared. The Clipboard also is not cleared after pasting, so multiple pastings can be done from one copy into the Clipboard.

To copy a cell's contents, select the cells or cell range and then click the Copy command. Select the destination cell or cell range and click the Paste command. The selected source range must be a single, continuous, rectangular area. After the Copy command is selected, the specified range will be marked. In defining the destination range, it is only necessary to specify the starting cell. The Paste command will paste the contents in the cells following the order of the source cells.

When the Copy command is normally used, the Clipboard will show only the size of the cells that were transferred. A special copy command—Copy Picture—is required when the Clipboard is used to transfer worksheet data to external programs. To use this command, pull down the Edit menu, *hold down the Shift key,* and the Copy command becomes Copy Picture. Click it to transfer the display image of the worksheet to the Clipboard.

PASTE

The Paste command is used with the Cut or Copy commands to move or copy data from one cell into another or from one part of the formula bar into another. The Paste command is not active until a cut or copy selection is made. Multiple pastes can be made with a single Copy command, but only one paste can be made with a Cut command. All cell properties of the source cell are moved or copied, including values, formulas, and format. If you need to copy only a portion of these, use the Paste Special command.

In a cut-and-paste operation, the source and destination cell ranges must be of the same size.

CLEAR

The Clear command is used to clear values, formulas, or formats from a cell or range of cells. To clear a cell or cell range, select the cells and then click the Clear command. The dialog box shown in Figure B.11 appears. It has the following options:

- **All** clears values, formulas, and formats from the selected cells.
- **Formats** clears only the formats of the selected cells, returning the cells to the General template.
- **Formulas** clears values and formulas without clearing formats.

You can retrieve cleared cells with the Undo command if no other command has been used since the clear.

PASTE SPECIAL

The Paste Special command permits you to complete a copy selectively; that is, you can copy all of the selected area's contents or just its formulas, values, or formats. The copy operation is initiated with the Copy command. The destination area is then selected, and the Paste Special command is clicked. In the dialog box shown in Figure B.12, the following options are available:

- **All** copies all cell properties, as with a normal Paste command.
- **Formulas** copies only formulas into the destination cells.
- **Values** copies only values into the destination cells.
- **Formats** copies only formats into the destination cells.

The Operation part of the dialog box can be used to perform operations on the data in the source cells, posting the results in the destination cells. The following operations are permitted: addition, subtraction, multiplication, and division. If the destination cells are blank, their value is assumed to be zero.

DELETE

The Delete command removes the selected cell or cell range from the worksheet. If row or column designators are used to select the range to be deleted, there will be no dialog box. If a portion of a column or row is selected, a dialog box (Figure B.13) will be displayed, asking how the

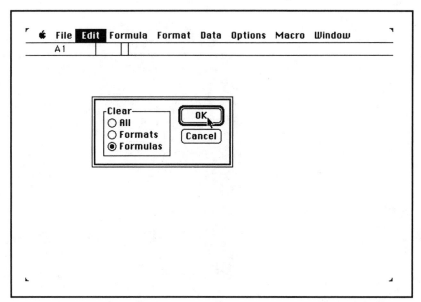

Figure B.11: Clearing cells

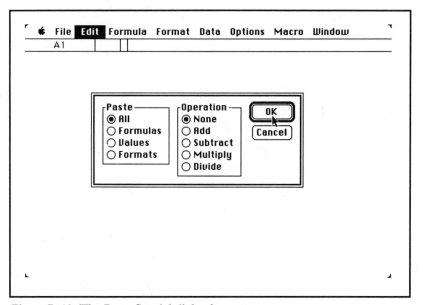

Figure B.12: The Paste Special dialog box

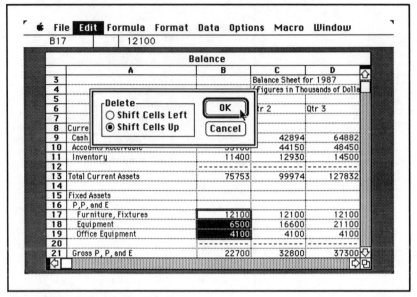

Figure B.13: Deleting a cell range

remaining rows and columns should be shifted to adjust for the deletion. Select the desired option and click OK.

INSERT

The Insert command inserts a blank cell or cell range into the worksheet. If row or column designators are used to select the insert area, there will be no dialog box. If a portion of a column or row is selected, a dialog box (Figure B.14) will be displayed, asking how the remaining rows and columns should be shifted to adjust for the insertion. Select the desired option and click OK.

FILL RIGHT

The Fill Right command provides a fast copy operation that can be used if the copy is from one cell range to a range to the right of the selected cells. You may use single or multiple selections. If multiple selections are made, each copy is performed separately. Formulas, values, and formats are copied.

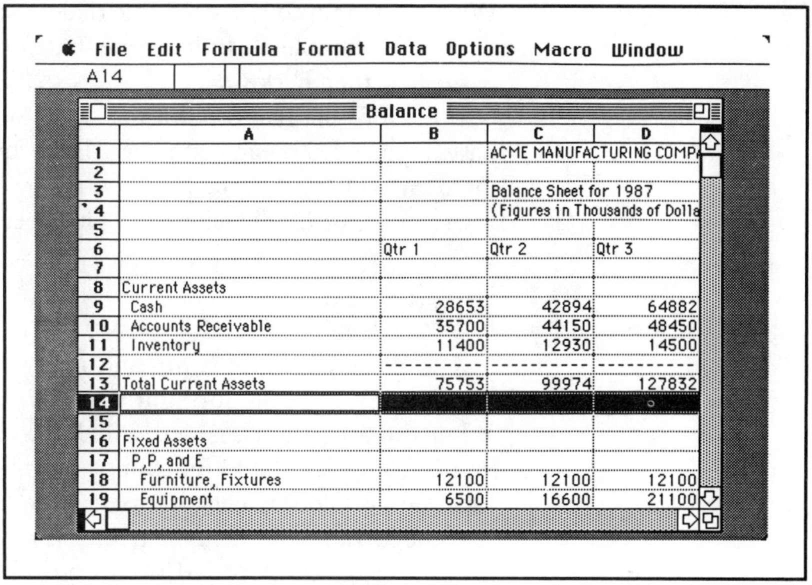

Figure B.14: Inserting a cell range

FILL DOWN

The Fill Down command provides a fast copy operation that can be used if the copy is from one cell range to a range below the selected cells. You may use single or multiple selections. If multiple selections are made, each copy is performed separately. Formulas, values, and formats are copied.

THE FORMULA MENU

The Formula menu is used to create complex formulas. It contains the commands for naming cells and pasting names. This menu also contains the commands for quickly moving to specific cells.

PASTE NAME

The Paste Name command can be used to paste a name into a formula in the formula bar from a list of names previously defined.

When the command is used, the dialog box shown in Figure B.15 is displayed. Double-click the name that you want to paste or click the name and then click OK.

If the formula bar is not active, it is made active and the name is pasted, preceded by an equal sign. If the formula bar is already active, the name is pasted at the insertion point. If no operator precedes the insertion point, Excel will insert a plus operator.

PASTE FUNCTION

The Paste Function command is used to paste a function name into a formula in the formula bar from the list of active functions. When the command is issued, a dialog box (Figure B.16) that lists the names of the available functions is displayed. Scroll to the desired function and double-click it, or click the name and click OK.

If the formula bar is not active, it is made active and the function name is pasted preceded by an equal sign. If the formula bar is already active, the function name is pasted at the insertion point.

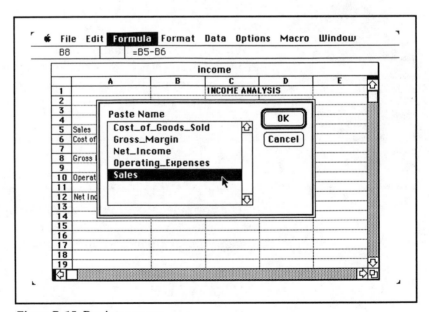

Figure B.15: Pasting a name

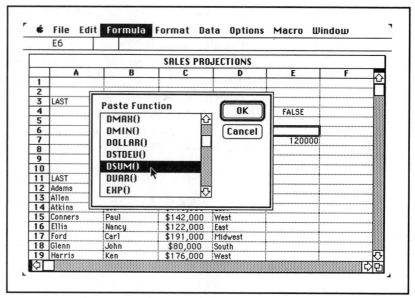

Figure B.16: The Paste Function dialog box

If no operator precedes the insertion point, Excel will insert a plus operator.

If you have defined any function macros and the macro sheets are open, these functions also will appear in the dialog box.

REFERENCE

The Reference command changes the type of references in the formula bar, if the formula bar is active. Relative cell references are changed to absolute, absolute to mixed, and mixed back to relative. If you select a reference before using the command, only the selected reference is converted. If only an insertion point is specified, the reference before the insertion point is converted.

DEFINE NAME

The Define Name command assigns a name to a specified cell or cell range. This command is also used to edit and delete names that have already been assigned. To define a name, the cell or cell range is normally selected before the command is used. The selection can be made, however, by typing it into the Refers To box after the command is clicked. Multiple selections can be made by using the Command key.

When the command is used, the window shown in Figure B.17 is displayed. Names that have already been defined are displayed in the window. The window can be moved so that you can view any part of the worksheet. The following entries are available:

- **Name** is the box that is used to enter the name that you are assigning to the cell or cell range. If there is text in the selected cell when the command is used, the text is proposed as a name. You can click any name in the scroll box and it will move into the Name box. Then, you can delete or edit that name. When creating a new name, you can enter any name into this box. It must begin with a letter and should not contain spaces.

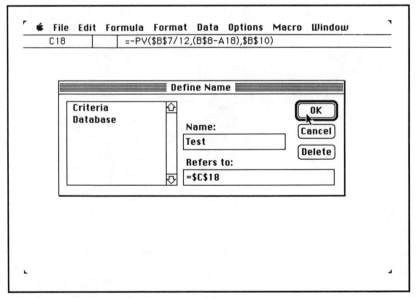

Figure B.17: The Define Name window

- **Refers To** is the box that is used to enter the cell or cell range to which the name is to be assigned. If a cell or cell range was active when the command was used, it will be shown in the box. You can move the cursor to this box and click cells to enter their references. You also can enter constants here if you wish to assign a name to a constant. Editing this box is like editing the formula bar—you can paste names or functions into it and use all the Edit menu commands.

- **Delete** is the button to use to delete a name previously defined. Click the name to move it to the Name box, then click the Delete button.

If you use this command when a macro sheet is active, the displayed window is slightly different, as shown in Figure B.18. At the bottom of the window is a Macro box that is used to identify the macro as a function or command macro. If the macro is a command macro, you can assign a keystroke sequence to it.

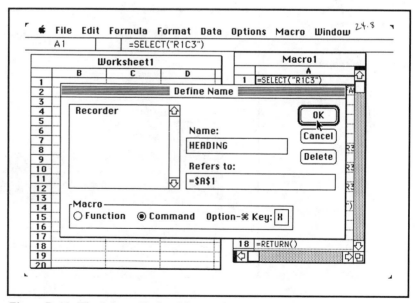

Figure B.18: The Macro Define Name window

CREATE NAMES

The Create Names command is used to assign names to several areas of the worksheet with a single command. The row or column titles are used as the names in the definition. To use the command, select one or more rows (if the row titles are to be the names) or one or more columns (if the column titles are to be the names) and click the command. You can also use both options at once.

When the command is used, the dialog box shown in Figure B.19 is displayed. Click one or both options, then click OK. If the name has already been assigned, you will be prompted and asked if the name is to be reassigned.

GOTO

The Goto command is used to quickly move to a specified cell or cell range. When the command is used, the dialog box shown in Figure B.20 is displayed. Click the name of the destination cell or cell range or enter a cell reference in the Reference box. The worksheet

In using this command, be sure that you have selected row or column designators and that text appears in the first cell of each specified range. If there are spaces in the text, they will be converted to underlines in the name.

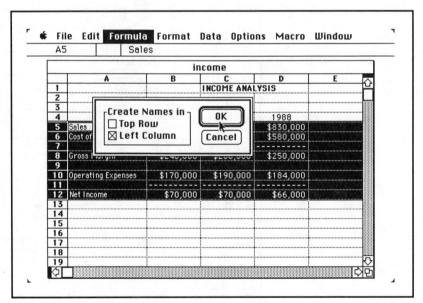

Figure B.19: Creating names

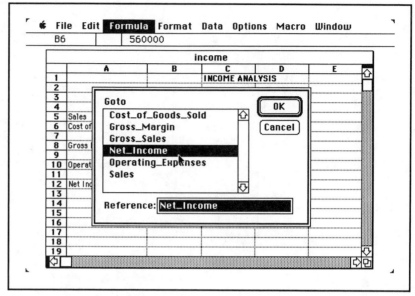

Figure B.20: The Goto dialog box

will quickly scroll to the specified area. You can also scroll to a cell in another open document by entering its reference preceded by the worksheet name and an exclamation point.

FIND

The Find command is used to locate specific text or values in a worksheet and to make the cells that contain them active. It is particularly useful for finding #REF! error messages after a worksheet is edited. If a cell range is selected, only the range is searched. If no range is selected, the entire worksheet is searched.

When the command is used, the dialog box shown in Figure B.21 is displayed. In the Find What box, you enter the value or text to locate. Wild-card characters (? and *) can be used, as well as comparison operators (see Chapter 4). The following options are available:

- **Look In** allows you to specify a search in formulas or on values only.

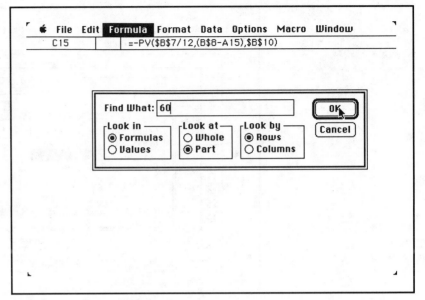

Figure B.21: The Find dialog box

- **Look At** permits selecting a match with the entire cell contents or with a part of the cell contents.

- **Look By** permits searching by row or column. This selection speeds up searches on large worksheets.

When you have made your selection, click OK. Press the Command and H keys to search for repeated occurrences (bypassing the dialog box).

SELECT LAST CELL

The Select Last Cell command scrolls immediately to the last cell in the worksheet. Since the amount of memory used is determined by the size of the worksheet, this command is useful for memory management.

SHOW ACTIVE CELL

The Show Active Cell command scrolls the worksheet until the active cell is visible on the display. Use this command if you scrolled away from the active cell and wish to return to it quickly.

THE FORMAT MENU

The Format menu permits you to select how data will be displayed in the specified cells.

NUMBER

The Number command permits you to specify the template for how numbers, dates, and times will be displayed. To specify how a cell range is to be displayed, first select the range and then click the Number command. When the command is used, a dialog box (Figure B.22) that contains a scroll box with available templates is displayed. Double-click the template desired or click the template and click OK. You can also create your own templates using the Format Number box (see Chapter 6). All cells default to the General template.

ALIGNMENT

The Alignment command controls the alignment for text and values in the selected cells. Select the range to be aligned and click the

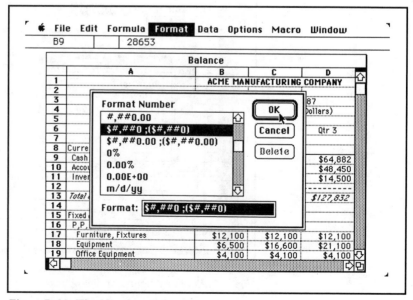

Figure B.22: The Number dialog box

command. The Alignment dialog box (Figure B.23) is displayed. Select the alignment and click OK. All cells default to a General alignment—text is left-justified, and values are right-justified.

STYLE

The Style command changes the style of the selected cell range. Select the range and click the command. The dialog box shown in Figure B.24 is displayed. Click one or both options and click OK.

BORDER

The Border command permits you to display and print borders around the selected cells. Select the range to border, then click the command. The dialog box shown in Figure B.25 will be displayed. The following options are available:

- **Outline** puts a border around the selected range.

- **Left** puts a border on the left edge of each cell in the range.

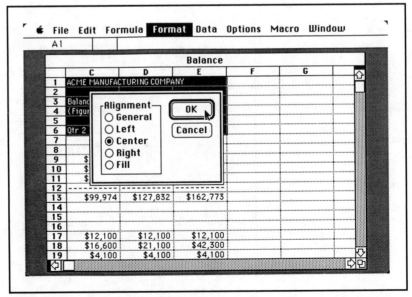

Figure B.23: The Alignment dialog box

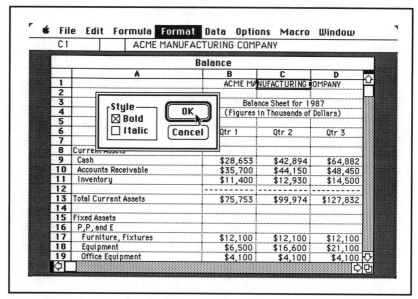

Figure B.24: The Style dialog box

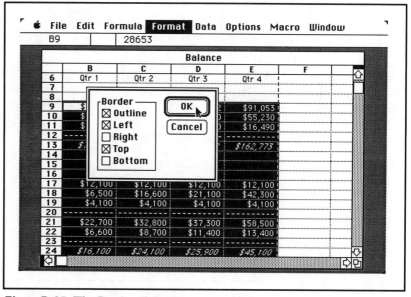

Figure B.25: The Border dialog box

- **Right** puts a border on the right edge of each cell in the range.
- **Top** puts a border on the top edge of each cell in the range.
- **Bottom** puts a border on the bottom edge of each cell in the range.

You can combine two or more of the above options. If the grid lines are displayed on the screen, it will be difficult to see the borders. You can use the Display command on the Options menu to turn off the grid lines.

CELL PROTECTION

The Cell Protection command permits you to lock cells to prevent them from being altered or to hide cells so that the formulas used in the calculation are not visible in the formula bar (see Chapter 13). To use the command, first select the cells to unlock or hide. Then, click the command. The dialog box shown in Figure B.26 is displayed. Click the desired option and click OK. To complete the protection, use the Protect Document command on the Options menu.

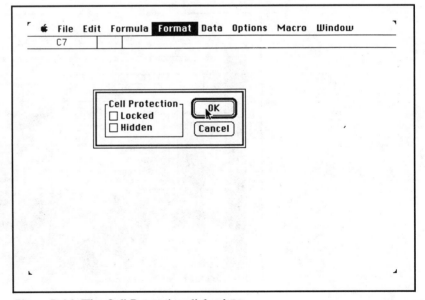

Figure B.26: The Cell Protection dialog box

Cells normally default to a locked status and are not hidden. The command is used, then, to unlock or to hide cells.

COLUMN WIDTH

The Column Width command is used to change the width of a specified column or columns. To change the width of a column, select any part of the column and click the command. You also can select multiple columns. The dialog box shown in Figure B.27 is then displayed. Click either standard width (10 characters) or enter the desired column width. The number must be between 0 and 72. You also can define the column width in decimal fractions (such as 2.5 characters).

Another way to change a column width is by clicking the bar to the right of the column designator and dragging it to the desired width.

THE DATA MENU

The Data menu contains the database commands.

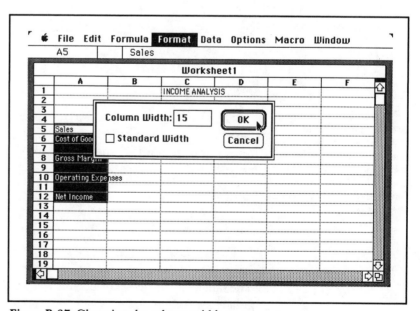

Figure B.27: Changing the column width

FIND

The Find command is used to locate records in a database that match the specified criteria (see Chapter 11). The criteria must be specified before the command is used. After using the command, the scroll box will change from white to striped. You can then scroll to find the matching records. To exit the command, choose any other command or click Exit Find on the Data menu. You can also press the Command and F keys to quickly move to the next matching record.

EXTRACT

In an extraction, the extracted records will overwrite any values, text, or formulas that were previously in the cells in the destination area.

The Extract command is used to extract records that match a specified criterion from a database (see Chapter 11). To use the command, set the database and criteria areas and then specify the criteria. You must also specify a destination area (with the field names) for the extracted records. It is not necessary to copy all fields. The extracted records are copied to a specified area on the current worksheet or another active worksheet. The command displays a dialog box (Figure B.28) from which you can select to copy all records or unique records only. If you select to copy only unique records, a record will be extracted only once, even if it matches more than one criterion.

DELETE

You cannot undo a Delete command. Use the Find command before you use the Delete command to see which records will be deleted. Save the worksheet before the deletion.

The Delete command is used to delete records in the current database that meet the specified criteria. The rest of the database is shifted up to recover the lost space. The remainder of the worksheet is not affected.

SET DATABASE

The Set Database command is used to define the range of cells to be assigned to the database. Only one database can be defined at a time. The range selected must include the row with the field names. To define a database, select the range and then click the Set Database command. Excel will assign the name Database to the specified range. The name can then be used for pasting, just like any other name.

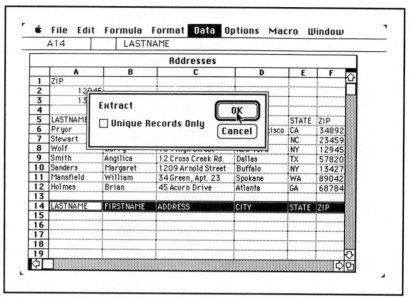

Figure B.28: The Extract dialog box

SET CRITERIA

The Set Criteria command is used to define the range of cells that are used to define the criteria for finding, extracting, and deleting records from the database. The name is also used with the database functions (see Chapter 11) to define the records to which a function is applied.

The criteria range consists of one row with the field names and one or more rows with the criteria. Criteria in the same row are ANDed; criteria in separate rows are ORed. You can use formulas, values, and comparison operators in defining the criteria. You can also use wild-card specifications (* and ?) in text criteria.

SORT

The Sort command is used to sort the rows or columns in a database in a specified order. When the command is issued, a Sort window (Figure B.29) is displayed. The following options are available:

- **Sort By** lets you sort by rows to reorder the records or by columns to reorder the fields.

You cannot undo a Sort command. If an undo is necessary, either save the worksheet first or create a new column with the record numbers before sorting. This column can then be used to initiate a sort to undo another sort.

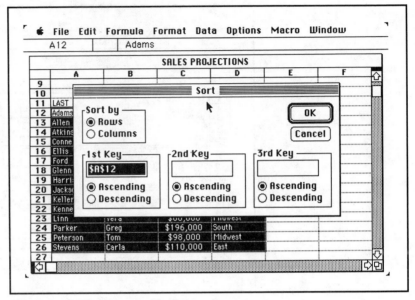

Figure B.29: The Sort window

- **1st, 2nd, and 3rd Keys** are used to specify the rows or columns used to control the sort. Up to three keys can be entered, with each creating an ascending or descending sort (to use more than three keys, use additional sorts).

When sorting a database, be sure not to include the field names.

SERIES

The Series command is used to fill a range of cells with a series of numbers. The command will fill by rows or by columns. To use the command, enter the value into the first cell and then select the range for the series. Click the Series command, and the dialog box shown in Figure B.30 appears. The following options are available:

- **Series In** defines the direction for the fill.
- **Type** defines the type of series for the fill.
- **Date Unit** is only active if a Date type is selected. It determines the type of increment for the date series.

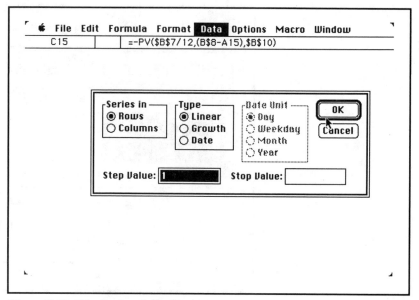

Figure B.30: The Series dialog box

- **Step Value** determines the increment value for each cell in the series.
- **Stop Value** determines the end value for the series.

For more information on using the Series command, see Chapter 14.

TABLE

The Table command is used to create tables (see Chapter 13). To create a table, define the range for the table and then click the Table command. The window shown in Figure B.31 is displayed.

For a one-input table, enter the reference of either the row input or column input cell. For a two-input table, define the row input cell as one input and the column input cell as the second input.

THE OPTIONS MENU

The Options menu is used to change display characteristics that affect the entire worksheet.

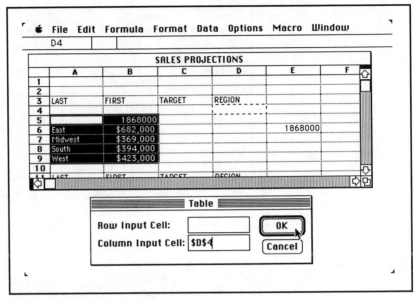

Figure B.31: The Table window

SET PRINT AREA

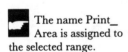
The name Print_ Area is assigned to the selected range.

The Set Print Area command is used to set the range of the worksheet that will be printed with the Print command on the File menu. If no area is selected, the entire worksheet is printed. To use the command, select the range and click the Set Print Area command.

SET PRINT TITLES

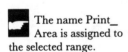
The name Print_ Titles is assigned to the selected range.

The Set Print Titles command is used to define the text that will be used as page titles with the Print command. The rows or columns that you define as titles will be printed on each page of the worksheet that contains any cells in that row or column. You can assign multiple rows or columns as titles. To use the command, select the rows or columns and then click the command.

SET PAGE BREAK

The Set Page Break command is used to set manual page breaks when the worksheet is printed. To use the command, select a cell and click the command. A manual page break will be inserted just before the selected cell, and the selected cell will be the first cell on the new page.

REMOVE PAGE BREAK

The Remove Page Break command is used to remove manual page breaks that have been set with the Set Page Break command. To remove a page break, select the cell that is the first cell on the new page and click the command. The page break before that cell will be removed.

FONT

The Font command is used to change the font and font size of the entire worksheet. When the command is used, the dialog box shown in Figure B.32 is displayed. The following options are available:

- **Font** selects from the fonts that are on the startup disk.

- **Size** selects from the font sizes available. You can scroll for additional font sizes.

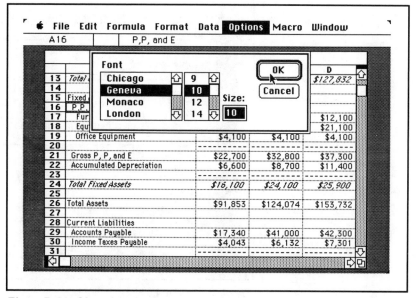

Figure B.32: Changing the font

You can use the DA/Font Mover program on your system disk to add fonts to the system.

DISPLAY

The Display command is used to control the screen display of formulas, grid lines, and row designators. When the command is used, the dialog box shown in Figure B.33 is displayed. Select one or more options and click OK.

If the Formulas option is selected, the formulas will be displayed and can be printed with the Print command. The Gridlines and Row & Column Headings selections affect only the screen display. To switch these on the printed copy, use the Page Setup command on the File menu.

PROTECT DOCUMENT/ UNPROTECT DOCUMENT

The Protect Document command is used to complete a worksheet protection assigned by the Cell Protection command on the Format menu. After a cell or cell range is assigned as locked or hidden, the Protect Document command is used to lock or hide the specified cells. The dialog box shown in Figure B.34 is displayed. Enter the password and click OK.

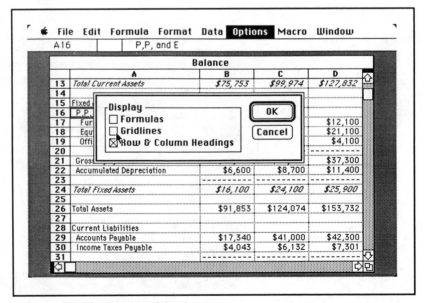

Figure B.33: The Display dialog box

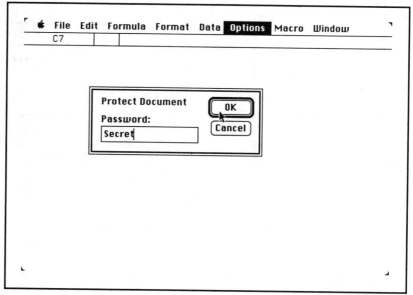

Figure B.34: Protecting the document

The document is then protected, and the menu changes to include an Unprotect Document command. To unprotect the document, select the Unprotect Document command, and the dialog box shown in Figure B.35 appears. Enter the password and click OK.

The Cell Protection command affects only the specified range, and multiple ranges can be selected using the command several times. The Protect Document command affects the entire worksheet, implementing the desired protection selections.

You can only unprotect a document if you know the password. If you forget the password, you cannot unprotect the document. Keep a record of the passwords that you use.

PRECISION AS DISPLAYED/FULL PRECISION

The Precision As Displayed/Full Precision command controls the precision with which the calculations are done and how the results are stored. Normally, all calculations are done at a full 14-digit precision, and the values are saved with this precision. If Precision As Displayed is selected, calculations are only done with the precision with which they are displayed, and the numbers are saved with this precision. However, you cannot change the precision of numbers that use the General template.

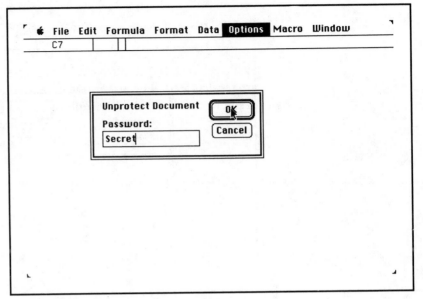

Figure B.35: Unprotecting the document

R1C1/A1

The R1C1/A1 command changes the method of cell reference. Excel normally uses the A1 format, in which columns are designated by letters and rows by numbers. Some spreadsheet programs use an R1C1 format, in which both rows and columns use numeric designators. This command permits you to switch the designator mode. Formulas are adjusted to the selected mode.

CALCULATE NOW

The Calculate Now command forces a recalculation of a worksheet or chart; it is used to complete the calculations if the manual mode is selected with the Calculation command. This command is not necessary if you are using the default automatic calculation.

You can also use the Calculate Now command to replace a formula in the formula bar with a value. If the formula bar is active and you begin an entry with an equal sign, Calculate Now will calculate the formula and replace the cell entry with the resulting value.

CALCULATION

The Calculation command controls when Excel recalculates formulas in the open documents. In the default automatic mode, whenever a cell is changed, all formulas and values that depend on that cell are recalculated. The amount of time required depends upon the size of the worksheet and the complexity of the formulas.

While creating a worksheet, you may find the calculations cannot keep up with the data entry on a large worksheet. In this case, use the Calculation command to switch off the calculations until the data entry is completed.

When the command is used, the dialog box shown in Figure B.36 is displayed. The following calculation options are available:

- **Automatic** calculates all values that depend on a cell each time that the cell contents are changed.

- **Automatic Except Tables** calculates all values except table values when the cell contents are changed.

- **Manual** calculates the worksheet only with the Calculate Now command.

Table calculations take much longer than others to calculate. Using the Automatic Except Tables option can speed up creating and editing worksheets that contain tables.

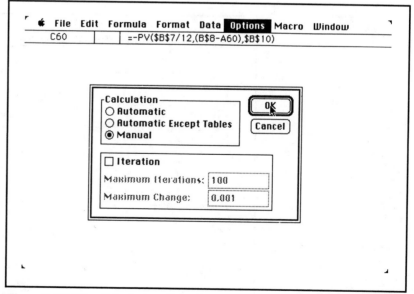

Figure B.36: The Calculation dialog box

The **Iteration** option in the Calculation dialog box is used to control iterative calculations when circular references are used on the worksheet. The default condition is no iteration, and Excel will display error messages when you use circular references. If you need to use circular references, click Iteration and select the desired parameters.

THE MACRO MENU

The Macro menu is used to create and execute function and command macros.

RUN

The Run command is used to initiate a previously defined command macro. The macro sheet must be open. When the command is executed, the dialog box shown in Figure B.37 is displayed. Double-click the desired macro or click the name and click OK. You can also execute a macro by entering in the Reference box the reference to the first cell on the macro sheet.

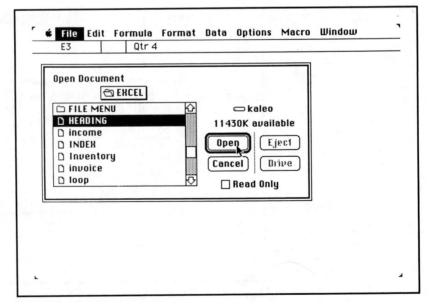

Figure B.37: Initiating a macro

START RECORDER/STOP RECORDER

The Start Recorder command initiates the recording of worksheet actions on a macro sheet in a range previously defined by the Set Recorder command. The Stop Recorder command terminates the recording. Cell references are recorded, by default, as relative references. If an attempt is made to record over a cell that already has an entry, an alert box will be displayed.

ABSOLUTE RECORD/RELATIVE RECORD

The Absolute Record/Relative Record command determines the type of cell references that are stored when the recorder is started.

SET RECORDER

The Set Recorder command is used to specify the range to be used by the recorder on the macro sheet (see Chapter 17). A range is selected on the macro sheet, and the Set Recorder command is clicked. Then, commands will be stored in the specified range.

THE WINDOW MENU

The Window menu is used to show the Clipboard, to switch between active windows quickly, and to open additional windows on the same document.

SHOW CLIPBOARD

The Show Clipboard command opens the Clipboard window. If the Clipboard contains worksheet cells, only the size of the cell range is shown. If the Copy Picture command has been used, the Clipboard will show the worksheet range.

NEW WINDOW

The New Window command opens a new window on the currently active document. The number of windows that can be open is limited only by your computer's memory.

ACTIVATE WINDOW

The Window menu will always show an entry for each open document. You can use the Activate Window command to switch quickly between open documents.

EXCEL'S CHART MENUS ARE AVAILABLE WHENEVER an existing chart is open or the New command on the File menu is used to create a chart. There are eight chart menus: Apple, File, Edit, Gallery, Chart, Format, Macro, and Window.

THE APPLE MENU

The Apple menu is identical to the Apple menu for the worksheet. It includes an About Microsoft Excel command that provides information about memory usage and about the listed help topics.

THE FILE MENU

The chart File menu is identical to the File menu for the worksheet except that the Page Setup command has some different options. It does not include the options for row and column designators or grid lines. Also, margins cannot be specified; instead, you can specify the size of the chart (see Figure C.1).

The chart Page Setup command also gives you the option of selecting either screen size or fit to page. If the **Fit to Page** option is set, the chart is printed as specified, regardless of the screen chart size. If the **Screen Size** option is selected, the chart will be printed at the screen size, and as much of the image as possible will be printed with the specified print width and height.

THE EDIT MENU

The Edit menu is used to edit charts, much as the familiar Macintosh Edit menu commands are used in other application programs.

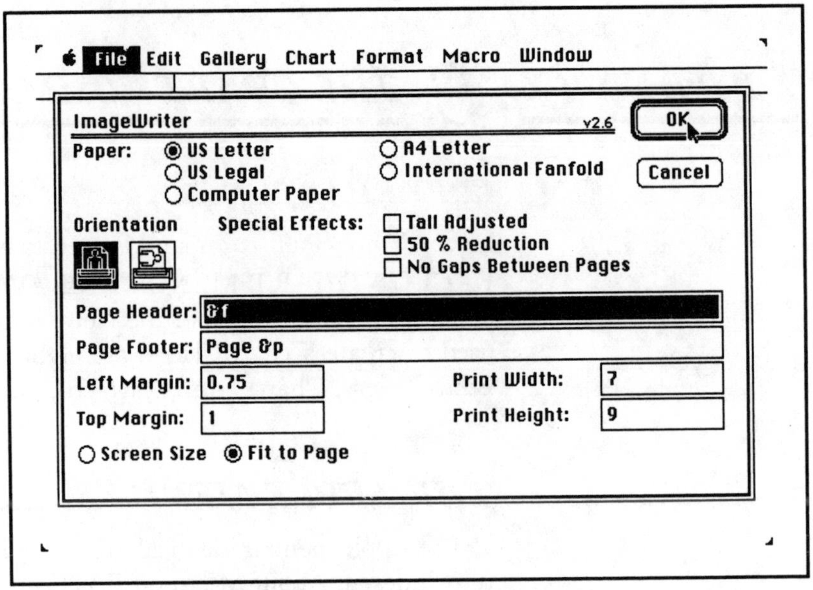

Figure C.1: The Page Setup dialog box for charts

UNDO

The Undo command is used to undo editing commands. Any Edit menu command can be undone until another command is selected. The menu displays the type of undo available.

CUT

The Cut command can be used to edit the chart formula bar. When your selections are cut, they are moved to the Clipboard. You cannot cut from the chart itself with this command.

COPY

The Copy command copies the data series and format of a chart onto the Clipboard, where it can be pasted into another chart. To copy a chart, the graph is first selected with the Select Chart command on the Chart menu. Then, the Copy command is used to move the data on the chart to the Clipboard. You can activate the destination chart and use the Paste or Paste Special command to copy the graph into it.

COPY CHART

The Copy Chart command is used to copy a chart into the Clipboard when you wish to move it to other Macintosh documents. When the command is selected, a dialog box (Figure C.2) is displayed. From this dialog box, you can select whether to copy the chart onto the Clipboard as it is displayed on the screen or as it would be printed. If you select to copy it as printed, you can control the size of the Clipboard image using the Page Setup command on the File menu.

PASTE

The Paste command is used to paste a data series from a worksheet or chart into another chart. To copy from a worksheet, select the data

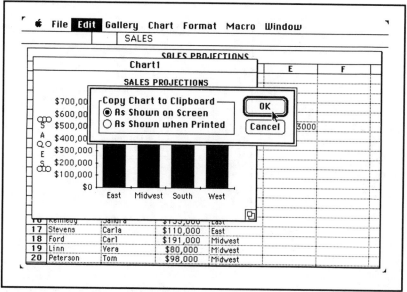

Figure C.2: The Copy Chart dialog box

series and use the Copy command to copy the data series into the Clipboard. Then, use the Paste command to paste the data series into a chart. To copy from another chart, use the Select Chart command on the Chart menu and the Copy command to copy the data series into the Clipboard. Then, use the Paste command to copy it from the Clipboard into the chart.

You can also use the Cut and Paste commands in the chart formula bar to edit a formula.

CLEAR

The Clear command is used to clear the formula bar or a chart data series. If the formula bar is active, the command will clear whatever is selected in the formula bar.

To clear a chart, first use the Select Chart command on the Chart menu to select the chart, then use the Clear command. A dialog box (Figure C.3) will be displayed. It provides the following options:

- **All** clears the data format and data series.

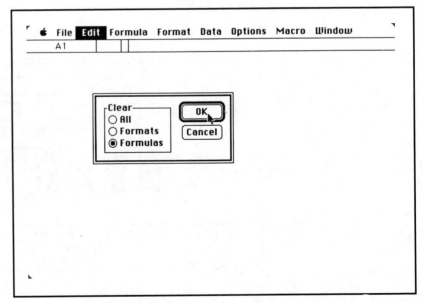

Figure C.3: The Clear dialog box

- **Formats** clears the format, but not the data series (the chart reverts to the preferred format).

- **Formulas** clears the data series, but not the format.

PASTE SPECIAL

The Paste Special command permits the user to control how the data series is defined when pasting. The Paste command does not permit the user to control the data series definition (see Chapter 19). The Copy command is used first to move the data series onto the Clipboard. The chart is then selected, and the Paste Special command is used. The dialog box shown in Figure C.4 is displayed. Select how you wish to define the data series and click OK.

The following options are available:

- **Values In** is the option to click to indicate if the data series is in a row or a column.

- **Series Names in First Column,** if checked, has Excel use the contents of the cell in the first column of each row as the

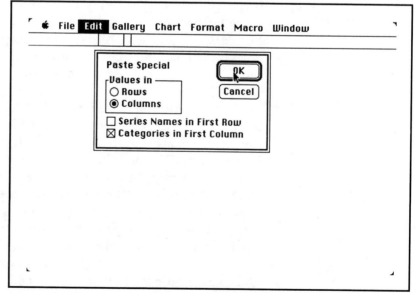

Figure C.4: The chart Paste Special dialog box

name of the data series for that row. If it is not checked, the contents of the first column are assumed to be the first value in the data series.

- **Categories in First Row,** if checked, has Excel use the text in each cell in the first row as the category for the series in the column. If it is not checked, the first row is the first data series.

- **Series Names in First Row,** if checked, has Excel use the contents of the cell in the first row of each column as the name of the data series for that column. If it is not checked, the contents of the first row are assumed to be the first value in the data series.

- **Categories in First Column,** if checked, has Excel use the text in each cell in the first column as the category for the series in the row. If it is not checked, the first column is the first data series.

GALLERY MENU

The Gallery menu is used to select the chart type. The active chart is changed to the specified type. Click the desired type, and then select the chart format within that type from the dialog box displayed. Figures C.5 through C.10 show the dialog boxes for the six basic types of charts. Figure C.11 shows the four combination types that can be used if two data series are charted.

The Preferred command changes the format of the currently displayed chart to the preferred format. Whenever a chart is first created from a data series, it is always displayed in the preferred format. It can then be changed to an alternate type by using a command on the Gallery menu. The default, preferred format, is the column type.

You can change the preferred format with the Set Preferred Format command on the Chart menu. The Preferred and Set Preferred Format commands are useful if you need to remember the currently displayed format while you experiment with other formats. Use the Set Preferred Format command to select the current format as the preferred format, then experiment as you wish. To return to the initial format, use the Preferred command.

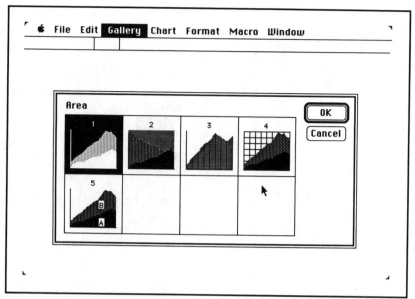

Figure C.5: Area chart formats

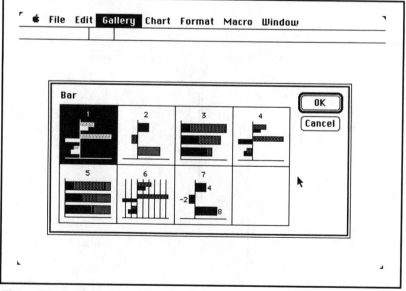

Figure C.6: Bar chart formats

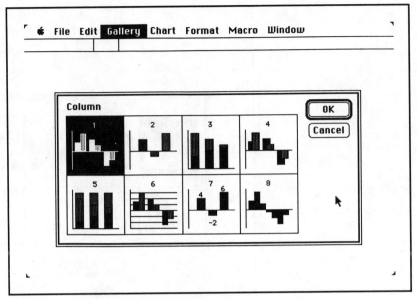

Figure C.7: Column chart formats

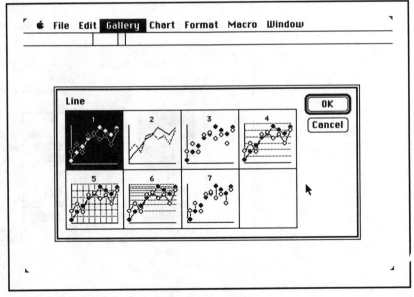

Figure C.8: Line chart formats

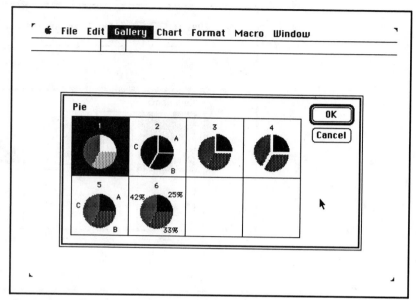

Figure C.9: Pie chart formats

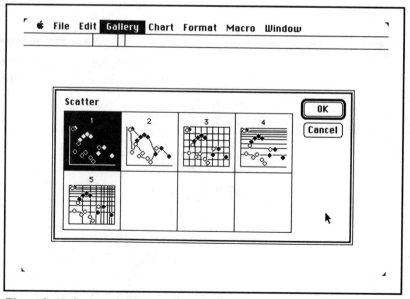

Figure C.10: Scatter chart formats

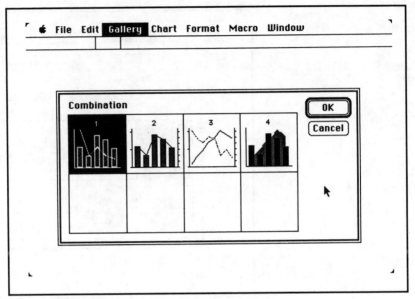

Figure C.11: Combination chart formats

CHART MENU

The Chart menu is used to control the chart type and the objects (legend, axes labels, titles, etc.) displayed on the chart.

MAIN CHART TYPE

The Main Chart Type command changes the basic type of the main chart. When the command is selected, the dialog box shown in Figure C.12 is displayed. Click the desired option, then click OK.

OVERLAY CHART TYPE

The Overlay Chart Type command changes the basic type of the overlay chart. When the command is selected, the dialog box shown in Figure C.13 is displayed. Click the desired option and click OK.

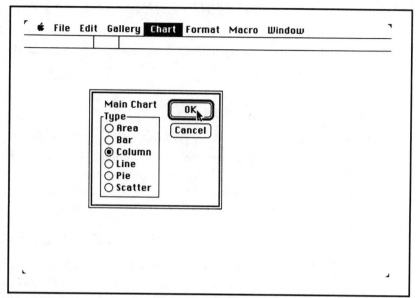

Figure C.12: The Main Chart Type dialog box

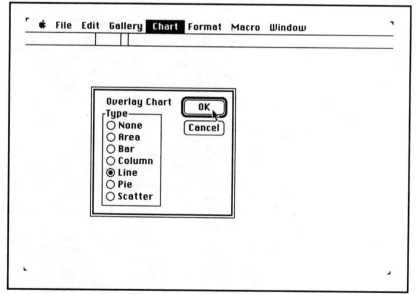

Figure C.13: The Overlay Chart Type dialog box

SET PREFERRED FORMAT

The Set Preferred Format command saves the format of the currently active chart as the preferred format (see the Preferred command in the Gallery menu section).

AXES

The Axes command controls the display of the axes and grid lines. You can control the weight of the lines with the Format Patterns command. When the Axes command is selected, the dialog box shown in Figure C.14 is displayed. Select the desired options and click OK.

ADD LEGEND/DELETE LEGEND

The Add Legend command adds a legend to the chart. On a pie chart, the category titles are the legend text. On other graphs, the data-series names are used as the legend titles. The chart is redrawn to accommodate the legend. You can format and position the legend

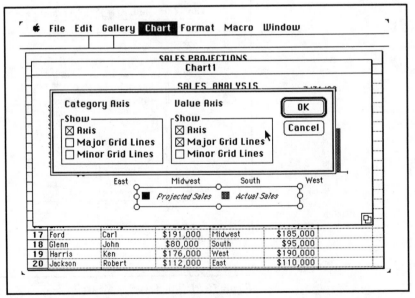

Figure C.14: The Axes dialog box

with the Text and Legend commands on the Format menu. You can also change the legend titles by editing the data-series formulas in the formula bar (see Chapter 19).

Use the Delete Legend command to remove the legend.

ATTACH TEXT

The Attach Text command is used to attach text to defined parts of the chart. To add attached text, click the command. The dialog box shown in Figure C.15 is displayed. Click the area to which you wish to attach the text, then click OK. Enter the text into the formula bar and click the enter box or press the Return key.

You can use this command to attach text to a title, either axis, or a data series. You can also attach text to a data point.

ADD ARROW

The Add Arrow command is used to add an arrow to highlight any point of the chart. The command puts an arrow in the upper left of

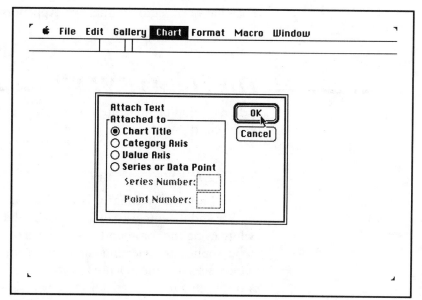

Figure C.15: The Attach Text dialog box

the chart. You can then drag the arrow to any point in the chart and format it with the Patterns command on the Format menu. You can add as many arrows as you want to a chart.

SELECT CHART

The Select Chart command selects the entire chart. Once selected, you can use the Patterns command on the Format menu to alter the patterns, clear the chart with the Clear command on the Edit menu, or copy the chart with the Copy command on the Edit menu.

SELECT PLOT AREA

The Select Plot Area command selects the plot area of the chart. You can then use the Patterns command on the Format menu to change the patterns.

CALCULATE NOW

The Calculate Now command redraws the chart if the calculation mode has been set to manual (see Appendix B).

THE FORMAT MENU

The Format menu controls the format of the chart and the objects on the chart.

PATTERNS

The Patterns command is used to control the patterns of the marker and the intensity of lines on the chart (grid lines, axes, etc.). Before using the command, select the area to which the command is to be applied by selecting the chart (using the Select Chart command), selecting the plot area (using the Select Plot Area command), or by clicking the desired object. Then, click the Patterns command.

The dialog box shown in Figure C.16 is displayed. The options available in this dialog box depend on the object that you selected before using the Patterns command. Select from the following options:

- **Invisible** removes the object from visibility on the chart.

- **Automatic** assigns patterns automatically.

- **Apply to All** applies the selection to all data points or series (for a data point or data-series selection only).

- **Patterns** controls the patterns of the background, border, area, line, axis, and arrows.

- **Marker Patterns** controls the markers in a line chart.

- **Weight** controls the weight of a selected line, border, arrowshaft, or axis.

- **Border Style** changes the normal border of a chart, text, or legend to a border with a shadow at the bottom and right sides.

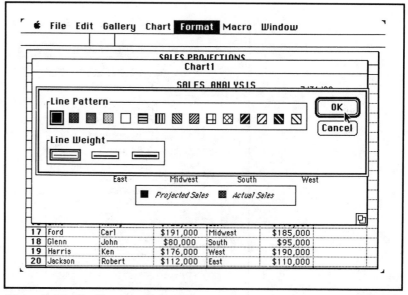

Figure C.16: The Patterns dialog box

- **Type of Tickmarks** controls the appearance of the tick marks.

- **Arrowhead** controls the width, length, and style of an arrowhead.

MAIN CHART

The Main Chart command controls other formatting features of the main chart that cannot be controlled by the Patterns command. The dialog box displayed varies with the type of chart. The Column Chart dialog box is shown in Figure C.17. The following features are available:

- **Stacked** adds the second data series to the first data series as a stacked graph.

- **100%** normalizes the category values to 100%. The absolute values do not appear on the chart.

For some objects, you need to use special commands to remove them from a chart. The Axes command on the Chart menu controls the axes, tick marks, labels, and grid lines. The Main Chart and Overlay Chart commands on the Format menu control the drop and hi-lo lines.

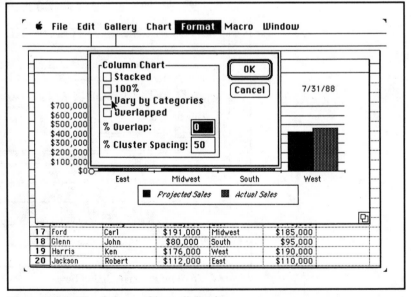

Figure C.17: The Column Chart dialog box

- **Vary by Categories** varies the pattern for each data point (for single series only).

- **Drop Lines** extends drop lines from the highest value in each category to the axis.

- **Hi-Lo Lines** extends lines from the highest value in each category to the lowest.

- **Overlapped** overlaps bar and column charts.

- **% Overlap** controls the amount of overlap.

- **% Cluster Spacing** controls spacing between bars.

- **Angle of First Slice** controls the angle of the first edge of the first slice from the vertical (pie chart).

OVERLAY CHART

The Overlay Chart command formats the overlay chart. Use this command after you select the overlay chart type. The dialog box displayed varies with the type of chart selected. Figure C.18 shows the

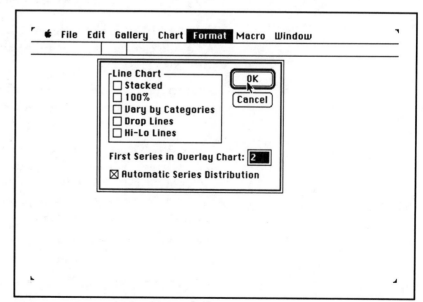

Figure C.18: The Overlay Chart dialog box

one for a line chart. These dialog boxes are the same as the ones displayed by the Main Chart command, with the exception of these two additional options:

- **First Series in Overlay Chart** controls the series selected for the overlay chart.

- **Automatic Series Distribution** divides the data series evenly between the main and overlay charts.

AXIS

The Axis command controls the order of the categories or values, intervals for tick-mark labels, and the scale of the axis. If an overlay chart is used, the dialog box shows only the main axis or overlay axis, depending upon which is selected. Use this command after you select the desired axis. The dialog box displayed varies depending upon the axis selected.

CATEGORY AXIS   The dialog box displayed for a category axis is shown in Figure C.19. The following options are available:

- **Value Axis Crosses at Category Number** controls the number of the category at which the value axis crosses the category axis. This defaults to 1.

- **Number of Categories Between Tick Labels** controls the number of categories for each tick-mark label. This defaults to 1.

- **Value Axis Crosses Between Categories** controls the value axis crossing. Normally, the value axis crosses through the center of the category indicated in the Value Axis Crosses at Category Number box. If this option is clicked, the value axis crosses between two categories.

- **Value Axis Crosses at Maximum Category**, if clicked, has the value axis cross the category axis at the last category.

- **Categories in Reverse Order** reverses the category order.

- **Tick Label Position** moves the position of the tick-mark labels (they normally appear next to the axis and tick marks).

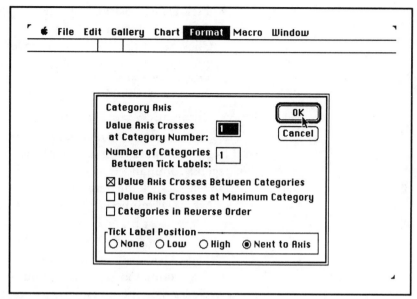

Figure C.19: The Category Axis dialog box

VALUE AXIS   The dialog box displayed for a value axis is shown in Figure C.20. The scaling is normally set to automatic for all five of the first categories, but you can override the automatic values and enter your own. The dialog box offers the following options:

- **Minimum** controls the range of values accepted. Values below the minimum do not appear on the chart.

- **Maximum** controls the range of values accepted. Values above the maximum do not appear on the chart.

- **Major Unit** controls the major divisions on the axis.

- **Minor Unit** controls the minor divisions on the axis.

- **Category Axis Crosses At** controls the point at which the category axis crosses the value axis.

- **Logarithmic Scale**, if checked, makes the axis values logarithmic.

- **Values in Reverse Order**, if checked, reverses the order of the values on the value axis.

- **Tick Label Position** controls the position of the labels for the tick marks. Normally, they are near the tick marks and axis. Click here to move them to the low or high end of the category axis.

LEGEND

The Legend command determines the position of the legend if the Add Legend command on the Chart menu has been selected. When the Legend command is selected, the dialog box shown in Figure C.21 appears. Click the desired option and click OK. The chart will be redrawn to accommodate the new position.

TEXT

The Text command is used to control the font, font size, alignment, style, and orientation of any text on the screen. The Text dialog box is shown in Figure C.22. The following options are available:

- **Font and Font Size** control the type and size of the font. You can add fonts using the DA/Font Mover program external to Excel.
- **Style** selects boldface, italic, both, or normal.
- **Automatic Text** restores default text created with the Attach Text command.
- **Automatic Size** restores the border to the default border.
- **Show Key** keys text attached to data points to the legend.
- **Show Value** labels a data point with the value of the data point.
- **Orientation** controls the orientation of the text (vertical or horizontal).
- **Horizontal Alignment** controls the horizontal alignment of text.
- **Vertical Alignment** controls the vertical alignment of text.

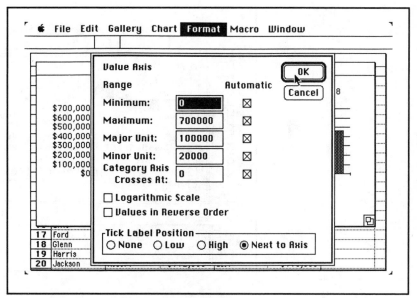

Figure C.20: The Value Axis dialog box

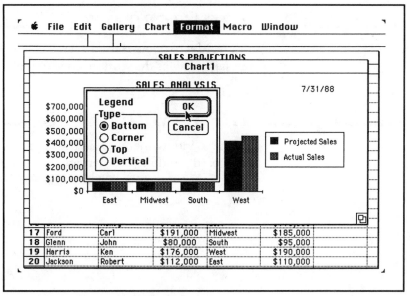

Figure C.21: Moving the legend

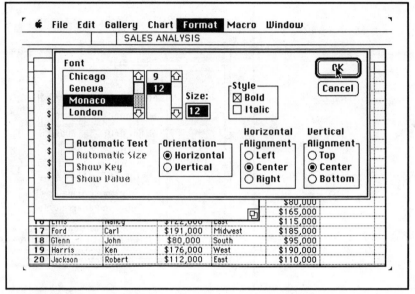

Figure C.22: Formatting text

THE MACRO MENU

The Macro menu is used to create and execute macros. It works in the same way as the worksheet Macro menu.

THE WINDOW MENU

The Window menu is used to switch active windows, open the Clipboard window, or open another window on the same chart. It works in the same way as the worksheet Window menu.

APPENDIX **D** *ERROR VALUES*

EXCEL ENTERS ERROR VALUES INTO A CELL WHEN, for some reason, it cannot process the formula for that cell. There are seven error values, as described below.

ERROR VALUE	CAUSE
#DIV/0!	An attempt was made to divide by zero.
#NAME?	A name was used in a formula that has not yet been defined. It generally means that you forgot the quotation marks.
#N/A	No value is available.
#NULL!	An intersection was specified (using a space operator) that does not exist, e.g., A3 C5.
#NUM!	A number is too large or too small or a function is used incorrectly.
#REF!	A cell was referenced that is not on the worksheet or has been deleted.
#VALUE!	The wrong type of argument or operand was used.

APPENDIX *E* USING EXCEL WITH LOTUS 1-2-3

WHEN A FILE IS TRANSFERRED IN EITHER DIRECTION between Lotus 1-2-3 and Excel, the following convert:

- Cell values, formulas, and formats
- Names

The following do not convert:

- Window properties
- Macros
- Lotus 1-2-3 charts to Excel graphs

Although many functions in Lotus 1-2-3 have a different order of arguments, they will still convert, and the worksheet will operate properly when transferred in either direction. See Chapter 20 for information about how to convert files. Here are some additional notes:

- Some Lotus 1-2-3 formulas cannot be converted, and you will be alerted by a dialog box when these are encountered. Some Excel functions are not in Lotus 1-2-3.

- Lotus 1-2-3 does not support arrays, and Excel arrays cannot be converted.

- Lotus 1-2-3 represents logical values somewhat differently than Excel represents them. Use caution with conversions of logical values.

- Excel permits the use of text as constants in formulas; Lotus 1-2-3 does not. Any Excel formula containing a text argument or operand will not convert.

- Excel permits the use of reference to multiple areas; Lotus 1-2-3 does not.

- Excel has more extensive capabilities in the use of names than Lotus 1-2-3 does.
- Excel has more operators (including union, intersection, concatenaton, and %) than Lotus 1-2-3 does.

FUNCTIONS

The following functions are the same in Lotus 1-2-3 and Excel:

ABS( )

ACOS( )

ASIN( )

ATAN( )

ATAN2( )

COS( )

EXP( )

FALSE( )

IF( )

ISNA( )

LN( )

LOG( )

NA( )

NOT( )

PI( )

RAND( )

ROUND( )

SIN( )

SQRT( )

TAN( )

TRUE( )

The following functions are in Excel, but not in Lotus 1-2-3:

AREAS( )
COLUMN( )
COLUMNS( )
DOLLAR( )
FIXED( )
GROWTH( )
HOUR( )
INDEX( )
ISREF( )
LEN( )
LINEST( )
LOGEST( )
LOOKUP( )
MATCH( )
MID( )
MINUTE( )
MIRR( )
NPER( )
RATE( )
REPT( )
ROW( )
ROWS( )
SECOND( )
SIGN( )
TEXT( )
TIME( )
TRANSPOSE( )

TREND( )

TYPE( )

VALUE( )

WEEKDAY( )

The following functions are in both Excel and Lotus 1-2-3, but have variations, such as the argument order or name:

AVG( )

COUNT( )

LOG10( )

MAX( )

MIN( )

STD( )

SUM( )

VAR( )

CHOOSE( )	(Excel is limited to 14 arguments; the index argument is different)
DATE( )	(see TODAY)
DAY( )	(see TODAY)
MONTH( )	(see TODAY)
TODAY( ), NOW( )	(A serial number is used to represent Excel dates so that you can calculate date differences)
YEAR( )	(see TODAY)
DAVG( )	(Lotus' *offset* is 0-based, Excel's *field-index* is 1-based)
DCOUNT( )	(see DAVG)
DMAX( )	(see DAVG)
DMIN( )	(see DAVG)
DSTD( )	(see DAVG)
DSUM( )	(see DAVG)

DVAR( )	(see DAVG)
ERR( )	(in Excel, it is #VALUE!)
FV( )	(see PV)
PMT( )	(see PV)
PV( )	(the order of the arguments is changed, and there are some sign changes)
HLOOKUP( )	(some argument definition variation)
VLOOKUP( )	(some argument definition variation)
INT( )	(Excel rounds down; Lotus rounds toward zero)
IRR( )	(the argument order is changed)
ISERR( )	
MOD( )	(MOD uses INT, and the variation follows the INT notes)
NPV( )	(Excel permits up to 13 arguments; Lotus 1-2-3 allows only 1)

FORMATTING

In converting, the templating information will be maintained as much as possible. In converting from Excel to Lotus 1-2-3, the alignment for text cells is maintained. All nontext cells will be right-aligned.

MISCELLANEOUS

The locking of cells is maintained, but Lotus 1-2-3 does not support hidden cells. Both Excel and Lotus 1-2-3 support iterations, but with Excel you can control the number of iterations. Excel has more extensive table-processing capability. The database commands and functions of both programs are very similar, however Excel interprets input criteria differently.

APPENDIX **F** *THE SWITCHER*

THE SWITCHER IS A MACINTOSH PROGRAM THAT permits Excel to reside in the computer memory with other application programs, such as Microsoft Word or Write. This allows a user to move data from one application program to another quickly, without having to constantly reload the program.

INSTALLING THE SWITCHER

To install the switcher and launch Excel:

1. Double-click the Switcher icon. The Switcher will load and display the Application Switcher window (Figure F.1). This window is used to launch, or start, different applications.

2. Switch the Clipboard so that a common Clipboard is used by all applications by pulling down the Switcher menu and clicking Options. Be sure that Always Convert Clipboard is selected (see Figure F.2), then click OK.

3. Launch Excel by double-clicking the first icon in the application window. When the dialog box is displayed (see Figure F.3), click the Excel program to start it.

Excel will start and an empty worksheet will be displayed.

LAUNCHING ADDITIONAL APPLICATIONS

After Excel is started, the menu bar is slightly different, with a double arrow in the upper right (see Figure F.4). To launch additional applications, click the middle of this arrow and the Application

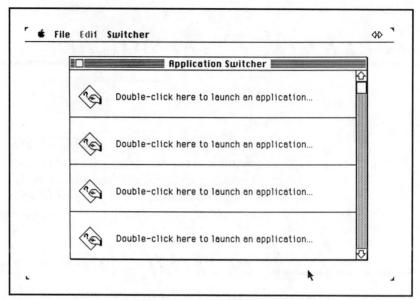

Figure F.1: The Applications Switcher window

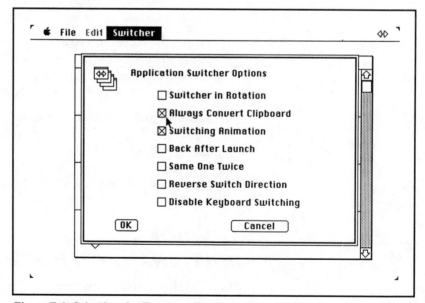

Figure F.2: Selecting the Excel application program

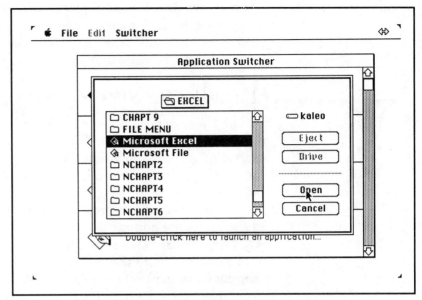

Figure F.3: Selecting Excel

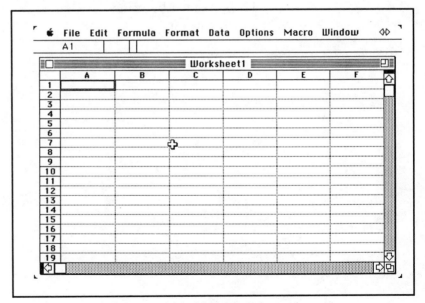

Figure F.4: The Excel menu bar with the Switcher active

Switcher window will be displayed. You can then launch another application by clicking the second icon and clicking the program name, just as you did when starting Excel.

USING THE SWITCHER

Once your applications are started, you can scroll between them by using the arrows at the right of the menu bar. Clicking the central part displays the Application Window, permitting you to launch another application. A maximum of four can be launched if you have adequate memory.

Quitting an application removes it from the Switcher. You can exit the Switcher by quitting all active applications and then choosing Quit from the Switcher's File menu.

You can monitor the memory space used by a particular application by returning to the Application Window, where the program icons show memory usage. If you prefer a graphic display, click Show Info Window on the Switcher's File menu.

You can also control the memory allocated to an application during launch by using the Configure then Install option of the Switcher menu.

APPENDIX *G* *KEYBOARD COMMANDS*

MANY OF THE MOST FREQUENTLY USED COMMANDS can be executed from the keyboard without the mouse. Using the keyboard command codes is often quicker than using the menus. This appendix lists the available keyboard commands. In the following table, the hyphen indicates that the keys are to be pressed at the same time.

COMMAND	KEYS
About Excel	Command-?
Activate Next Window	Command-M
Activate Previous Window	Shift-Command-M
Calculate Now	Command- =
Cancel	Command-.
Clear	Command-B
Copy	Command-C
Copy Picture	Shift-Command-C
Cut	Command-X
Data Find Next	Command-F
Data Find Previous	Shift-Command-F
Define Name	Command-L
Delete	Command-K
Enter Array Formula	Command-Return
Extract	Command-E
Fill Down	Command-D

COMMAND	KEYS
Fill Right	Command-R
Fill Selection with Formula	Option-Enter
Formula Find Next	Command-H
Formula Find Previous	Shift-Command-H
Goto	Command-G
Insert	Command-I
New	Command-N
Open	Command-O
Paste	Command-V
Print	Command-P
Quit	Command-Q
Reference	Command-T
Save	Command-S
Select All Cells	Command-A
Select Chart	Command-A
Undo	Command-Z

THERE ARE 86 FUNCTIONS AVAILABLE TO THE EXCEL user. These can be classified into nine types: mathematical, statistical, database, trigonometric, logical, text, financial, date, and special-purpose.

MATHEMATICAL FUNCTIONS

FUNCTION	*DESCRIPTION*
ABS(*number*)	Returns the absolute value of *number*.
EXP(*number*)	Returns e raised to the power of *number*. EXP is the reverse of the *LN* (natural logarithm) function. To calculate the power to other bases, use the exponentiation operator.
INT(*number*)	Returns the largest integer less than or equal to *number*. For example: INT(7.6) is 7.
LN(*number*)	Returns the natural logarithm of *number*. *Number* must be positive. LN is the inverse of EXP.
LOG10(*number*)	Returns the base 10 logarithm of *number*.
MOD(*number, divisor number*)	Returns the remainder after *number* is divided by *divisor number*. The

	result has the same sign as divisor number.
PI( )	Returns the value of pi. There is no argument.
RAND( )	Returns a random number between 0 and 0.999.... The value will change each time the worksheet is recalculated. There is no argument.
ROUND(*number, number of digits*)	Returns *number* rounded to *number of digits.*
SIGN(*number*)	Returns 1 if *number* is positive, 0 if *number* is 0, and -1 if *number* is negative.
SQRT(*number*)	Returns the square root of *number. Number* must be positive.

STATISTICAL FUNCTIONS

FUNCTION	DESCRIPTION
AVERAGE(*number 1, number 2, …*)	Returns the average of the numeric arguments.
COUNT(*number 1, number 2, …*)	Returns the number of numbers in a list of arguments. Example: COUNT(A1:A5,A8) equals 6.
GROWTH(*Y array, X array, x array*)	Returns an array with the y values as the exponential curve of regression $y = b*m \wedge x$ for two variables represented by *X array* and *Y array.*
LINEST(*Y array, X array*)	Returns the horizontal array of two elements, the slope and y intercept of the line of regression for $y = mx + b$ for two variables X

	and Y represented by *X array* and *Y array.*
LOGEST(*Y array, X array*)	Returns a horizontal array of two elements, the parameters of m and b in the exponential curve of regression y = b*m ^ x for two variables represented by *X array* and *Y array.*
MAX(*number 1, number 2, ...*)	Returns the largest number in a list of arguments.
MIN(*number 1, number 2, ...*)	Returns the smallest number in a list of arguments.
STDEV(*number 1, number 2, ...*)	Returns the standard deviation of the numbers in a list of arguments.
SUM(*number 1, number 2, ...*)	Returns the sum of the numbers in a list of arguments.
TREND(*Y array, X array, x array*)	Returns an array, the y values on the line of regression, y = mx + b, for the two variables X and Y represented by X array and Y array.
VAR(*number 1, number 2, ...*)	Returns the variance of the numbers in the list of arguments.

DATABASE FUNCTIONS

FUNCTION	*DESCRIPTION*
DAVERAGE(*database, field name, criteria*)	Returns the average of the numbers in a particular field of the database that meet the specified criteria.
DCOUNT(*database, field name, criteria*)	Returns the count of the numbers in a particular field of a database that meet the specified criteria.

DMAX(*database, field name, criteria*)	Returns the largest of the numbers in a particular field of a database that meet the specified criteria.
DMIN(*database, field name, criteria*)	Returns the smallest of the numbers in a particular field of a database that meet the specified criteria.
DSTDEV(*database, field name, criteria*)	Returns the standard deviation of the numbers in a particular field of a database that meet the specified criteria.
DSUM(*database, field name, criteria*)	Returns the sum of the numbers in a particular field of a database that meet the specified criteria.
DVAR(*database, field name, criteria*)	Returns the variance of the numbers in a particular field of a database that meet the specified criteria.

TRIGONOMETRIC FUNCTIONS

FUNCTION	*DESCRIPTION*
ACOS(*number*)	Returns the arccosine of *number*. The value is returned in radians. To convert to degrees, multiply by 180/PI().
ASIN(*number*)	Returns the arcsine of number (see ACOS).
ATAN(*number*)	Returns the arctangent of number (see ACOS).
ATAN2(*x number, y number*)	Returns the arctangent of *x number* and *y number*.
COS(*number*)	Returns the cosine of *number*.
SIN(*number*)	Returns the sine of *number*.
TAN(*number*)	Returns the tangent of *number*.

LOGICAL FUNCTIONS

FUNCTION	DESCRIPTION
AND(*logical 1, logical 2, ...*)	Returns TRUE if all logical values in the list of arguments are true. If any of the values are false, the function will return a value of FALSE.
CHOOSE(*index, value 1, value 2, ...*)	Returns the value from the list of arguments based on the value of *index*. If *index* is 1, *value 1* is returned.
FALSE( )	Returns the value of FALSE. Useful as an argument in the CHOOSE function.
IF(*logical, value if true, value if false*)	Returns *value if true* if *logical* is TRUE, otherwise returns *value if false*.
ISERROR(*value*)	Returns TRUE if *value* is any Excel error value, otherwise returns FALSE.
ISNA(*value*)	Returns TRUE if *value* is #N/A, (not available— see Appendix D), otherwise returns FALSE.
ISREF(*value*)	Returns TRUE if *value* is a reference or reference formula, otherwise returns FALSE.
NOT(*logical*)	Returns FALSE if *logical* is TRUE, TRUE if *logical* is FALSE.
OR(*logical 1, logical 2, ...*)	Returns TRUE if any of the logical values in the list of arguments is TRUE. If all logical values in the list are FALSE, it returns FALSE.
TRUE( )	Returns a logical value of TRUE. Used with CHOOSE function. There is no argument.

TEXT FUNCTIONS

FUNCTION	DESCRIPTION
DOLLAR(*number, number of digits*)	Rounds *number* to *number of digits*, formats it to currency format, and returns a text result.
FIXED(*number, number of digits*)	Rounds *number* to *number of digits*, formats to a decimal format with commas, and returns a text result.
LEN(*text*)	Returns a number equal to the length of *text*.
MID(*text, start position, number of characters*)	Extracts *number of characters* from *text*, starting with *start position*.
REPT(*text, number of times*)	Repeats *text* for *number of times*.
TEXT(*number, format text*)	Formats *number* to *format text* and returns it as text.
VALUE(*text*)	Converts *text* to a number. (Not necessary to use in a formula, as Excel converts it automatically if necessary.)

FINANCIAL FUNCTIONS

FUNCTION	DESCRIPTION
FV(*rate, nper, pmt, pv, type*)	Returns the future value of an investment (see PV).
IRR(*values, guess*)	Returns internal rate of return of a series of cash flows, represented by values. *Guess* is an optional argument, specifying the starting point for the iteration. If *guess* is omitted, it is assumed to be 0.1 or 10%. *Values* should be an array or reference that contains numbers.

MIRR(*values, safe, risk*)   Returns a modified internal rate of return of a series of cash flows, represented by the numbers in *values*, given *safe* and *risk*. *Safe* is the rate returned by the investment that will finance the negative cash flows. *Risk* is the rate at which the positive cash flows can be reinvested.

NPER(*rate, pmt, pv, fv, type*)   Returns the number of periods of an investment involving constant cash flows (see PV).

NPV(*rate, values 1, values 2, ...*)   Returns net present value of a series of future cash flows, represented by the numbers in the list of values, discounted at a constant interest rate specified by *rate*.

PMT(*rate, nper, pv, fv, type*)   Returns the periodic payment on an investment involving constant cash flows (see PV and the example in this chapter).

PV(*rate, nper, pmt, fv, type*)   Returns the present value. The arguments are as follows:
rate: interest rate per period
nper: number of periods
pmt: periodic payment
fv: future value
type: indicates whether payments occur at the beginning or end of the period. If *type* = 0, first payment is at the end of the first period. If *type* = 1, payment is at beginning. If argument is omitted, it is assumed to be 0.

RATE(*nper, pmt, pv, fv, type, guess*)   Returns the interest rate per period of an investment involving constant cash flows. (See PV.)

Guess is an optional argument that specifies the starting value for the iteration. If omitted, it is assumed to be 0.1 or 10%.

DATE FUNCTIONS

FUNCTION	DESCRIPTION
DATE(*year, month, day*)	Returns the serial number of the specified day.
DAY(*serial number*)	Converts *serial number* to the day of the month.
HOUR(*serial number*)	Converts *serial number* to an hour of the day.
MINUTE(*serial number*)	Converts *serial number* to a minute.
MONTH(*serial number*)	Converts *serial number* to a month of the year.
NOW( )	Returns the *serial number* of the current date and time. There is no argument.
SECOND(*serial number*)	Converts *serial number* to second.
TIME(*hour, minute, second*)	Returns the *serial number* for the specified time.
WEEKDAY(*serial number*)	Converts *serial number* to the day of the week.
YEAR(*serial number*)	Converts *serial number* to a year.

SPECIAL-PURPOSE FUNCTIONS

FUNCTION	DESCRIPTION
AREAS(*ref*)	Returns the number of areas in *ref*. *Ref* can refer to multiple areas.

	Example: AREAS(A1:A5,B1) equals 2.
COLUMN(*ref*)	Returns the column number of *ref*. If *ref* is omitted, it returns the column number of the current cell. *Ref* cannot refer to multiple areas.
COLUMNS(*array*)	Returns the number of columns in *array*.
HLOOKUP(*lookup value, compare array, index number*)	Searches the first row of *compare array* for the largest value that is less than or equal to *lookup value*. The function moves down the column by the amount specified by *index number* and returns the value found there.
INDEX(*ref, row, column, area*)	Returns the cell that is defined in *ref* by row and column. If *ref* refers to multiple areas, *area* defines the areas from which the cell is to be obtained.
INDEX(*array, row, column*)	Returns the value of a single element within *array*, selected by *row* and *column*.
LOOKUP(*lookup value, compare vector, result vector*)	Searches *compare vector* for largest value less than or equal to *lookup value*. The function returns the corresponding value of *result vector*. The values in *compare vector* can be text, numbers, or logical, but they must be in ascending order. Microsoft recommends using this version of LOOKUP rather than the next one.
LOOKUP(*lookup value, compare array*)	Searches first row or column of *compare array* for largest value that

is less than or equal to *lookup value*. The function returns the corresponding value in the last row or column of *compare array*. Whether the first row or column is searched depends on the size of the array. If it is square or has more rows than columns, LOOKUP searches the first column and gives a value from the corresponding last column. If there are more columns than rows, the first row is searched and LOOKUP gives the value of the corresponding cell in the last row. The values in the array can be text, numbers, or logical, but they must be in ascending order.

MATCH(*lookup value, compare vector, type*)

Returns the corresponding number of the comparison value in *compare vector* that matches *lookup value*. Example: If the look-up value matches the second comparison value, MATCH returns a 2.

NA( )

Returns the error value of #N/A (value not available—see Appendix D). There is no argument.

ROW(*ref*)

Returns the row number of *ref* if *ref* references a single cell. If *ref* refers to a range of cells, a vertical array is returned. If the argument is omitted, the row of the current cell is returned. ROW cannot refer to multiple areas.

ROWS(*array*)

Returns the number of rows in *array*.

TRANSPOSE(*array*)	Returns an array that is the transpose of *array*. That is, the rows become columns and the columns become rows.
TYPE(*value*)	Returns a code defining the type of *value:* 1 for number, 2 for text, 4 for logical, 16 for error, and 64 for an array.
VLOOKUP(*lookup value, compare array, index number*)	Identical to HLOOKUP, except that it searches the first column of *compare array,* moving right in that row by the amount specified by *index number.*

INDEX